FROM THE WORLD OF FABLEWOOD...

FICTION SQUAD

JENKINS & BACHS & PACIAROTTI

BOOM! STUDIOS

FICTION SQUAD, October 2015. Published by BOOM! Studios, a division of Boom Entertainment, Inc. Fiction Squad is ™ & © 2015 Fiction Farm. Originally published in single magazine form as FICTION SQUAD No. 1-6. ™ & © 2015 Fiction Farm. All Rights Reserved. BOOM! Studios™ and the BOOM! Studios logo are trademarks of Boom Entertainment, Inc., registered in various countries and categories. All characters, events, and institutions depicted herein are fictional. Any similarity between any of the names, characters, persons, events, and/or institutions in this publication to actual names, characters, and persons, whether living or dead, events, and/or institutions is unintended and purely coincidental. BOOM! Studios does not read or accept unsolicited submissions of ideas, stories, or artwork.

A catalog record of this book is available from OCLC and from the BOOM! Studios website, www.boom-studios.com, on the Librarians Page.

BOOM! Studios, 5670 Wilshire Boulevard, Suite 450, Los Angeles, CA 90036-5679. Printed in China. First Printing.

Trade Paperback Edition
ISBN: 978-1-60886-760-8, eISBN: 978-1-61398-431-4

Hardcover Kickstarter Edition
ISBN: 978-1-60886-807-0, eISBN: 978-1-61398-478-9

Hardcover Kickstarter Case File Edition
ISBN: 978-1-60886-808-7, eISBN: 978-1-61398-479-6

FROM THE WORLD OF FABLEWOOD...

FICTION SQUAD

WRITTEN BY
PAUL JENKINS

ILLUSTRATED BY
RAMON BACHS

COLORS BY
LEONARDO PACIAROTTI

LETTERS BY
JIM CAMPBELL

KID DETECTIVE

WRITTEN BY
PAUL JENKINS

ILLUSTRATED BY
HUMBERTO RAMOS

COLORS BY
EDGAR DELGADO

LETTERS BY
ED DUKESHIRE

COVER BY
RAMON BACHS
WITH COLORS BY **EDGAR DELGADO**

CHARACTER DESIGNS BY
HUMBERTO RAMOS
& RAMON BACHS

DESIGNER
KARA LEOPARD
WITH **SCOTT NEWMAN**

ASSISTANT EDITOR
ALEX GALER

EDITOR
DAFNA PLEBAN

CHAPTER ONE

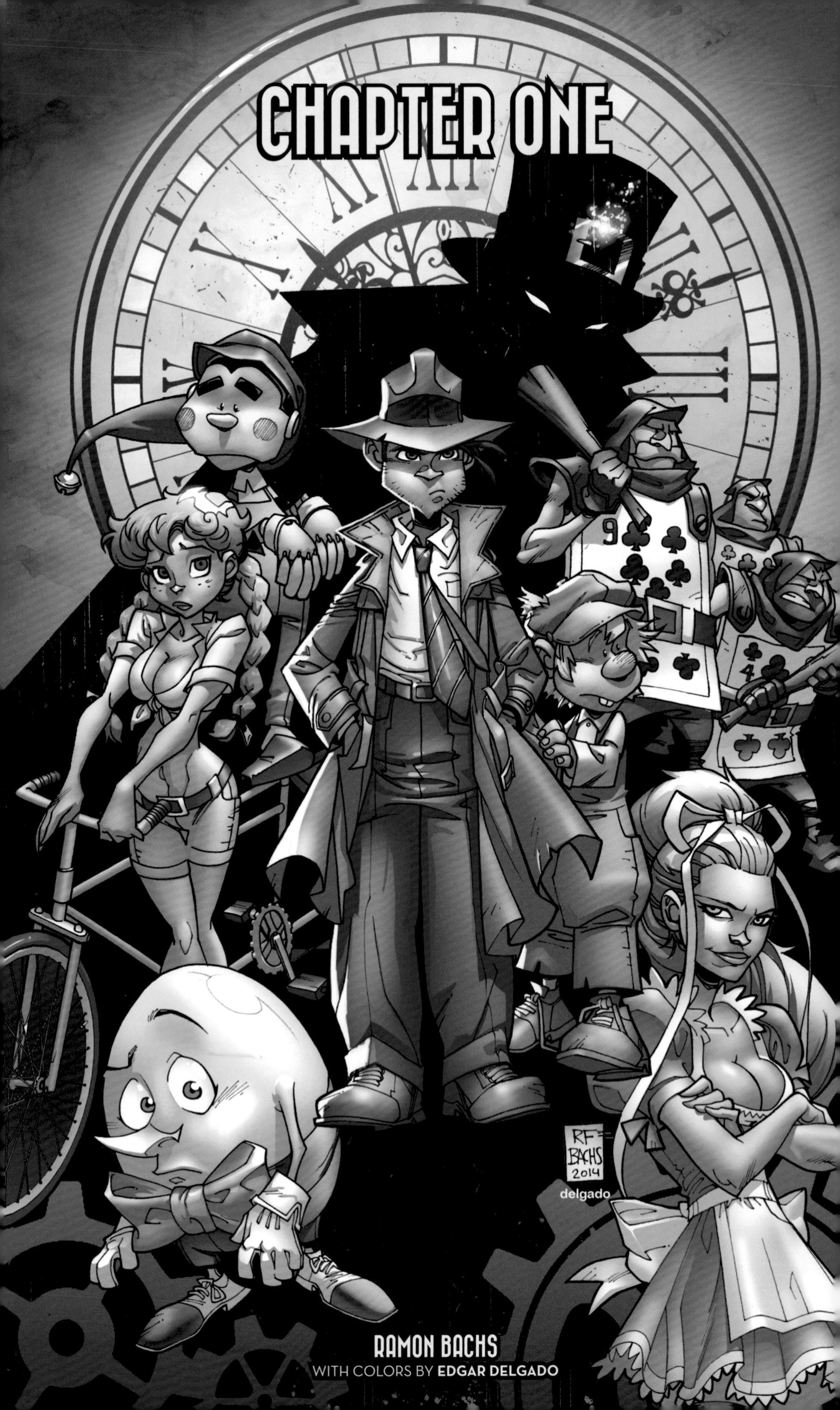
RF BACHS 2014
delgado

RAMON BACHS
WITH COLORS BY **EDGAR DELGADO**

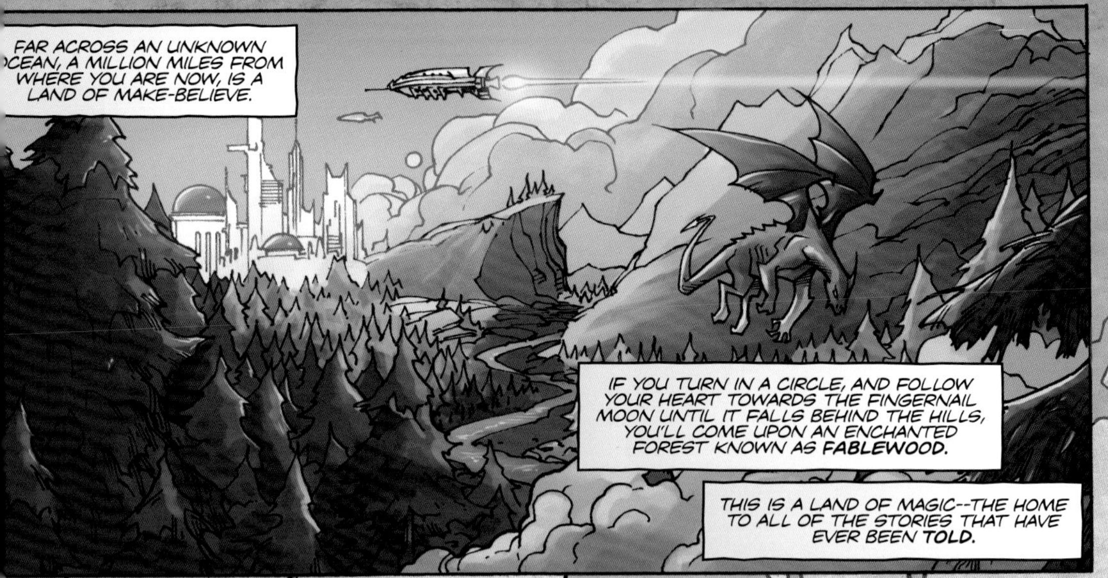
FAR ACROSS AN UNKNOWN OCEAN, A MILLION MILES FROM WHERE YOU ARE NOW, IS A LAND OF MAKE-BELIEVE.
IF YOU TURN IN A CIRCLE, AND FOLLOW YOUR HEART TOWARDS THE FINGERNAIL MOON UNTIL IT FALLS BEHIND THE HILLS, YOU'LL COME UPON AN ENCHANTED FOREST KNOWN AS **FABLEWOOD.**
THIS IS A LAND OF MAGIC--THE HOME TO ALL OF THE STORIES THAT HAVE EVER BEEN **TOLD.**

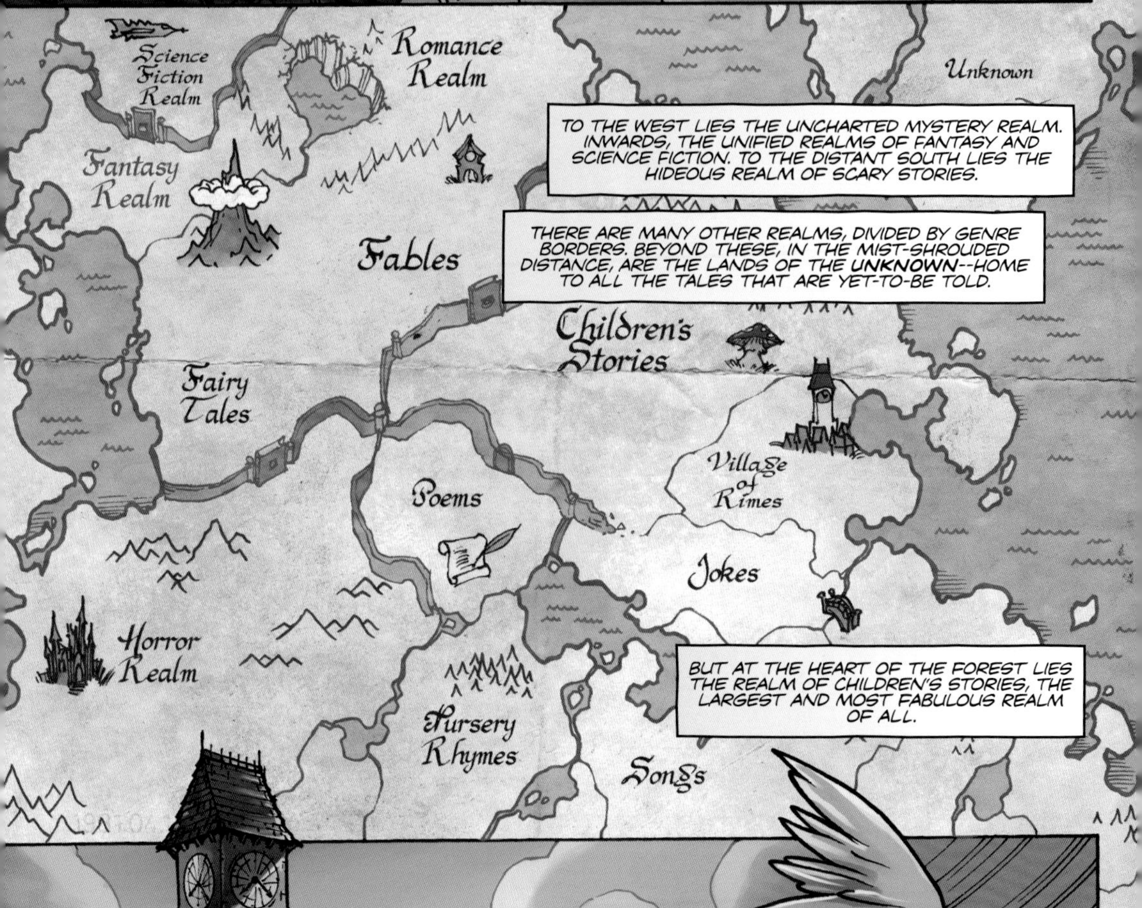
Science Fiction Realm
Romance Realm
Unknown
TO THE WEST LIES THE UNCHARTED MYSTERY REALM. INWARDS, THE UNIFIED REALMS OF FANTASY AND SCIENCE FICTION. TO THE DISTANT SOUTH LIES THE HIDEOUS REALM OF SCARY STORIES.
Fantasy Realm
THERE ARE MANY OTHER REALMS, DIVIDED BY GENRE BORDERS. BEYOND THESE, IN THE MIST-SHROUDED DISTANCE, ARE THE LANDS OF THE **UNKNOWN**--HOME TO ALL THE TALES THAT ARE YET-TO-BE TOLD.
Fables
Children's Stories
Fairy Tales
Village of Rimes
Poems
Jokes
Horror Realm
BUT AT THE HEART OF THE FOREST LIES THE REALM OF CHILDREN'S STORIES, THE LARGEST AND MOST FABULOUS REALM OF ALL.
Nursery Rhymes
Songs

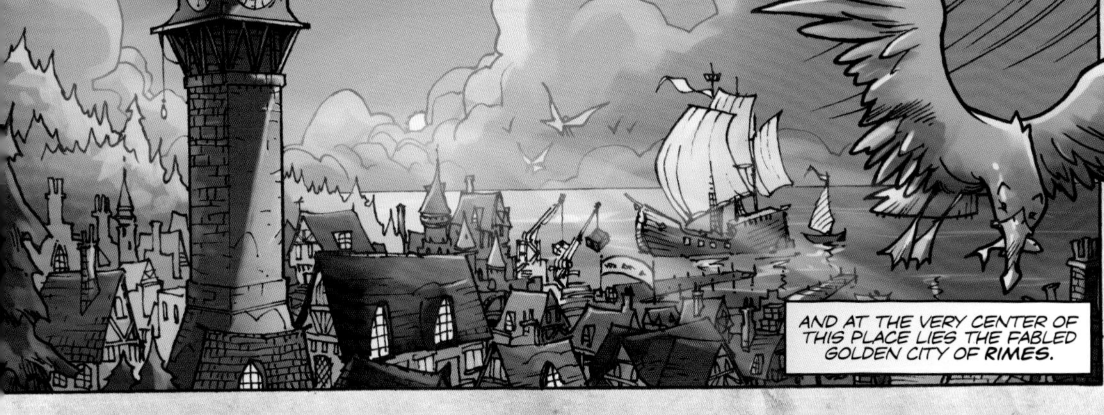
AND AT THE VERY CENTER OF THIS PLACE LIES THE FABLED GOLDEN CITY OF **RIMES.**

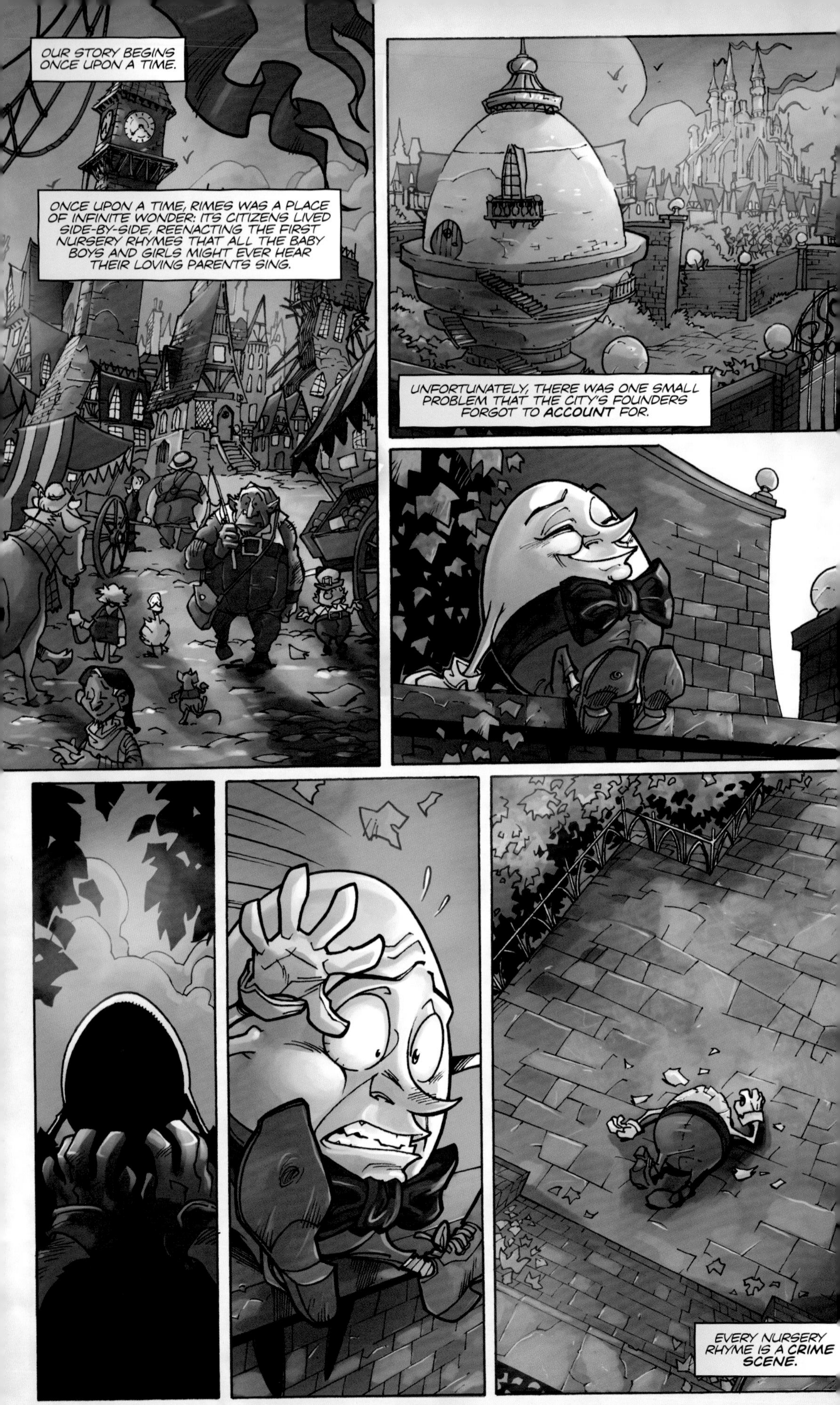
OUR STORY BEGINS ONCE UPON A TIME.
ONCE UPON A TIME, RIMES WAS A PLACE OF INFINITE WONDER: ITS CITIZENS LIVED SIDE-BY-SIDE, REENACTING THE FIRST NURSERY RHYMES THAT ALL THE BABY BOYS AND GIRLS MIGHT EVER HEAR THEIR LOVING PARENTS SING.
UNFORTUNATELY, THERE WAS ONE SMALL PROBLEM THAT THE CITY'S FOUNDERS FORGOT TO ACCOUNT FOR.
EVERY NURSERY RHYME IS A CRIME SCENE.

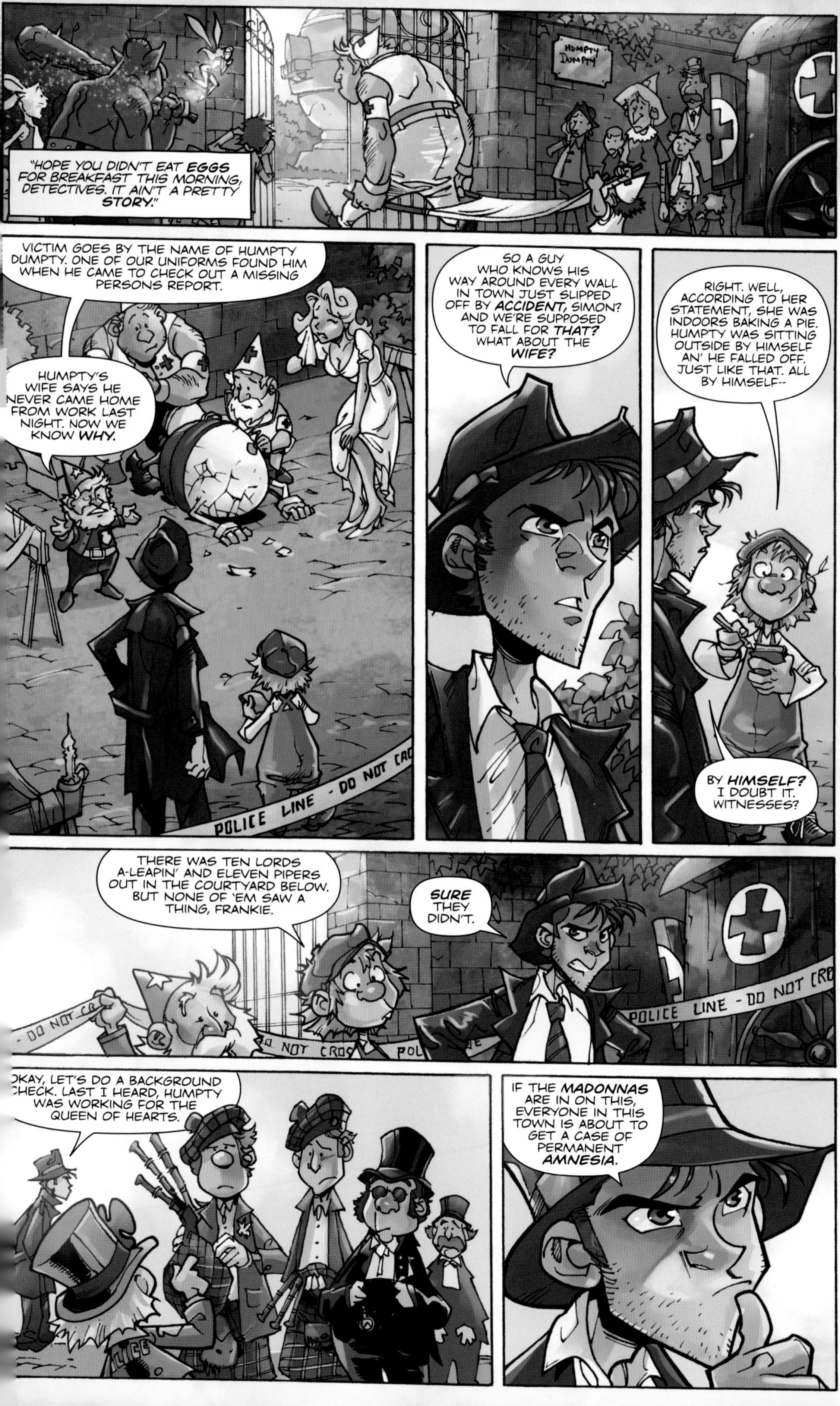
"HOPE YOU DIDN'T EAT EGGS FOR BREAKFAST THIS MORNING, DETECTIVES. IT AIN'T A PRETTY STORY."
HUMPTY DUMPTY
VICTIM GOES BY THE NAME OF HUMPTY DUMPTY. ONE OF OUR UNIFORMS FOUND HIM WHEN HE CAME TO CHECK OUT A MISSING PERSONS REPORT.
HUMPTY'S WIFE SAYS HE NEVER CAME HOME FROM WORK LAST NIGHT. NOW WE KNOW WHY.
POLICE LINE - DO NOT CRO
SO A GUY WHO KNOWS HIS WAY AROUND EVERY WALL IN TOWN JUST SLIPPED OFF BY ACCIDENT, SIMON? AND WE'RE SUPPOSED TO FALL FOR THAT? WHAT ABOUT THE WIFE?
RIGHT. WELL, ACCORDING TO HER STATEMENT, SHE WAS INDOORS BAKING A PIE. HUMPTY WAS SITTING OUTSIDE BY HIMSELF AN' HE FALLED OFF. JUST LIKE THAT. ALL BY HIMSELF--
BY HIMSELF? I DOUBT IT. WITNESSES?
THERE WAS TEN LORDS A-LEAPIN' AND ELEVEN PIPERS OUT IN THE COURTYARD BELOW. BUT NONE OF 'EM SAW A THING, FRANKIE.
SURE THEY DIDN'T.
POLICE LINE - DO NOT CR
OKAY, LET'S DO A BACKGROUND CHECK. LAST I HEARD, HUMPTY WAS WORKING FOR THE QUEEN OF HEARTS.
IF THE MADONNAS ARE IN ON THIS, EVERYONE IN THIS TOWN IS ABOUT TO GET A CASE OF PERMANENT AMNESIA.

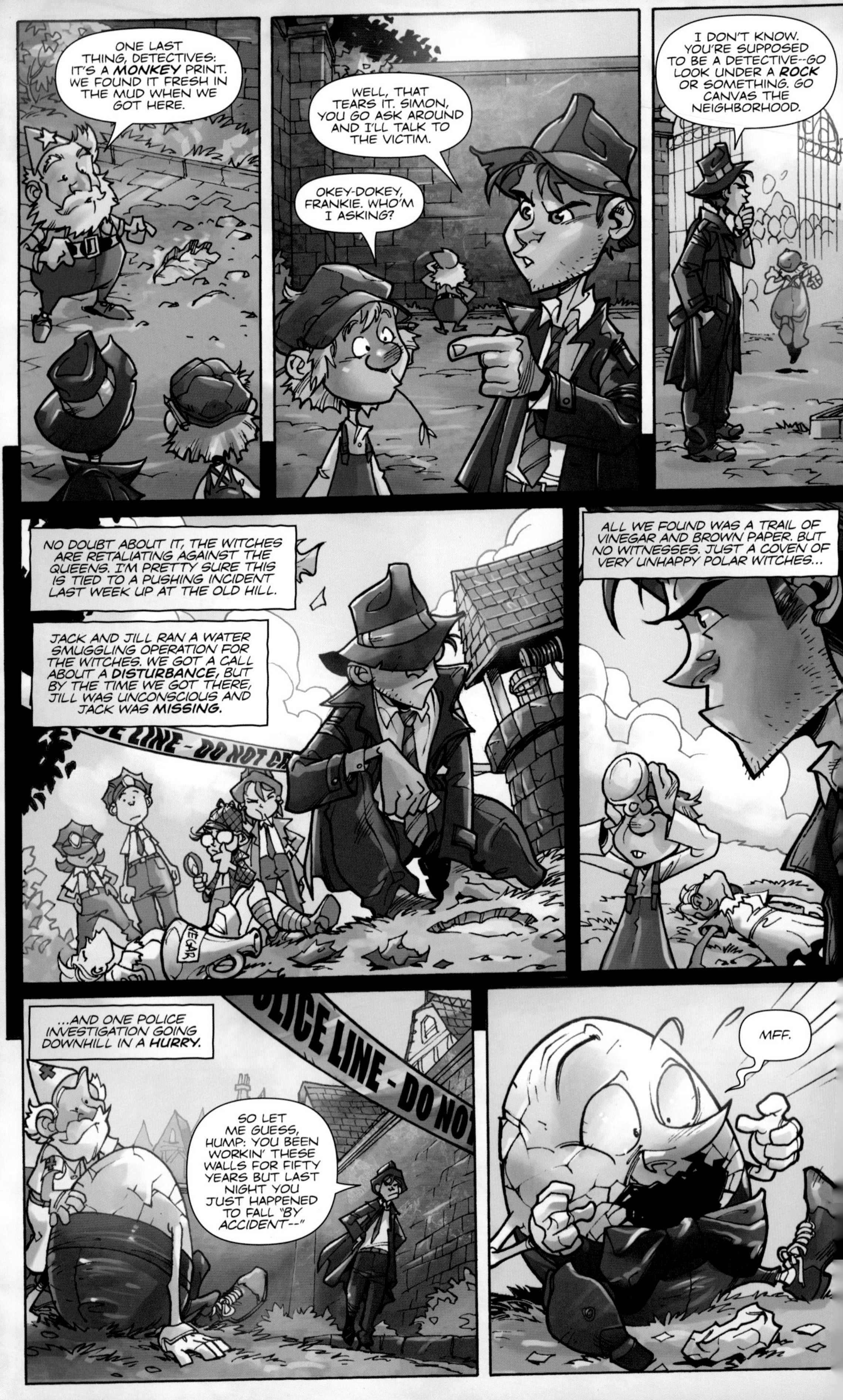
ONE LAST THING, DETECTIVES: IT'S A MONKEY PRINT. WE FOUND IT FRESH IN THE MUD WHEN WE GOT HERE.
WELL, THAT TEARS IT. SIMON, YOU GO ASK AROUND AND I'LL TALK TO THE VICTIM.
OKEY-DOKEY, FRANKIE. WHO'M I ASKING?
I DON'T KNOW. YOU'RE SUPPOSED TO BE A DETECTIVE--GO LOOK UNDER A ROCK OR SOMETHING. GO CANVAS THE NEIGHBORHOOD.
NO DOUBT ABOUT IT, THE WITCHES ARE RETALIATING AGAINST THE QUEENS. I'M PRETTY SURE THIS IS TIED TO A PUSHING INCIDENT LAST WEEK UP AT THE OLD HILL.
JACK AND JILL RAN A WATER SMUGGLING OPERATION FOR THE WITCHES. WE GOT A CALL ABOUT A DISTURBANCE, BUT BY THE TIME WE GOT THERE, JILL WAS UNCONSCIOUS AND JACK WAS MISSING.
ALL WE FOUND WAS A TRAIL OF VINEGAR AND BROWN PAPER. BUT NO WITNESSES. JUST A COVEN OF VERY UNHAPPY POLAR WITCHES...
...AND ONE POLICE INVESTIGATION GOING DOWNHILL IN A HURRY.
POLICE LINE - DO NOT
SO LET ME GUESS, HUMP: YOU BEEN WORKIN' THESE WALLS FOR FIFTY YEARS BUT LAST NIGHT YOU JUST HAPPENED TO FALL "BY ACCIDENT--"
MFF.

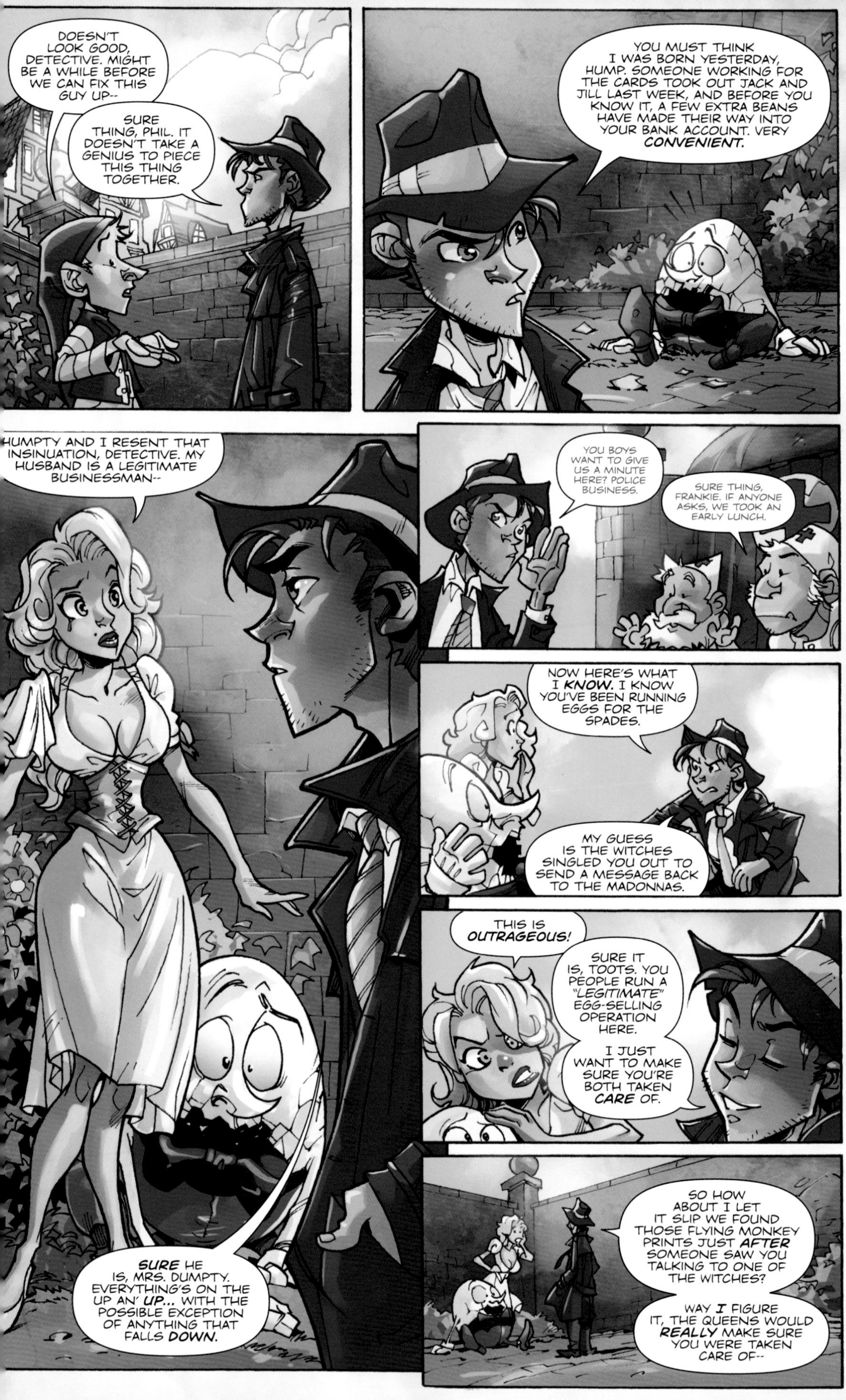

DOESN'T LOOK GOOD, DETECTIVE. MIGHT BE A WHILE BEFORE WE CAN FIX THIS GUY UP--
SURE THING, PHIL. IT DOESN'T TAKE A GENIUS TO PIECE THIS THING TOGETHER.
YOU MUST THINK I WAS BORN YESTERDAY, HUMP. SOMEONE WORKING FOR THE CARDS TOOK OUT JACK AND JILL LAST WEEK, AND BEFORE YOU KNOW IT, A FEW EXTRA BEANS HAVE MADE THEIR WAY INTO YOUR BANK ACCOUNT. VERY CONVENIENT.
HUMPTY AND I RESENT THAT INSINUATION, DETECTIVE. MY HUSBAND IS A LEGITIMATE BUSINESSMAN--
SURE HE IS, MRS. DUMPTY. EVERYTHING'S ON THE UP AN' UP... WITH THE POSSIBLE EXCEPTION OF ANYTHING THAT FALLS DOWN.
YOU BOYS WANT TO GIVE US A MINUTE HERE? POLICE BUSINESS.
SURE THING, FRANKIE. IF ANYONE ASKS, WE TOOK AN EARLY LUNCH.
NOW HERE'S WHAT I KNOW. I KNOW YOU'VE BEEN RUNNING EGGS FOR THE SPADES.
MY GUESS IS THE WITCHES SINGLED YOU OUT TO SEND A MESSAGE BACK TO THE MADONNAS.
THIS IS OUTRAGEOUS!
SURE IT IS, TOOTS. YOU PEOPLE RUN A "LEGITIMATE" EGG-SELLING OPERATION HERE.
I JUST WANT TO MAKE SURE YOU'RE BOTH TAKEN CARE OF.
SO HOW ABOUT I LET IT SLIP WE FOUND THOSE FLYING MONKEY PRINTS JUST AFTER SOMEONE SAW YOU TALKING TO ONE OF THE WITCHES?
WAY I FIGURE IT, THE QUEENS WOULD REALLY MAKE SURE YOU WERE TAKEN CARE OF--

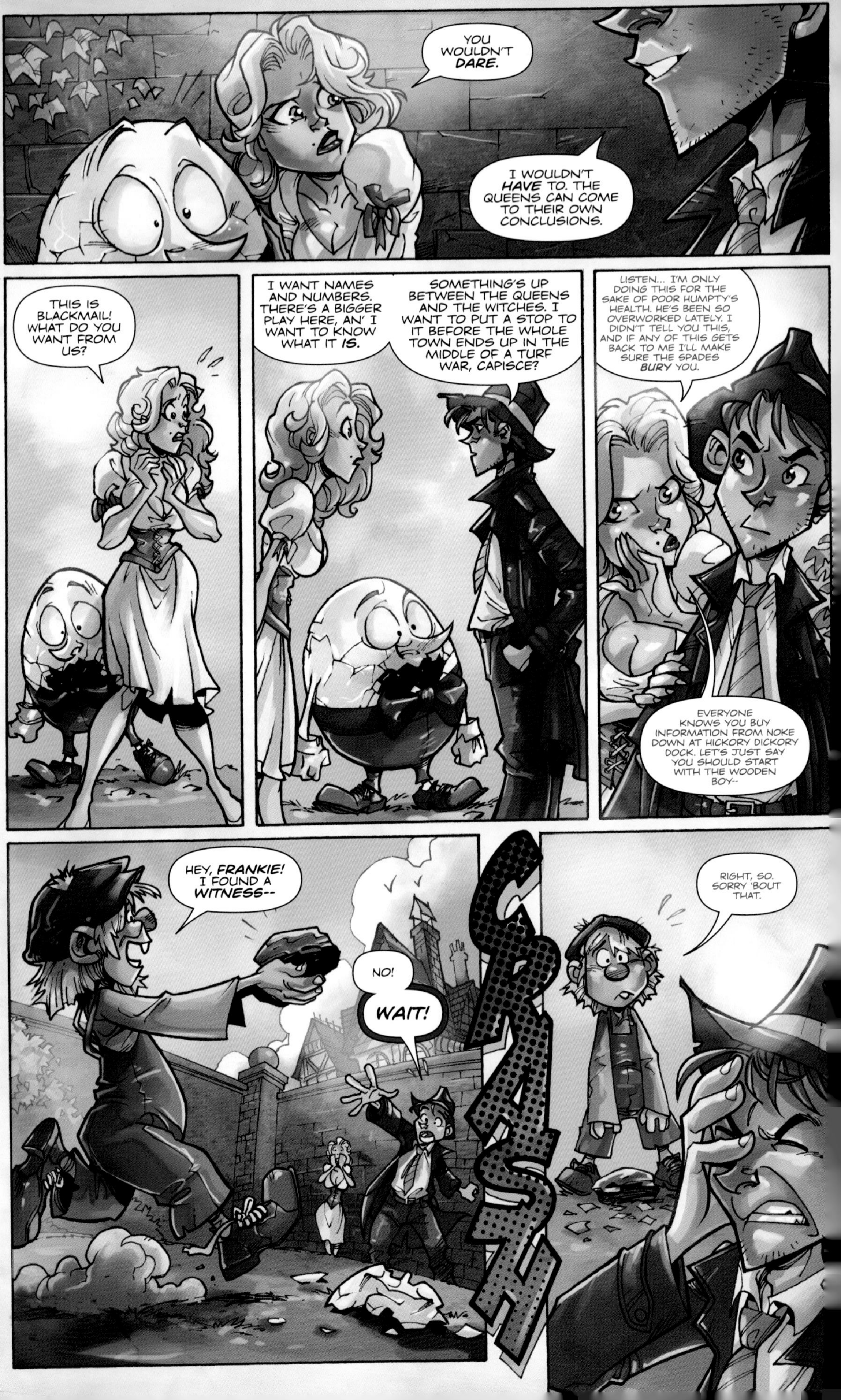

YOU WOULDN'T DARE.
I WOULDN'T HAVE TO. THE QUEENS CAN COME TO THEIR OWN CONCLUSIONS.
THIS IS BLACKMAIL! WHAT DO YOU WANT FROM US?
I WANT NAMES AND NUMBERS. THERE'S A BIGGER PLAY HERE, AN' I WANT TO KNOW WHAT IT IS.
SOMETHING'S UP BETWEEN THE QUEENS AND THE WITCHES. I WANT TO PUT A STOP TO IT BEFORE THE WHOLE TOWN ENDS UP IN THE MIDDLE OF A TURF WAR, CAPISCE?
LISTEN... I'M ONLY DOING THIS FOR THE SAKE OF POOR HUMPTY'S HEALTH. HE'S BEEN SO OVERWORKED LATELY. I DIDN'T TELL YOU THIS, AND IF ANY OF THIS GETS BACK TO ME I'LL MAKE SURE THE SPADES BURY YOU.
EVERYONE KNOWS YOU BUY INFORMATION FROM NOKE DOWN AT HICKORY DICKORY DOCK. LET'S JUST SAY YOU SHOULD START WITH THE WOODEN BOY--
HEY, FRANKIE! I FOUND A WITNESS--
NO!
WAIT!
CRASH
RIGHT, SO. SORRY 'BOUT THAT.

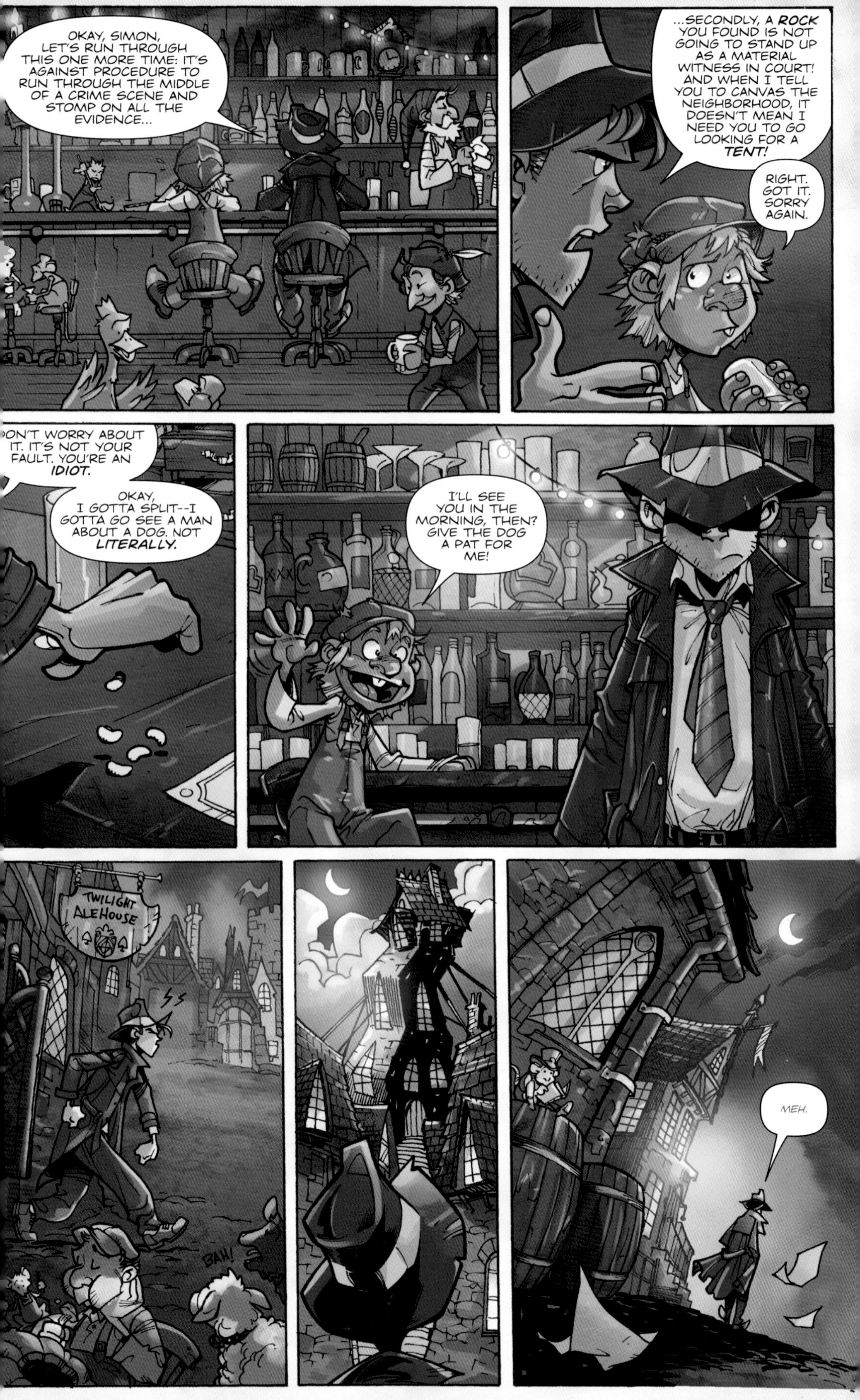
OKAY, SIMON, LET'S RUN THROUGH THIS ONE MORE TIME: IT'S AGAINST PROCEDURE TO RUN THROUGH THE MIDDLE OF A CRIME SCENE AND STOMP ON ALL THE EVIDENCE...
...SECONDLY, A ROCK YOU FOUND IS NOT GOING TO STAND UP AS A MATERIAL WITNESS IN COURT! AND WHEN I TELL YOU TO CANVAS THE NEIGHBORHOOD, IT DOESN'T MEAN I NEED YOU TO GO LOOKING FOR A TENT!
RIGHT. GOT IT. SORRY AGAIN.
ON'T WORRY ABOUT IT. IT'S NOT YOUR FAULT. YOU'RE AN IDIOT.
OKAY, I GOTTA SPLIT--I GOTTA GO SEE A MAN ABOUT A DOG. NOT LITERALLY.
I'LL SEE YOU IN THE MORNING, THEN? GIVE THE DOG A PAT FOR ME!
TWILIGHT ALEHOUSE
BAH!
MEH.

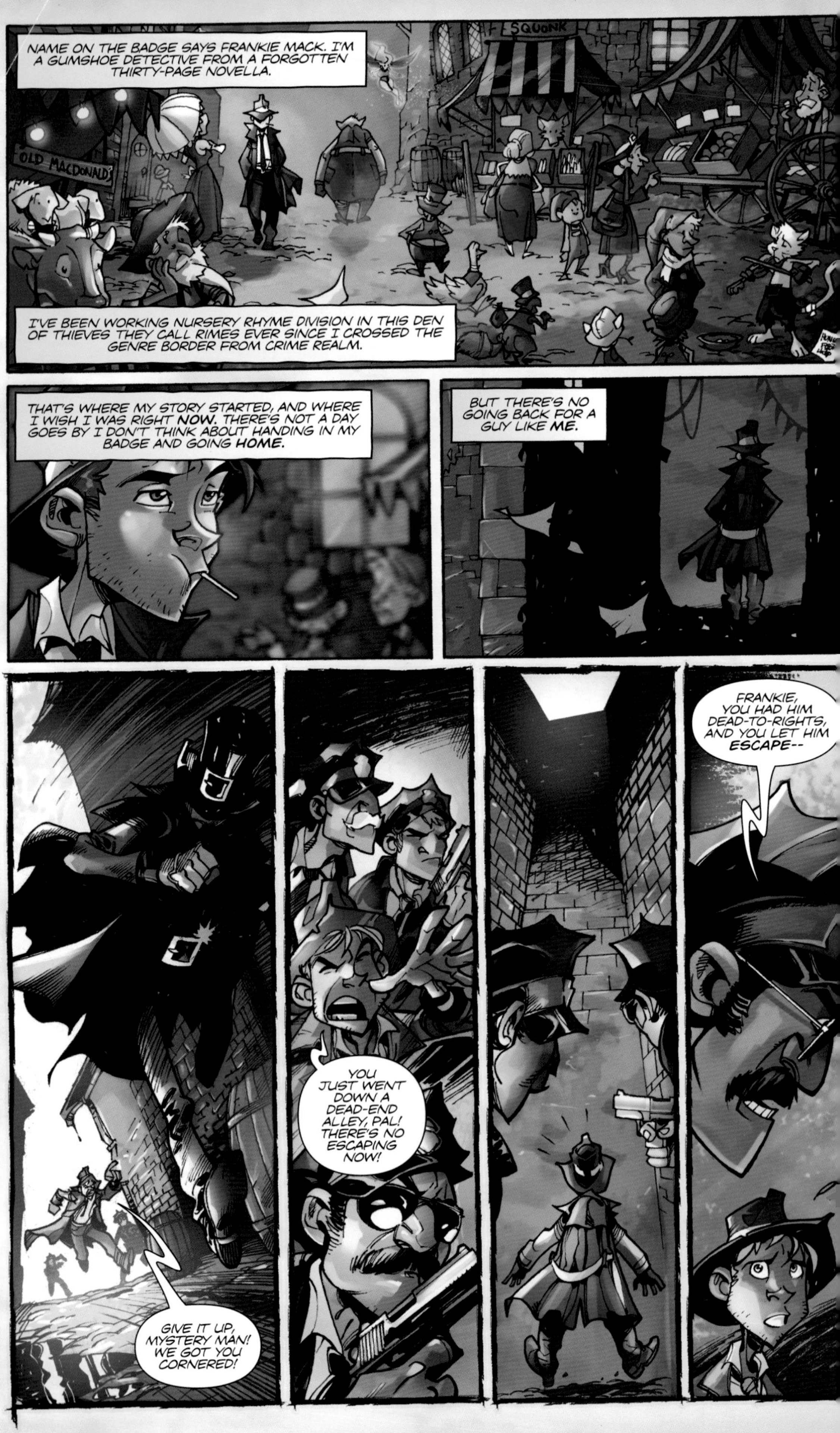

NAME ON THE BADGE SAYS FRANKIE MACK. I'M A GUMSHOE DETECTIVE FROM A FORGOTTEN THIRTY-PAGE NOVELLA.
SQUONK
OLD MACDONALD'S
I'VE BEEN WORKING NURSERY RHYME DIVISION IN THIS DEN OF THIEVES THEY CALL RIMES EVER SINCE I CROSSED THE GENRE BORDER FROM CRIME REALM.
THAT'S WHERE MY STORY STARTED, AND WHERE I WISH I WAS RIGHT NOW. THERE'S NOT A DAY GOES BY I DON'T THINK ABOUT HANDING IN MY BADGE AND GOING HOME.
BUT THERE'S NO GOING BACK FOR A GUY LIKE ME.
GIVE IT UP, MYSTERY MAN! WE GOT YOU CORNERED!
YOU JUST WENT DOWN A DEAD-END ALLEY, PAL! THERE'S NO ESCAPING NOW!
FRANKIE, YOU HAD HIM DEAD-TO-RIGHTS, AND YOU LET HIM ESCAPE--

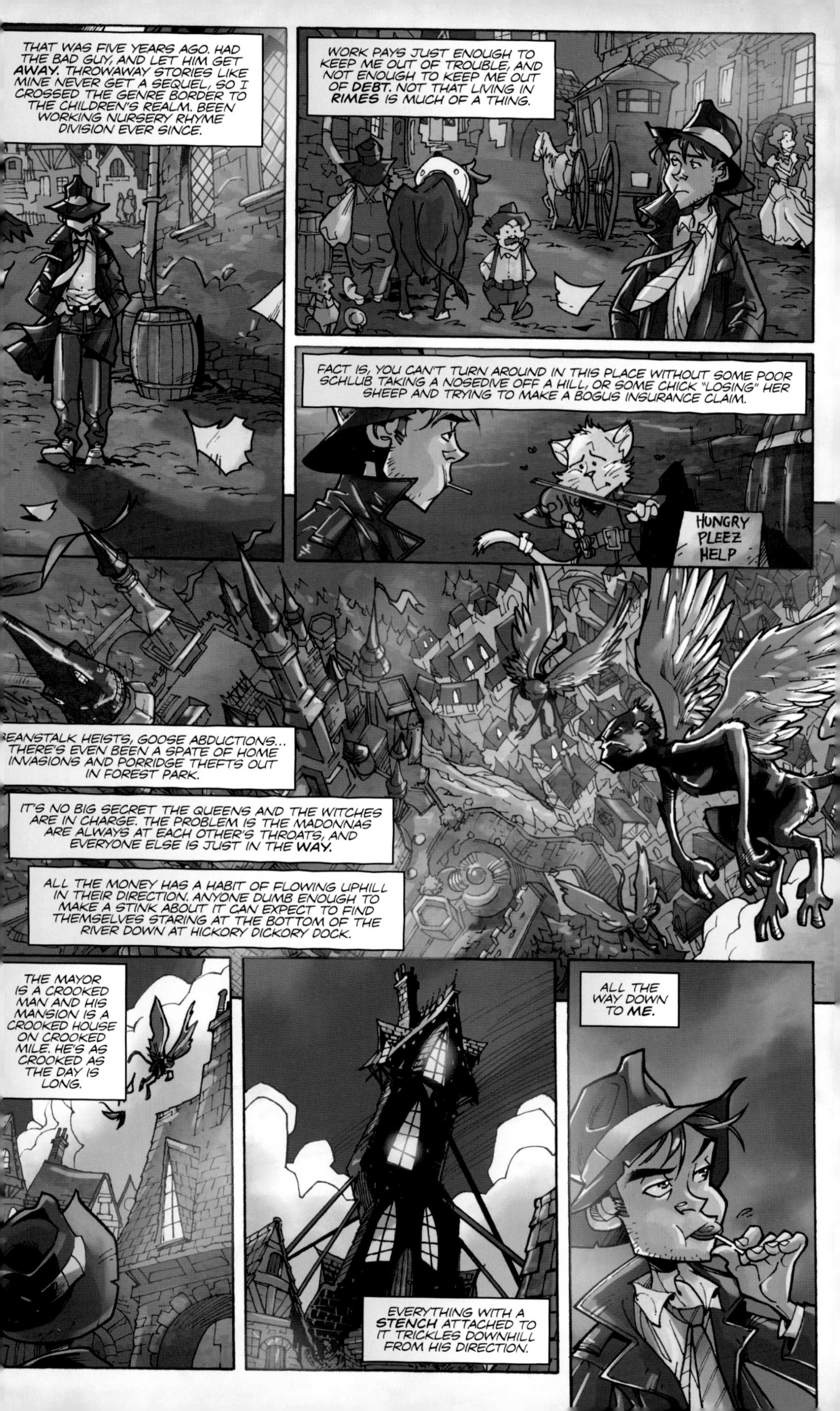
THAT WAS FIVE YEARS AGO. HAD THE BAD GUY, AND LET HIM GET AWAY. THROWAWAY STORIES LIKE MINE NEVER GET A SEQUEL, SO I CROSSED THE GENRE BORDER TO THE CHILDREN'S REALM. BEEN WORKING NURSERY RHYME DIVISION EVER SINCE.
WORK PAYS JUST ENOUGH TO KEEP ME OUT OF TROUBLE, AND NOT ENOUGH TO KEEP ME OUT OF DEBT. NOT THAT LIVING IN RIMES IS MUCH OF A THING.
FACT IS, YOU CAN'T TURN AROUND IN THIS PLACE WITHOUT SOME POOR SCHLUB TAKING A NOSEDIVE OFF A HILL, OR SOME CHICK "LOSING" HER SHEEP AND TRYING TO MAKE A BOGUS INSURANCE CLAIM.
HUNGRY PLEEZ HELP
EANSTALK HEISTS, GOOSE ABDUCTIONS... THERE'S EVEN BEEN A SPATE OF HOME INVASIONS AND PORRIDGE THEFTS OUT IN FOREST PARK.
IT'S NO BIG SECRET THE QUEENS AND THE WITCHES ARE IN CHARGE. THE PROBLEM IS THE MADONNAS ARE ALWAYS AT EACH OTHER'S THROATS, AND EVERYONE ELSE IS JUST IN THE WAY.
ALL THE MONEY HAS A HABIT OF FLOWING UPHILL IN THEIR DIRECTION. ANYONE DUMB ENOUGH TO MAKE A STINK ABOUT IT CAN EXPECT TO FIND THEMSELVES STARING AT THE BOTTOM OF THE RIVER DOWN AT HICKORY DICKORY DOCK.
THE MAYOR IS A CROOKED MAN AND HIS MANSION IS A CROOKED HOUSE ON CROOKED MILE. HE'S AS CROOKED AS THE DAY IS LONG.
EVERYTHING WITH A STENCH ATTACHED TO IT TRICKLES DOWNHILL FROM HIS DIRECTION.
ALL THE WAY DOWN TO ME.

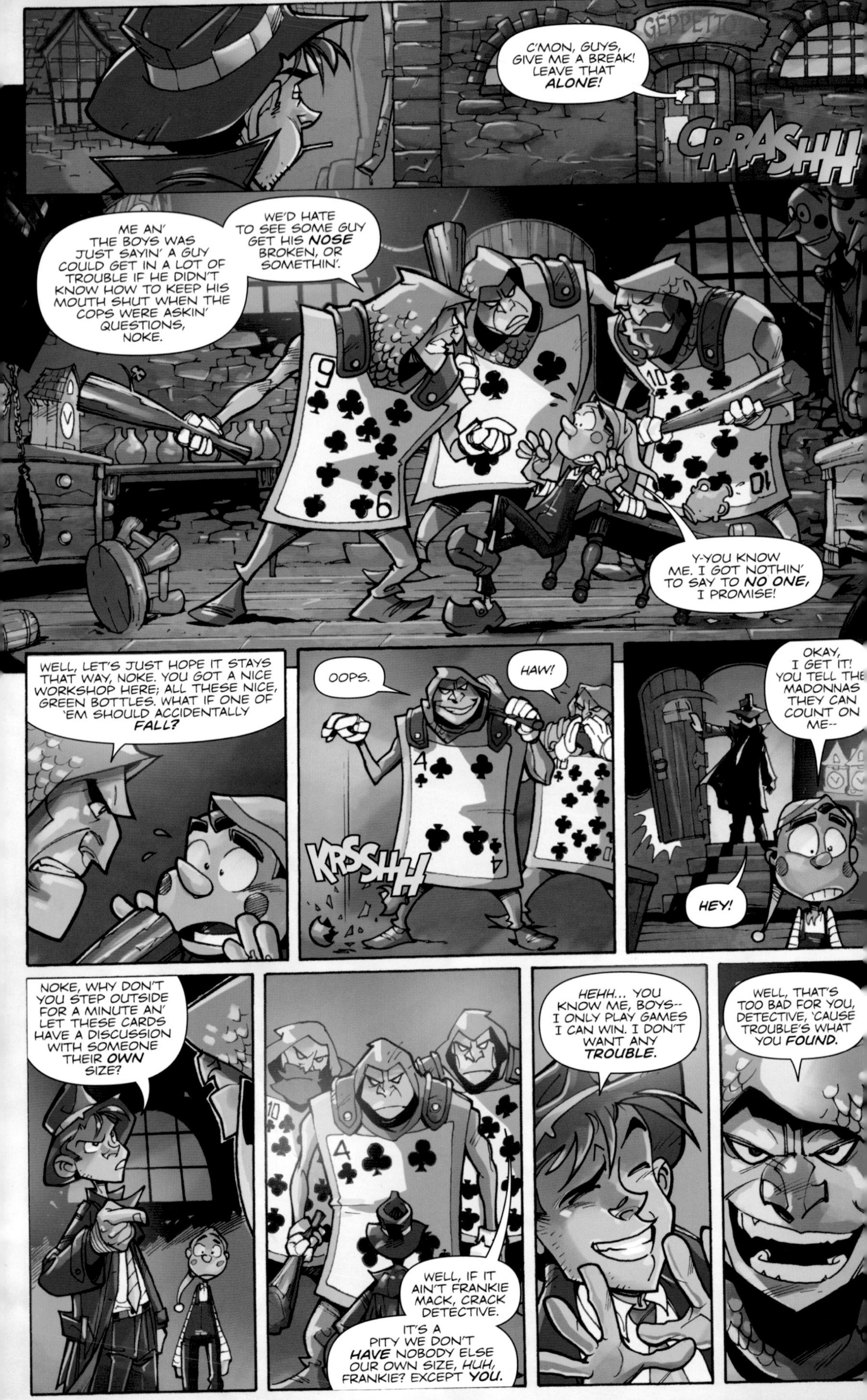
GEPPETTO
C'MON, GUYS, GIVE ME A BREAK! LEAVE THAT ALONE!
CRRASHH
ME AN' THE BOYS WAS JUST SAYIN' A GUY COULD GET IN A LOT OF TROUBLE IF HE DIDN'T KNOW HOW TO KEEP HIS MOUTH SHUT WHEN THE COPS WERE ASKIN' QUESTIONS, NOKE.
WE'D HATE TO SEE SOME GUY GET HIS NOSE BROKEN, OR SOMETHIN'.
Y-YOU KNOW ME. I GOT NOTHIN' TO SAY TO NO ONE, I PROMISE!
WELL, LET'S JUST HOPE IT STAYS THAT WAY, NOKE. YOU GOT A NICE WORKSHOP HERE; ALL THESE NICE, GREEN BOTTLES. WHAT IF ONE OF 'EM SHOULD ACCIDENTALLY FALL?
OOPS.
HAW!
KRSSHH
OKAY, I GET IT! YOU TELL THE MADONNAS THEY CAN COUNT ON ME--
HEY!
NOKE, WHY DON'T YOU STEP OUTSIDE FOR A MINUTE AN' LET THESE CARDS HAVE A DISCUSSION WITH SOMEONE THEIR OWN SIZE?
WELL, IF IT AIN'T FRANKIE MACK, CRACK DETECTIVE.
IT'S A PITY WE DON'T HAVE NOBODY ELSE OUR OWN SIZE, HUH, FRANKIE? EXCEPT YOU.
HEHH... YOU KNOW ME, BOYS-- I ONLY PLAY GAMES I CAN WIN. I DON'T WANT ANY TROUBLE.
WELL, THAT'S TOO BAD FOR YOU, DETECTIVE, 'CAUSE TROUBLE'S WHAT YOU FOUND.

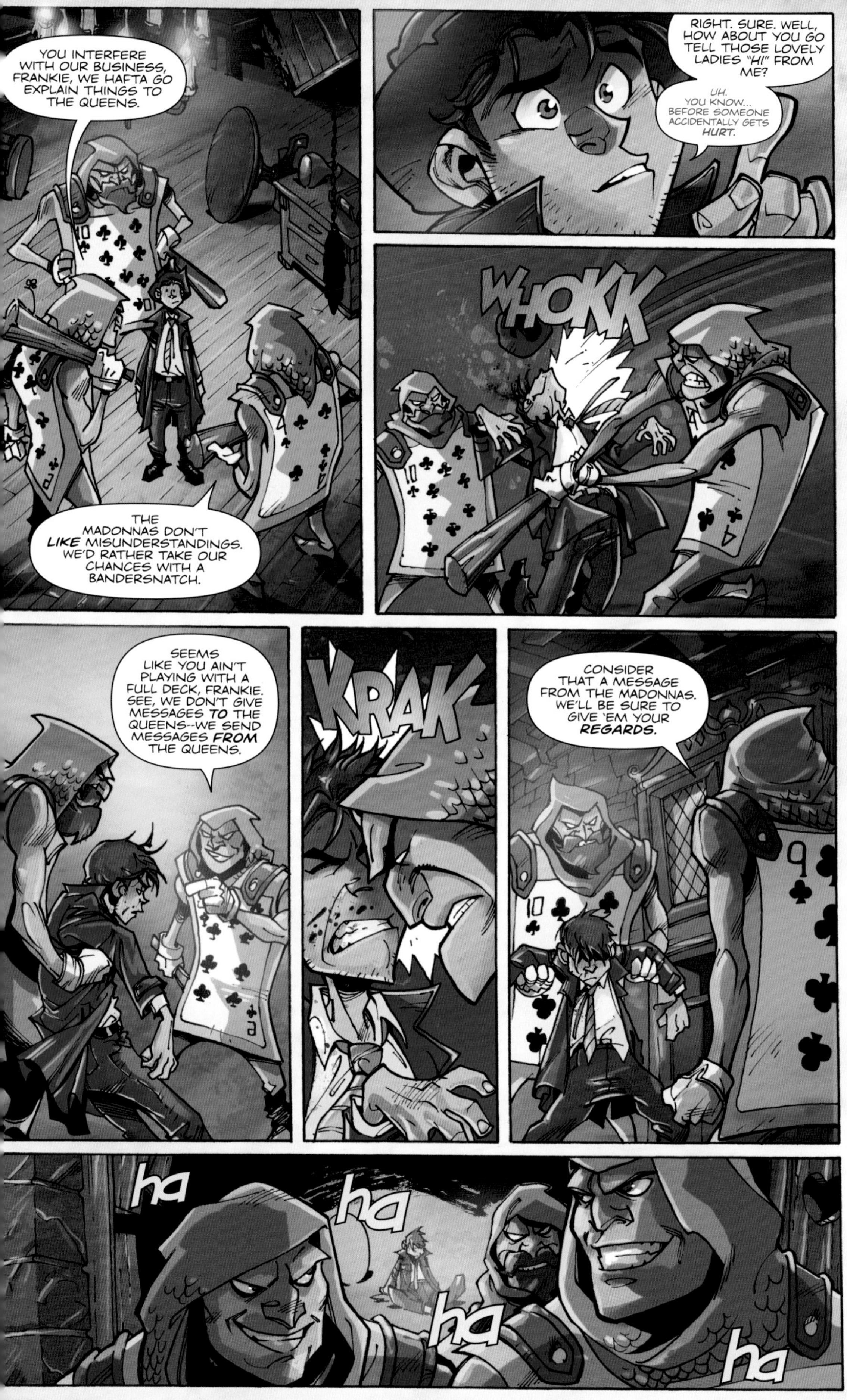
YOU INTERFERE WITH OUR BUSINESS, FRANKIE, WE HAFTA GO EXPLAIN THINGS TO THE QUEENS.
THE MADONNAS DON'T LIKE MISUNDERSTANDINGS. WE'D RATHER TAKE OUR CHANCES WITH A BANDERSNATCH.
RIGHT. SURE. WELL, HOW ABOUT YOU GO TELL THOSE LOVELY LADIES "HI" FROM ME?
UH. YOU KNOW... BEFORE SOMEONE ACCIDENTALLY GETS HURT.
WHOKK
SEEMS LIKE YOU AIN'T PLAYING WITH A FULL DECK, FRANKIE. SEE, WE DON'T GIVE MESSAGES TO THE QUEENS--WE SEND MESSAGES FROM THE QUEENS.
KRAK
CONSIDER THAT A MESSAGE FROM THE MADONNAS. WE'LL BE SURE TO GIVE 'EM YOUR REGARDS.
ha
ha
ha
ha

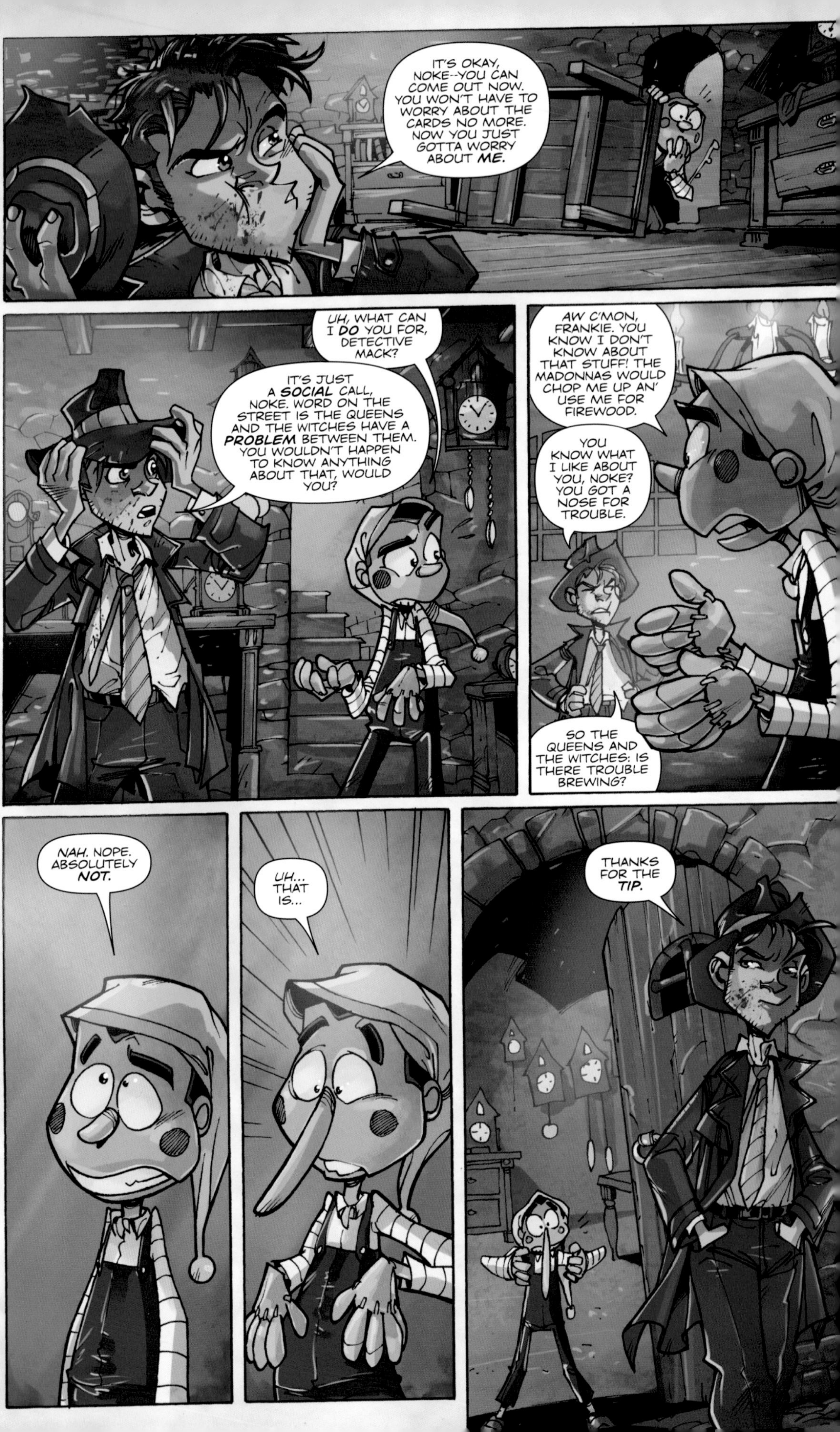

IT'S OKAY, NOKE--YOU CAN COME OUT NOW. YOU WON'T HAVE TO WORRY ABOUT THE CARDS NO MORE. NOW YOU JUST GOTTA WORRY ABOUT ***ME.***
UH, WHAT CAN I ***DO*** YOU FOR, DETECTIVE MACK?
IT'S JUST A ***SOCIAL*** CALL, NOKE. WORD ON THE STREET IS THE QUEENS AND THE WITCHES HAVE A ***PROBLEM*** BETWEEN THEM. YOU WOULDN'T HAPPEN TO KNOW ANYTHING ABOUT THAT, WOULD YOU?
AW C'MON, FRANKIE. YOU KNOW I DON'T KNOW ABOUT THAT STUFF! THE MADONNAS WOULD CHOP ME UP AN' USE ME FOR FIREWOOD.
YOU KNOW WHAT I LIKE ABOUT YOU, NOKE? YOU GOT A NOSE FOR TROUBLE.
SO THE QUEENS AND THE WITCHES: IS THERE TROUBLE BREWING?
NAH. NOPE. ABSOLUTELY ***NOT.***
UH... THAT IS...
THANKS FOR THE ***TIP.***

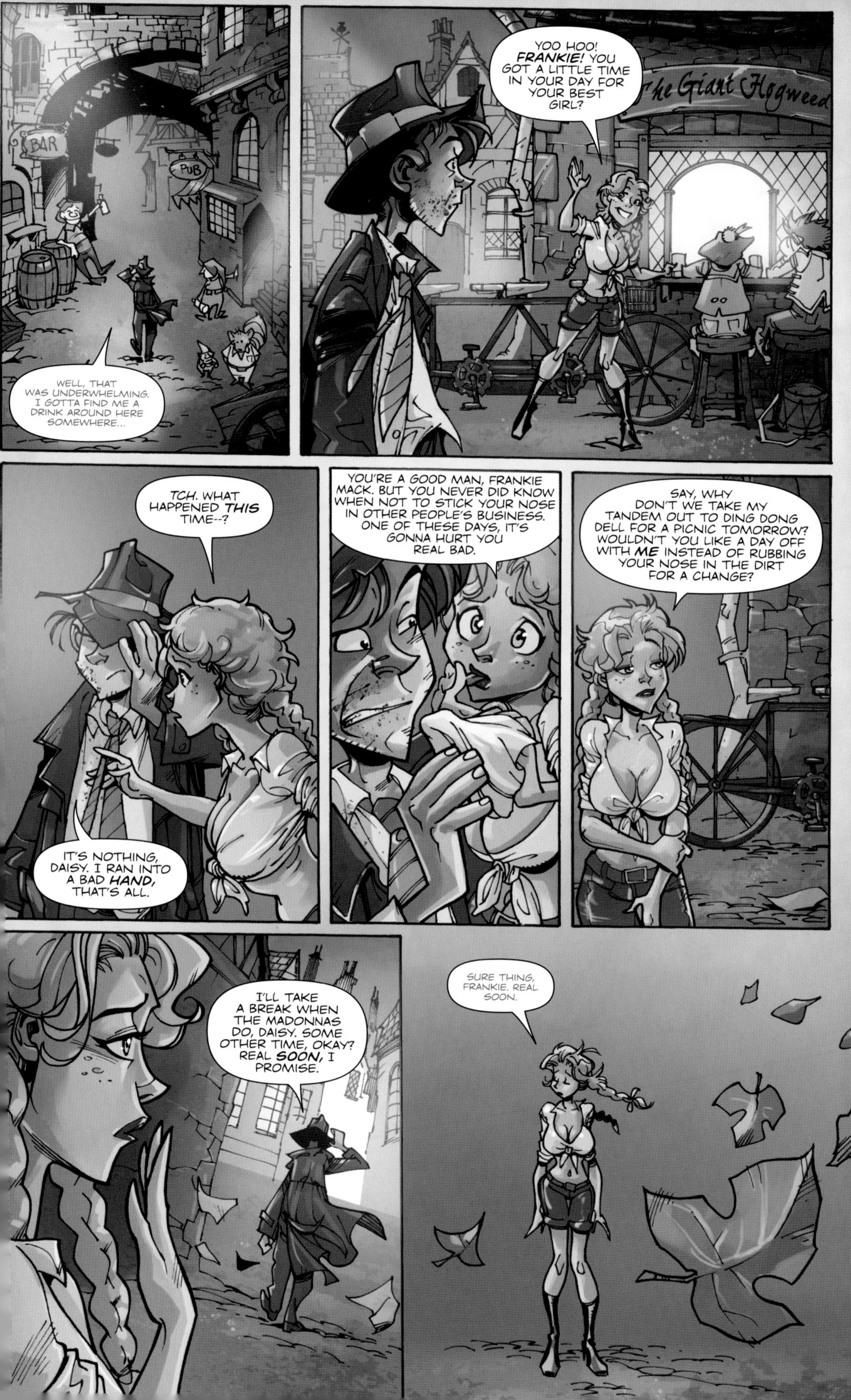
BAR
PUB
WELL, THAT WAS UNDERWHELMING. I GOTTA FIND ME A DRINK AROUND HERE SOMEWHERE...
YOO HOO! FRANKIE! YOU GOT A LITTLE TIME IN YOUR DAY FOR YOUR BEST GIRL?
The Giant Hogweed
TCH. WHAT HAPPENED THIS TIME--?
IT'S NOTHING, DAISY. I RAN INTO A BAD HAND, THAT'S ALL.
YOU'RE A GOOD MAN, FRANKIE MACK. BUT YOU NEVER DID KNOW WHEN NOT TO STICK YOUR NOSE IN OTHER PEOPLE'S BUSINESS. ONE OF THESE DAYS, IT'S GONNA HURT YOU REAL BAD.
SAY, WHY DON'T WE TAKE MY TANDEM OUT TO DING DONG DELL FOR A PICNIC TOMORROW? WOULDN'T YOU LIKE A DAY OFF WITH ME INSTEAD OF RUBBING YOUR NOSE IN THE DIRT FOR A CHANGE?
I'LL TAKE A BREAK WHEN THE MADONNAS DO, DAISY. SOME OTHER TIME, OKAY? REAL SOON, I PROMISE.
SURE THING, FRANKIE. REAL SOON.

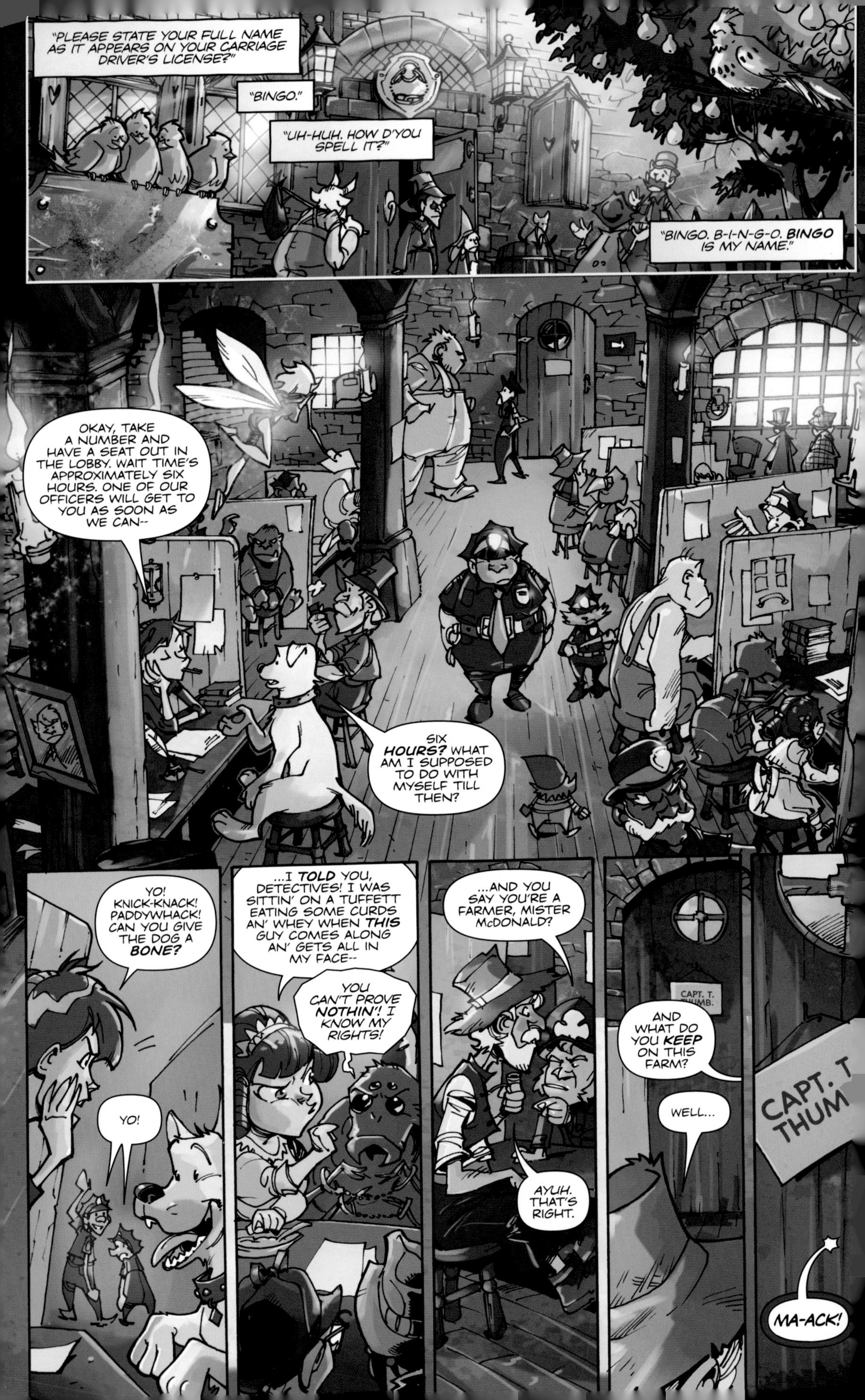
"PLEASE STATE YOUR FULL NAME AS IT APPEARS ON YOUR CARRIAGE DRIVER'S LICENSE?"
"BINGO."
"UH-HUH. HOW D'YOU SPELL IT?"
"BINGO. B-I-N-G-O. BINGO IS MY NAME."
OKAY, TAKE A NUMBER AND HAVE A SEAT OUT IN THE LOBBY. WAIT TIME'S APPROXIMATELY SIX HOURS. ONE OF OUR OFFICERS WILL GET TO YOU AS SOON AS WE CAN--
SIX HOURS? WHAT AM I SUPPOSED TO DO WITH MYSELF TILL THEN?
YO! KNICK-KNACK! PADDYWHACK! CAN YOU GIVE THE DOG A BONE?
YO!
...I TOLD YOU, DETECTIVES! I WAS SITTIN' ON A TUFFETT EATING SOME CURDS AN' WHEY WHEN THIS GUY COMES ALONG AN' GETS ALL IN MY FACE--
YOU CAN'T PROVE NOTHIN'! I KNOW MY RIGHTS!
...AND YOU SAY YOU'RE A FARMER, MISTER McDONALD?
AYUH. THAT'S RIGHT.
CAPT. T. THUMB.
AND WHAT DO YOU KEEP ON THIS FARM?
WELL...
CAPT. T THUM
MA-ACK!

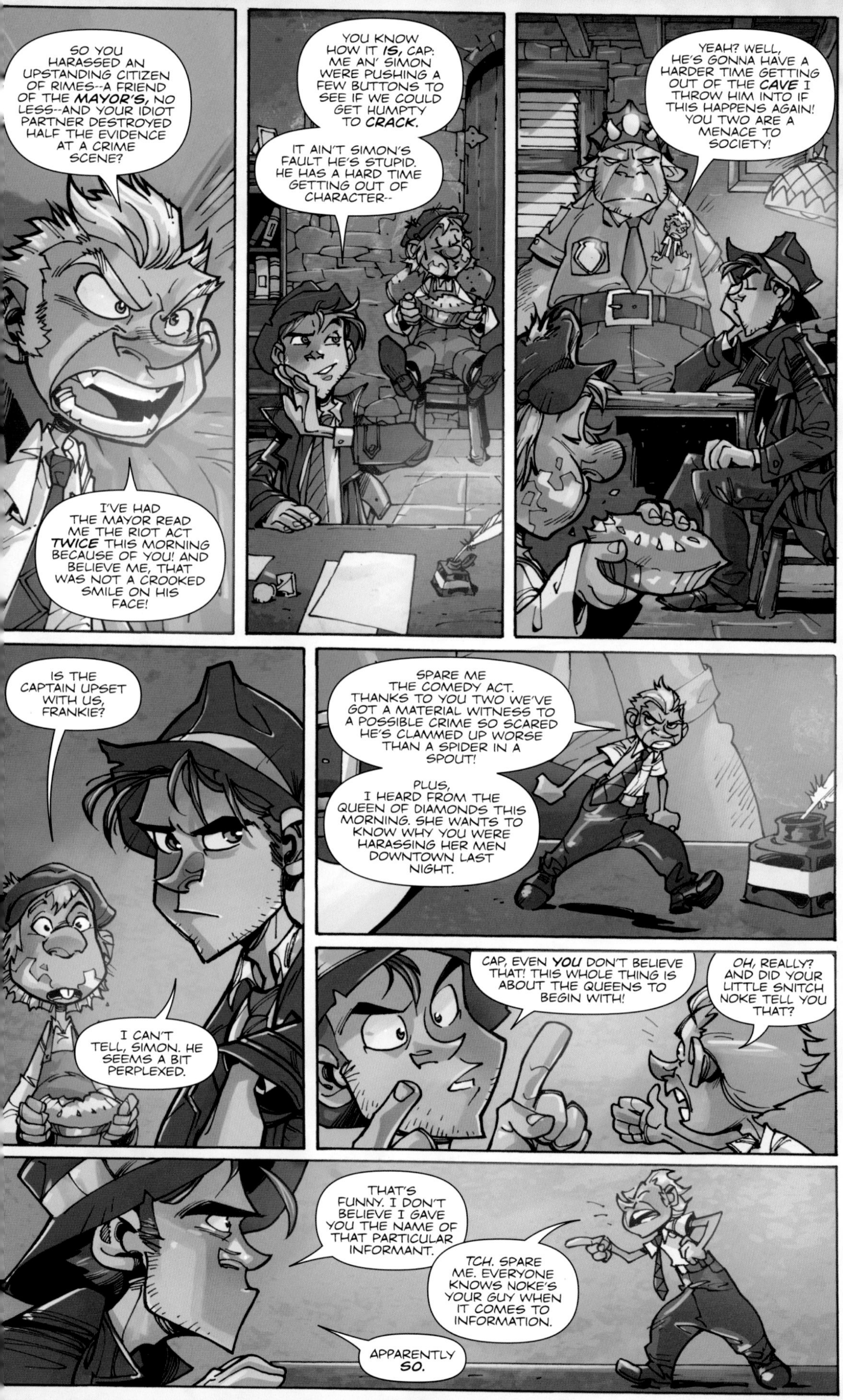
SO YOU HARASSED AN UPSTANDING CITIZEN OF RIMES--A FRIEND OF THE MAYOR'S, NO LESS--AND YOUR IDIOT PARTNER DESTROYED HALF THE EVIDENCE AT A CRIME SCENE?
I'VE HAD THE MAYOR READ ME THE RIOT ACT TWICE THIS MORNING BECAUSE OF YOU! AND BELIEVE ME, THAT WAS NOT A CROOKED SMILE ON HIS FACE!
YOU KNOW HOW IT IS, CAP: ME AN' SIMON WERE PUSHING A FEW BUTTONS TO SEE IF WE COULD GET HUMPTY TO CRACK.
IT AIN'T SIMON'S FAULT HE'S STUPID. HE HAS A HARD TIME GETTING OUT OF CHARACTER--
YEAH? WELL, HE'S GONNA HAVE A HARDER TIME GETTING OUT OF THE CAVE I THROW HIM INTO IF THIS HAPPENS AGAIN! YOU TWO ARE A MENACE TO SOCIETY!
IS THE CAPTAIN UPSET WITH US, FRANKIE?
I CAN'T TELL, SIMON. HE SEEMS A BIT PERPLEXED.
SPARE ME THE COMEDY ACT. THANKS TO YOU TWO WE'VE GOT A MATERIAL WITNESS TO A POSSIBLE CRIME SO SCARED HE'S CLAMMED UP WORSE THAN A SPIDER IN A SPOUT!
PLUS, I HEARD FROM THE QUEEN OF DIAMONDS THIS MORNING. SHE WANTS TO KNOW WHY YOU WERE HARASSING HER MEN DOWNTOWN LAST NIGHT.
CAP, EVEN YOU DON'T BELIEVE THAT! THIS WHOLE THING IS ABOUT THE QUEENS TO BEGIN WITH!
OH, REALLY? AND DID YOUR LITTLE SNITCH NOKE TELL YOU THAT?
THAT'S FUNNY. I DON'T BELIEVE I GAVE YOU THE NAME OF THAT PARTICULAR INFORMANT.
TCH. SPARE ME. EVERYONE KNOWS NOKE'S YOUR GUY WHEN IT COMES TO INFORMATION.
APPARENTLY SO.

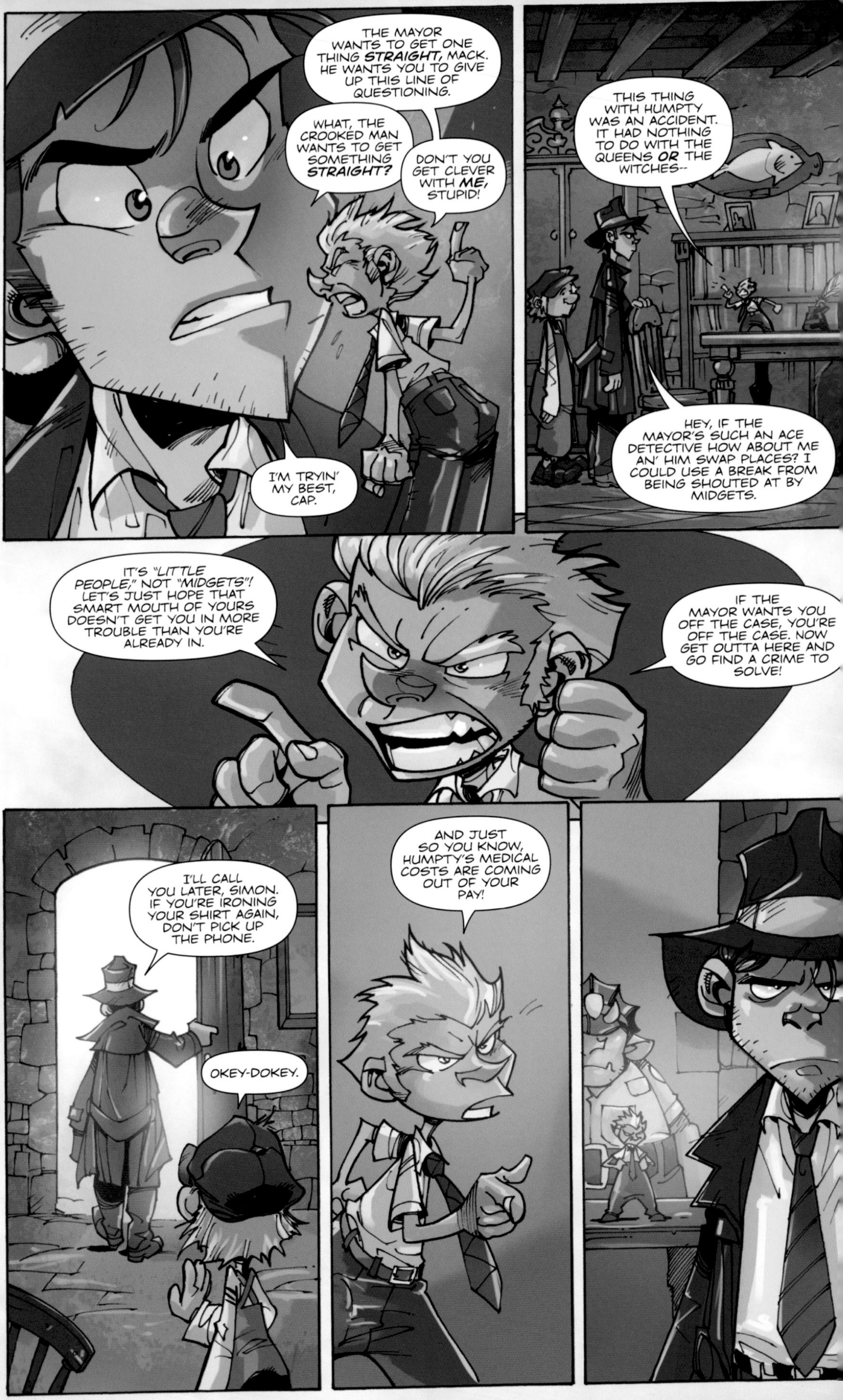

THE MAYOR WANTS TO GET ONE THING STRAIGHT, MACK. HE WANTS YOU TO GIVE UP THIS LINE OF QUESTIONING.
WHAT, THE CROOKED MAN WANTS TO GET SOMETHING STRAIGHT?
DON'T YOU GET CLEVER WITH ME, STUPID!
I'M TRYIN' MY BEST, CAP.
THIS THING WITH HUMPTY WAS AN ACCIDENT. IT HAD NOTHING TO DO WITH THE QUEENS OR THE WITCHES--
HEY, IF THE MAYOR'S SUCH AN ACE DETECTIVE HOW ABOUT ME AN' HIM SWAP PLACES? I COULD USE A BREAK FROM BEING SHOUTED AT BY MIDGETS.
IT'S "LITTLE PEOPLE," NOT "MIDGETS"! LET'S JUST HOPE THAT SMART MOUTH OF YOURS DOESN'T GET YOU IN MORE TROUBLE THAN YOU'RE ALREADY IN.
IF THE MAYOR WANTS YOU OFF THE CASE, YOU'RE OFF THE CASE. NOW GET OUTTA HERE AND GO FIND A CRIME TO SOLVE!
I'LL CALL YOU LATER, SIMON. IF YOU'RE IRONING YOUR SHIRT AGAIN, DON'T PICK UP THE PHONE.
OKEY-DOKEY.
AND JUST SO YOU KNOW, HUMPTY'S MEDICAL COSTS ARE COMING OUT OF YOUR PAY!

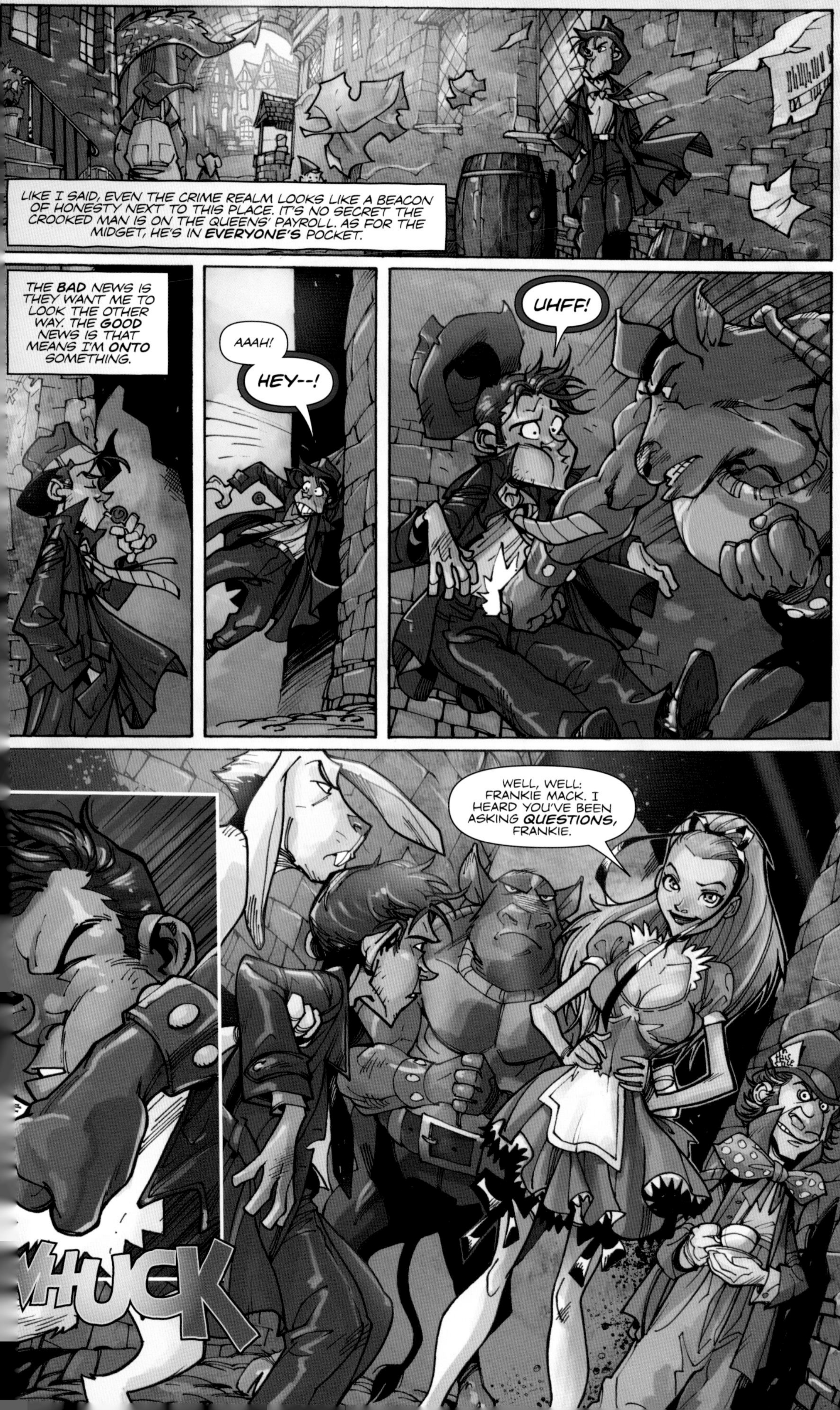
LIKE I SAID, EVEN THE CRIME REALM LOOKS LIKE A BEACON OF HONESTY NEXT TO THIS PLACE. IT'S NO SECRET THE CROOKED MAN IS ON THE QUEENS' PAYROLL. AS FOR THE MIDGET, HE'S IN **EVERYONE'S** POCKET.
THE **BAD** NEWS IS THEY WANT ME TO LOOK THE OTHER WAY. THE **GOOD** NEWS IS THAT MEANS I'M **ONTO** SOMETHING.
AAAH!
HEY--!
UHFF!
WHUCK
WELL, WELL: FRANKIE MACK. I HEARD YOU'VE BEEN ASKING **QUESTIONS,** FRANKIE.

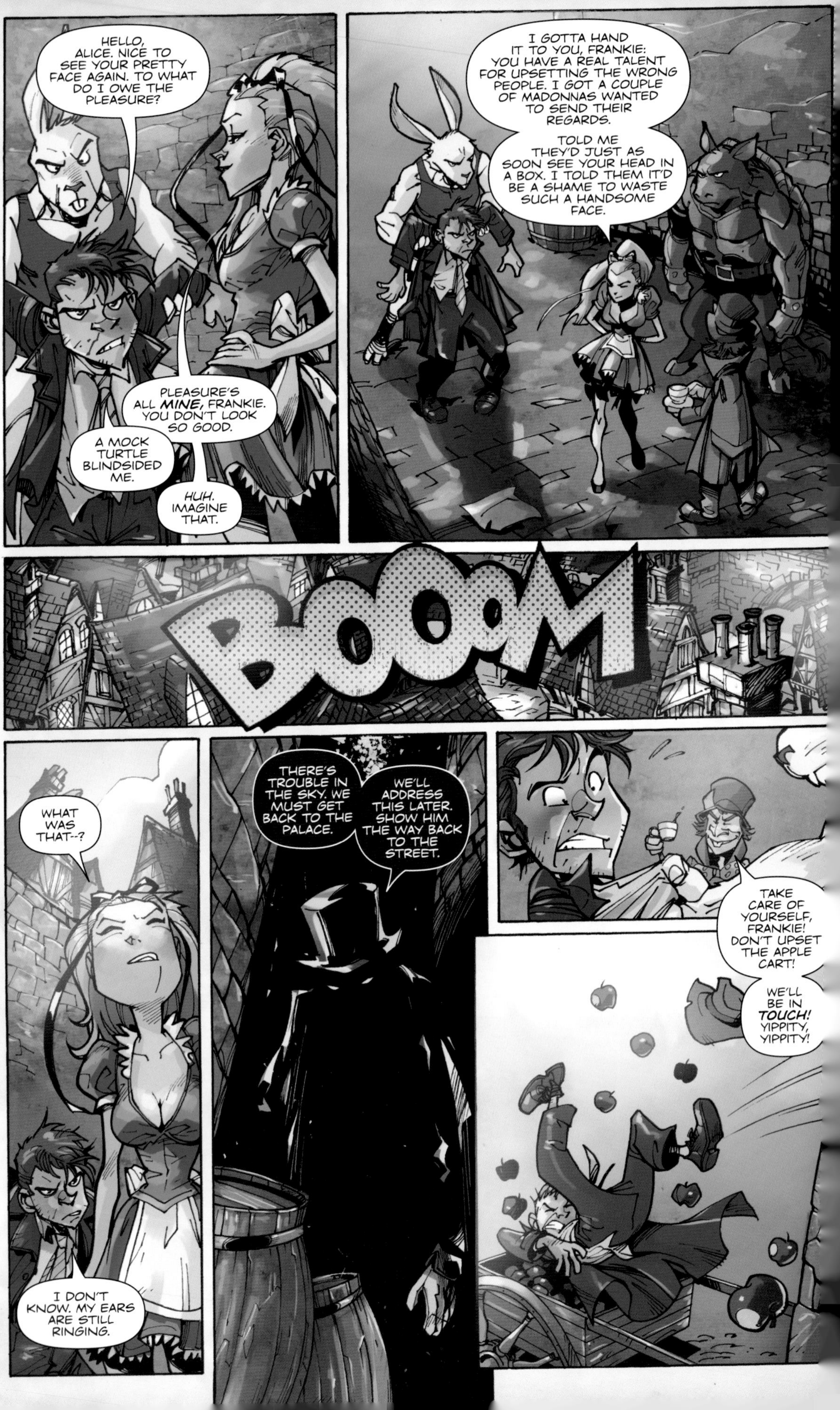
HELLO, ALICE. NICE TO SEE YOUR PRETTY FACE AGAIN. TO WHAT DO I OWE THE PLEASURE?
PLEASURE'S ALL MINE, FRANKIE. YOU DON'T LOOK SO GOOD.
A MOCK TURTLE BLINDSIDED ME.
HUH. IMAGINE THAT.
I GOTTA HAND IT TO YOU, FRANKIE: YOU HAVE A REAL TALENT FOR UPSETTING THE WRONG PEOPLE. I GOT A COUPLE OF MADONNAS WANTED TO SEND THEIR REGARDS.
TOLD ME THEY'D JUST AS SOON SEE YOUR HEAD IN A BOX. I TOLD THEM IT'D BE A SHAME TO WASTE SUCH A HANDSOME FACE.
BOOOM
WHAT WAS THAT--?
I DON'T KNOW. MY EARS ARE STILL RINGING.
THERE'S TROUBLE IN THE SKY. WE MUST GET BACK TO THE PALACE.
WE'LL ADDRESS THIS LATER. SHOW HIM THE WAY BACK TO THE STREET.
TAKE CARE OF YOURSELF, FRANKIE! DON'T UPSET THE APPLE CART!
WE'LL BE IN TOUCH! YIPPITY, YIPPITY!

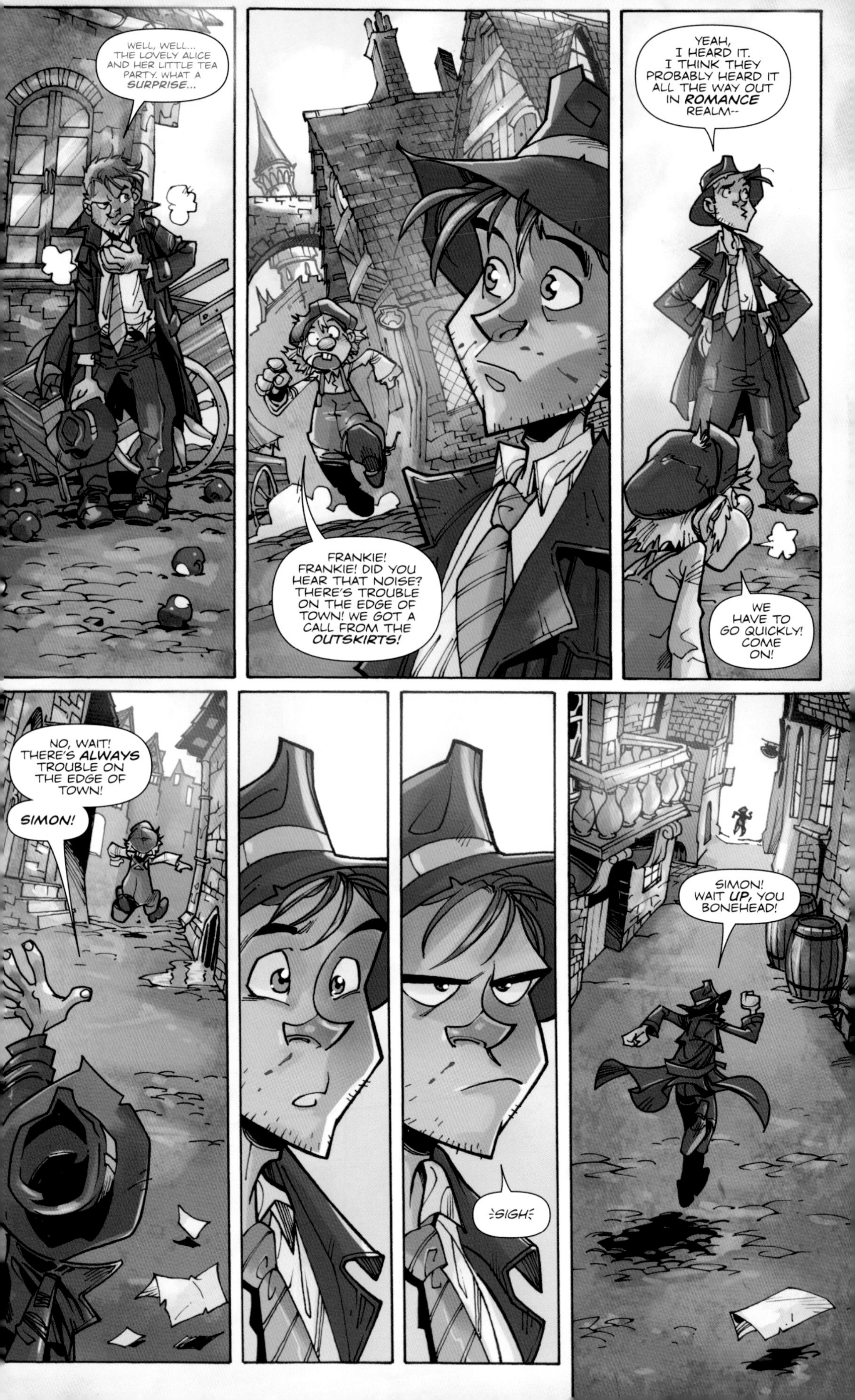
WELL, WELL... THE LOVELY ALICE AND HER LITTLE TEA PARTY. WHAT A SURPRISE...
FRANKIE! FRANKIE! DID YOU HEAR THAT NOISE? THERE'S TROUBLE ON THE EDGE OF TOWN! WE GOT A CALL FROM THE OUTSKIRTS!
YEAH, I HEARD IT. I THINK THEY PROBABLY HEARD IT ALL THE WAY OUT IN ROMANCE REALM--
WE HAVE TO GO QUICKLY! COME ON!
NO, WAIT! THERE'S ALWAYS TROUBLE ON THE EDGE OF TOWN!
SIMON!
SIGH
SIMON! WAIT UP, YOU BONEHEAD!

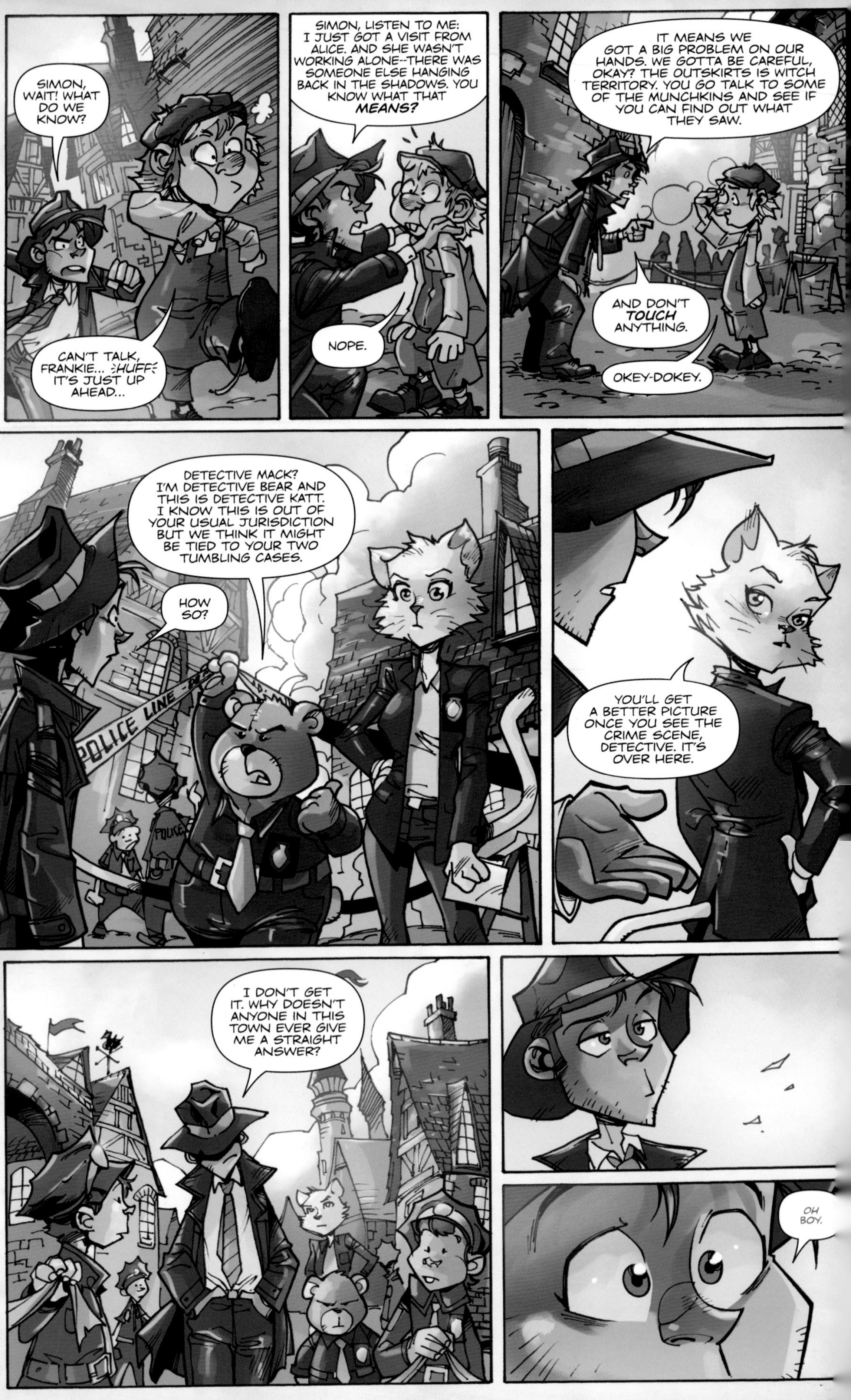
SIMON, WAIT! WHAT DO WE KNOW?
CAN'T TALK, FRANKIE... *HUFF* IT'S JUST UP AHEAD...
SIMON, LISTEN TO ME: I JUST GOT A VISIT FROM ALICE. AND SHE WASN'T WORKING ALONE--THERE WAS SOMEONE ELSE HANGING BACK IN THE SHADOWS. YOU KNOW WHAT THAT MEANS?
NOPE.
IT MEANS WE GOT A BIG PROBLEM ON OUR HANDS. WE GOTTA BE CAREFUL, OKAY? THE OUTSKIRTS IS WITCH TERRITORY. YOU GO TALK TO SOME OF THE MUNCHKINS AND SEE IF YOU CAN FIND OUT WHAT THEY SAW.
AND DON'T TOUCH ANYTHING.
OKEY-DOKEY.
DETECTIVE MACK? I'M DETECTIVE BEAR AND THIS IS DETECTIVE KATT. I KNOW THIS IS OUT OF YOUR USUAL JURISDICTION BUT WE THINK IT MIGHT BE TIED TO YOUR TWO TUMBLING CASES.
HOW SO?
POLICE LINE
POLICE
YOU'LL GET A BETTER PICTURE ONCE YOU SEE THE CRIME SCENE, DETECTIVE. IT'S OVER HERE.
I DON'T GET IT. WHY DOESN'T ANYONE IN THIS TOWN EVER GIVE ME A STRAIGHT ANSWER?
OH BOY.

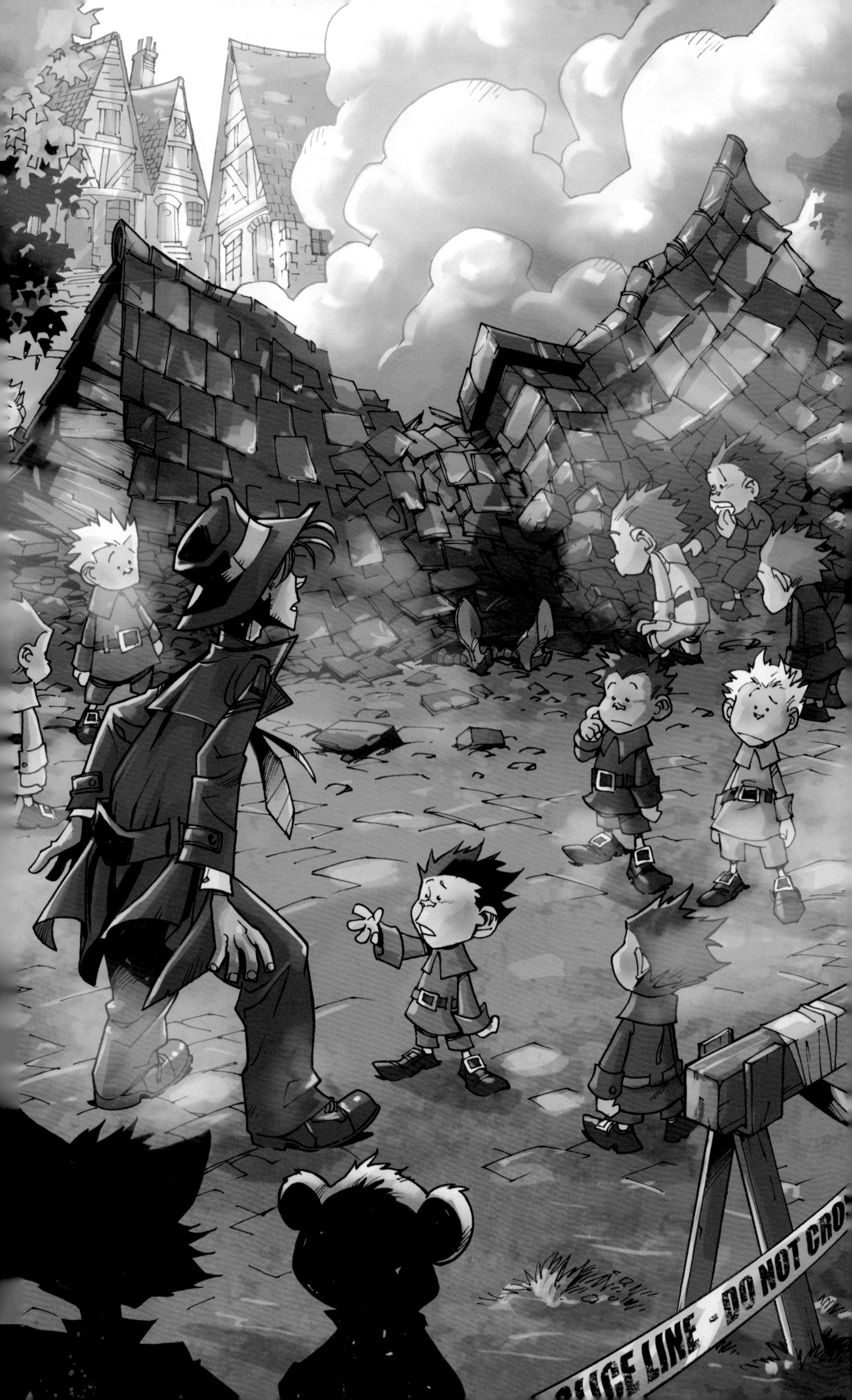
ICE LINE - DO NOT CRO

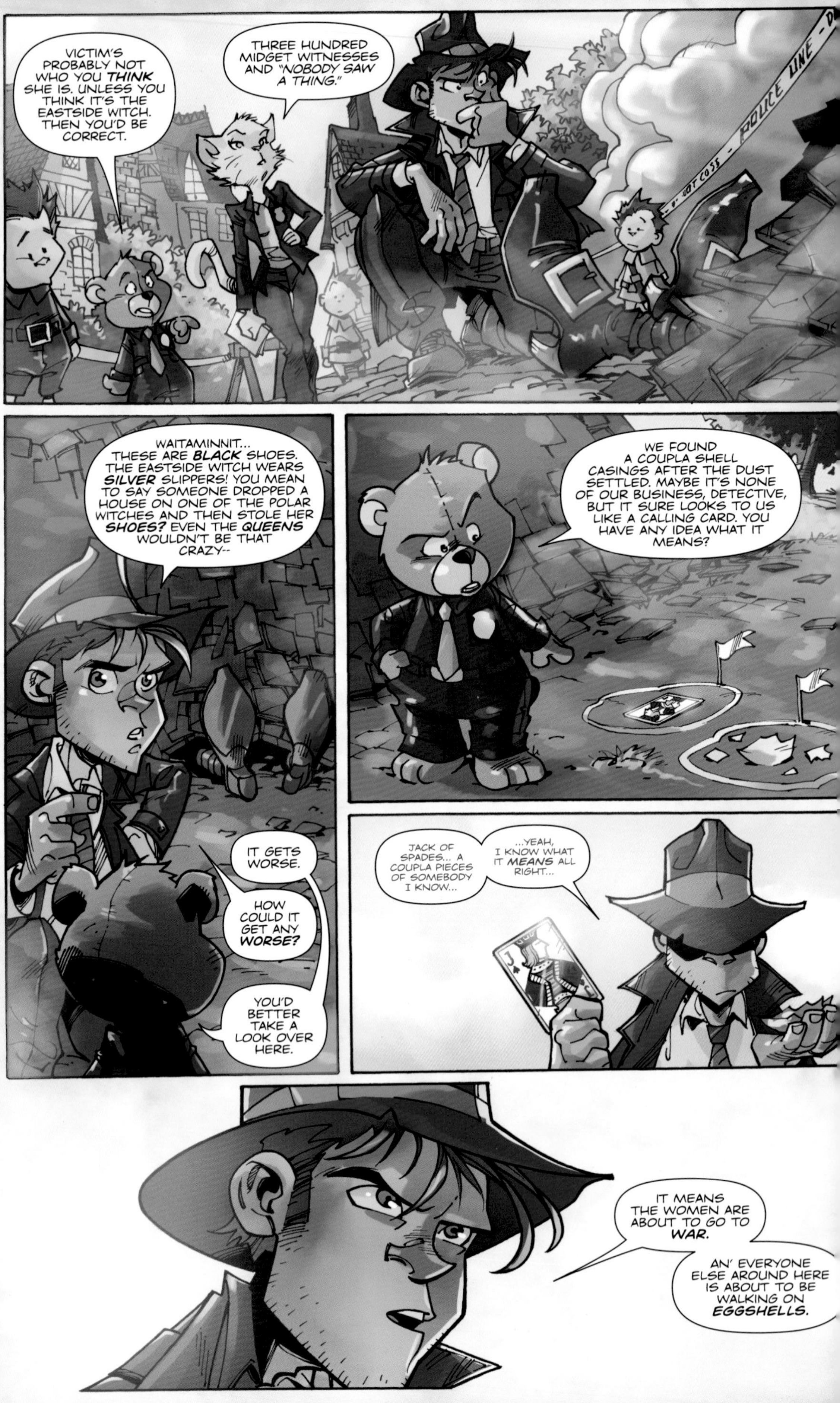

VICTIM'S PROBABLY NOT WHO YOU THINK SHE IS. UNLESS YOU THINK IT'S THE EASTSIDE WITCH. THEN YOU'D BE CORRECT.
THREE HUNDRED MIDGET WITNESSES AND "NOBODY SAW A THING."
POLICE LINE
WAITAMINNIT... THESE ARE BLACK SHOES. THE EASTSIDE WITCH WEARS SILVER SLIPPERS! YOU MEAN TO SAY SOMEONE DROPPED A HOUSE ON ONE OF THE POLAR WITCHES AND THEN STOLE HER SHOES? EVEN THE QUEENS WOULDN'T BE THAT CRAZY--
IT GETS WORSE.
HOW COULD IT GET ANY WORSE?
YOU'D BETTER TAKE A LOOK OVER HERE.
WE FOUND A COUPLA SHELL CASINGS AFTER THE DUST SETTLED. MAYBE IT'S NONE OF OUR BUSINESS, DETECTIVE, BUT IT SURE LOOKS TO US LIKE A CALLING CARD. YOU HAVE ANY IDEA WHAT IT MEANS?
JACK OF SPADES... A COUPLA PIECES OF SOMEBODY I KNOW...
...YEAH, I KNOW WHAT IT MEANS ALL RIGHT...
IT MEANS THE WOMEN ARE ABOUT TO GO TO WAR.
AN' EVERYONE ELSE AROUND HERE IS ABOUT TO BE WALKING ON EGGSHELLS.

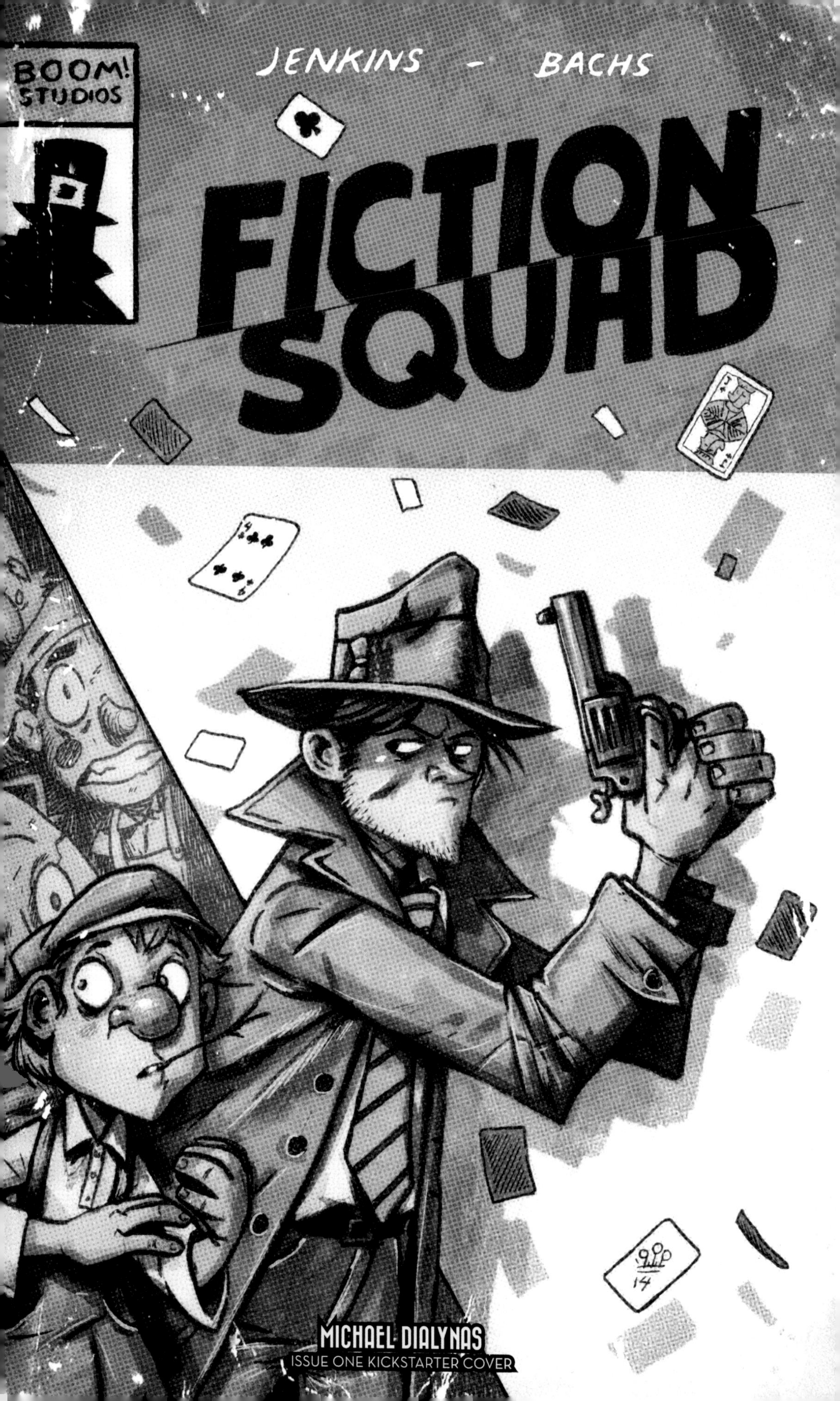
BOOM! STUDIOS
JENKINS - BACHS
FICTION SQUAD
MICHAEL DIALYNAS
ISSUE ONE KICKSTARTER COVER

CHAPTER TWO

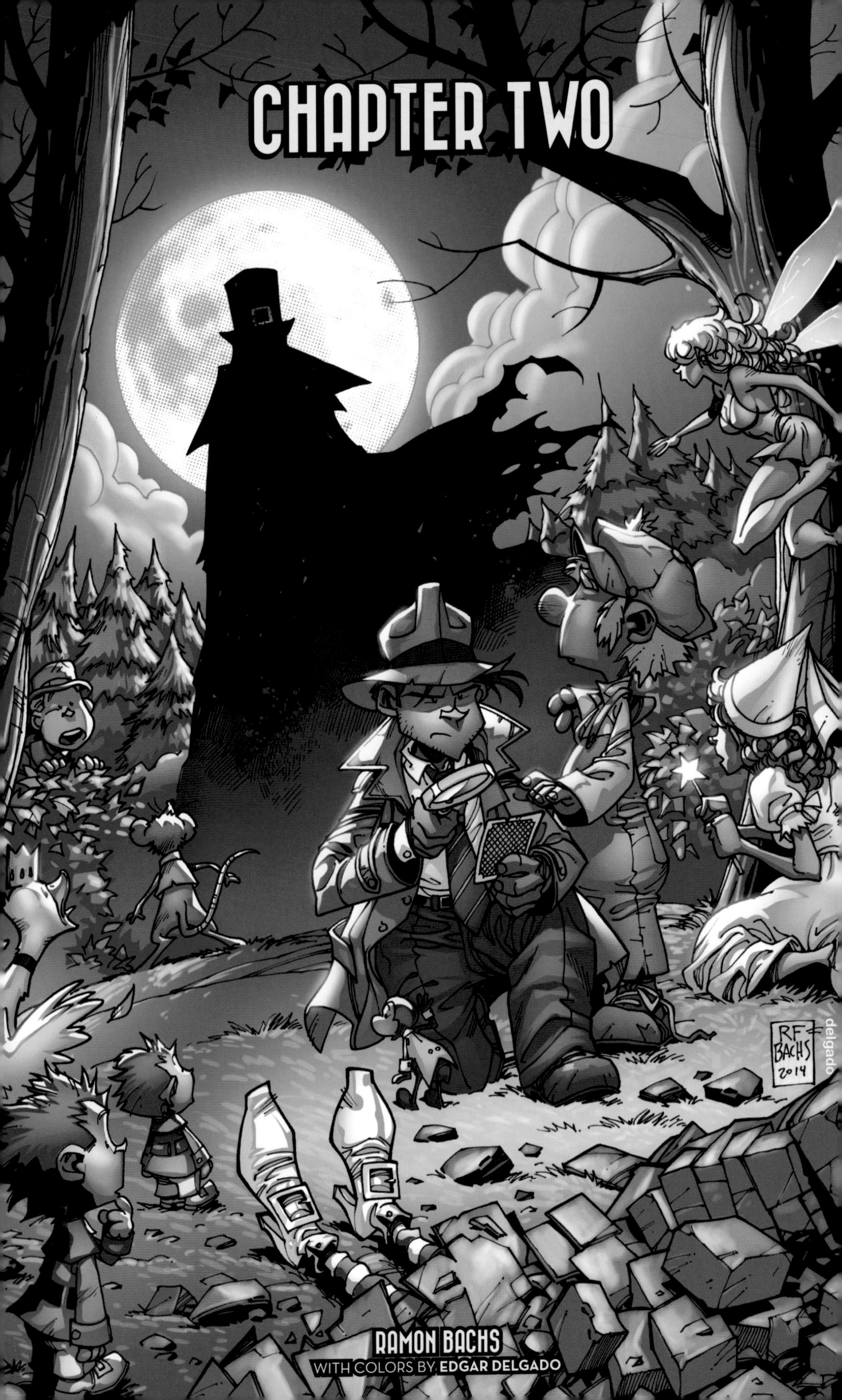
RF BACHS 2014
delgado

RAMON BACHS

WITH COLORS BY EDGAR DELGADO

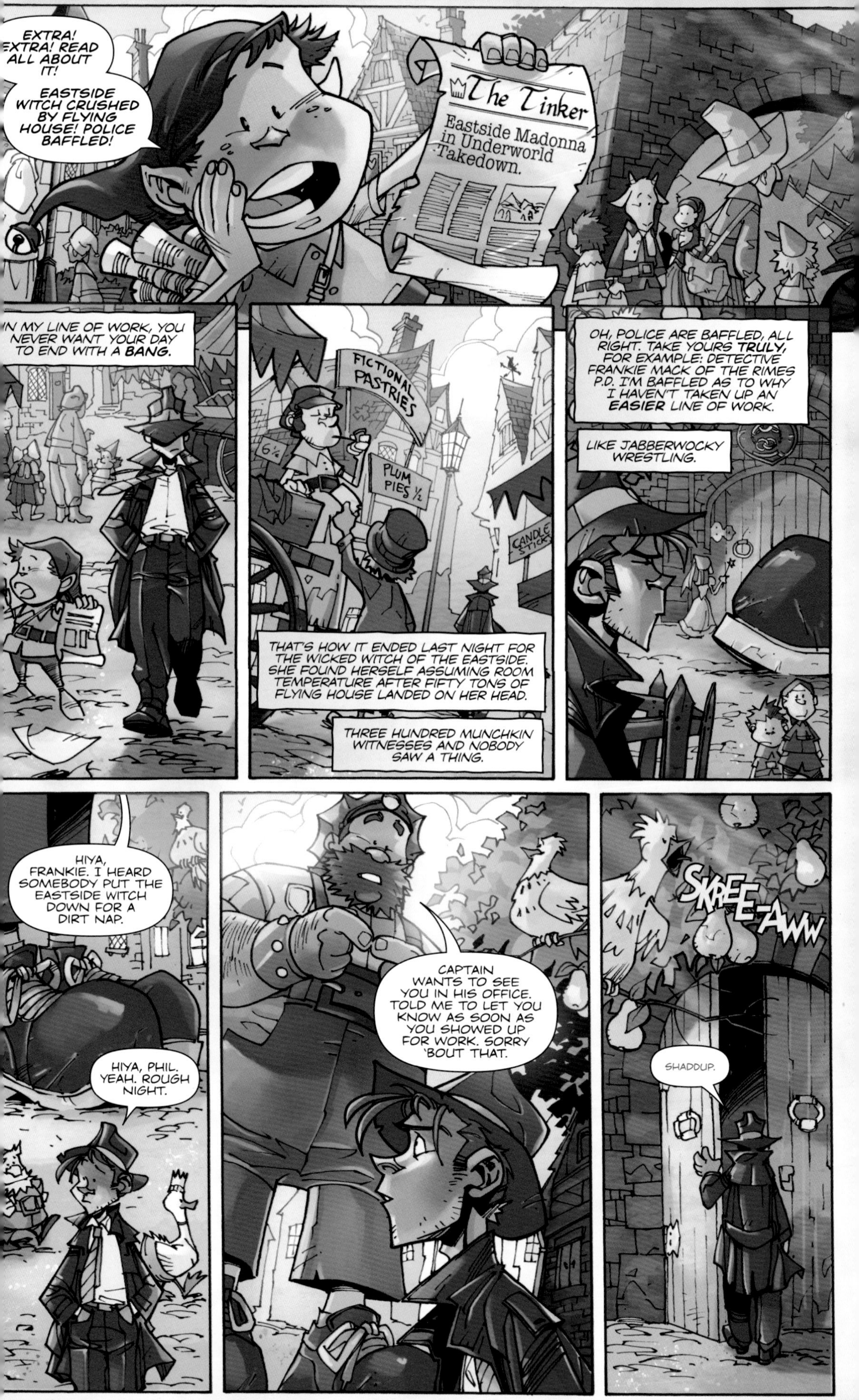
EXTRA! EXTRA! READ ALL ABOUT IT!
EASTSIDE WITCH CRUSHED BY FLYING HOUSE! POLICE BAFFLED!
The Tinker
Eastside Madonna in Underworld Takedown.
IN MY LINE OF WORK, YOU NEVER WANT YOUR DAY TO END WITH A BANG.
FICTIONAL PASTRIES
6½
PLUM PIES ½
CANDLE STICKS
THAT'S HOW IT ENDED LAST NIGHT FOR THE WICKED WITCH OF THE EASTSIDE. SHE FOUND HERSELF ASSUMING ROOM TEMPERATURE AFTER FIFTY TONS OF FLYING HOUSE LANDED ON HER HEAD.
THREE HUNDRED MUNCHKIN WITNESSES AND NOBODY SAW A THING.
OH, POLICE ARE BAFFLED, ALL RIGHT. TAKE YOURS TRULY, FOR EXAMPLE: DETECTIVE FRANKIE MACK OF THE RIMES P.D. I'M BAFFLED AS TO WHY I HAVEN'T TAKEN UP AN EASIER LINE OF WORK.
LIKE JABBERWOCKY WRESTLING.
HIYA, FRANKIE. I HEARD SOMEBODY PUT THE EASTSIDE WITCH DOWN FOR A DIRT NAP.
HIYA, PHIL. YEAH. ROUGH NIGHT.
CAPTAIN WANTS TO SEE YOU IN HIS OFFICE. TOLD ME TO LET YOU KNOW AS SOON AS YOU SHOWED UP FOR WORK. SORRY 'BOUT THAT.
SKREEE-AWW
SHADDUP.

SOMEBODY NEEDS TO CHOP DOWN THAT PEAR TREE OUT FRONT--

HIYA, FRANKIE. CHIEF SAYS HE NEEDS TO SEE US. DID WE MESS UP AGAIN?

I DON'T KNOW, SIMON. JUST LET ME DO THE TALKING, OKAY?

CAPT. T. THUMB

OKEY-DOKEY.

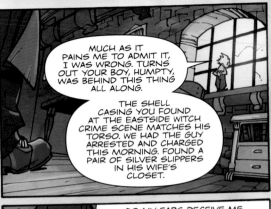

MUCH AS IT PAINS ME TO ADMIT IT, I WAS WRONG. TURNS OUT YOUR BOY, HUMPTY, WAS BEHIND THIS THING ALL ALONG.

THE SHELL CASING YOU FOUND AT THE EASTSIDE WITCH CRIME SCENE MATCHES HIS TORSO. WE HAD THE GUY ARRESTED AND CHARGED THIS MORNING. FOUND A PAIR OF SILVER SLIPPERS IN HIS WIFE'S CLOSET.

DO MY EARS DECEIVE ME, SIMON, OR DID OUR ILLUSTRIOUS CAPTAIN JUST SAY HE WAS WRONG?

UHM. I DIDN'T REALLY UNDERSTAND WHAT HE SAID.

THE EASTSIDE WITCH CASE IS *CLOSED*, DETECTIVES.

I'VE SPOKEN PERSONALLY WITH THE QUEEN OF HEARTS AND SHE ASSURES ME THE CARDS FULLY DISASSOCIATE THEMSELVES WITH MISTER DUMPTY'S ACTIONS.

WE HAVE OUR PRIME SUSPECT IN CUSTODY. THE EVIDENCE IS CLEAR.

ALL WE NEED NOW IS A *CONFESSION*.

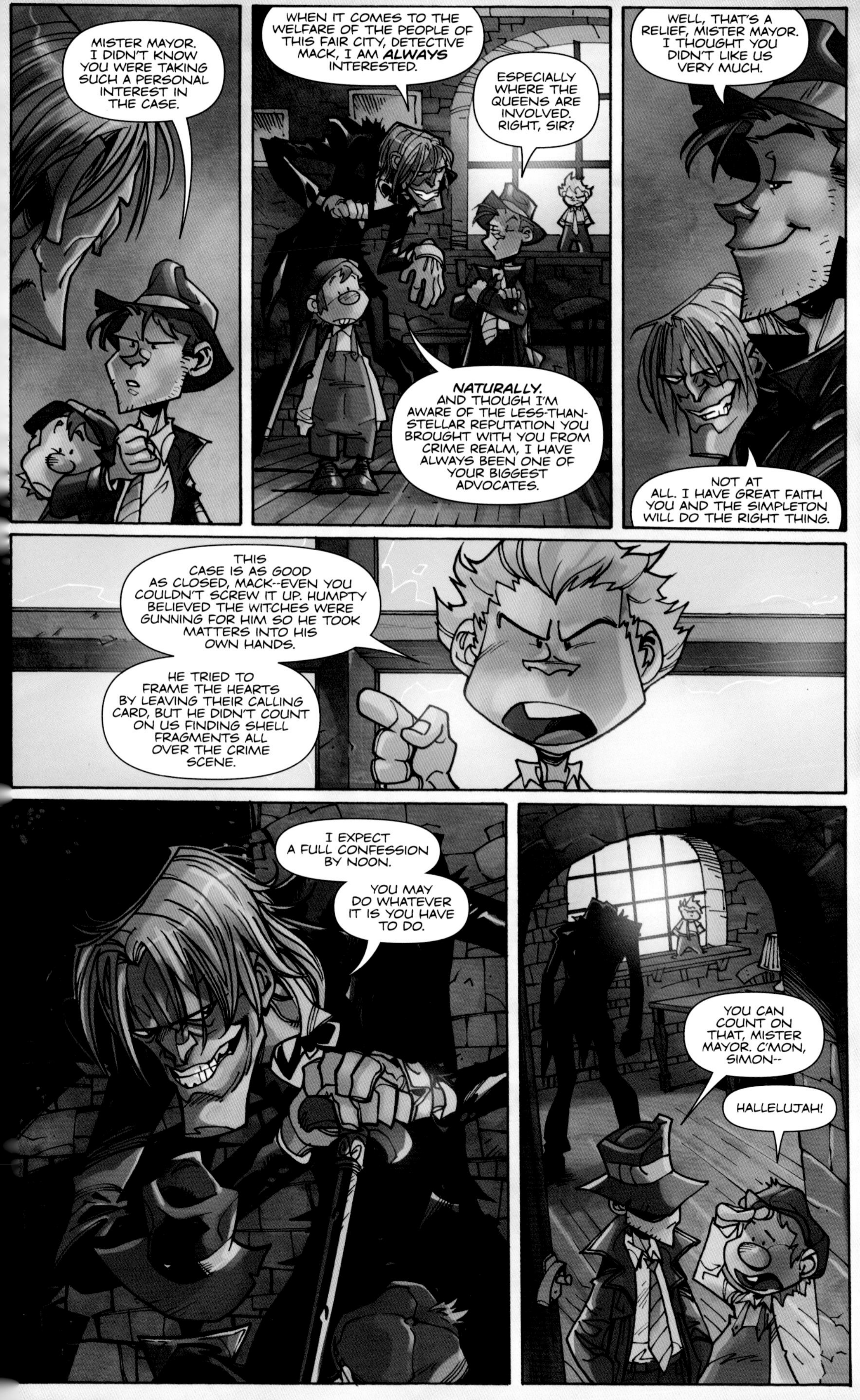

MISTER MAYOR. I DIDN'T KNOW YOU WERE TAKING SUCH A PERSONAL INTEREST IN THE CASE.
WHEN IT COMES TO THE WELFARE OF THE PEOPLE OF THIS FAIR CITY, DETECTIVE MACK, I AM ALWAYS INTERESTED.
ESPECIALLY WHERE THE QUEENS ARE INVOLVED. RIGHT, SIR?
NATURALLY. AND THOUGH I'M AWARE OF THE LESS-THAN-STELLAR REPUTATION YOU BROUGHT WITH YOU FROM CRIME REALM, I HAVE ALWAYS BEEN ONE OF YOUR BIGGEST ADVOCATES.
WELL, THAT'S A RELIEF, MISTER MAYOR. I THOUGHT YOU DIDN'T LIKE US VERY MUCH.
NOT AT ALL. I HAVE GREAT FAITH YOU AND THE SIMPLETON WILL DO THE RIGHT THING.
THIS CASE IS AS GOOD AS CLOSED, MACK--EVEN YOU COULDN'T SCREW IT UP. HUMPTY BELIEVED THE WITCHES WERE GUNNING FOR HIM SO HE TOOK MATTERS INTO HIS OWN HANDS.
HE TRIED TO FRAME THE HEARTS BY LEAVING THEIR CALLING CARD, BUT HE DIDN'T COUNT ON US FINDING SHELL FRAGMENTS ALL OVER THE CRIME SCENE.
I EXPECT A FULL CONFESSION BY NOON.
YOU MAY DO WHATEVER IT IS YOU HAVE TO DO.
YOU CAN COUNT ON THAT, MISTER MAYOR. C'MON, SIMON--
HALLELUJAH!

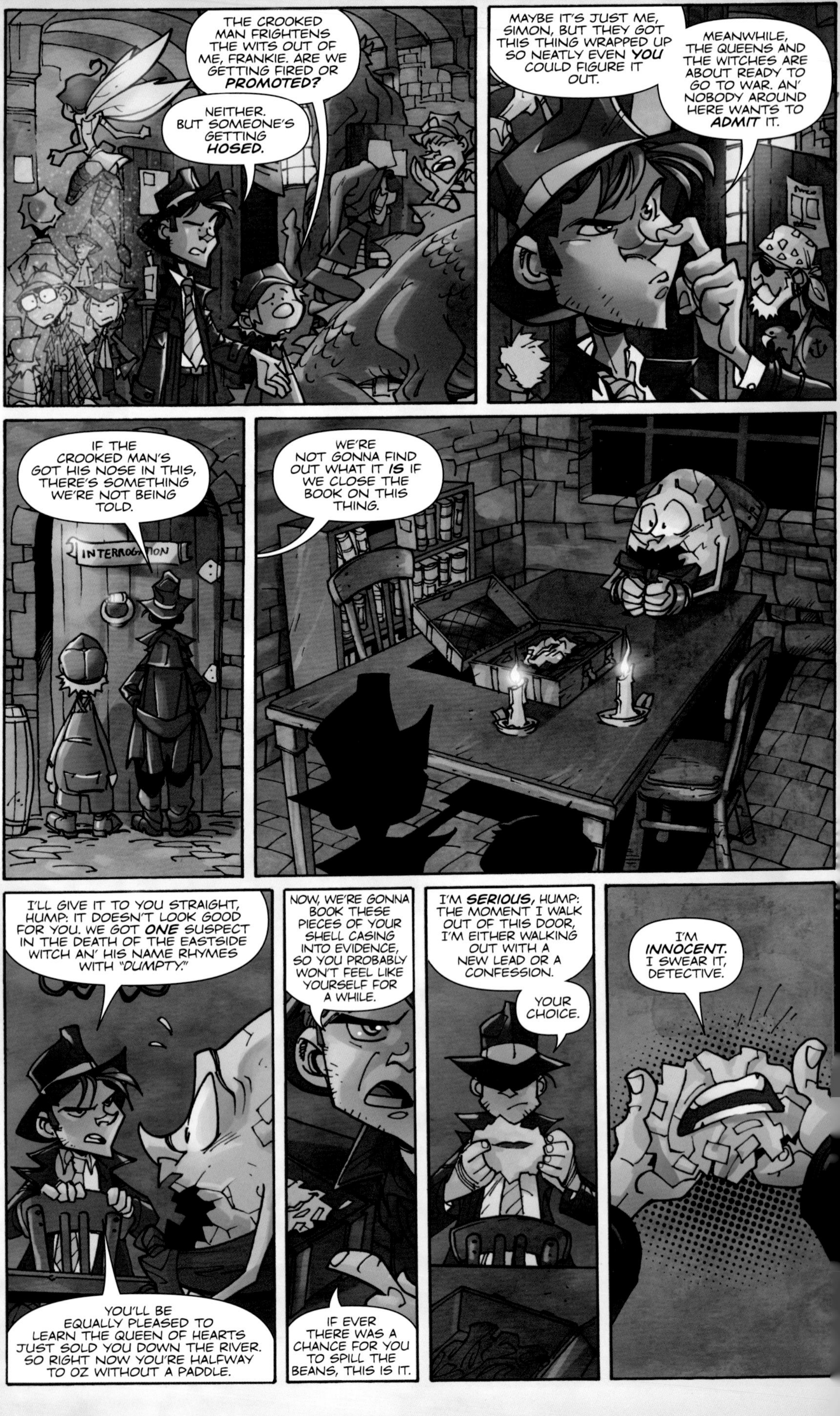
THE CROOKED MAN FRIGHTENS THE WITS OUT OF ME, FRANKIE. ARE WE GETTING FIRED OR PROMOTED?
NEITHER. BUT SOMEONE'S GETTING HOSED.
MAYBE IT'S JUST ME, SIMON, BUT THEY GOT THIS THING WRAPPED UP SO NEATLY EVEN YOU COULD FIGURE IT OUT.
MEANWHILE, THE QUEENS AND THE WITCHES ARE ABOUT READY TO GO TO WAR. AN' NOBODY AROUND HERE WANTS TO ADMIT IT.
IF THE CROOKED MAN'S GOT HIS NOSE IN THIS, THERE'S SOMETHING WE'RE NOT BEING TOLD.
INTERROGATION
WE'RE NOT GONNA FIND OUT WHAT IT IS IF WE CLOSE THE BOOK ON THIS THING.
I'LL GIVE IT TO YOU STRAIGHT, HUMP: IT DOESN'T LOOK GOOD FOR YOU. WE GOT ONE SUSPECT IN THE DEATH OF THE EASTSIDE WITCH AN' HIS NAME RHYMES WITH "DUMPTY."
YOU'LL BE EQUALLY PLEASED TO LEARN THE QUEEN OF HEARTS JUST SOLD YOU DOWN THE RIVER. SO RIGHT NOW YOU'RE HALFWAY TO OZ WITHOUT A PADDLE.
NOW, WE'RE GONNA BOOK THESE PIECES OF YOUR SHELL CASING INTO EVIDENCE, SO YOU PROBABLY WON'T FEEL LIKE YOURSELF FOR A WHILE.
IF EVER THERE WAS A CHANCE FOR YOU TO SPILL THE BEANS, THIS IS IT.
I'M SERIOUS, HUMP: THE MOMENT I WALK OUT OF THIS DOOR, I'M EITHER WALKING OUT WITH A NEW LEAD OR A CONFESSION.
YOUR CHOICE.
I'M INNOCENT. I SWEAR IT, DETECTIVE.

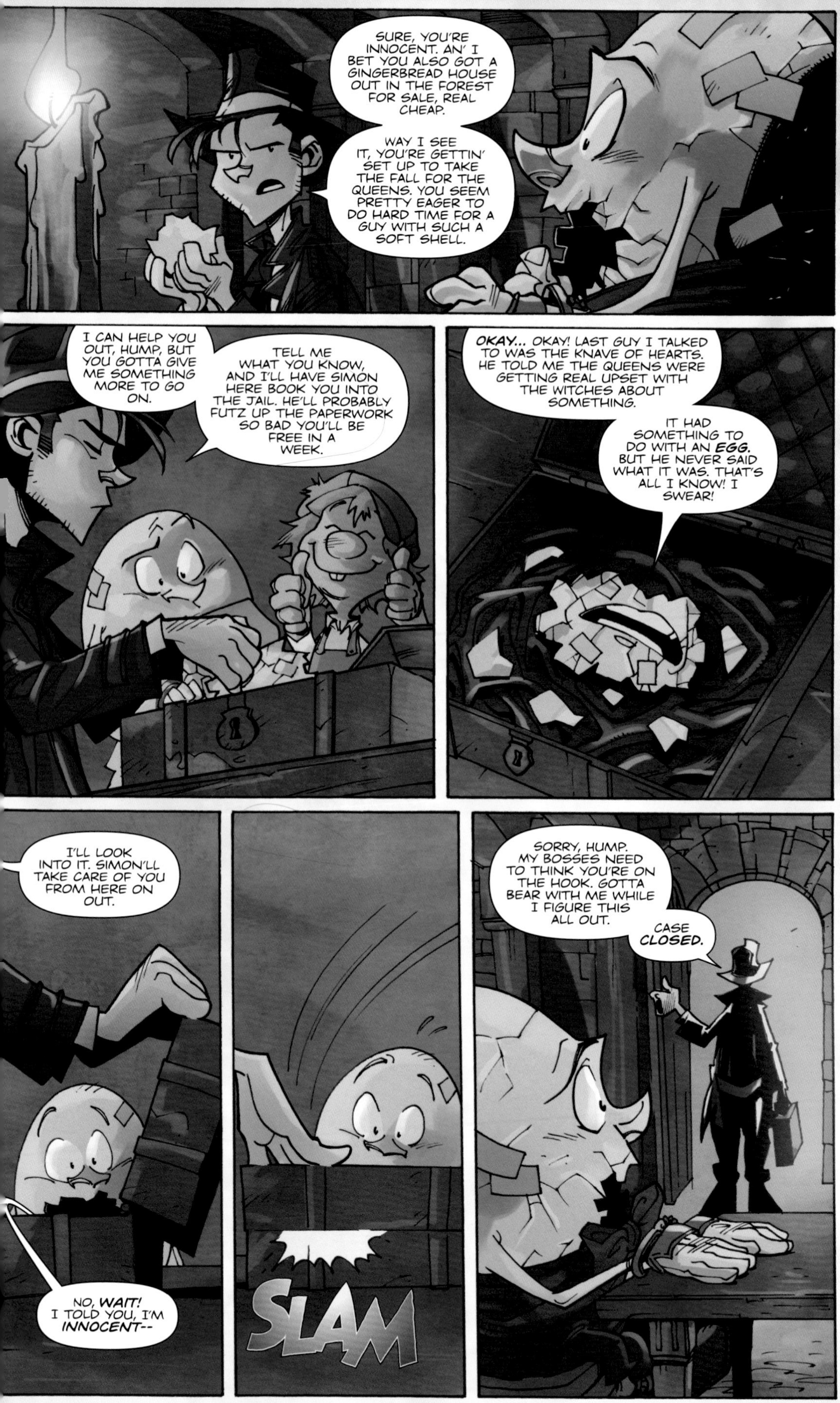
SURE, YOU'RE INNOCENT. AN' I BET YOU ALSO GOT A GINGERBREAD HOUSE OUT IN THE FOREST FOR SALE, REAL CHEAP.
WAY I SEE IT, YOU'RE GETTIN' SET UP TO TAKE THE FALL FOR THE QUEENS. YOU SEEM PRETTY EAGER TO DO HARD TIME FOR A GUY WITH SUCH A SOFT SHELL.
I CAN HELP YOU OUT, HUMP, BUT YOU GOTTA GIVE ME SOMETHING MORE TO GO ON.
TELL ME WHAT YOU KNOW, AND I'LL HAVE SIMON HERE BOOK YOU INTO THE JAIL. HE'LL PROBABLY FUTZ UP THE PAPERWORK SO BAD YOU'LL BE FREE IN A WEEK.
OKAY... OKAY! LAST GUY I TALKED TO WAS THE KNAVE OF HEARTS. HE TOLD ME THE QUEENS WERE GETTING REAL UPSET WITH THE WITCHES ABOUT SOMETHING.
IT HAD SOMETHING TO DO WITH AN **EGG.** BUT HE NEVER SAID WHAT IT WAS. THAT'S ALL I KNOW! I SWEAR!
I'LL LOOK INTO IT. SIMON'LL TAKE CARE OF YOU FROM HERE ON OUT.
NO, **WAIT!** I TOLD YOU, I'M **INNOCENT--**
SLAM
SORRY, HUMP. MY BOSSES NEED TO THINK YOU'RE ON THE HOOK. GOTTA BEAR WITH ME WHILE I FIGURE THIS ALL OUT.
CASE **CLOSED.**

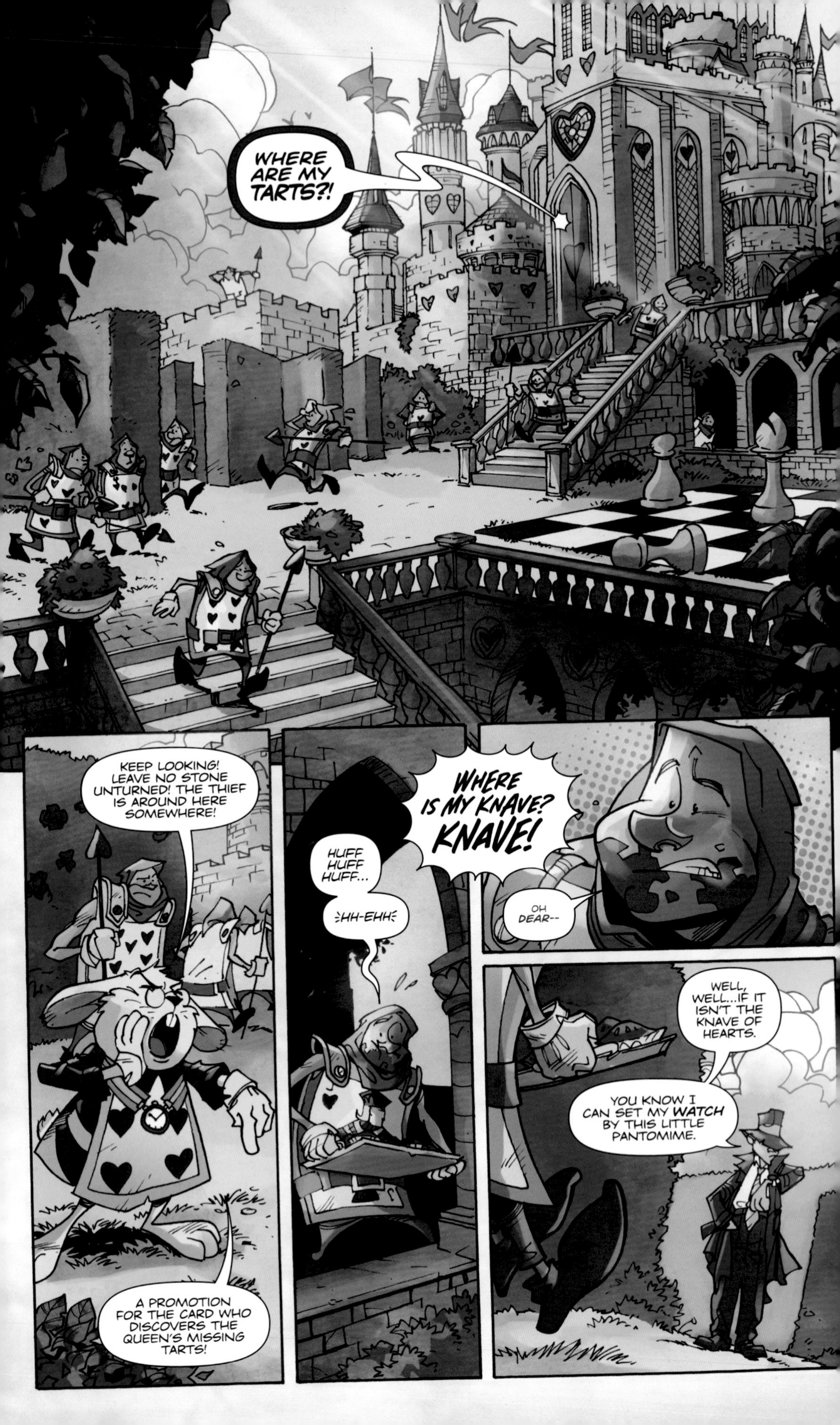
WHERE ARE MY TARTS?!
KEEP LOOKING! LEAVE NO STONE UNTURNED! THE THIEF IS AROUND HERE SOMEWHERE!
A PROMOTION FOR THE CARD WHO DISCOVERS THE QUEEN'S MISSING TARTS!
WHERE IS MY KNAVE? KNAVE!
HUFF HUFF HUFF...
HH-EHH
OH DEAR--
WELL, WELL...IF IT ISN'T THE KNAVE OF HEARTS.
YOU KNOW I CAN SET MY WATCH BY THIS LITTLE PANTOMIME.

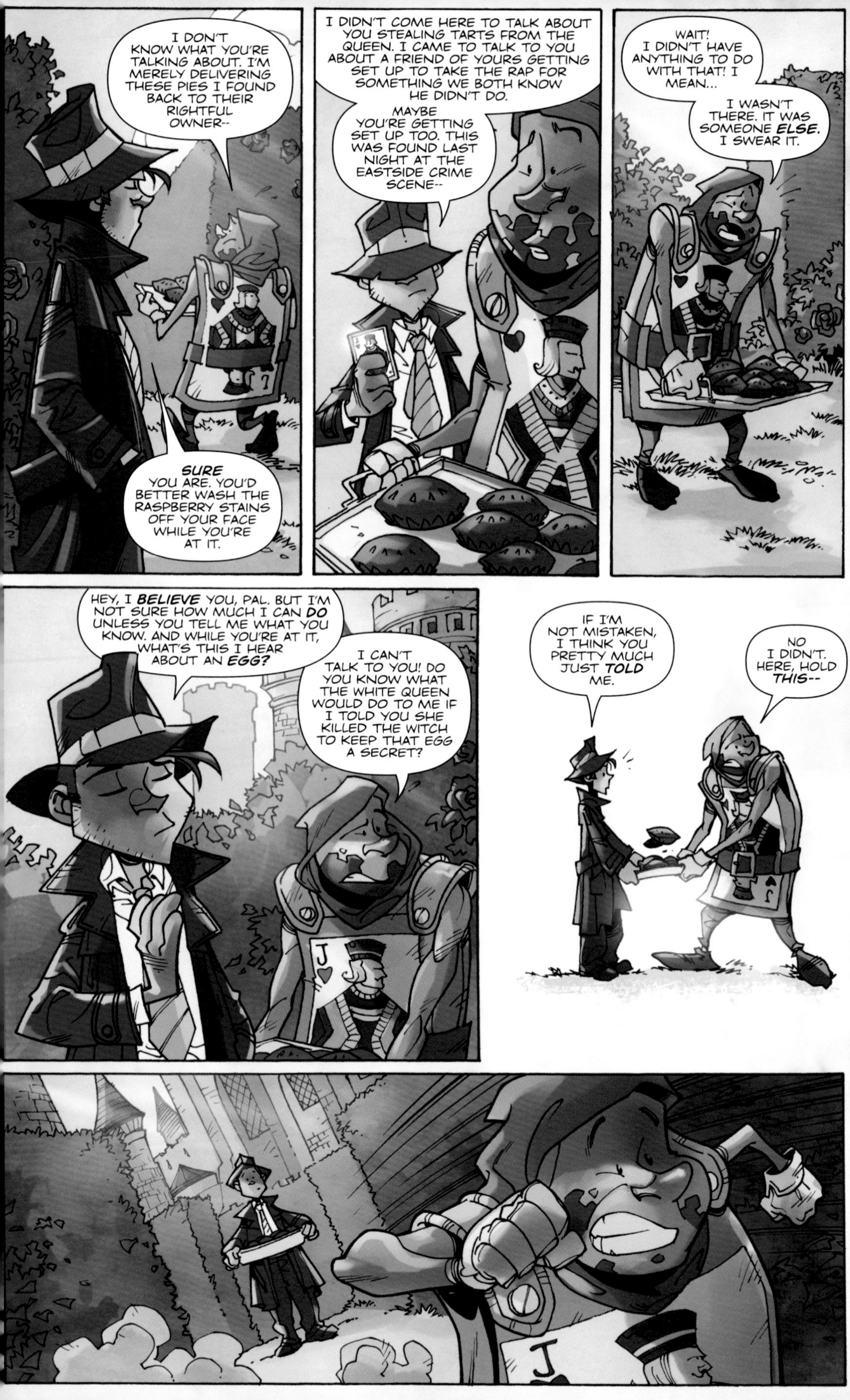
I DON'T KNOW WHAT YOU'RE TALKING ABOUT. I'M MERELY DELIVERING THESE PIES I FOUND BACK TO THEIR RIGHTFUL OWNER--
SURE YOU ARE. YOU'D BETTER WASH THE RASPBERRY STAINS OFF YOUR FACE WHILE YOU'RE AT IT.
I DIDN'T COME HERE TO TALK ABOUT YOU STEALING TARTS FROM THE QUEEN. I CAME TO TALK TO YOU ABOUT A FRIEND OF YOURS GETTING SET UP TO TAKE THE RAP FOR SOMETHING WE BOTH KNOW HE DIDN'T DO.
MAYBE YOU'RE GETTING SET UP TOO. THIS WAS FOUND LAST NIGHT AT THE EASTSIDE CRIME SCENE--
WAIT! I DIDN'T HAVE ANYTHING TO DO WITH THAT! I MEAN...
I WASN'T THERE. IT WAS SOMEONE **ELSE**. I SWEAR IT.
HEY, I **BELIEVE** YOU, PAL. BUT I'M NOT SURE HOW MUCH I CAN **DO** UNLESS YOU TELL ME WHAT YOU KNOW. AND WHILE YOU'RE AT IT, WHAT'S THIS I HEAR ABOUT AN **EGG?**
I CAN'T TALK TO YOU! DO YOU KNOW WHAT THE WHITE QUEEN WOULD DO TO ME IF I TOLD YOU SHE KILLED THE WITCH TO KEEP THAT EGG A SECRET?
IF I'M NOT MISTAKEN, I THINK YOU PRETTY MUCH JUST **TOLD** ME.
NO I DIDN'T. HERE, HOLD **THIS--**

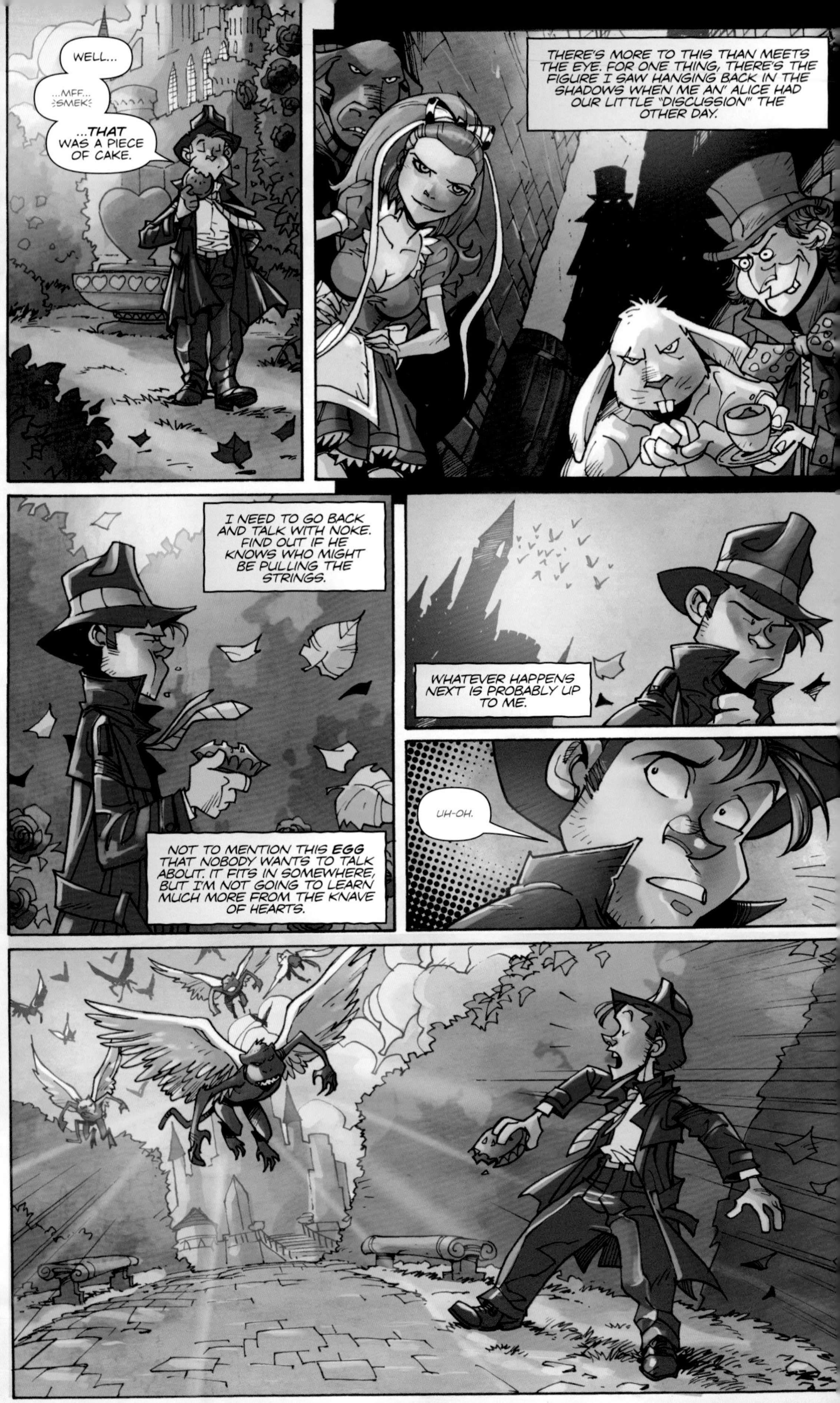
WELL...
...MFF... SMEK
...THAT WAS A PIECE OF CAKE.
THERE'S MORE TO THIS THAN MEETS THE EYE. FOR ONE THING, THERE'S THE FIGURE I SAW HANGING BACK IN THE SHADOWS WHEN ME AN' ALICE HAD OUR LITTLE "DISCUSSION" THE OTHER DAY.
I NEED TO GO BACK AND TALK WITH NOKE. FIND OUT IF HE KNOWS WHO MIGHT BE PULLING THE STRINGS.
NOT TO MENTION THIS EGG THAT NOBODY WANTS TO TALK ABOUT. IT FITS IN SOMEWHERE, BUT I'M NOT GOING TO LEARN MUCH MORE FROM THE KNAVE OF HEARTS.
WHATEVER HAPPENS NEXT IS PROBABLY UP TO ME.
UH-OH.

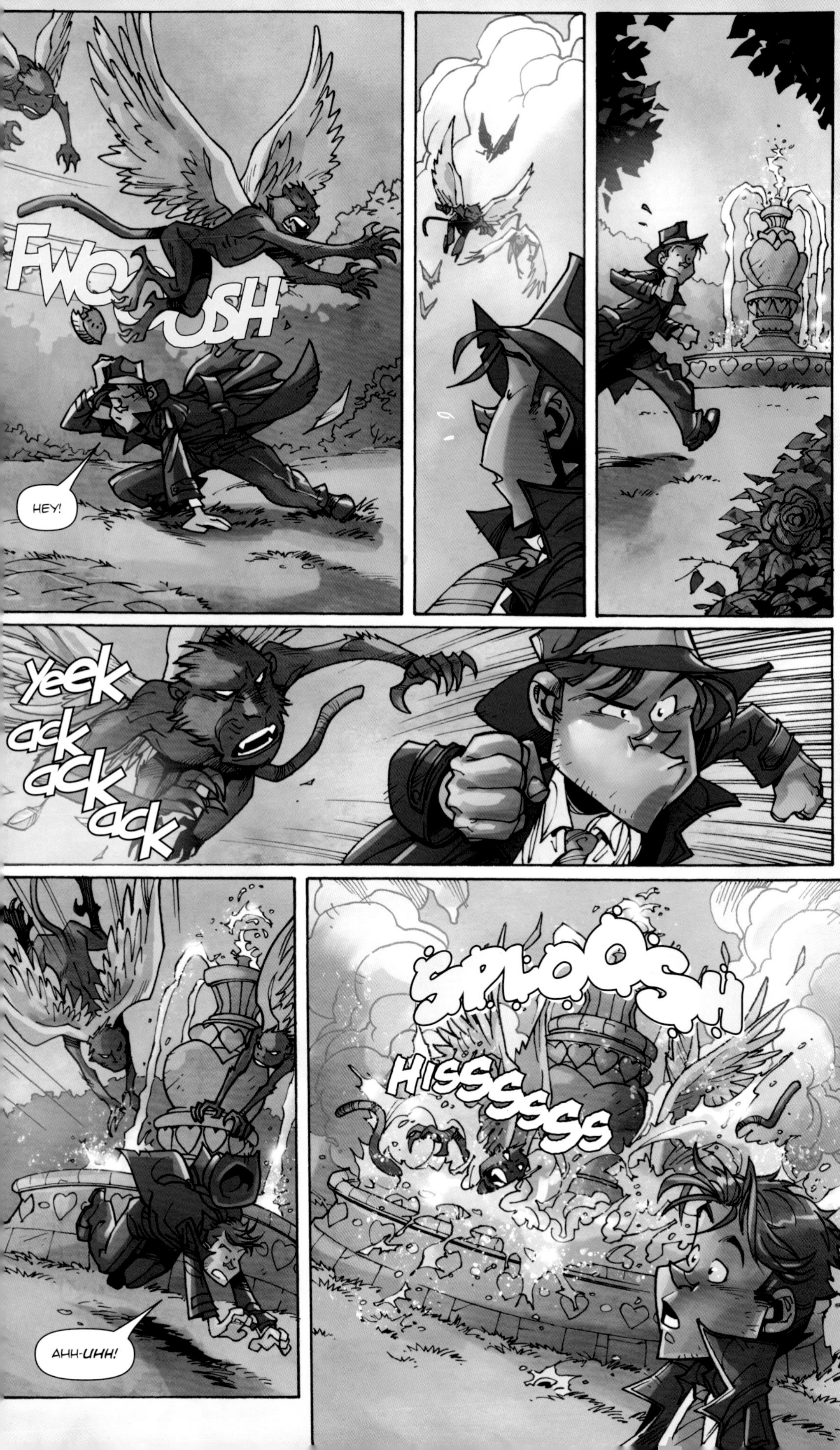
FWOOSH
HEY!
yeek ack ack ack
AHH-UHH!
SPLOOSH
HISSSSSSS

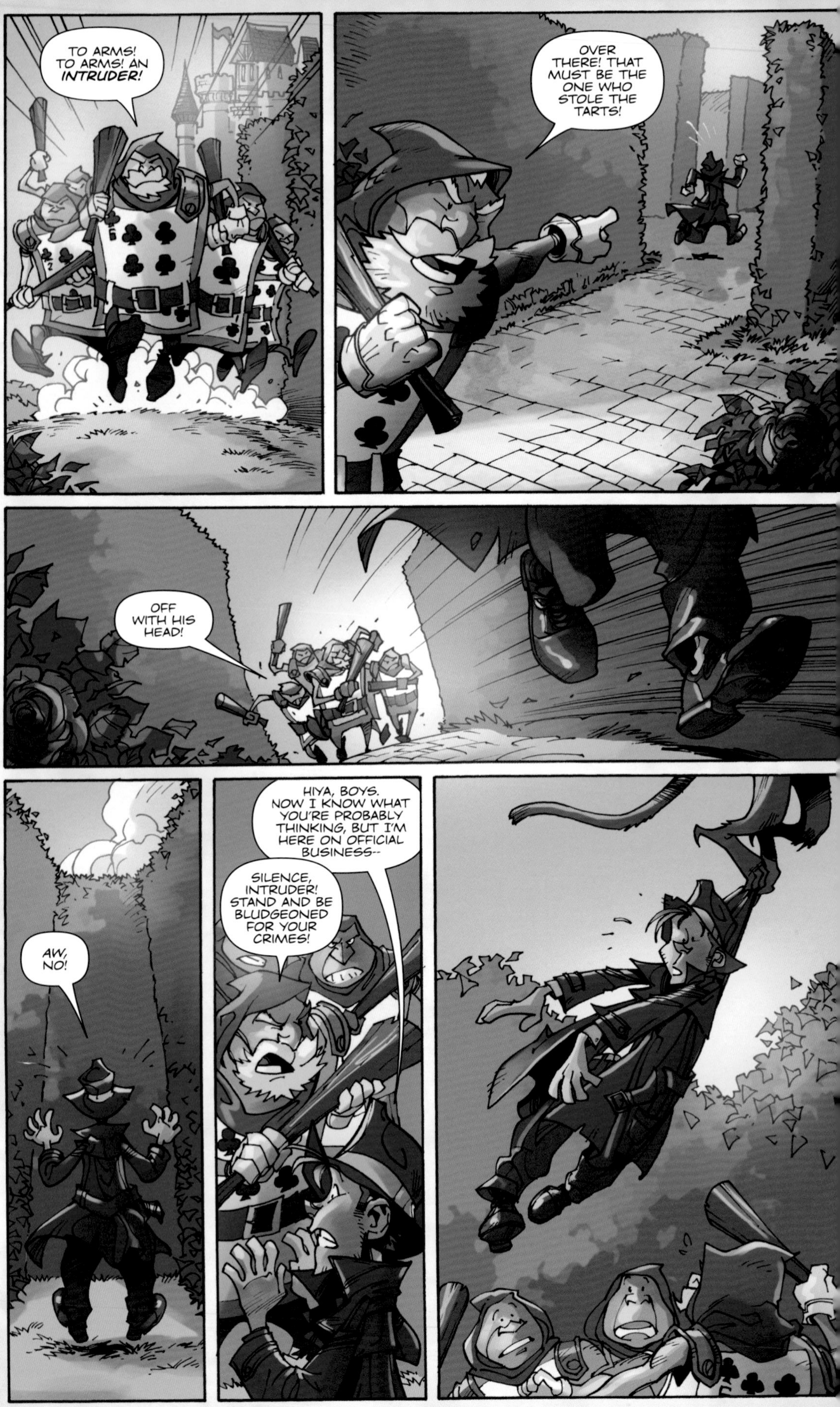
TO ARMS! TO ARMS! AN INTRUDER!
OVER THERE! THAT MUST BE THE ONE WHO STOLE THE TARTS!
OFF WITH HIS HEAD!
AW, NO!
HIYA, BOYS. NOW I KNOW WHAT YOU'RE PROBABLY THINKING, BUT I'M HERE ON OFFICIAL BUSINESS--
SILENCE, INTRUDER! STAND AND BE BLUDGEONED FOR YOUR CRIMES!

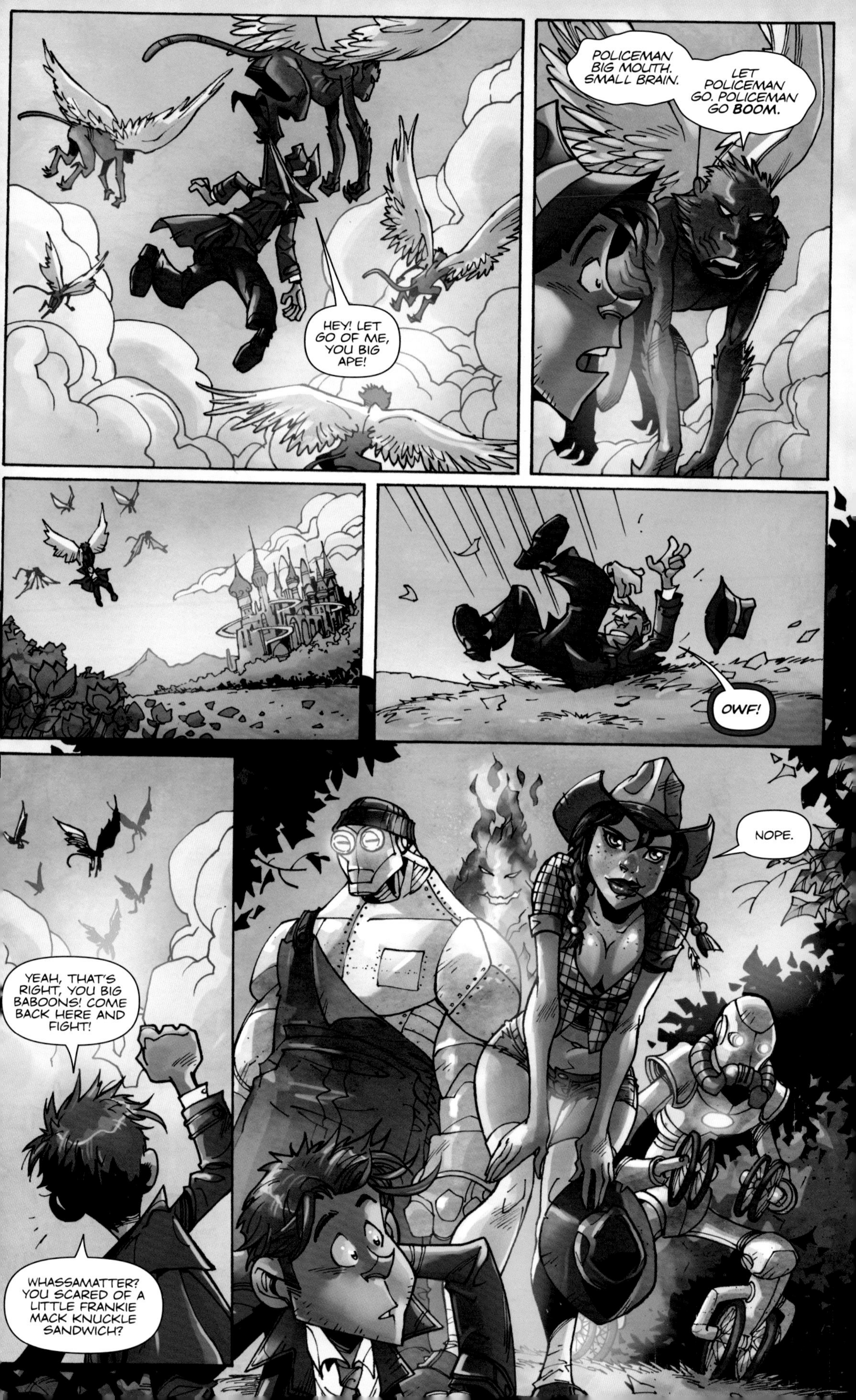
HEY! LET GO OF ME, YOU BIG APE!
POLICEMAN BIG MOUTH. SMALL BRAIN.
LET POLICEMAN GO. POLICEMAN GO BOOM.
OWF!
YEAH, THAT'S RIGHT, YOU BIG BABOONS! COME BACK HERE AND FIGHT!
WHASSAMATTER? YOU SCARED OF A LITTLE FRANKIE MACK KNUCKLE SANDWICH?
NOPE.

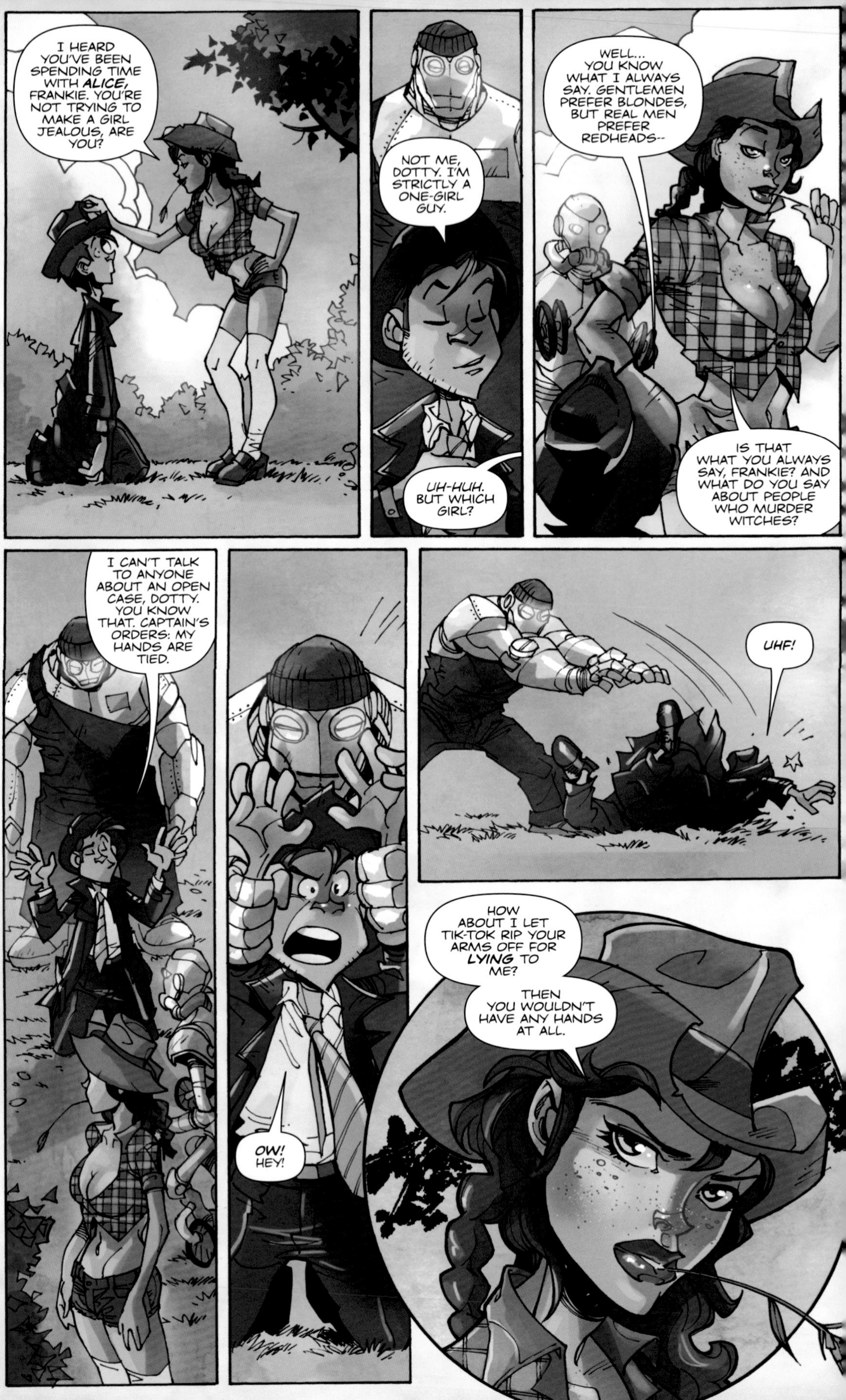
I HEARD YOU'VE BEEN SPENDING TIME WITH ALICE, FRANKIE. YOU'RE NOT TRYING TO MAKE A GIRL JEALOUS, ARE YOU?
NOT ME, DOTTY. I'M STRICTLY A ONE-GIRL GUY.
UH-HUH. BUT WHICH GIRL?
WELL... YOU KNOW WHAT I ALWAYS SAY. GENTLEMEN PREFER BLONDES, BUT REAL MEN PREFER REDHEADS--
IS THAT WHAT YOU ALWAYS SAY, FRANKIE? AND WHAT DO YOU SAY ABOUT PEOPLE WHO MURDER WITCHES?
I CAN'T TALK TO ANYONE ABOUT AN OPEN CASE, DOTTY. YOU KNOW THAT. CAPTAIN'S ORDERS: MY HANDS ARE TIED.
OW! HEY!
UHF!
HOW ABOUT I LET TIK-TOK RIP YOUR ARMS OFF FOR LYING TO ME?
THEN YOU WOULDN'T HAVE ANY HANDS AT ALL.

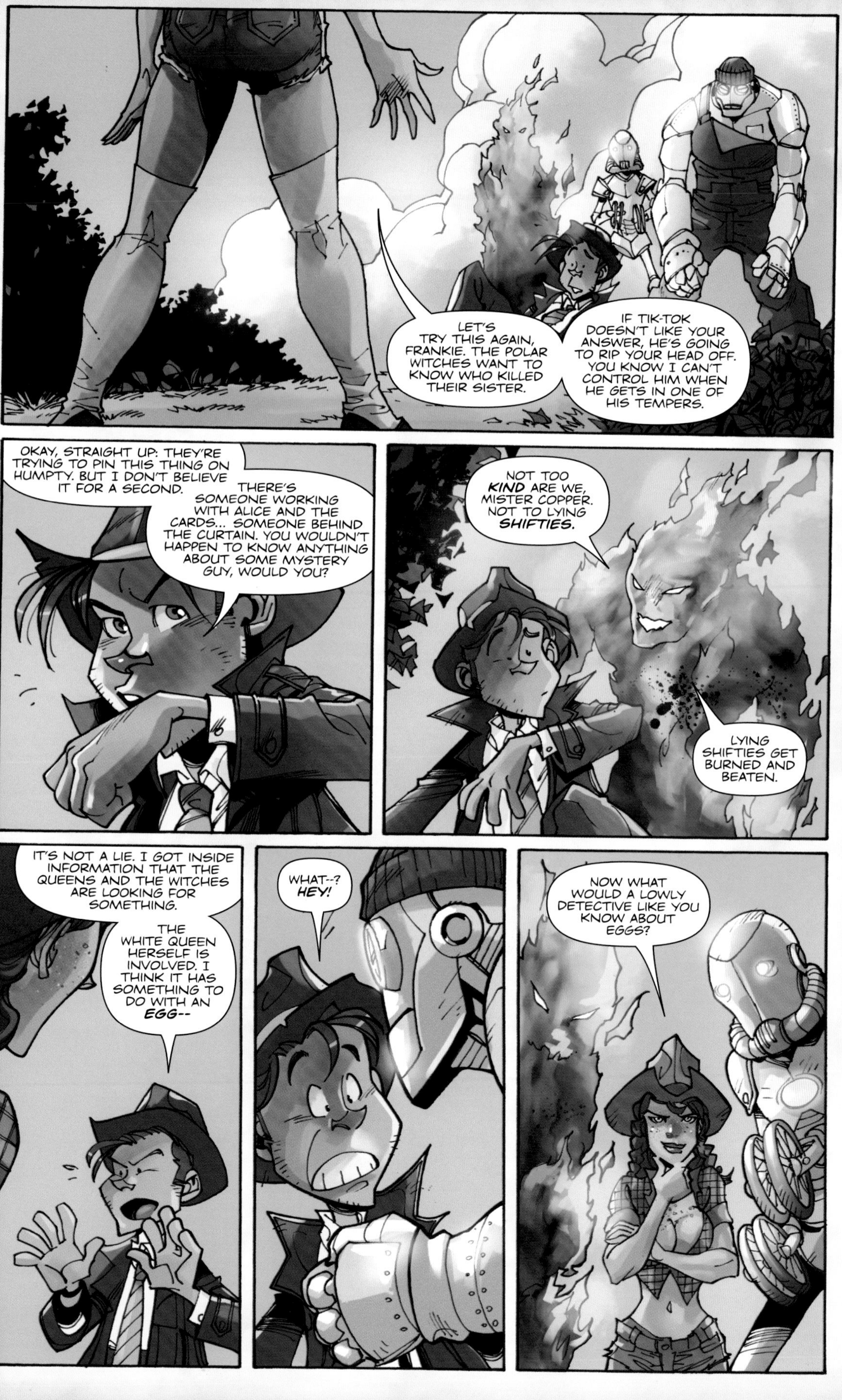
LET'S TRY THIS AGAIN, FRANKIE. THE POLAR WITCHES WANT TO KNOW WHO KILLED THEIR SISTER.
IF TIK-TOK DOESN'T LIKE YOUR ANSWER, HE'S GOING TO RIP YOUR HEAD OFF. YOU KNOW I CAN'T CONTROL HIM WHEN HE GETS IN ONE OF HIS TEMPERS.
OKAY, STRAIGHT UP: THEY'RE TRYING TO PIN THIS THING ON HUMPTY. BUT I DON'T BELIEVE IT FOR A SECOND.
THERE'S SOMEONE WORKING WITH ALICE AND THE CARDS... SOMEONE BEHIND THE CURTAIN. YOU WOULDN'T HAPPEN TO KNOW ANYTHING ABOUT SOME MYSTERY GUY, WOULD YOU?
NOT TOO **KIND** ARE WE, MISTER COPPER. NOT TO LYING **SHIFTIES.**
LYING SHIFTIES GET BURNED AND BEATEN.
IT'S NOT A LIE. I GOT INSIDE INFORMATION THAT THE QUEENS AND THE WITCHES ARE LOOKING FOR SOMETHING.
THE WHITE QUEEN HERSELF IS INVOLVED. I THINK IT HAS SOMETHING TO DO WITH AN **EGG--**
WHAT--? **HEY!**
NOW WHAT WOULD A LOWLY DETECTIVE LIKE YOU KNOW ABOUT EGGS?

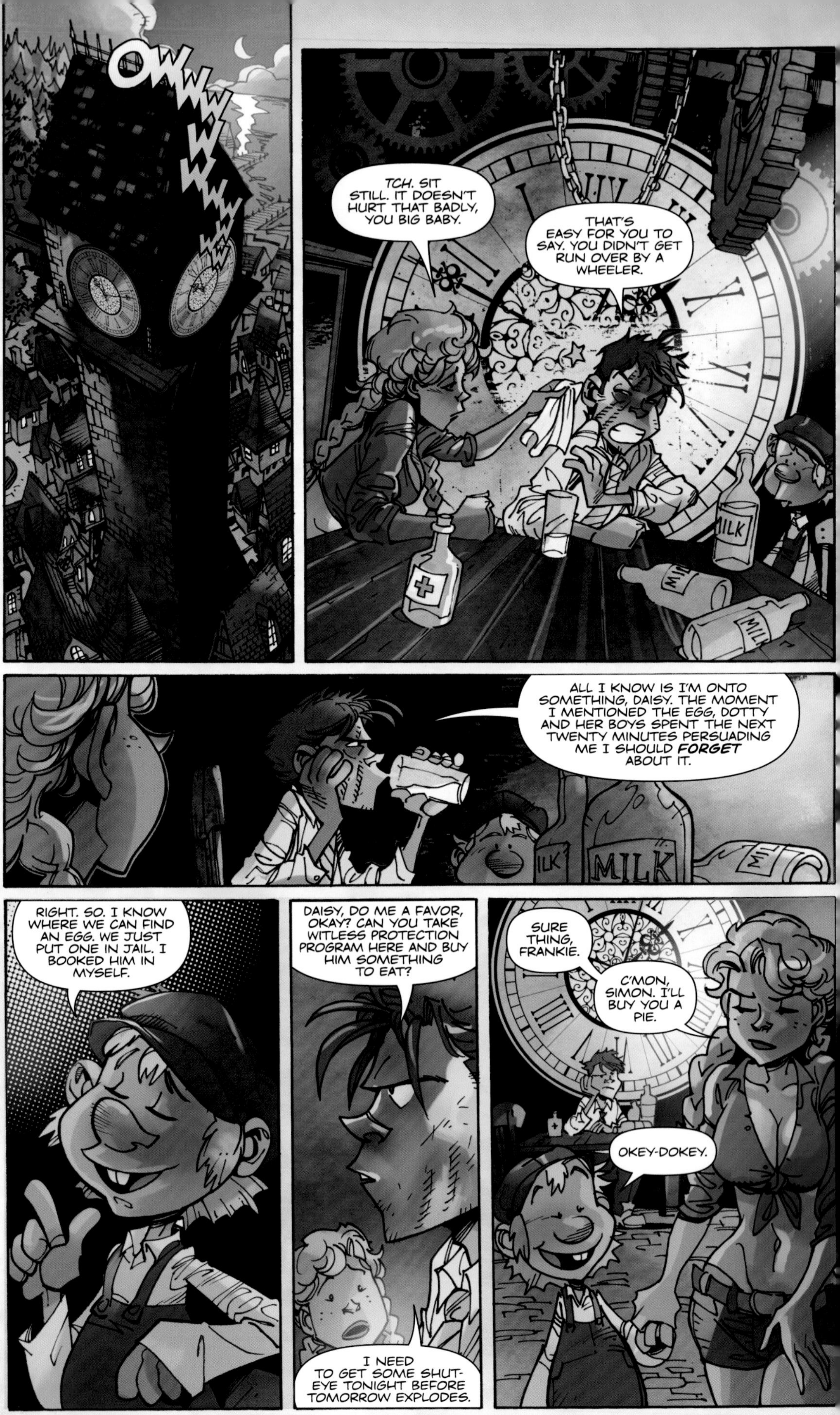
OWWWWWWWWWW
TCH. SIT STILL. IT DOESN'T HURT THAT BADLY, YOU BIG BABY.
THAT'S EASY FOR YOU TO SAY. YOU DIDN'T GET RUN OVER BY A WHEELER.
MILK
ALL I KNOW IS I'M ONTO SOMETHING, DAISY. THE MOMENT I MENTIONED THE EGG, DOTTY AND HER BOYS SPENT THE NEXT TWENTY MINUTES PERSUADING ME I SHOULD FORGET ABOUT IT.
MILK
RIGHT. SO. I KNOW WHERE WE CAN FIND AN EGG. WE JUST PUT ONE IN JAIL. I BOOKED HIM IN MYSELF.
DAISY, DO ME A FAVOR, OKAY? CAN YOU TAKE WITLESS PROTECTION PROGRAM HERE AND BUY HIM SOMETHING TO EAT?
I NEED TO GET SOME SHUT-EYE TONIGHT BEFORE TOMORROW EXPLODES.
SURE THING, FRANKIE.
C'MON, SIMON. I'LL BUY YOU A PIE.
OKEY-DOKEY.

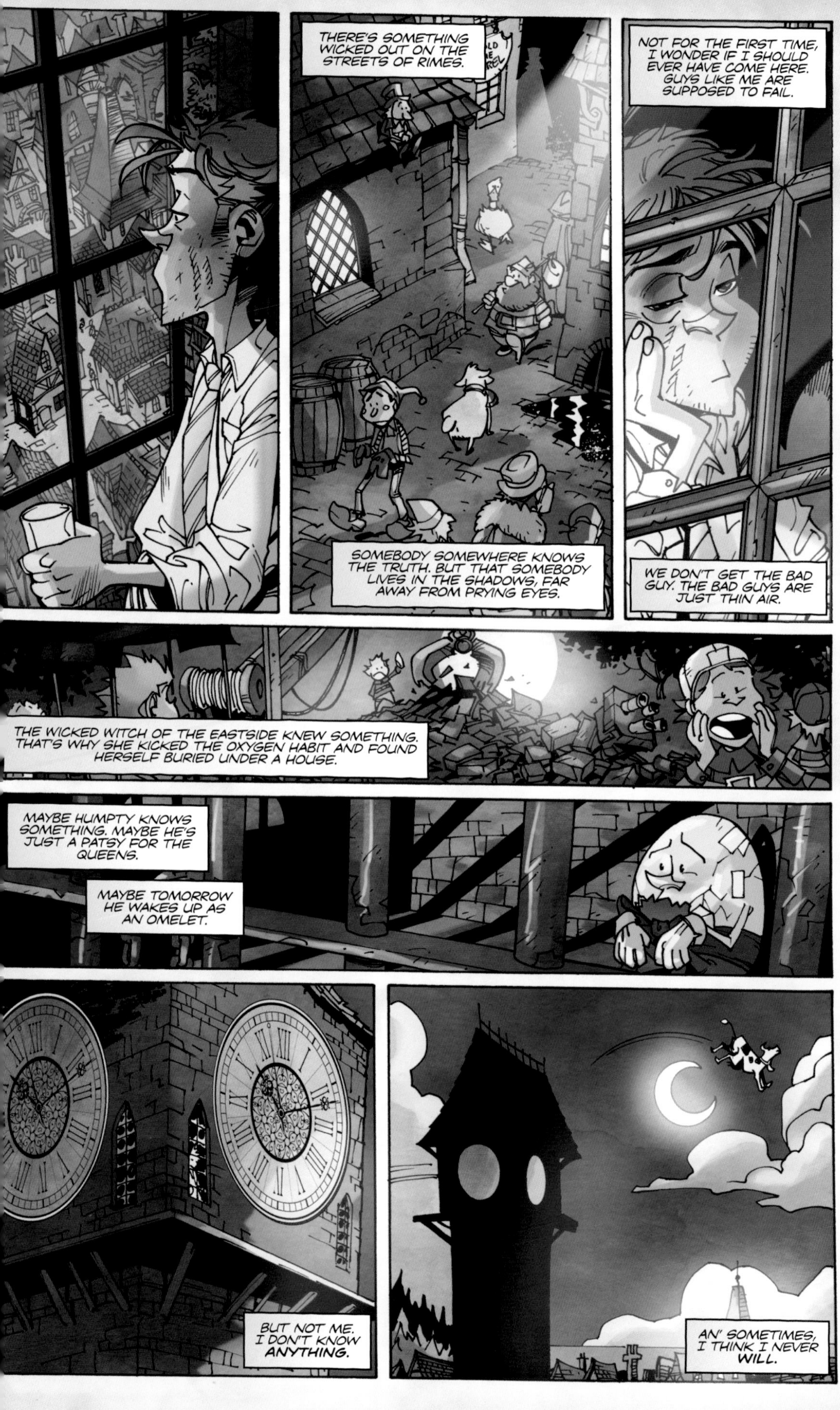

THERE'S SOMETHING WICKED OUT ON THE STREETS OF RIMES.
SOMEBODY SOMEWHERE KNOWS THE TRUTH. BUT THAT SOMEBODY LIVES IN THE SHADOWS, FAR AWAY FROM PRYING EYES.
NOT FOR THE FIRST TIME, I WONDER IF I SHOULD EVER HAVE COME HERE. GUYS LIKE ME ARE SUPPOSED TO FAIL.
WE DON'T GET THE BAD GUY. THE BAD GUYS ARE JUST THIN AIR.
THE WICKED WITCH OF THE EASTSIDE KNEW SOMETHING. THAT'S WHY SHE KICKED THE OXYGEN HABIT AND FOUND HERSELF BURIED UNDER A HOUSE.
MAYBE HUMPTY KNOWS SOMETHING. MAYBE HE'S JUST A PATSY FOR THE QUEENS.
MAYBE TOMORROW HE WAKES UP AS AN OMELET.
BUT NOT ME. I DON'T KNOW **ANYTHING**.
AN' SOMETIMES, I THINK I NEVER **WILL**.

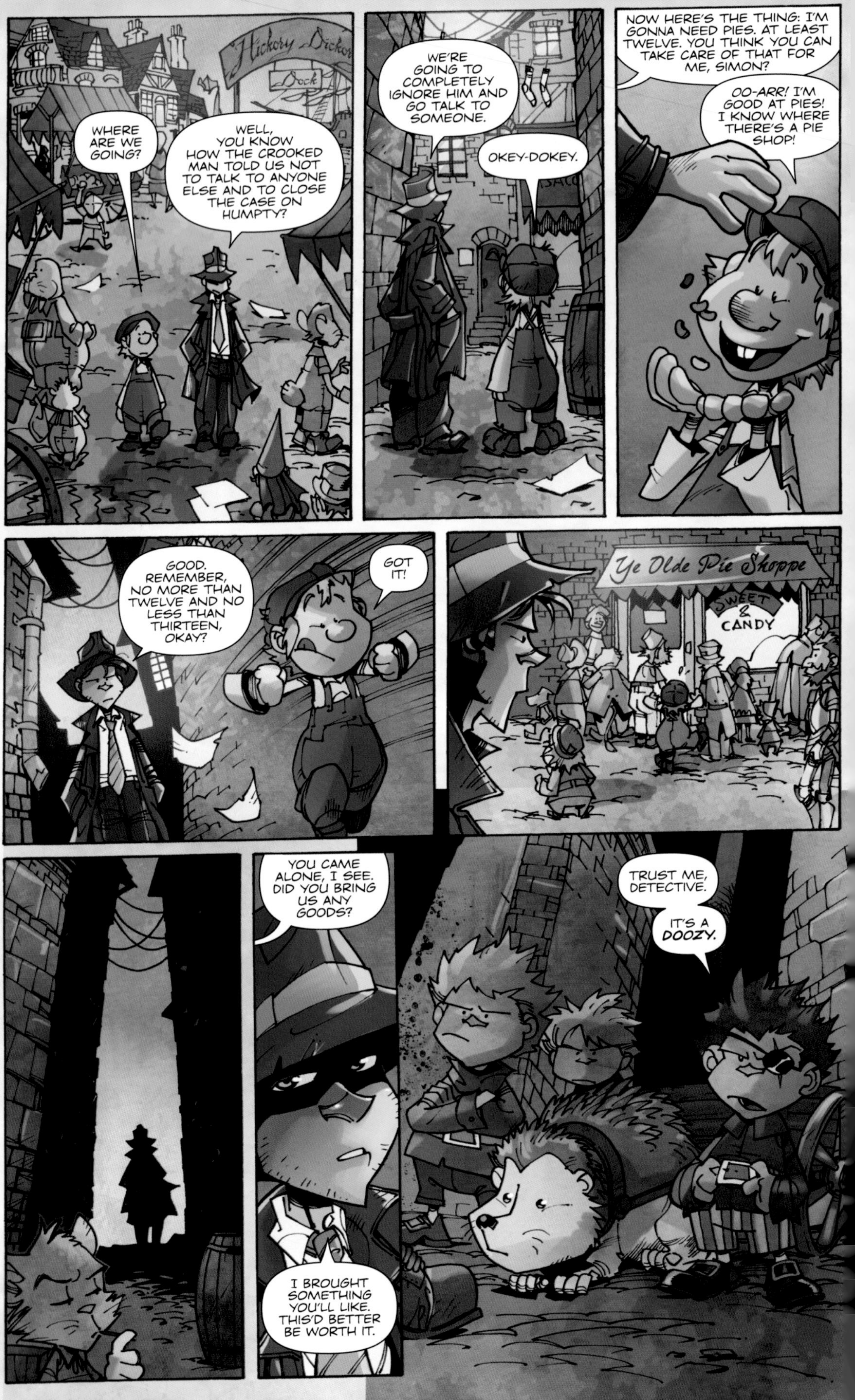
Hickory Dickory
Dock
WHERE ARE WE GOING?
WELL, YOU KNOW HOW THE CROOKED MAN TOLD US NOT TO TALK TO ANYONE ELSE AND TO CLOSE THE CASE ON HUMPTY?
WE'RE GOING TO COMPLETELY IGNORE HIM AND GO TALK TO SOMEONE.
OKEY-DOKEY.
NOW HERE'S THE THING: I'M GONNA NEED PIES. AT LEAST TWELVE. YOU THINK YOU CAN TAKE CARE OF THAT FOR ME, SIMON?
OO-ARR! I'M GOOD AT PIES! I KNOW WHERE THERE'S A PIE SHOP!
GOOD. REMEMBER, NO MORE THAN TWELVE AND NO LESS THAN THIRTEEN, OKAY?
GOT IT!
Ye Olde Pie Shoppe
SWEET & CANDY
YOU CAME ALONE, I SEE. DID YOU BRING US ANY GOODS?
I BROUGHT SOMETHING YOU'LL LIKE. THIS'D BETTER BE WORTH IT.
TRUST ME, DETECTIVE.
IT'S A DOOZY.

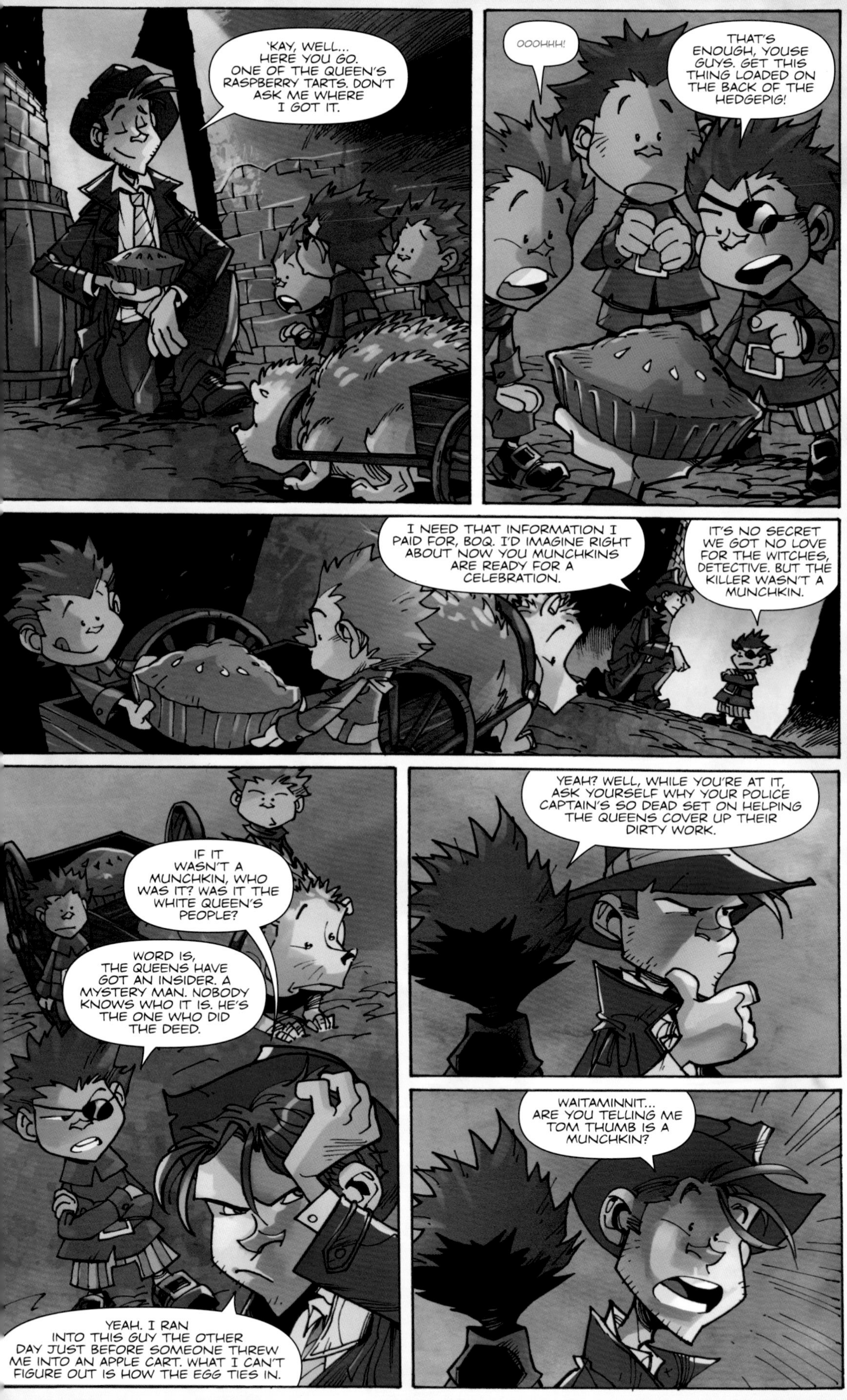
'KAY, WELL... HERE YOU GO. ONE OF THE QUEEN'S RASPBERRY TARTS. DON'T ASK ME WHERE I GOT IT.
OOOHHH!
THAT'S ENOUGH, YOUSE GUYS. GET THIS THING LOADED ON THE BACK OF THE HEDGEPIG!
I NEED THAT INFORMATION I PAID FOR, BOQ. I'D IMAGINE RIGHT ABOUT NOW YOU MUNCHKINS ARE READY FOR A CELEBRATION.
IT'S NO SECRET WE GOT NO LOVE FOR THE WITCHES, DETECTIVE. BUT THE KILLER WASN'T A MUNCHKIN.
IF IT WASN'T A MUNCHKIN, WHO WAS IT? WAS IT THE WHITE QUEEN'S PEOPLE?
WORD IS, THE QUEENS HAVE GOT AN INSIDER. A MYSTERY MAN. NOBODY KNOWS WHO IT IS. HE'S THE ONE WHO DID THE DEED.
YEAH. I RAN INTO THIS GUY THE OTHER DAY JUST BEFORE SOMEONE THREW ME INTO AN APPLE CART. WHAT I CAN'T FIGURE OUT IS HOW THE EGG TIES IN.
YEAH? WELL, WHILE YOU'RE AT IT, ASK YOURSELF WHY YOUR POLICE CAPTAIN'S SO DEAD SET ON HELPING THE QUEENS COVER UP THEIR DIRTY WORK.
WAITAMINNIT... ARE YOU TELLING ME TOM THUMB IS A MUNCHKIN?

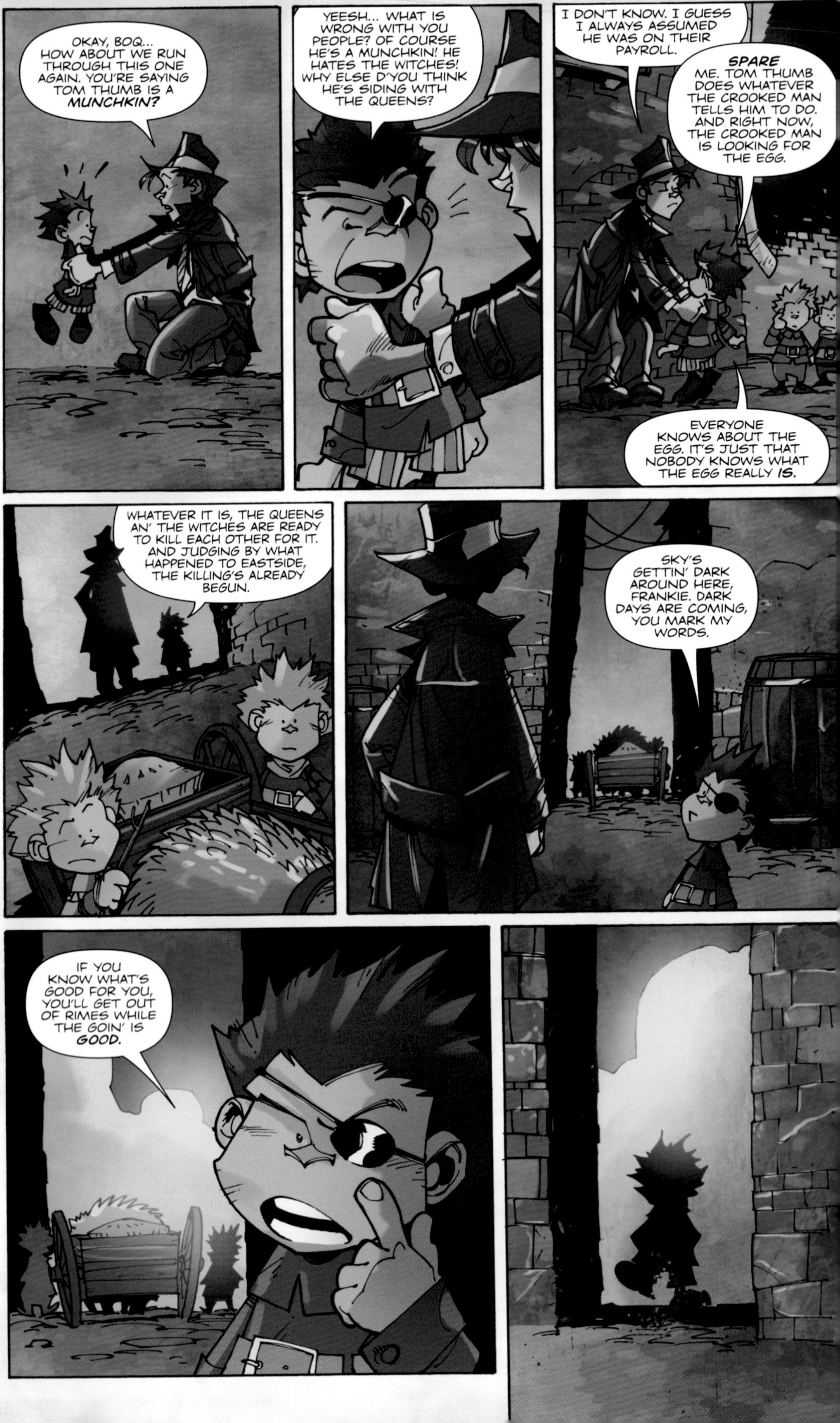
OKAY, BOQ... HOW ABOUT WE RUN THROUGH THIS ONE AGAIN. YOU'RE SAYING TOM THUMB IS A **MUNCHKIN?**
YEESH... WHAT IS WRONG WITH YOU PEOPLE? OF COURSE HE'S A MUNCHKIN! HE HATES THE WITCHES! WHY ELSE D'YOU THINK HE'S SIDING WITH THE QUEENS?
I DON'T KNOW. I GUESS I ALWAYS ASSUMED HE WAS ON THEIR PAYROLL.
SPARE ME. TOM THUMB DOES WHATEVER THE CROOKED MAN TELLS HIM TO DO. AND RIGHT NOW, THE CROOKED MAN IS LOOKING FOR THE EGG.
EVERYONE KNOWS ABOUT THE EGG. IT'S JUST THAT NOBODY KNOWS WHAT THE EGG REALLY ***IS.***
WHATEVER IT IS, THE QUEENS AN' THE WITCHES ARE READY TO KILL EACH OTHER FOR IT. AND JUDGING BY WHAT HAPPENED TO EASTSIDE, THE KILLING'S ALREADY BEGUN.
SKY'S GETTIN' DARK AROUND HERE, FRANKIE. DARK DAYS ARE COMING, YOU MARK MY WORDS.
IF YOU KNOW WHAT'S GOOD FOR YOU, YOU'LL GET OUT OF RIMES WHILE THE GOIN' IS ***GOOD.***

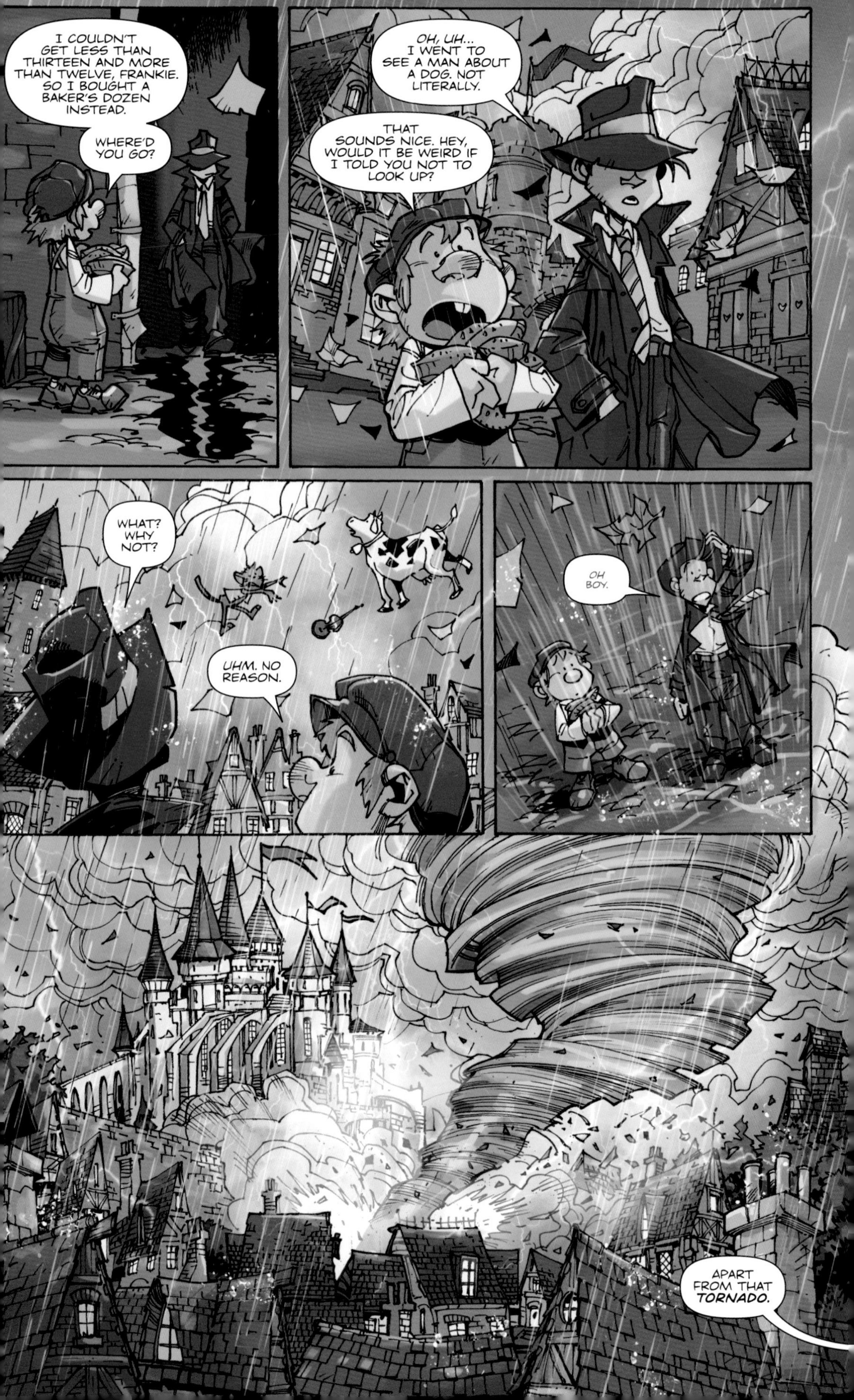
I COULDN'T GET LESS THAN THIRTEEN AND MORE THAN TWELVE, FRANKIE. SO I BOUGHT A BAKER'S DOZEN INSTEAD.
WHERE'D YOU GO?
OH, UH... I WENT TO SEE A MAN ABOUT A DOG. NOT LITERALLY.
THAT SOUNDS NICE. HEY, WOULD IT BE WEIRD IF I TOLD YOU NOT TO LOOK UP?
WHAT? WHY NOT?
UHM. NO REASON.
OH BOY.
APART FROM THAT *TORNADO.*

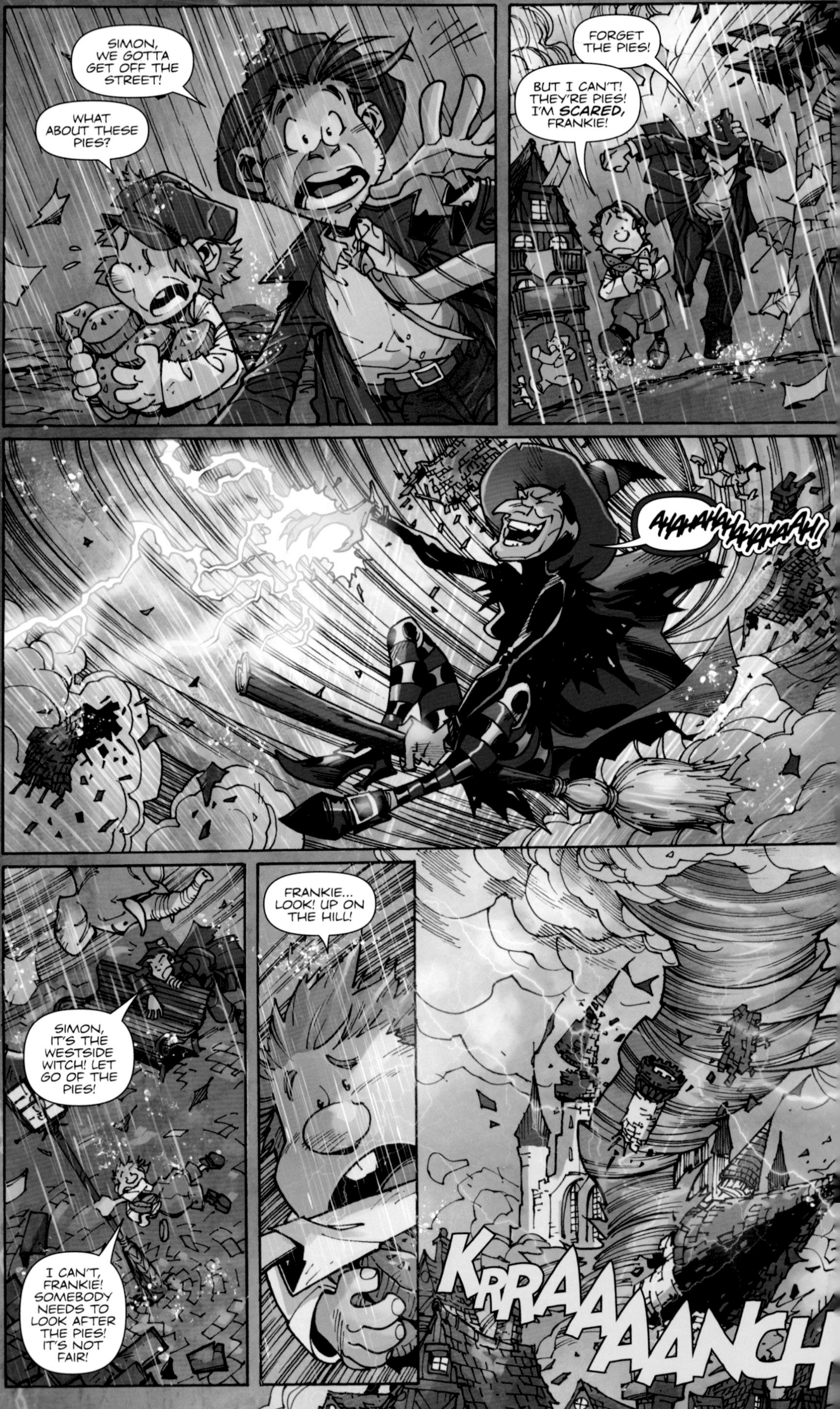
SIMON, WE GOTTA GET OFF THE STREET!
WHAT ABOUT THESE PIES?
FORGET THE PIES!
BUT I CAN'T! THEY'RE PIES! I'M SCARED, FRANKIE!
AHAHAHAHAHAHAAH!
SIMON, IT'S THE WESTSIDE WITCH! LET GO OF THE PIES!
I CAN'T, FRANKIE! SOMEBODY NEEDS TO LOOK AFTER THE PIES! IT'S NOT FAIR!
FRANKIE... LOOK! UP ON THE HILL!
KRRAAAAANCH

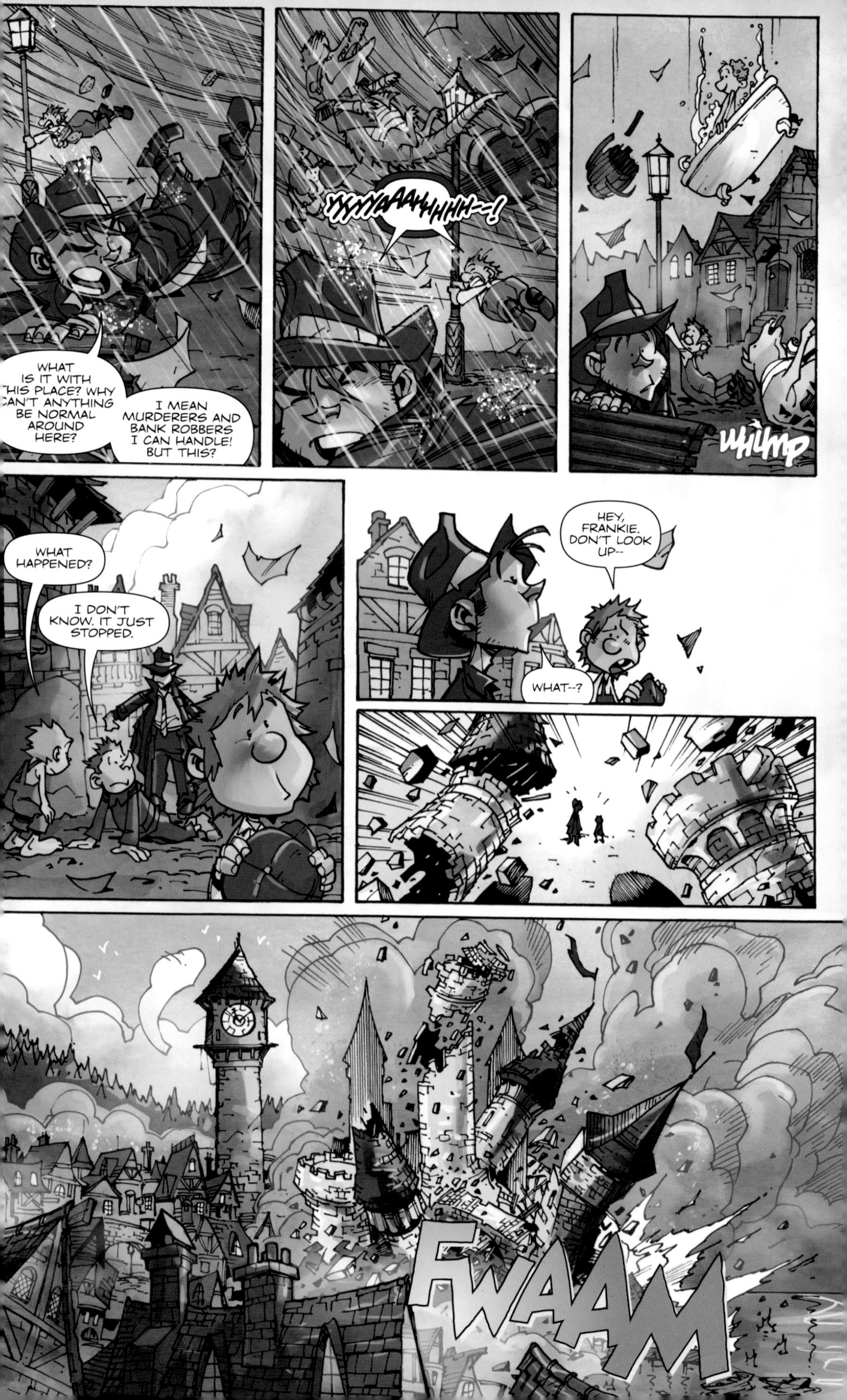
WHAT IS IT WITH THIS PLACE? WHY CAN'T ANYTHING BE NORMAL AROUND HERE?
I MEAN MURDERERS AND BANK ROBBERS I CAN HANDLE! BUT THIS?
YYYYYAAAHHHHH--!
WHUMP
WHAT HAPPENED?
I DON'T KNOW. IT JUST STOPPED.
HEY, FRANKIE. DON'T LOOK UP--
WHAT--?
FWAAM

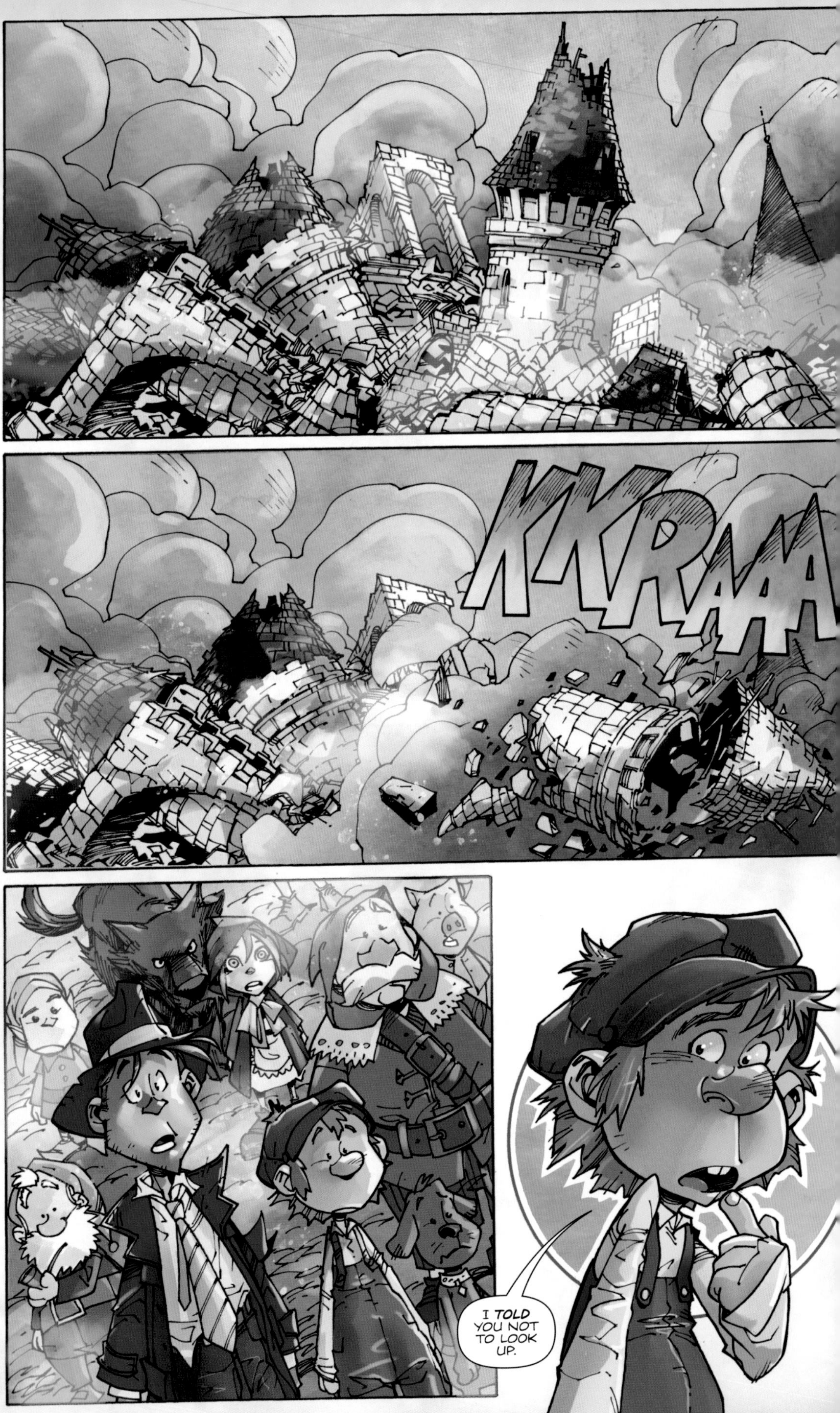
KKRAAA
I TOLD YOU NOT TO LOOK UP.

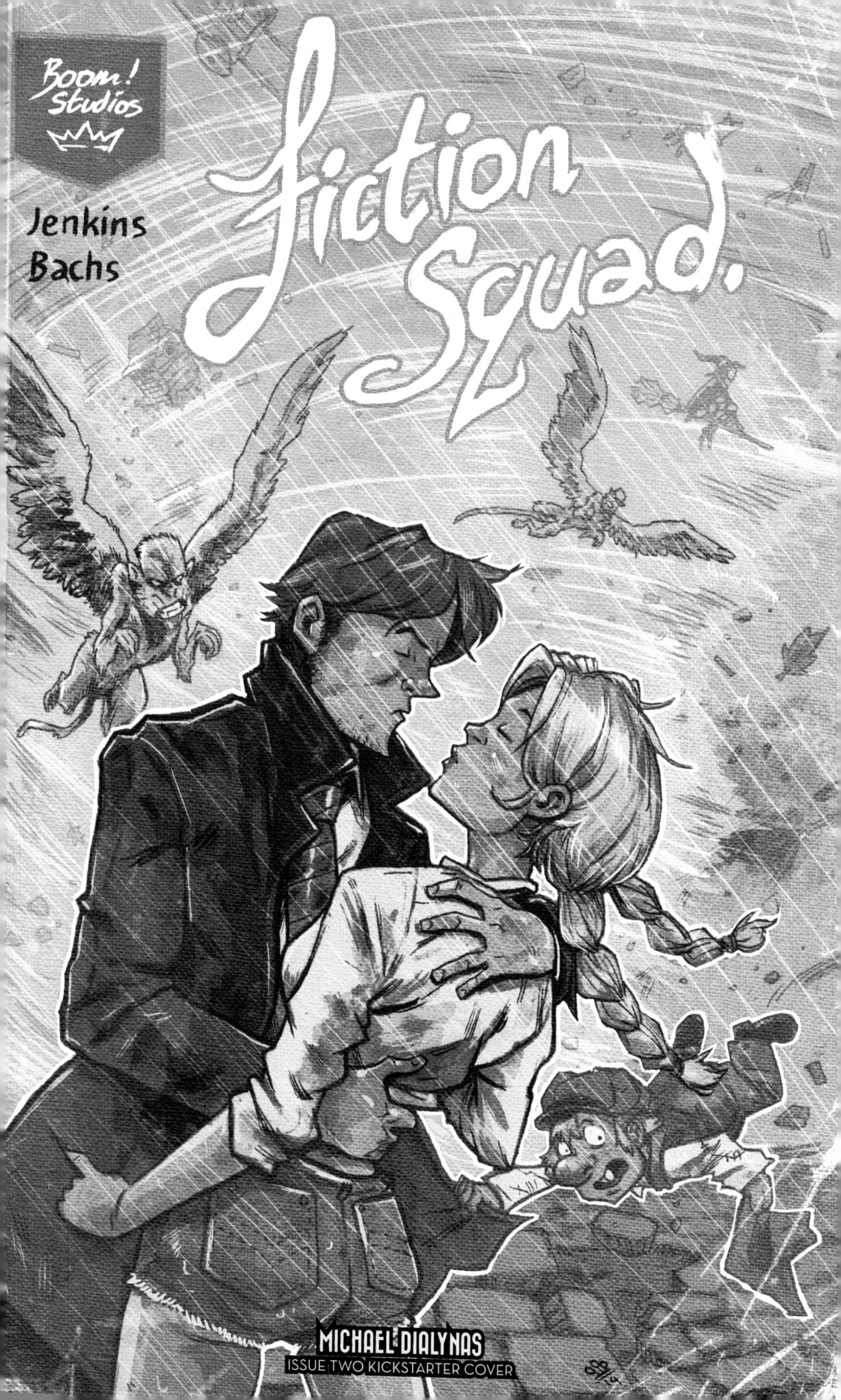

Boom! Studios
Fiction Squad.
Jenkins
Bachs
MICHAEL DIALYNAS
ISSUE TWO KICKSTARTER COVER

CHAPTER THREE

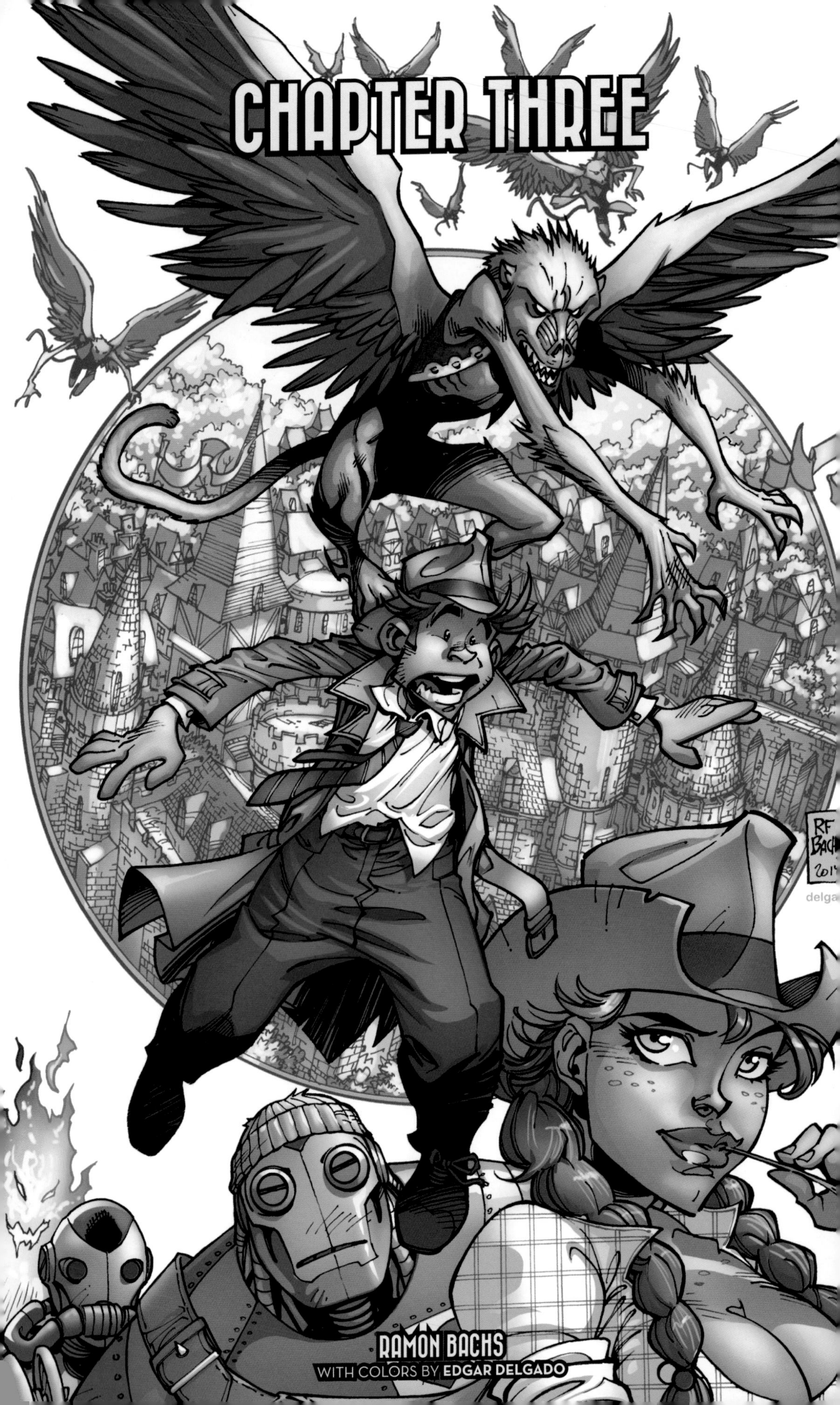

RAMON BACHS
WITH COLORS BY EDGAR DELGADO

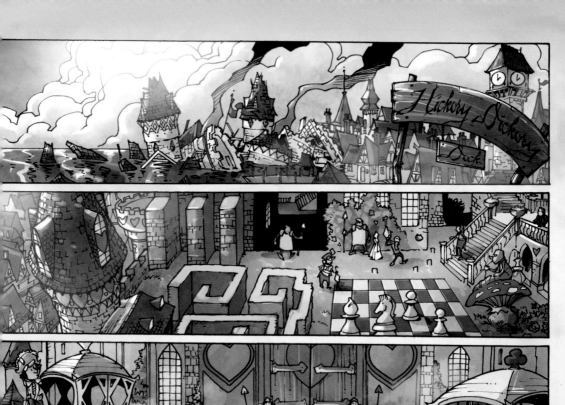

SISTERS. IT WOULD SEEM A PERSON OF UNRELIABLE CHARACTER HAS ADDED TO OUR BURDENS.

LET US DISCUSS THIS "THING" THAT HAS HAPPENED.

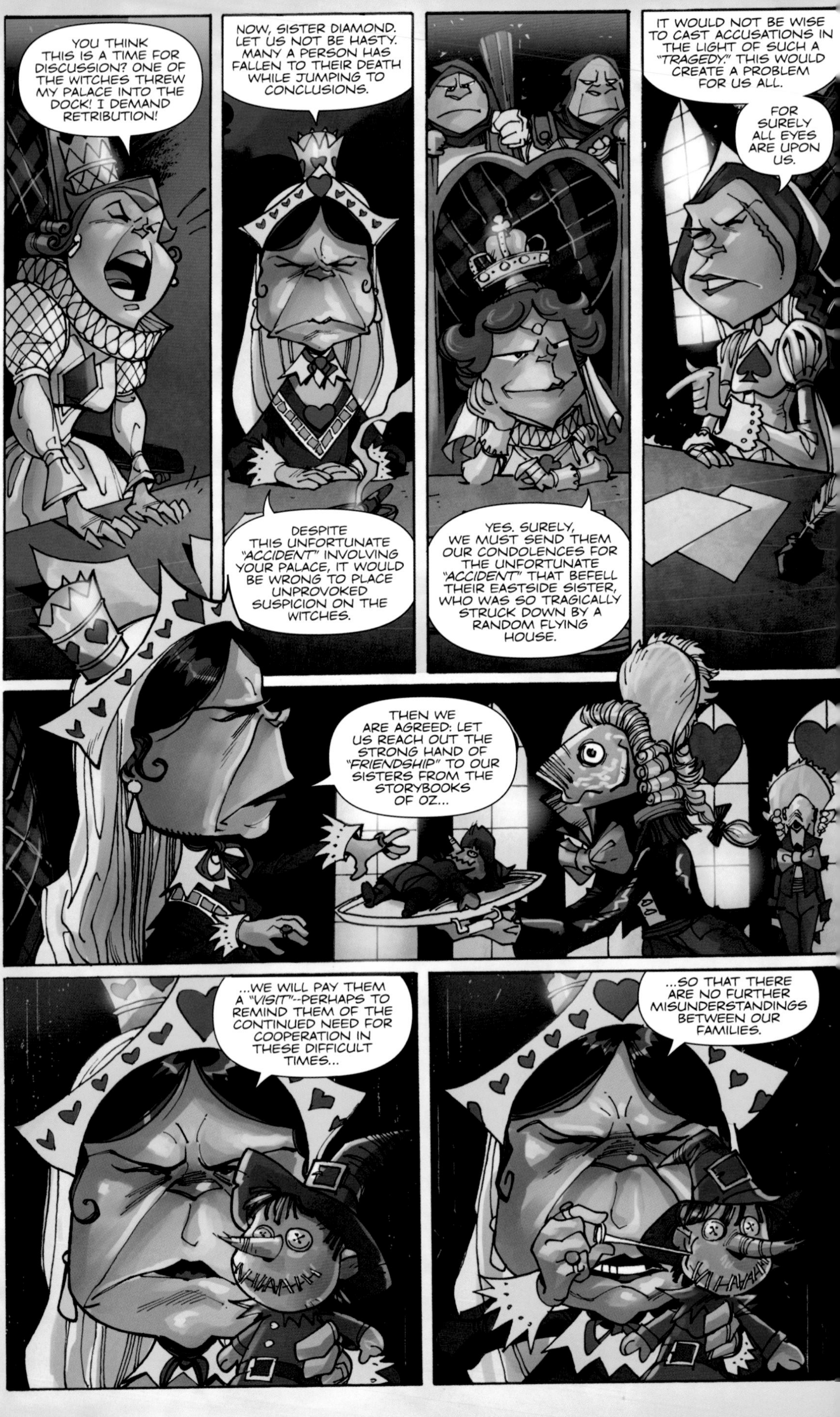
YOU THINK THIS IS A TIME FOR DISCUSSION? ONE OF THE WITCHES THREW MY PALACE INTO THE DOCK! I DEMAND RETRIBUTION!
NOW, SISTER DIAMOND. LET US NOT BE HASTY. MANY A PERSON HAS FALLEN TO THEIR DEATH WHILE JUMPING TO CONCLUSIONS.
IT WOULD NOT BE WISE TO CAST ACCUSATIONS IN THE LIGHT OF SUCH A "TRAGEDY." THIS WOULD CREATE A PROBLEM FOR US ALL.
FOR SURELY ALL EYES ARE UPON US.
DESPITE THIS UNFORTUNATE "ACCIDENT" INVOLVING YOUR PALACE, IT WOULD BE WRONG TO PLACE UNPROVOKED SUSPICION ON THE WITCHES.
YES. SURELY, WE MUST SEND THEM OUR CONDOLENCES FOR THE UNFORTUNATE "ACCIDENT" THAT BEFELL THEIR EASTSIDE SISTER, WHO WAS SO TRAGICALLY STRUCK DOWN BY A RANDOM FLYING HOUSE.
THEN WE ARE AGREED: LET US REACH OUT THE STRONG HAND OF "FRIENDSHIP" TO OUR SISTERS FROM THE STORYBOOKS OF OZ...
...WE WILL PAY THEM A "VISIT"--PERHAPS TO REMIND THEM OF THE CONTINUED NEED FOR COOPERATION IN THESE DIFFICULT TIMES...
...SO THAT THERE ARE NO FURTHER MISUNDERSTANDINGS BETWEEN OUR FAMILIES.

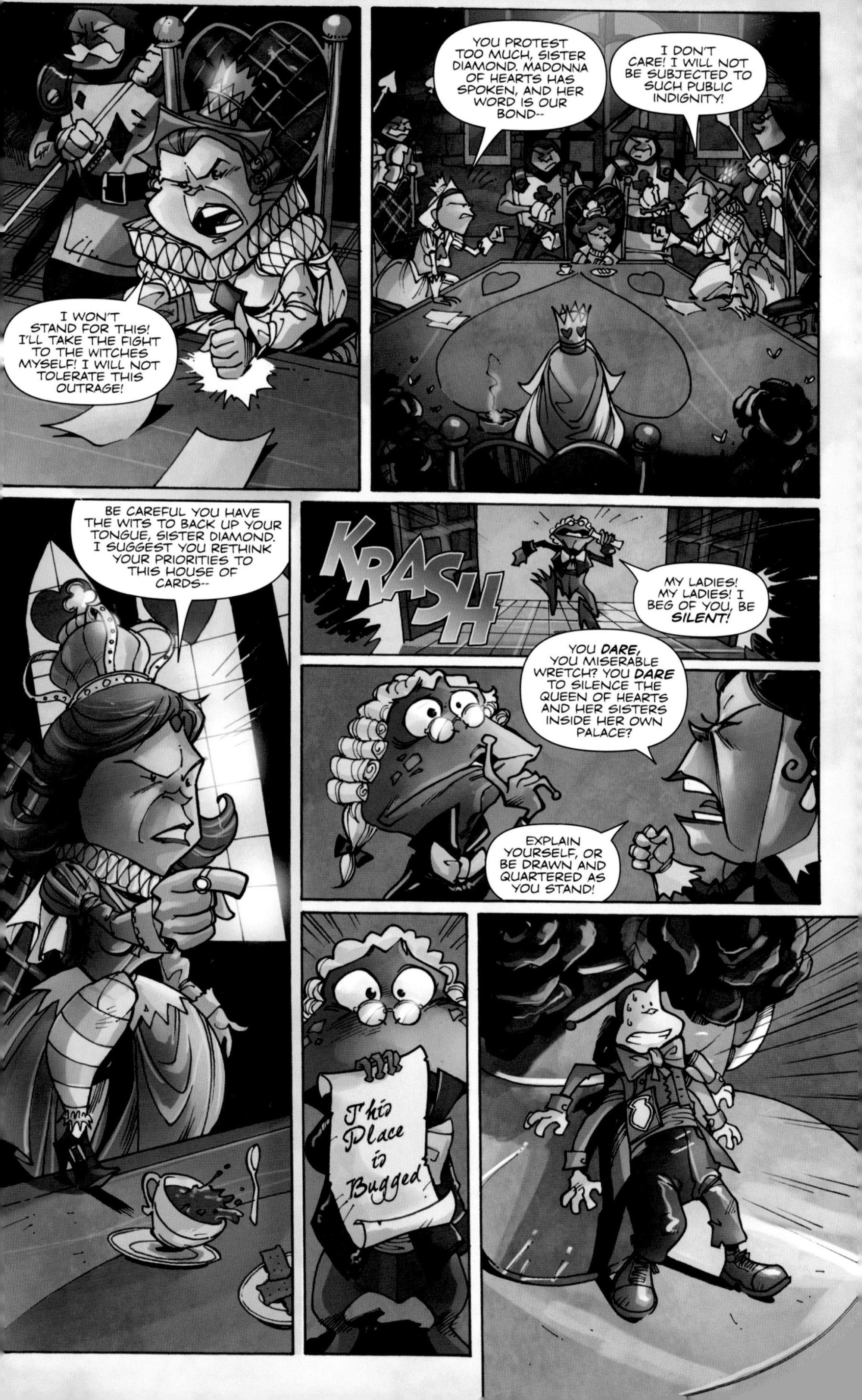
I WON'T STAND FOR THIS! I'LL TAKE THE FIGHT TO THE WITCHES MYSELF! I WILL NOT TOLERATE THIS OUTRAGE!
YOU PROTEST TOO MUCH, SISTER DIAMOND. MADONNA OF HEARTS HAS SPOKEN, AND HER WORD IS OUR BOND--
I DON'T CARE! I WILL NOT BE SUBJECTED TO SUCH PUBLIC INDIGNITY!
BE CAREFUL YOU HAVE THE WITS TO BACK UP YOUR TONGUE, SISTER DIAMOND. I SUGGEST YOU RETHINK YOUR PRIORITIES TO THIS HOUSE OF CARDS--
KRASH
MY LADIES! MY LADIES! I BEG OF YOU, BE **SILENT!**
YOU **DARE,** YOU MISERABLE WRETCH? YOU **DARE** TO SILENCE THE QUEEN OF HEARTS AND HER SISTERS INSIDE HER OWN PALACE?
EXPLAIN YOURSELF, OR BE DRAWN AND QUARTERED AS YOU STAND!
This Place is Bugged

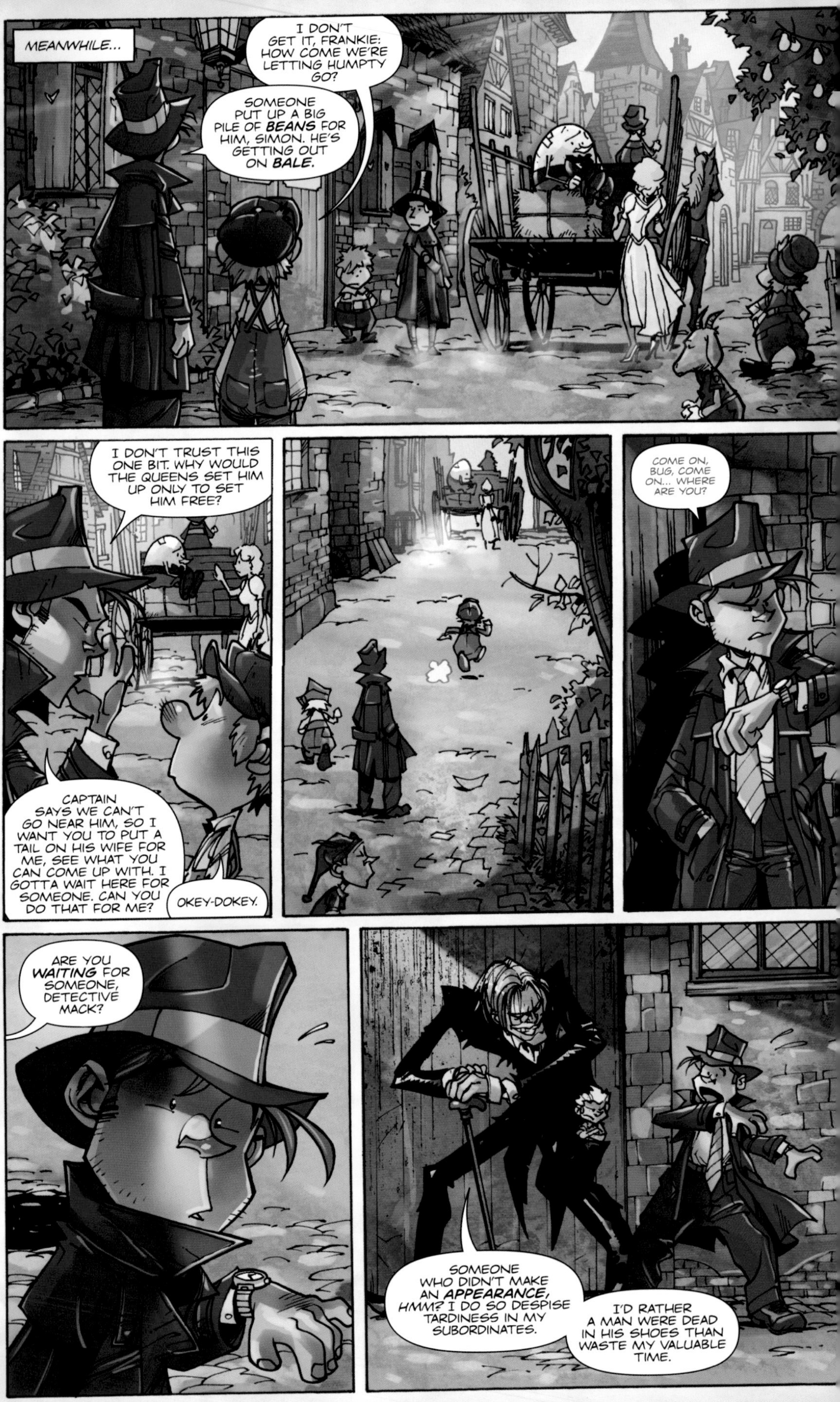
MEANWHILE...
I DON'T GET IT, FRANKIE: HOW COME WE'RE LETTING HUMPTY GO?
SOMEONE PUT UP A BIG PILE OF BEANS FOR HIM, SIMON. HE'S GETTING OUT ON BALE.
I DON'T TRUST THIS ONE BIT. WHY WOULD THE QUEENS SET HIM UP ONLY TO SET HIM FREE?
CAPTAIN SAYS WE CAN'T GO NEAR HIM, SO I WANT YOU TO PUT A TAIL ON HIS WIFE FOR ME, SEE WHAT YOU CAN COME UP WITH. I GOTTA WAIT HERE FOR SOMEONE. CAN YOU DO THAT FOR ME?
OKEY-DOKEY.
COME ON, BUG, COME ON... WHERE ARE YOU?
ARE YOU WAITING FOR SOMEONE, DETECTIVE MACK?
SOMEONE WHO DIDN'T MAKE AN APPEARANCE, HMM? I DO SO DESPISE TARDINESS IN MY SUBORDINATES.
I'D RATHER A MAN WERE DEAD IN HIS SHOES THAN WASTE MY VALUABLE TIME.

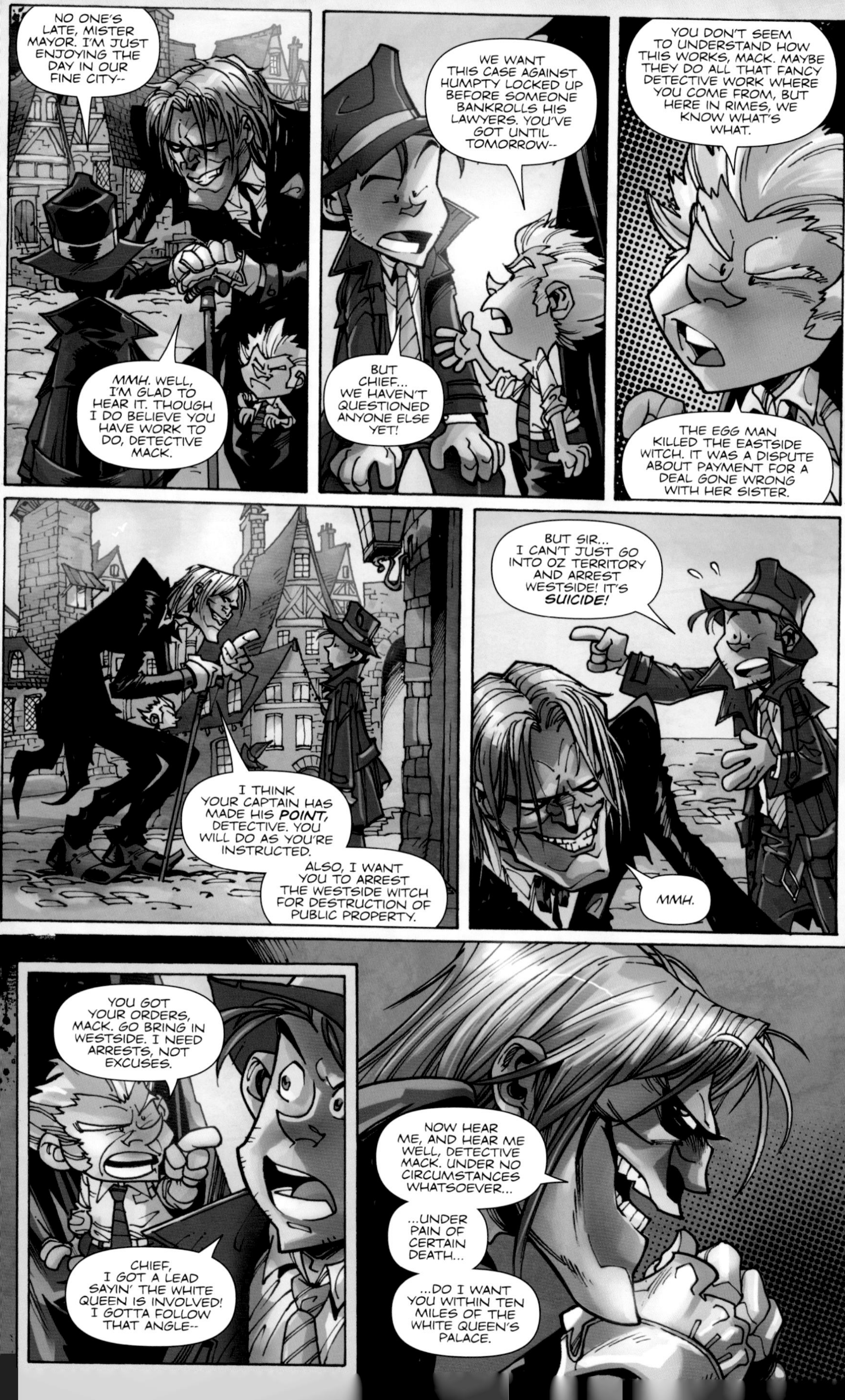

NO ONE'S LATE, MISTER MAYOR. I'M JUST ENJOYING THE DAY IN OUR FINE CITY--
MMH. WELL, I'M GLAD TO HEAR IT. THOUGH I DO BELIEVE YOU HAVE WORK TO DO, DETECTIVE MACK.
WE WANT THIS CASE AGAINST HUMPTY LOCKED UP BEFORE SOMEONE BANKROLLS HIS LAWYERS. YOU'VE GOT UNTIL TOMORROW--
BUT CHIEF... WE HAVEN'T QUESTIONED ANYONE ELSE YET!
YOU DON'T SEEM TO UNDERSTAND HOW THIS WORKS, MACK. MAYBE THEY DO ALL THAT FANCY DETECTIVE WORK WHERE YOU COME FROM, BUT HERE IN RIMES, WE KNOW WHAT'S WHAT.
THE EGG MAN KILLED THE EASTSIDE WITCH. IT WAS A DISPUTE ABOUT PAYMENT FOR A DEAL GONE WRONG WITH HER SISTER.
I THINK YOUR CAPTAIN HAS MADE HIS POINT, DETECTIVE. YOU WILL DO AS YOU'RE INSTRUCTED.
ALSO, I WANT YOU TO ARREST THE WESTSIDE WITCH FOR DESTRUCTION OF PUBLIC PROPERTY.
BUT SIR... I CAN'T JUST GO INTO OZ TERRITORY AND ARREST WESTSIDE! IT'S SUICIDE!
MMH.
YOU GOT YOUR ORDERS, MACK. GO BRING IN WESTSIDE. I NEED ARRESTS, NOT EXCUSES.
CHIEF, I GOT A LEAD SAYIN' THE WHITE QUEEN IS INVOLVED! I GOTTA FOLLOW THAT ANGLE--
NOW HEAR ME, AND HEAR ME WELL, DETECTIVE MACK. UNDER NO CIRCUMSTANCES WHATSOEVER...
...UNDER PAIN OF CERTAIN DEATH...
...DO I WANT YOU WITHIN TEN MILES OF THE WHITE QUEEN'S PALACE.

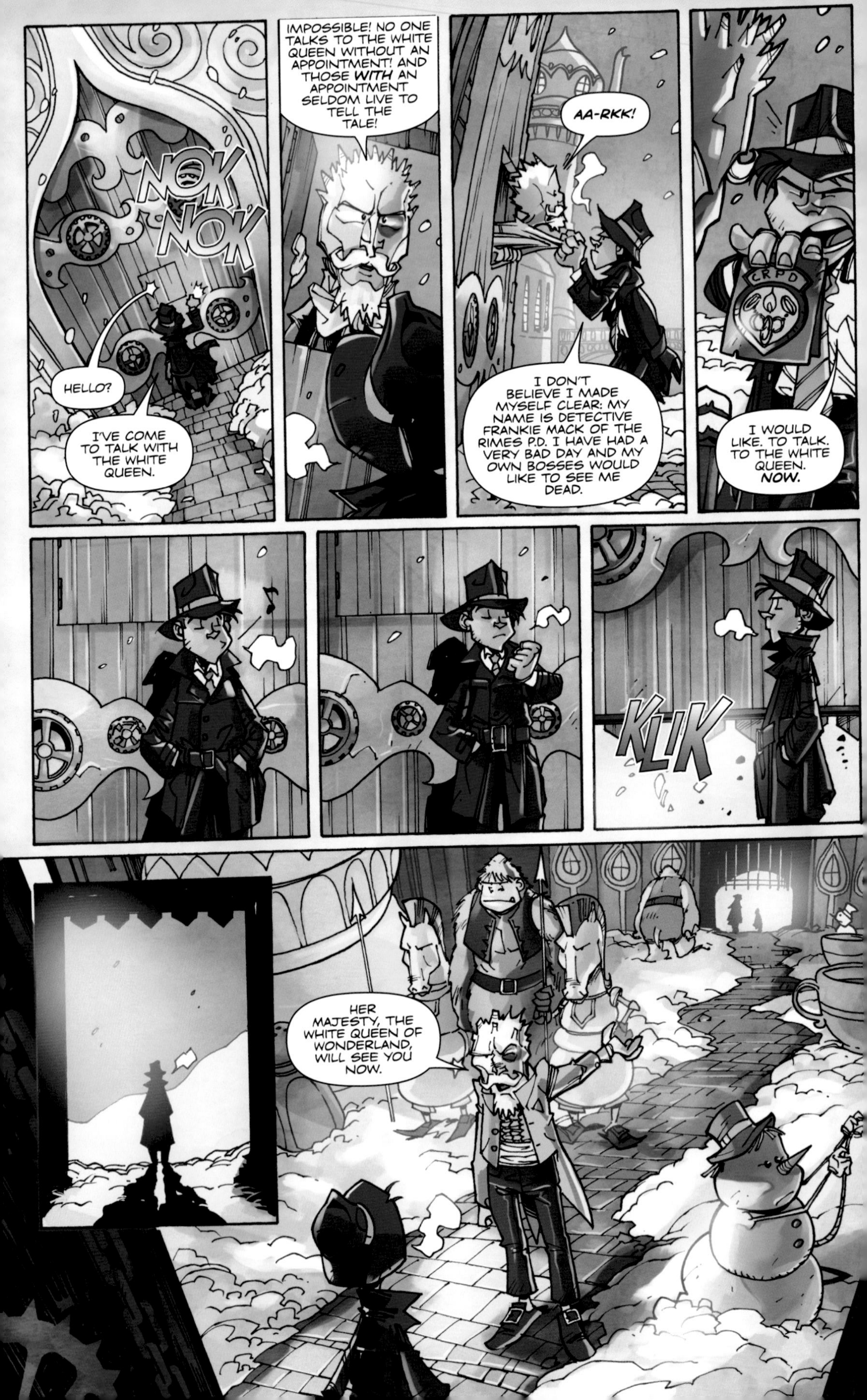
NOK NOK
HELLO?
I'VE COME TO TALK WITH THE WHITE QUEEN.
IMPOSSIBLE! NO ONE TALKS TO THE WHITE QUEEN WITHOUT AN APPOINTMENT! AND THOSE **WITH** AN APPOINTMENT SELDOM LIVE TO TELL THE TALE!
AA-RKK!
I DON'T BELIEVE I MADE MYSELF CLEAR: MY NAME IS DETECTIVE FRANKIE MACK OF THE RIMES P.D. I HAVE HAD A VERY BAD DAY AND MY OWN BOSSES WOULD LIKE TO SEE ME DEAD.
CRPD
I WOULD LIKE. TO TALK. TO THE WHITE QUEEN. **NOW.**
KLIK
HER MAJESTY, THE WHITE QUEEN OF WONDERLAND, WILL SEE YOU NOW.

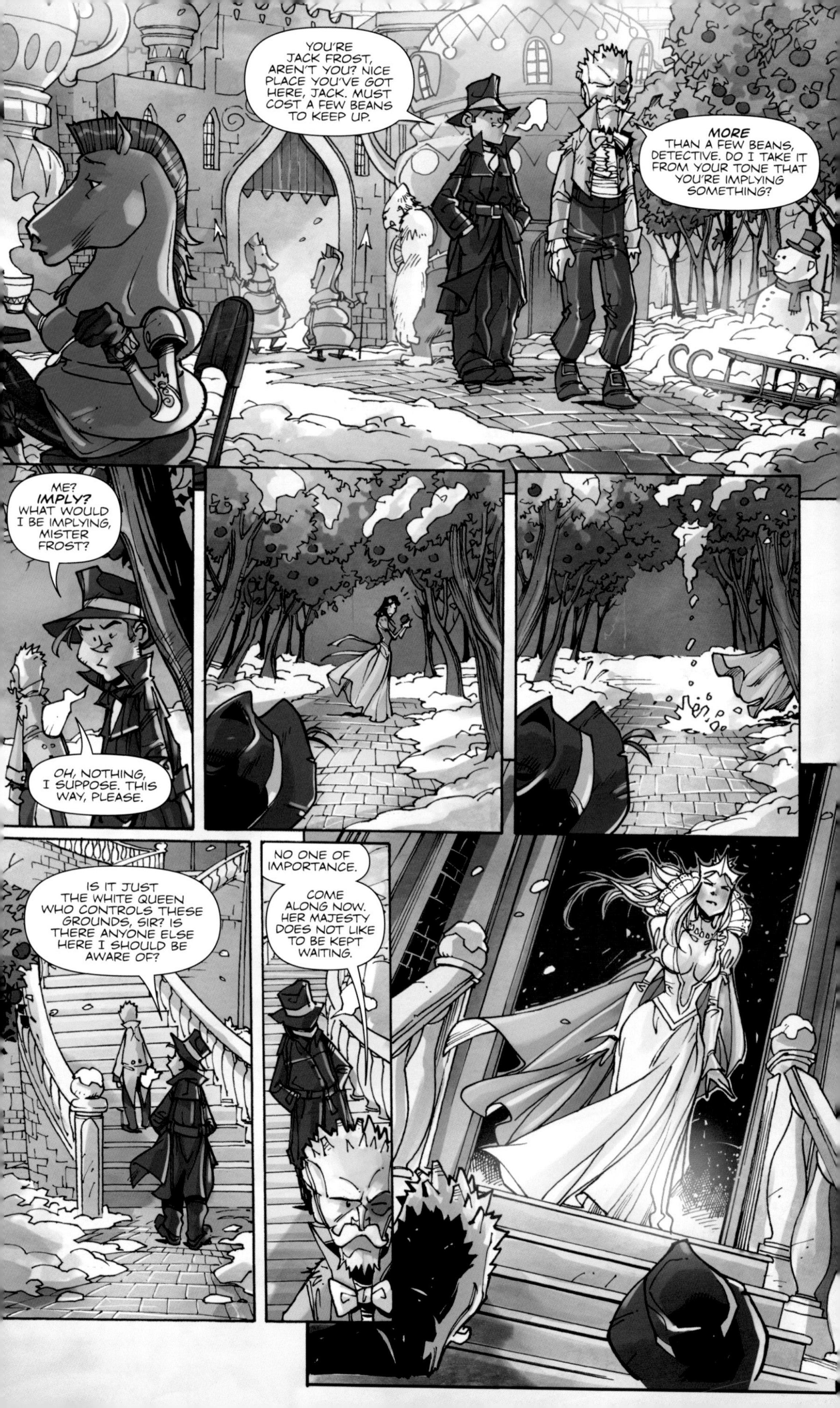
YOU'RE JACK FROST, AREN'T YOU? NICE PLACE YOU'VE GOT HERE, JACK. MUST COST A FEW BEANS TO KEEP UP.
MORE THAN A FEW BEANS, DETECTIVE. DO I TAKE IT FROM YOUR TONE THAT YOU'RE IMPLYING SOMETHING?
ME? IMPLY? WHAT WOULD I BE IMPLYING, MISTER FROST?
OH, NOTHING, I SUPPOSE. THIS WAY, PLEASE.
IS IT JUST THE WHITE QUEEN WHO CONTROLS THESE GROUNDS, SIR? IS THERE ANYONE ELSE HERE I SHOULD BE AWARE OF?
NO ONE OF IMPORTANCE.
COME ALONG NOW. HER MAJESTY DOES NOT LIKE TO BE KEPT WAITING.

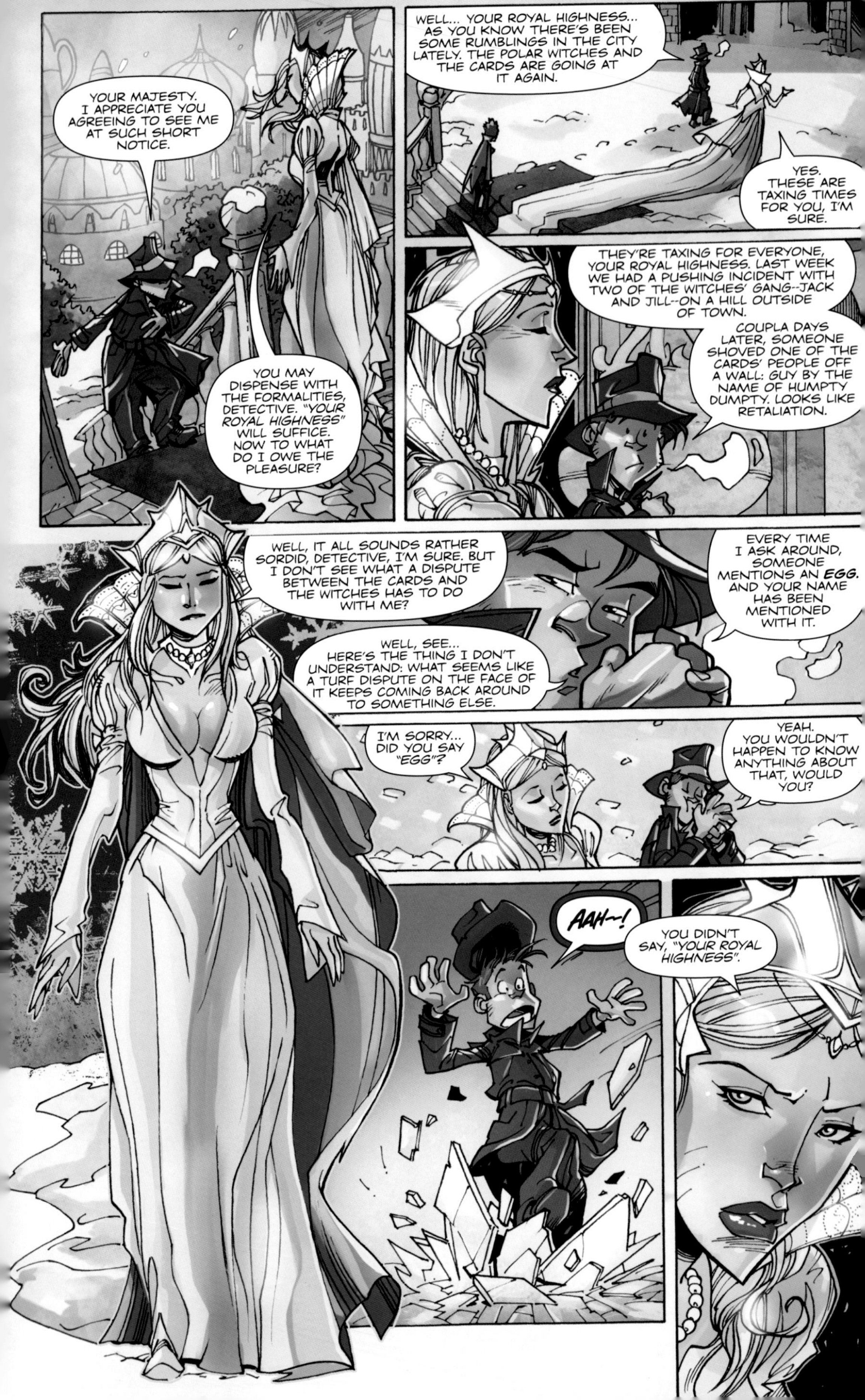
YOUR MAJESTY. I APPRECIATE YOU AGREEING TO SEE ME AT SUCH SHORT NOTICE.
YOU MAY DISPENSE WITH THE FORMALITIES, DETECTIVE. "YOUR ROYAL HIGHNESS" WILL SUFFICE. NOW TO WHAT DO I OWE THE PLEASURE?
WELL... YOUR ROYAL HIGHNESS... AS YOU KNOW THERE'S BEEN SOME RUMBLINGS IN THE CITY LATELY. THE POLAR WITCHES AND THE CARDS ARE GOING AT IT AGAIN.
YES. THESE ARE TAXING TIMES FOR YOU, I'M SURE.
THEY'RE TAXING FOR EVERYONE, YOUR ROYAL HIGHNESS. LAST WEEK WE HAD A PUSHING INCIDENT WITH TWO OF THE WITCHES' GANG--JACK AND JILL--ON A HILL OUTSIDE OF TOWN.
COUPLA DAYS LATER, SOMEONE SHOVED ONE OF THE CARDS' PEOPLE OFF A WALL: GUY BY THE NAME OF HUMPTY DUMPTY. LOOKS LIKE RETALIATION.
WELL, IT ALL SOUNDS RATHER SORDID, DETECTIVE, I'M SURE. BUT I DON'T SEE WHAT A DISPUTE BETWEEN THE CARDS AND THE WITCHES HAS TO DO WITH ME?
WELL, SEE... HERE'S THE THING I DON'T UNDERSTAND: WHAT SEEMS LIKE A TURF DISPUTE ON THE FACE OF IT KEEPS COMING BACK AROUND TO SOMETHING ELSE.
EVERY TIME I ASK AROUND, SOMEONE MENTIONS AN EGG. AND YOUR NAME HAS BEEN MENTIONED WITH IT.
I'M SORRY... DID YOU SAY "EGG"?
YEAH. YOU WOULDN'T HAPPEN TO KNOW ANYTHING ABOUT THAT, WOULD YOU?
AAH--!
YOU DIDN'T SAY, "YOUR ROYAL HIGHNESS".

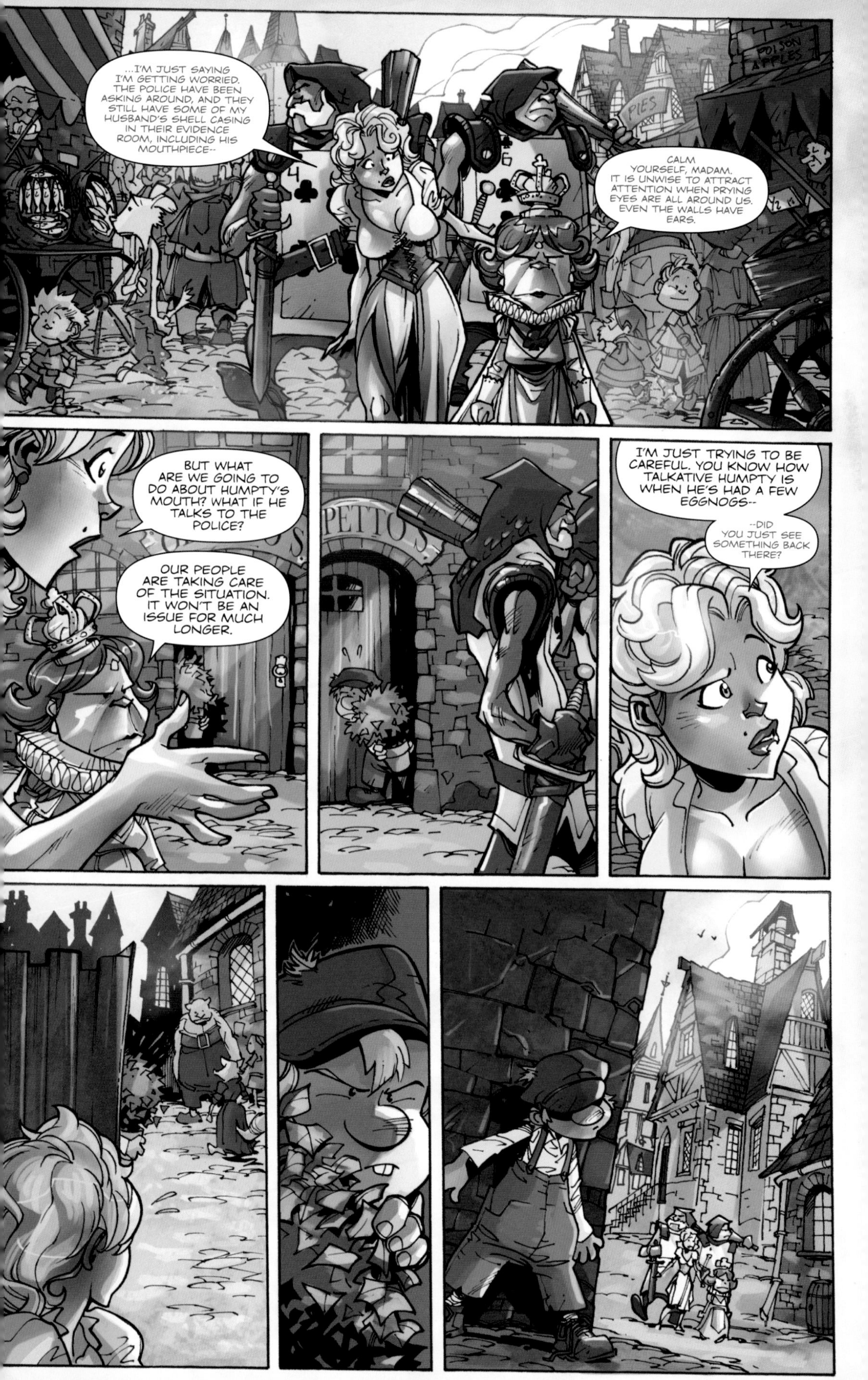

...I'M JUST SAYING I'M GETTING WORRIED. THE POLICE HAVE BEEN ASKING AROUND, AND THEY STILL HAVE SOME OF MY HUSBAND'S SHELL CASING IN THEIR EVIDENCE ROOM, INCLUDING HIS MOUTHPIECE--
POISON APPLES
PIES
CALM YOURSELF, MADAM. IT IS UNWISE TO ATTRACT ATTENTION WHEN PRYING EYES ARE ALL AROUND US. EVEN THE WALLS HAVE EARS.
BUT WHAT ARE WE GOING TO DO ABOUT HUMPTY'S MOUTH? WHAT IF HE TALKS TO THE POLICE?
OUR PEOPLE ARE TAKING CARE OF THE SITUATION. IT WON'T BE AN ISSUE FOR MUCH LONGER.
I'M JUST TRYING TO BE CAREFUL. YOU KNOW HOW TALKATIVE HUMPTY IS WHEN HE'S HAD A FEW EGGNOGS--
--DID YOU JUST SEE SOMETHING BACK THERE?

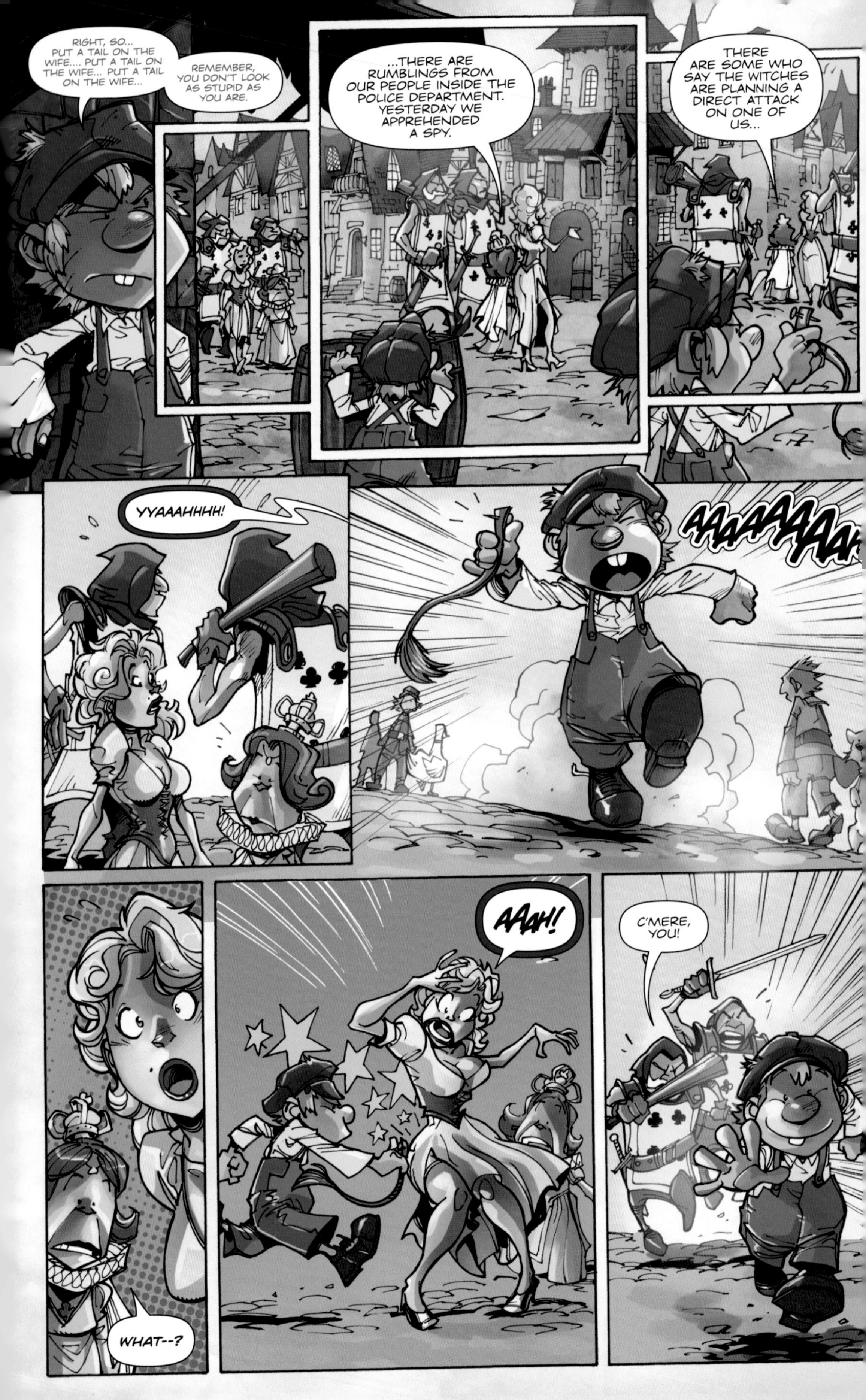
RIGHT, SO... PUT A TAIL ON THE WIFE.... PUT A TAIL ON THE WIFE... PUT A TAIL ON THE WIFE...
REMEMBER, YOU DON'T LOOK AS STUPID AS YOU ARE.
...THERE ARE RUMBLINGS FROM OUR PEOPLE INSIDE THE POLICE DEPARTMENT. YESTERDAY WE APPREHENDED A SPY.
THERE ARE SOME WHO SAY THE WITCHES ARE PLANNING A DIRECT ATTACK ON ONE OF US...
YYAAAHHHH!
AAAAAAAAAH
WHAT--?
AAAH!
C'MERE, YOU!

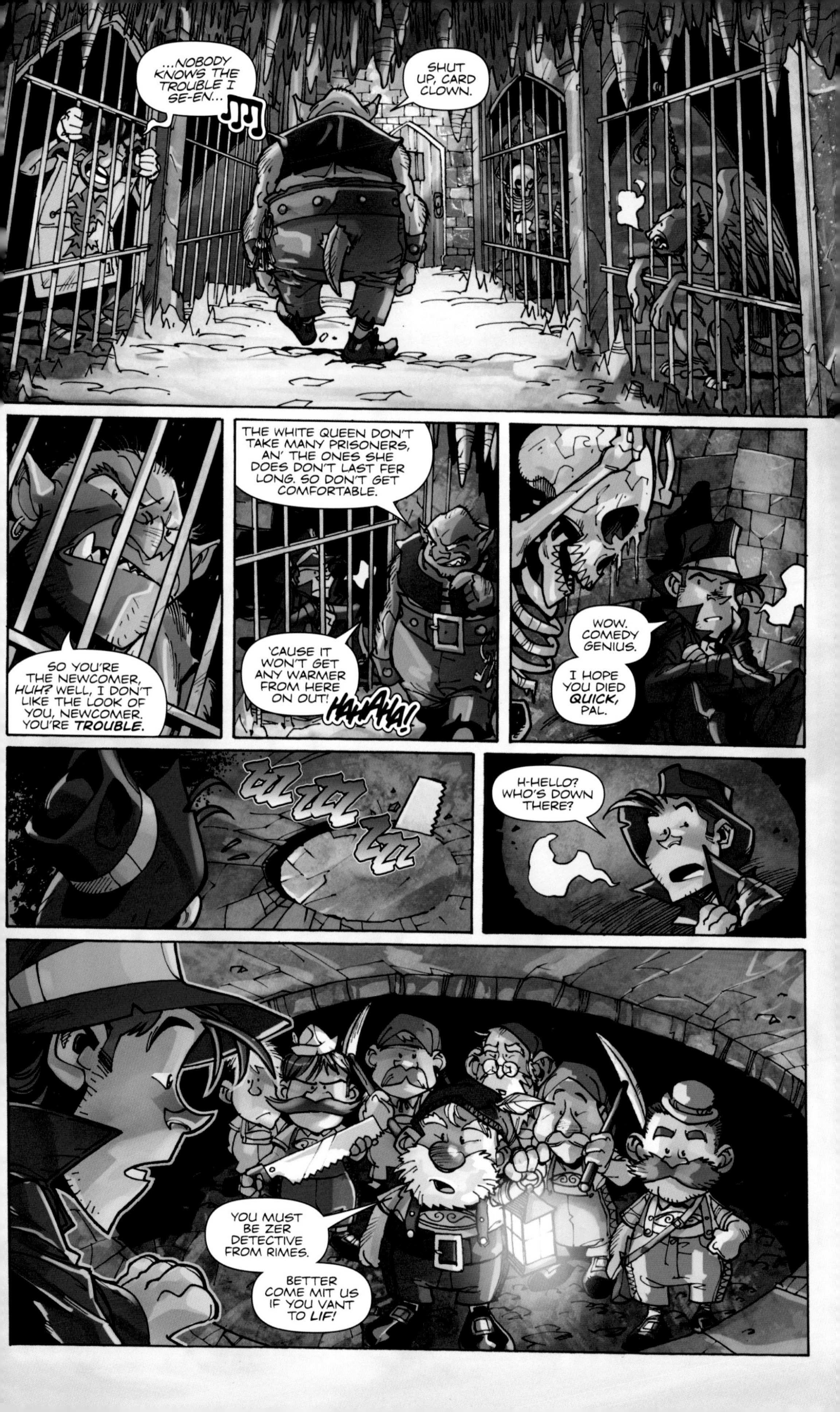
...NOBODY KNOWS THE TROUBLE I SE-EN...
SHUT UP, CARD CLOWN.
SO YOU'RE THE NEWCOMER, HUH? WELL, I DON'T LIKE THE LOOK OF YOU, NEWCOMER. YOU'RE TROUBLE.
THE WHITE QUEEN DON'T TAKE MANY PRISONERS, AN' THE ONES SHE DOES DON'T LAST FER LONG. SO DON'T GET COMFORTABLE.
'CAUSE IT WON'T GET ANY WARMER FROM HERE ON OUT!
HAHAHA!
WOW. COMEDY GENIUS.
I HOPE YOU DIED QUICK, PAL.
H-HELLO? WHO'S DOWN THERE?
YOU MUST BE ZER DETECTIVE FROM RIMES.
BETTER COME MIT US IF YOU VANT TO LIF!

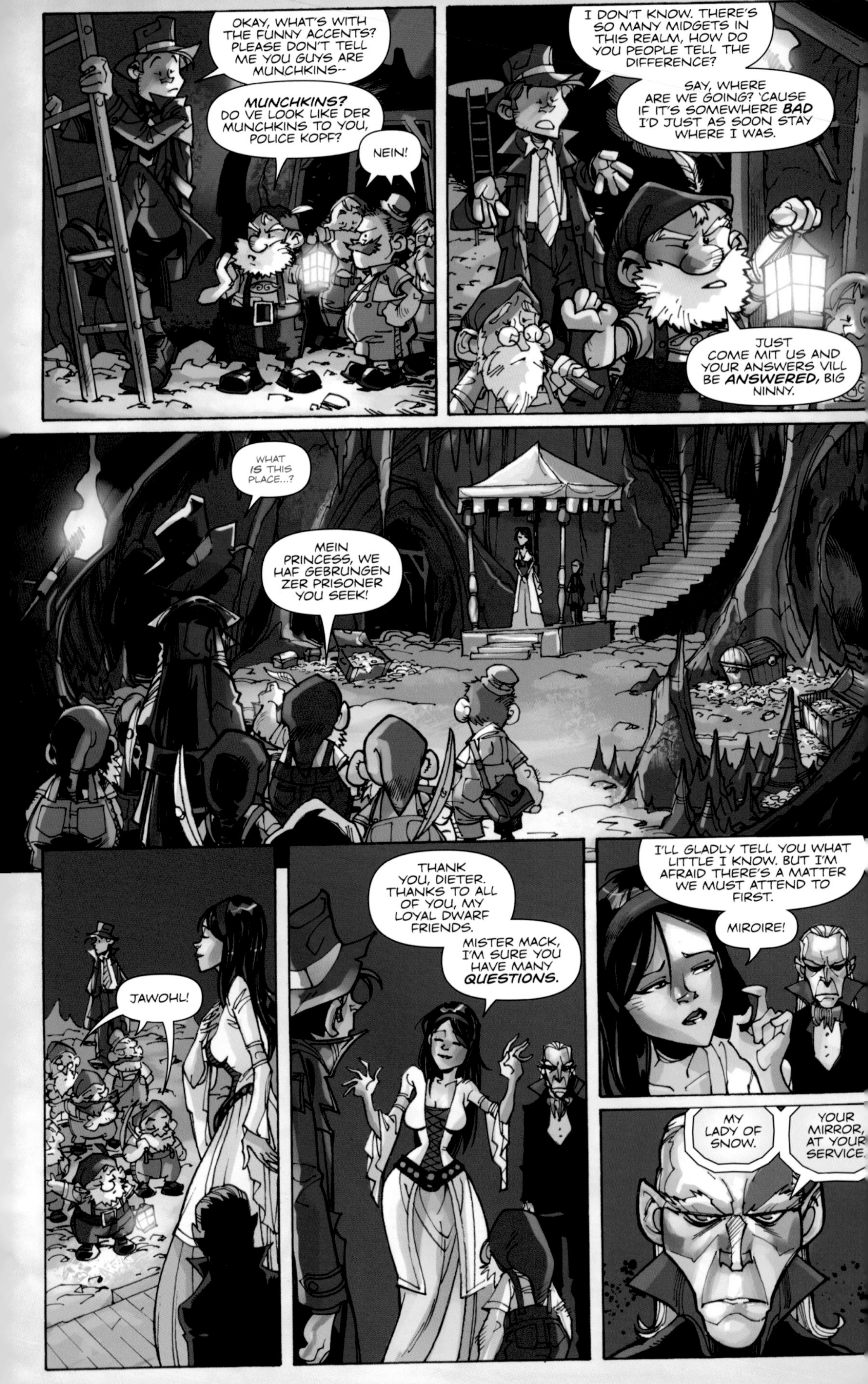
OKAY, WHAT'S WITH THE FUNNY ACCENTS? PLEASE DON'T TELL ME YOU GUYS ARE MUNCHKINS--
MUNCHKINS? DO VE LOOK LIKE DER MUNCHKINS TO YOU, POLICE KOPF?
NEIN!
I DON'T KNOW. THERE'S SO MANY MIDGETS IN THIS REALM, HOW DO YOU PEOPLE TELL THE DIFFERENCE?
SAY, WHERE ARE WE GOING? 'CAUSE IF IT'S SOMEWHERE BAD I'D JUST AS SOON STAY WHERE I WAS.
JUST COME MIT US AND YOUR ANSWERS VILL BE ANSWERED, BIG NINNY.
WHAT IS THIS PLACE...?
MEIN PRINCESS, WE HAF GEBRUNGEN ZER PRISONER YOU SEEK!
JAWOHL!
THANK YOU, DIETER. THANKS TO ALL OF YOU, MY LOYAL DWARF FRIENDS.
MISTER MACK, I'M SURE YOU HAVE MANY QUESTIONS.
I'LL GLADLY TELL YOU WHAT LITTLE I KNOW. BUT I'M AFRAID THERE'S A MATTER WE MUST ATTEND TO FIRST.
MIROIRE!
MY LADY OF SNOW.
YOUR MIRROR, AT YOUR SERVICE.

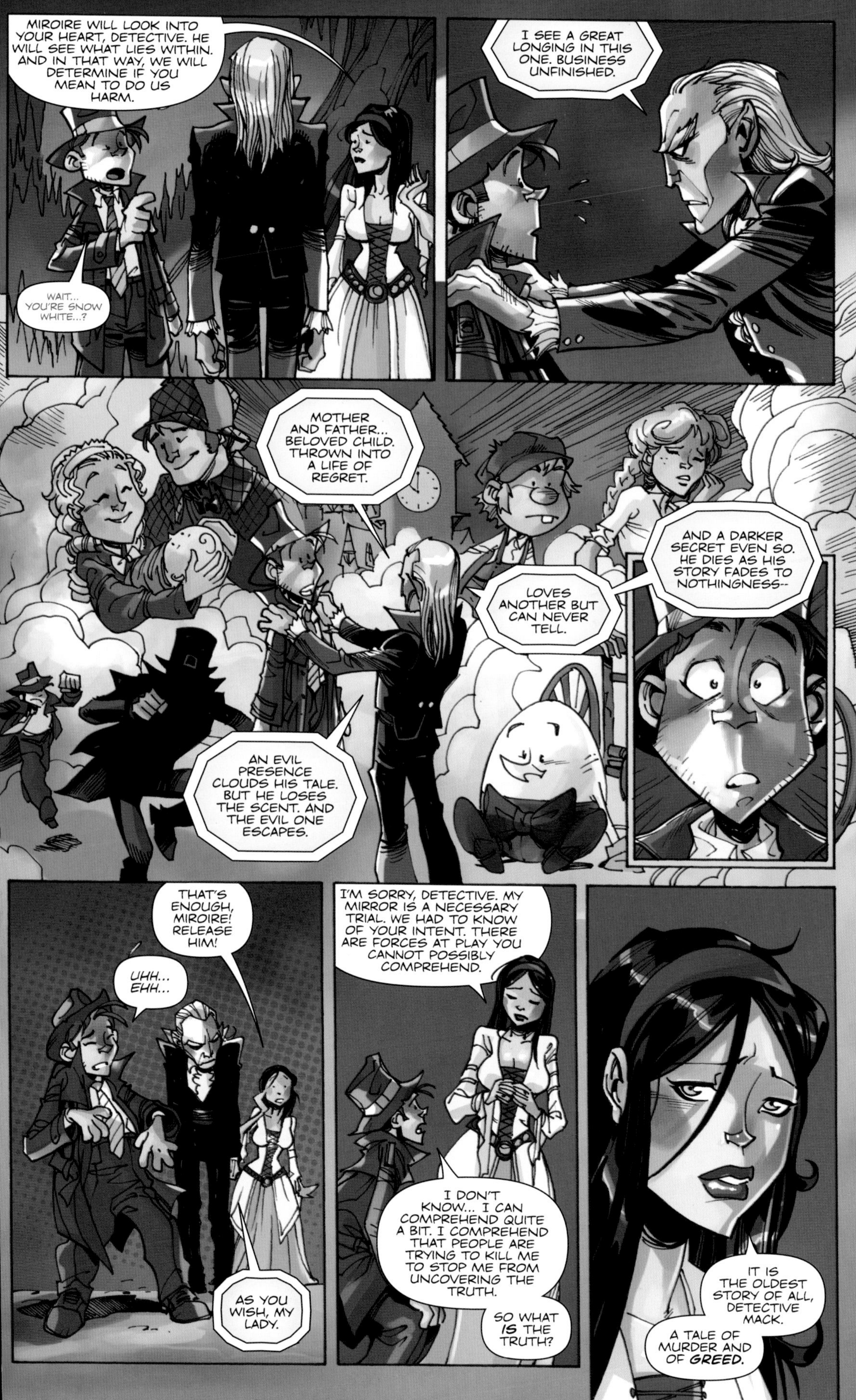
MIROIRE WILL LOOK INTO YOUR HEART, DETECTIVE. HE WILL SEE WHAT LIES WITHIN. AND IN THAT WAY, WE WILL DETERMINE IF YOU MEAN TO DO US HARM.
WAIT... YOU'RE SNOW WHITE...?
I SEE A GREAT LONGING IN THIS ONE. BUSINESS UNFINISHED.
MOTHER AND FATHER... BELOVED CHILD. THROWN INTO A LIFE OF REGRET.
LOVES ANOTHER BUT CAN NEVER TELL.
AND A DARKER SECRET EVEN SO. HE DIES AS HIS STORY FADES TO NOTHINGNESS--
AN EVIL PRESENCE CLOUDS HIS TALE. BUT HE LOSES THE SCENT. AND THE EVIL ONE ESCAPES.
THAT'S ENOUGH, MIROIRE! RELEASE HIM!
UHH... EHH...
AS YOU WISH, MY LADY.
I'M SORRY, DETECTIVE. MY MIRROR IS A NECESSARY TRIAL. WE HAD TO KNOW OF YOUR INTENT. THERE ARE FORCES AT PLAY YOU CANNOT POSSIBLY COMPREHEND.
I DON'T KNOW... I CAN COMPREHEND QUITE A BIT. I COMPREHEND THAT PEOPLE ARE TRYING TO KILL ME TO STOP ME FROM UNCOVERING THE TRUTH.
SO WHAT IS THE TRUTH?
IT IS THE OLDEST STORY OF ALL, DETECTIVE MACK.
A TALE OF MURDER AND OF GREED.

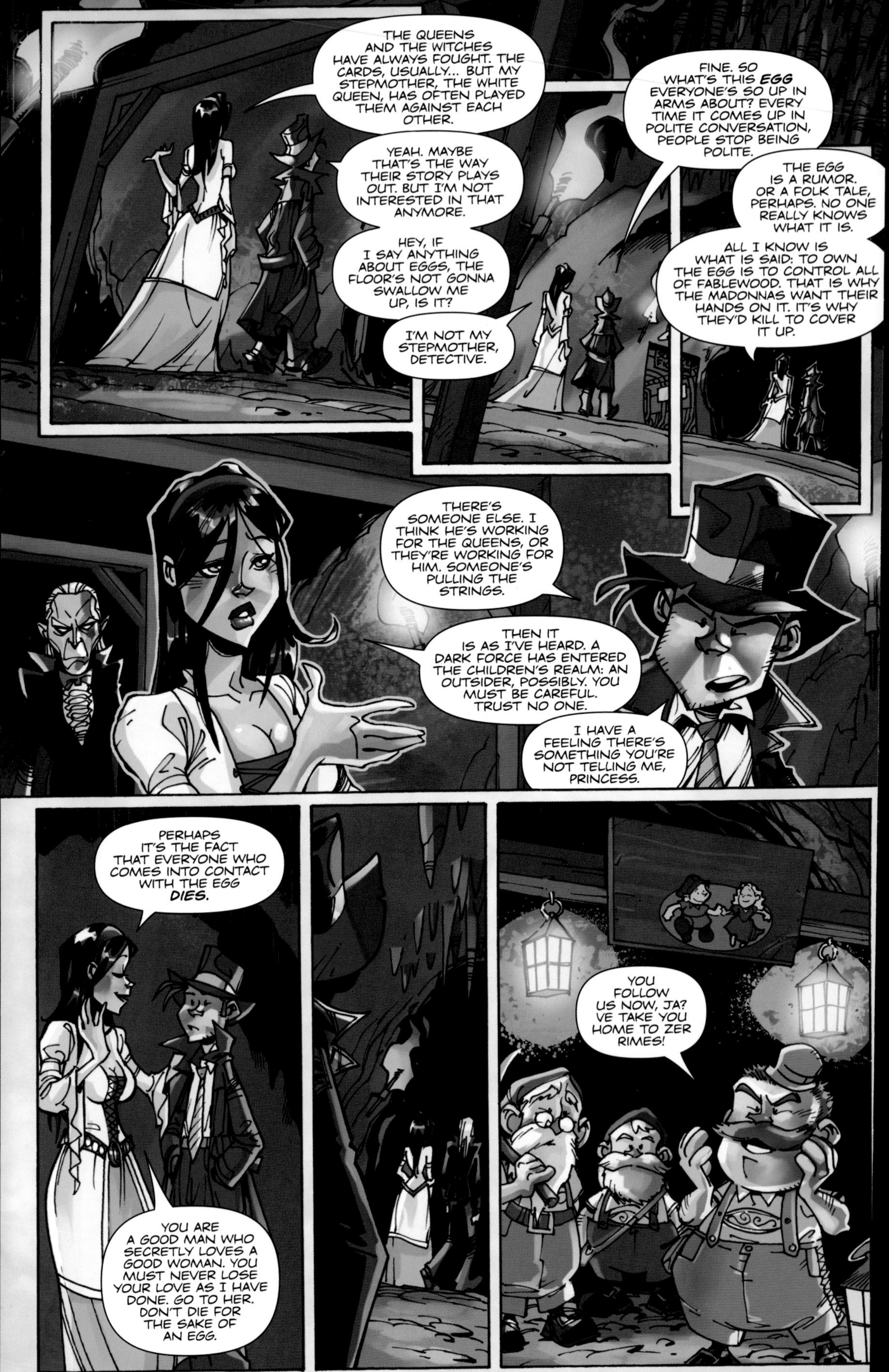

THE QUEENS AND THE WITCHES HAVE ALWAYS FOUGHT. THE CARDS, USUALLY... BUT MY STEPMOTHER, THE WHITE QUEEN, HAS OFTEN PLAYED THEM AGAINST EACH OTHER.
YEAH. MAYBE THAT'S THE WAY THEIR STORY PLAYS OUT. BUT I'M NOT INTERESTED IN THAT ANYMORE.
HEY, IF I SAY ANYTHING ABOUT EGGS, THE FLOOR'S NOT GONNA SWALLOW ME UP, IS IT?
I'M NOT MY STEPMOTHER, DETECTIVE.
FINE. SO WHAT'S THIS **EGG** EVERYONE'S SO UP IN ARMS ABOUT? EVERY TIME IT COMES UP IN POLITE CONVERSATION, PEOPLE STOP BEING POLITE.
THE EGG IS A RUMOR. OR A FOLK TALE, PERHAPS. NO ONE REALLY KNOWS WHAT IT IS.
ALL I KNOW IS WHAT IS SAID: TO OWN THE EGG IS TO CONTROL ALL OF FABLEWOOD. THAT IS WHY THE MADONNAS WANT THEIR HANDS ON IT. IT'S WHY THEY'D KILL TO COVER IT UP.
THERE'S SOMEONE ELSE. I THINK HE'S WORKING FOR THE QUEENS, OR THEY'RE WORKING FOR HIM. SOMEONE'S PULLING THE STRINGS.
THEN IT IS AS I'VE HEARD. A DARK FORCE HAS ENTERED THE CHILDREN'S REALM: AN OUTSIDER, POSSIBLY. YOU MUST BE CAREFUL. TRUST NO ONE.
I HAVE A FEELING THERE'S SOMETHING YOU'RE NOT TELLING ME, PRINCESS.
PERHAPS IT'S THE FACT THAT EVERYONE WHO COMES INTO CONTACT WITH THE EGG ***DIES.***
YOU ARE A GOOD MAN WHO SECRETLY LOVES A GOOD WOMAN. YOU MUST NEVER LOSE YOUR LOVE AS I HAVE DONE. GO TO HER. DON'T DIE FOR THE SAKE OF AN EGG.
YOU FOLLOW US NOW, JA? VE TAKE YOU HOME TO ZER RIMES!

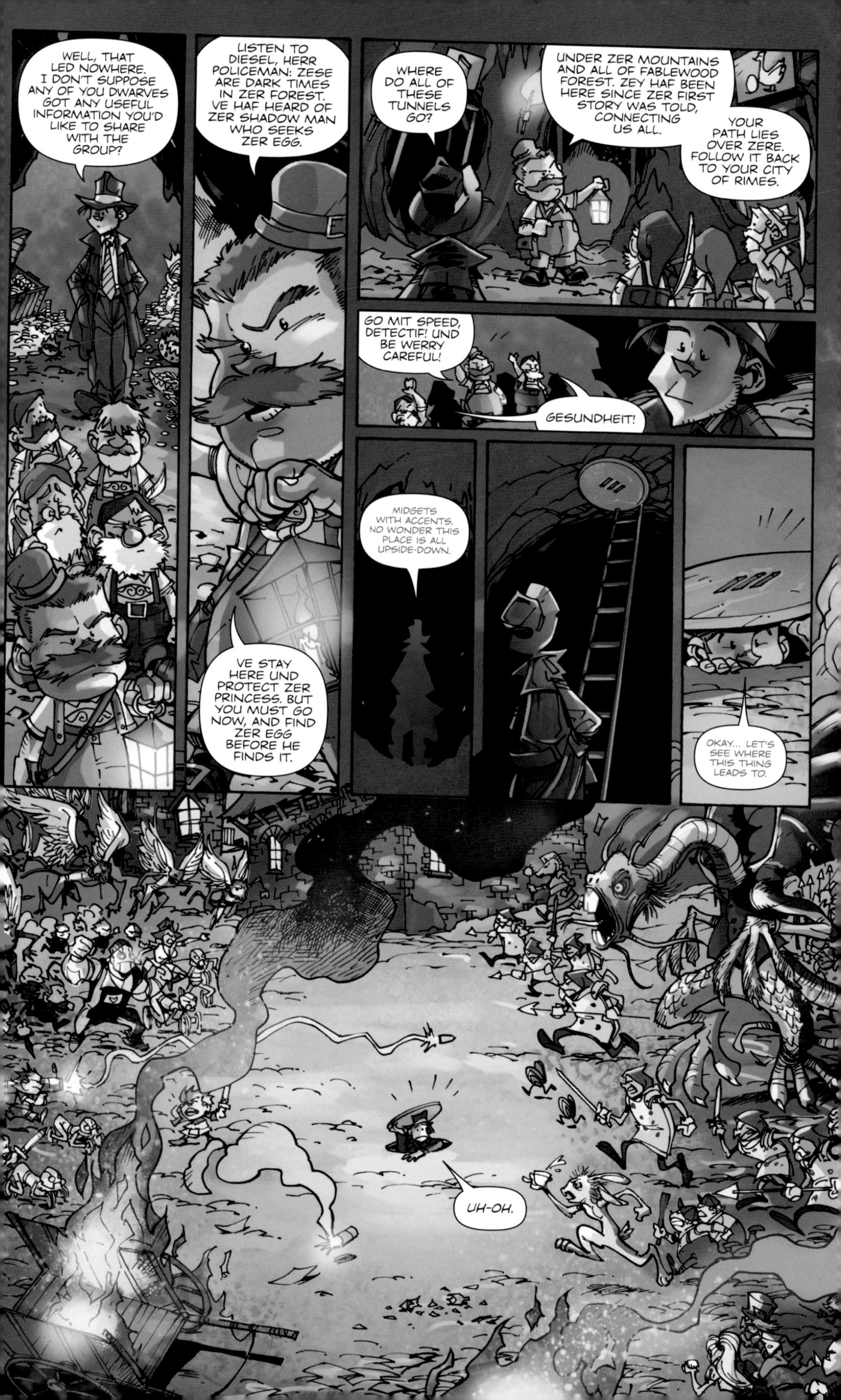
WELL, THAT LED NOWHERE. I DON'T SUPPOSE ANY OF YOU DWARVES GOT ANY USEFUL INFORMATION YOU'D LIKE TO SHARE WITH THE GROUP?
LISTEN TO DIESEL, HERR POLICEMAN: ZESE ARE DARK TIMES IN ZER FOREST. VE HAF HEARD OF ZER SHADOW MAN WHO SEEKS ZER EGG.
VE STAY HERE UND PROTECT ZER PRINCESS. BUT YOU MUST GO NOW, AND FIND ZER EGG BEFORE HE FINDS IT.
WHERE DO ALL OF THESE TUNNELS GO?
UNDER ZER MOUNTAINS AND ALL OF FABLEWOOD FOREST. ZEY HAF BEEN HERE SINCE ZER FIRST STORY WAS TOLD, CONNECTING US ALL.
YOUR PATH LIES OVER ZERE. FOLLOW IT BACK TO YOUR CITY OF RIMES.
GO MIT SPEED, DETECTIF! UND BE WERRY CAREFUL!
GESUNDHEIT!
MIDGETS WITH ACCENTS. NO WONDER THIS PLACE IS ALL UPSIDE-DOWN.
OKAY... LET'S SEE WHERE THIS THING LEADS TO.
UH-OH.

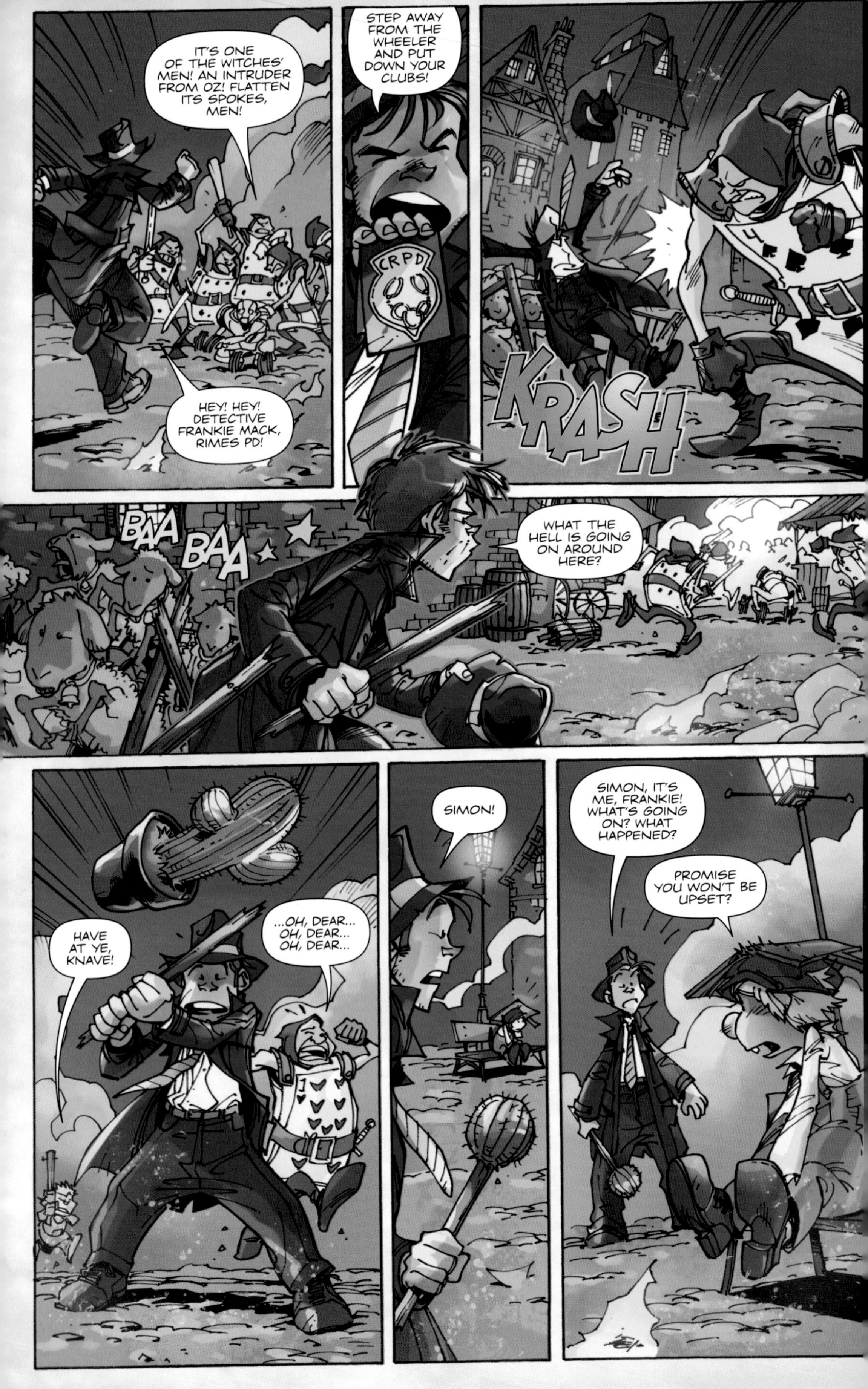
IT'S ONE OF THE WITCHES' MEN! AN INTRUDER FROM OZ! FLATTEN ITS SPOKES, MEN!
HEY! HEY! DETECTIVE FRANKIE MACK, RIMES PD!
STEP AWAY FROM THE WHEELER AND PUT DOWN YOUR CLUBS!
CRPD
KRASH
BAA BAA
WHAT THE HELL IS GOING ON AROUND HERE?
HAVE AT YE, KNAVE!
...OH, DEAR... OH, DEAR... OH, DEAR...
SIMON!
SIMON, IT'S ME, FRANKIE! WHAT'S GOING ON? WHAT HAPPENED?
PROMISE YOU WON'T BE UPSET?

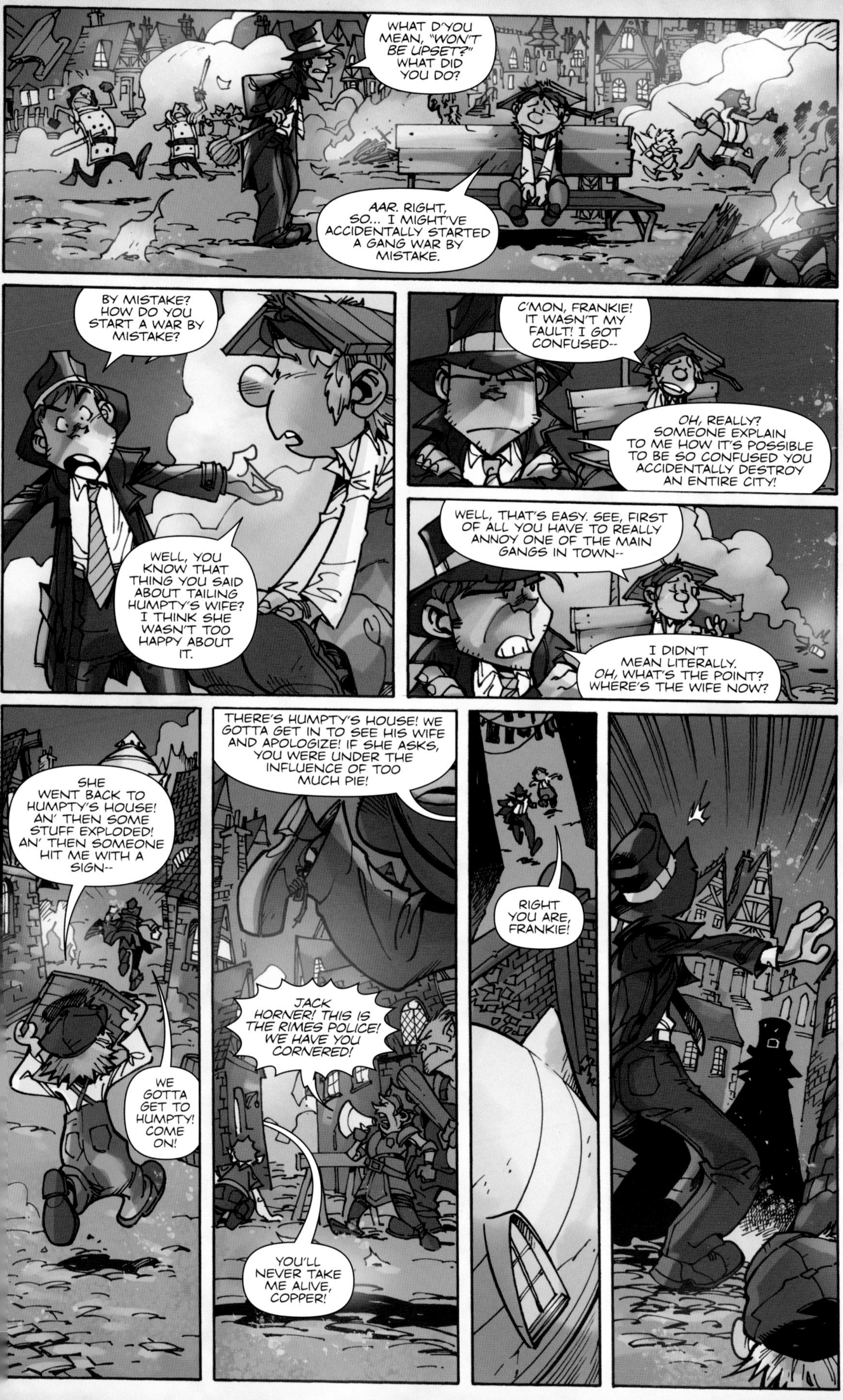
WHAT D'YOU MEAN, "WON'T BE UPSET?" WHAT DID YOU DO?
AAR. RIGHT, SO... I MIGHT'VE ACCIDENTALLY STARTED A GANG WAR BY MISTAKE.
BY MISTAKE? HOW DO YOU START A WAR BY MISTAKE?
WELL, YOU KNOW THAT THING YOU SAID ABOUT TAILING HUMPTY'S WIFE? I THINK SHE WASN'T TOO HAPPY ABOUT IT.
C'MON, FRANKIE! IT WASN'T MY FAULT! I GOT CONFUSED--
OH, REALLY? SOMEONE EXPLAIN TO ME HOW IT'S POSSIBLE TO BE SO CONFUSED YOU ACCIDENTALLY DESTROY AN ENTIRE CITY!
WELL, THAT'S EASY. SEE, FIRST OF ALL YOU HAVE TO REALLY ANNOY ONE OF THE MAIN GANGS IN TOWN--
I DIDN'T MEAN LITERALLY. OH, WHAT'S THE POINT? WHERE'S THE WIFE NOW?
SHE WENT BACK TO HUMPTY'S HOUSE! AN' THEN SOME STUFF EXPLODED! AN' THEN SOMEONE HIT ME WITH A SIGN--
WE GOTTA GET TO HUMPTY! COME ON!
THERE'S HUMPTY'S HOUSE! WE GOTTA GET IN TO SEE HIS WIFE AND APOLOGIZE! IF SHE ASKS, YOU WERE UNDER THE INFLUENCE OF TOO MUCH PIE!
JACK HORNER! THIS IS THE RIMES POLICE! WE HAVE YOU CORNERED!
YOU'LL NEVER TAKE ME ALIVE, COPPER!
RIGHT YOU ARE, FRANKIE!

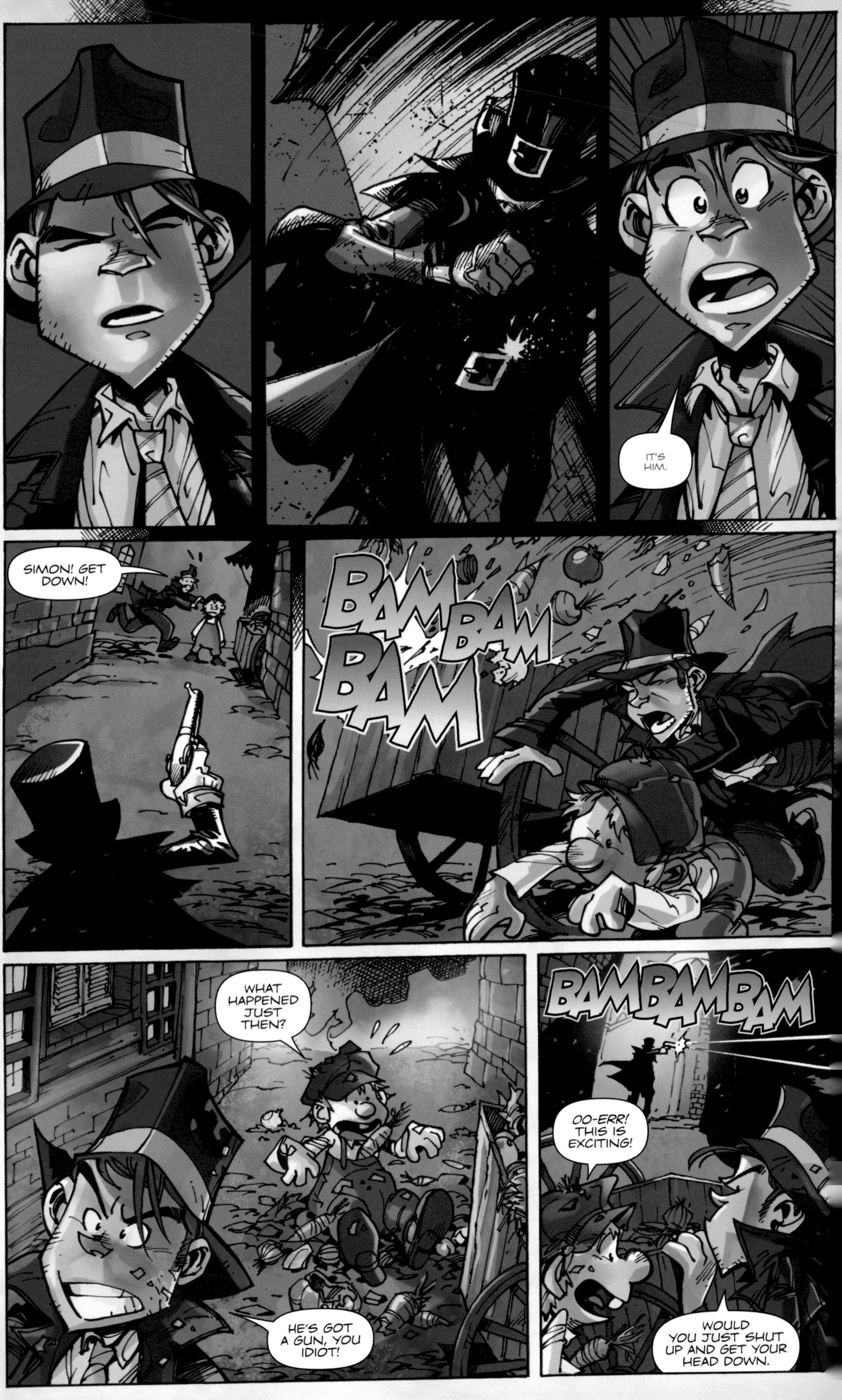
IT'S HIM.
SIMON! GET DOWN!
BAM BAM BAM
WHAT HAPPENED JUST THEN?
HE'S GOT A GUN, YOU IDIOT!
BAM BAM BAM
OO-ERR! THIS IS EXCITING!
WOULD YOU JUST SHUT UP AND GET YOUR HEAD DOWN.

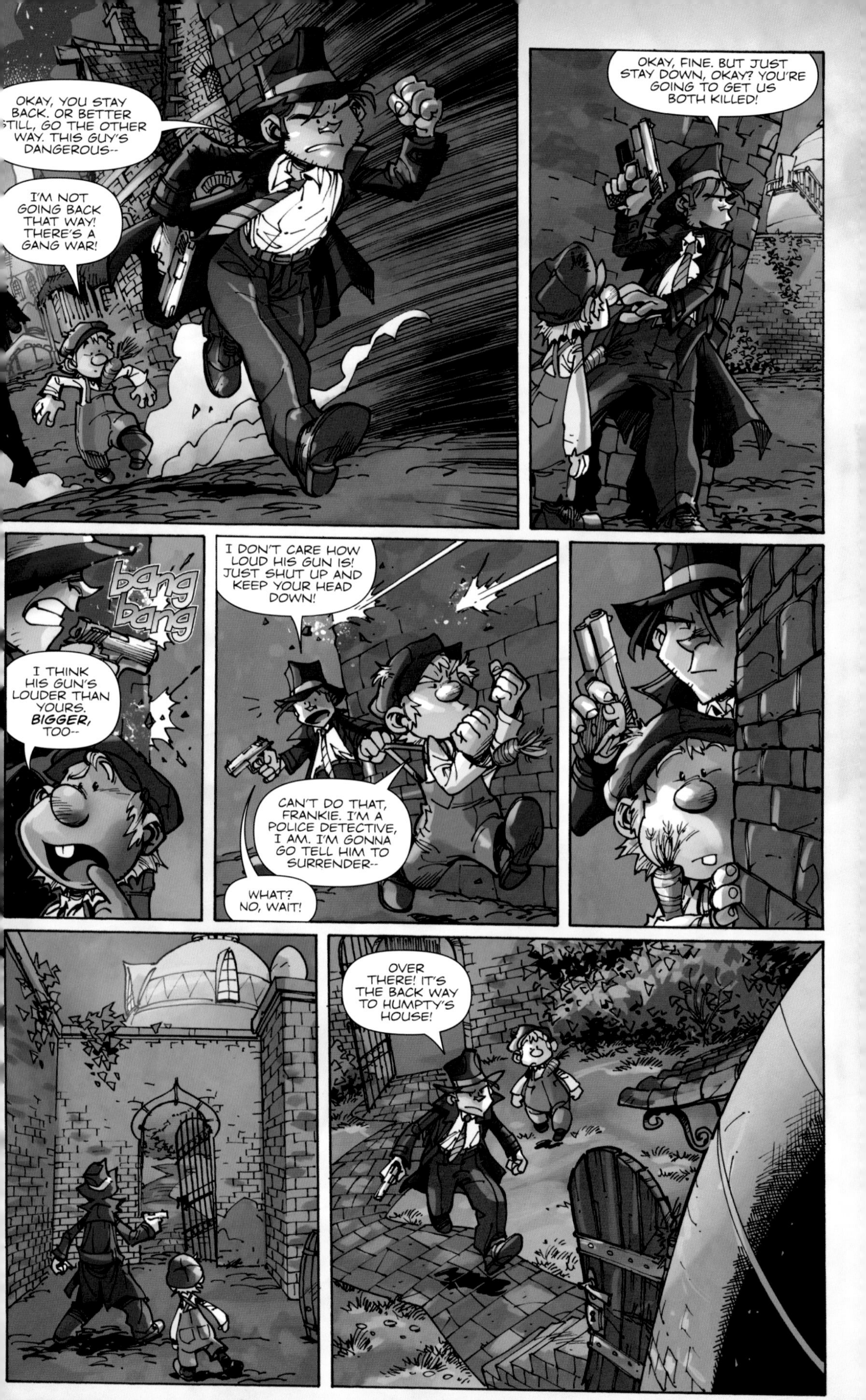

OKAY, YOU STAY BACK. OR BETTER STILL, GO THE OTHER WAY. THIS GUY'S DANGEROUS--
I'M NOT GOING BACK THAT WAY! THERE'S A GANG WAR!
OKAY, FINE. BUT JUST STAY DOWN, OKAY? YOU'RE GOING TO GET US BOTH KILLED!
bang bang
I THINK HIS GUN'S LOUDER THAN YOURS. BIGGER, TOO--
I DON'T CARE HOW LOUD HIS GUN IS! JUST SHUT UP AND KEEP YOUR HEAD DOWN!
CAN'T DO THAT, FRANKIE. I'M A POLICE DETECTIVE, I AM. I'M GONNA GO TELL HIM TO SURRENDER--
WHAT? NO, WAIT!
OVER THERE! IT'S THE BACK WAY TO HUMPTY'S HOUSE!

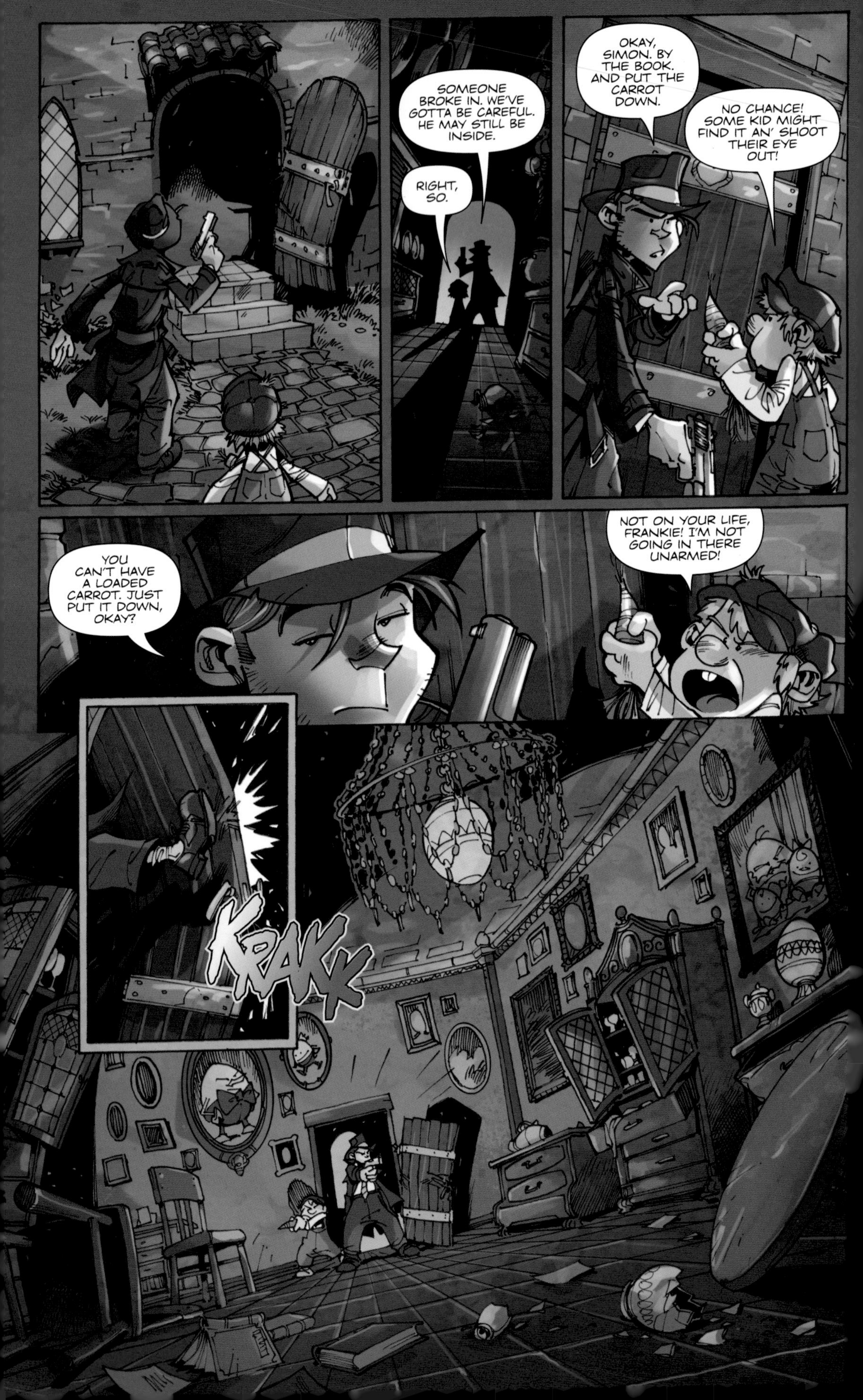
SOMEONE BROKE IN. WE'VE GOTTA BE CAREFUL. HE MAY STILL BE INSIDE.
RIGHT, SO.
OKAY, SIMON. BY THE BOOK. AND PUT THE CARROT DOWN.
NO CHANCE! SOME KID MIGHT FIND IT AN' SHOOT THEIR EYE OUT!
YOU CAN'T HAVE A LOADED CARROT. JUST PUT IT DOWN, OKAY?
NOT ON YOUR LIFE, FRANKIE! I'M NOT GOING IN THERE UNARMED!
KRAKK

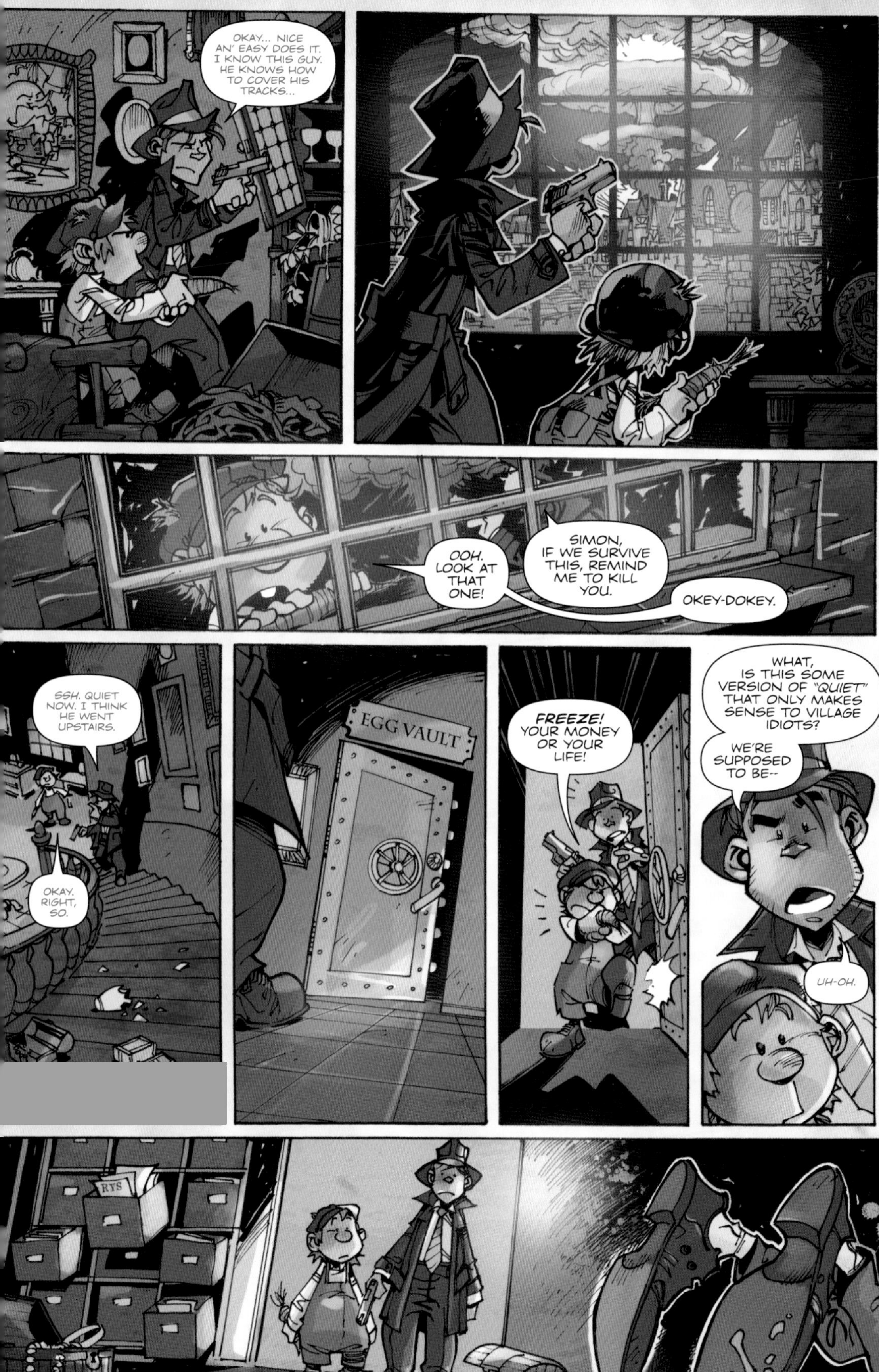
OKAY... NICE AN' EASY DOES IT. I KNOW THIS GUY. HE KNOWS HOW TO COVER HIS TRACKS...
SIMON, IF WE SURVIVE THIS, REMIND ME TO KILL YOU.
OOH. LOOK AT THAT ONE!
OKEY-DOKEY.
SSH. QUIET NOW. I THINK HE WENT UPSTAIRS.
OKAY. RIGHT, SO.
EGG VAULT
FREEZE! YOUR MONEY OR YOUR LIFE!
WHAT, IS THIS SOME VERSION OF "QUIET" THAT ONLY MAKES SENSE TO VILLAGE IDIOTS?
WE'RE SUPPOSED TO BE--
UH-OH.
RYS

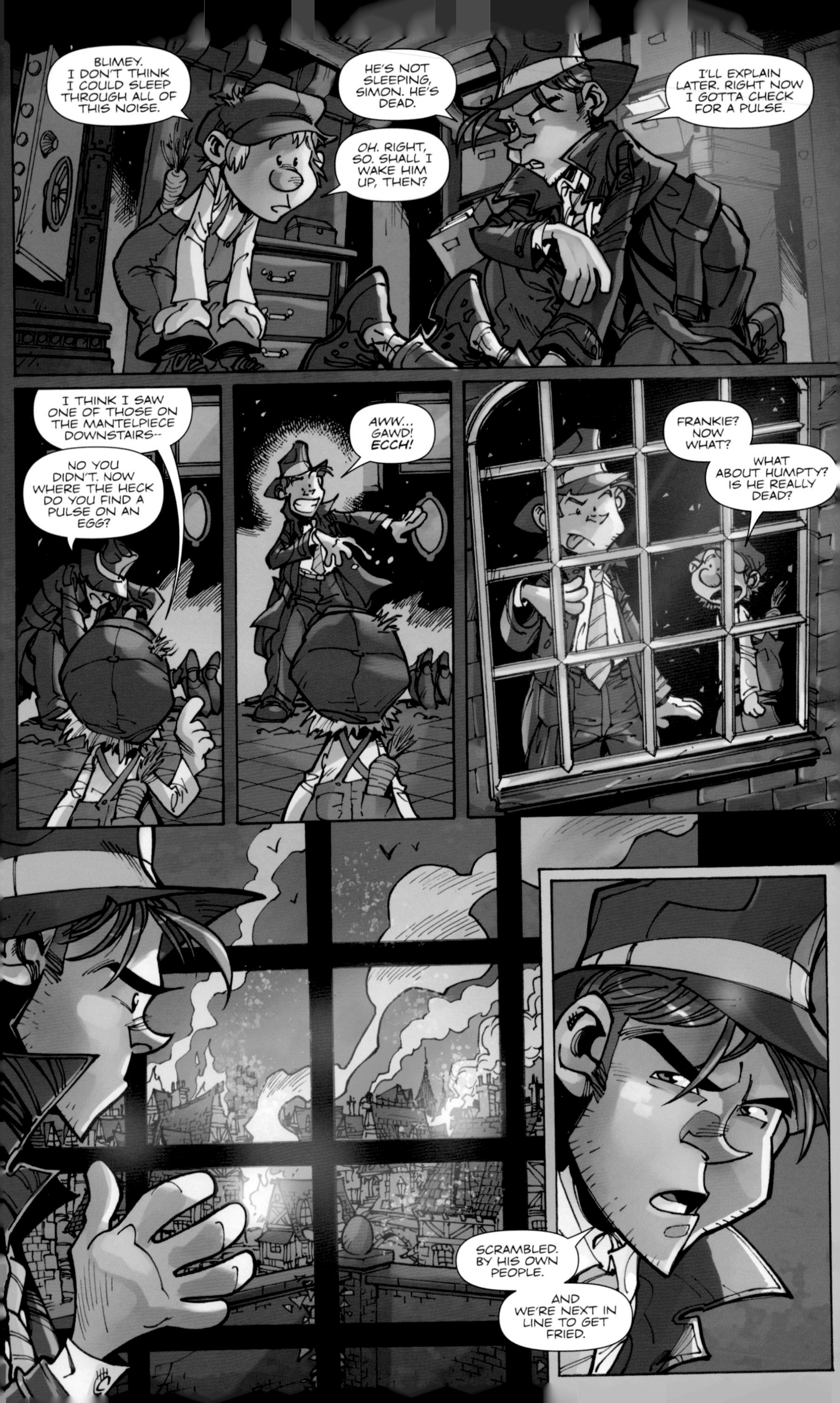
BLIMEY. I DON'T THINK I COULD SLEEP THROUGH ALL OF THIS NOISE.
HE'S NOT SLEEPING, SIMON. HE'S DEAD.
OH. RIGHT, SO. SHALL I WAKE HIM UP, THEN?
I'LL EXPLAIN LATER. RIGHT NOW I GOTTA CHECK FOR A PULSE.
I THINK I SAW ONE OF THOSE ON THE MANTELPIECE DOWNSTAIRS--
NO YOU DIDN'T. NOW WHERE THE HECK DO YOU FIND A PULSE ON AN EGG?
AWW... GAWD! *ECCH!*
FRANKIE? NOW WHAT?
WHAT ABOUT HUMPTY? IS HE REALLY DEAD?
SCRAMBLED. BY HIS OWN PEOPLE.
AND WE'RE NEXT IN LINE TO GET FRIED.

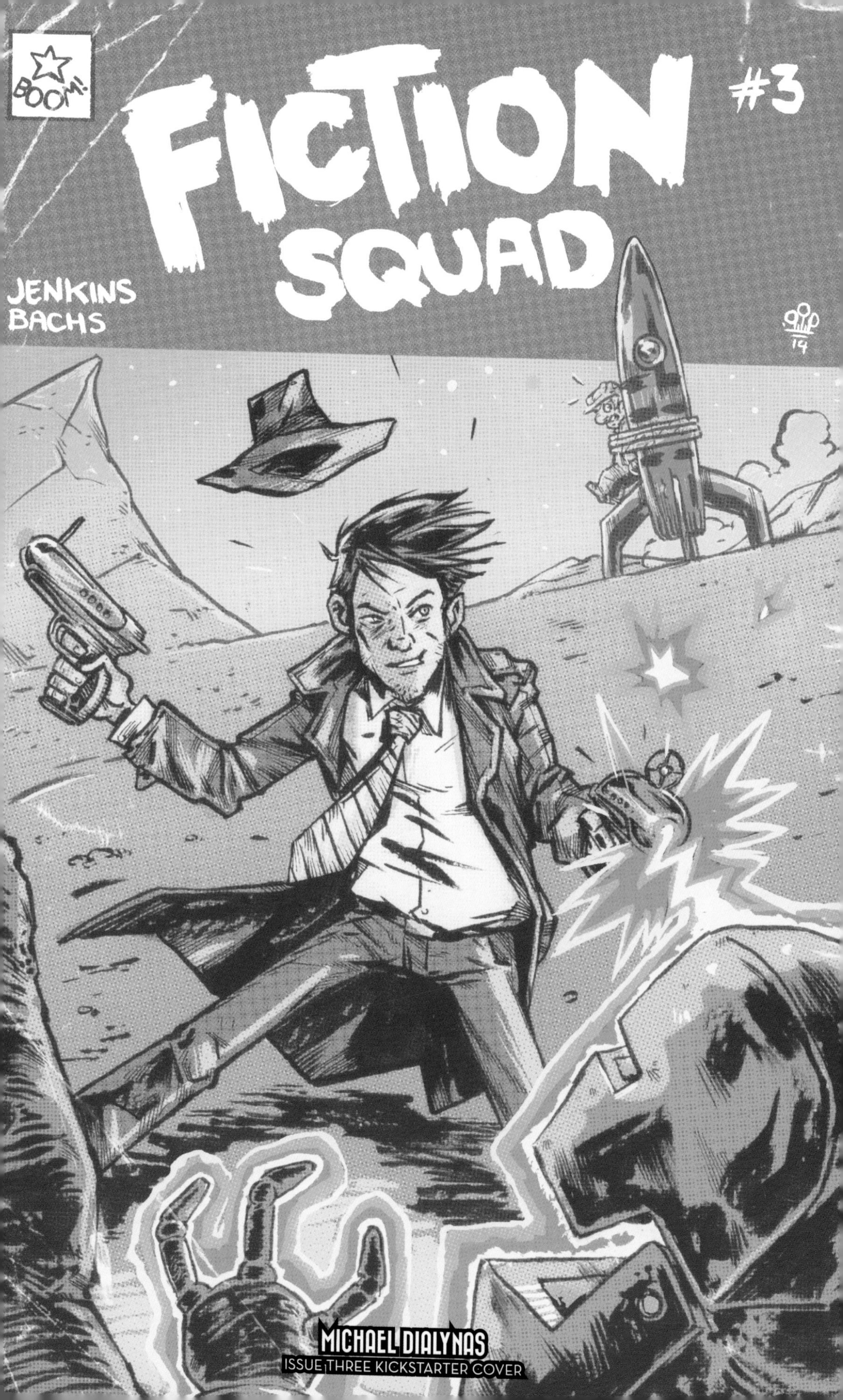

BOOM!
FICTION SQUAD
#3
JENKINS
BACHS
MICHAEL DIALYNAS
ISSUE THREE KICKSTARTER COVER

CHAPTER FOUR

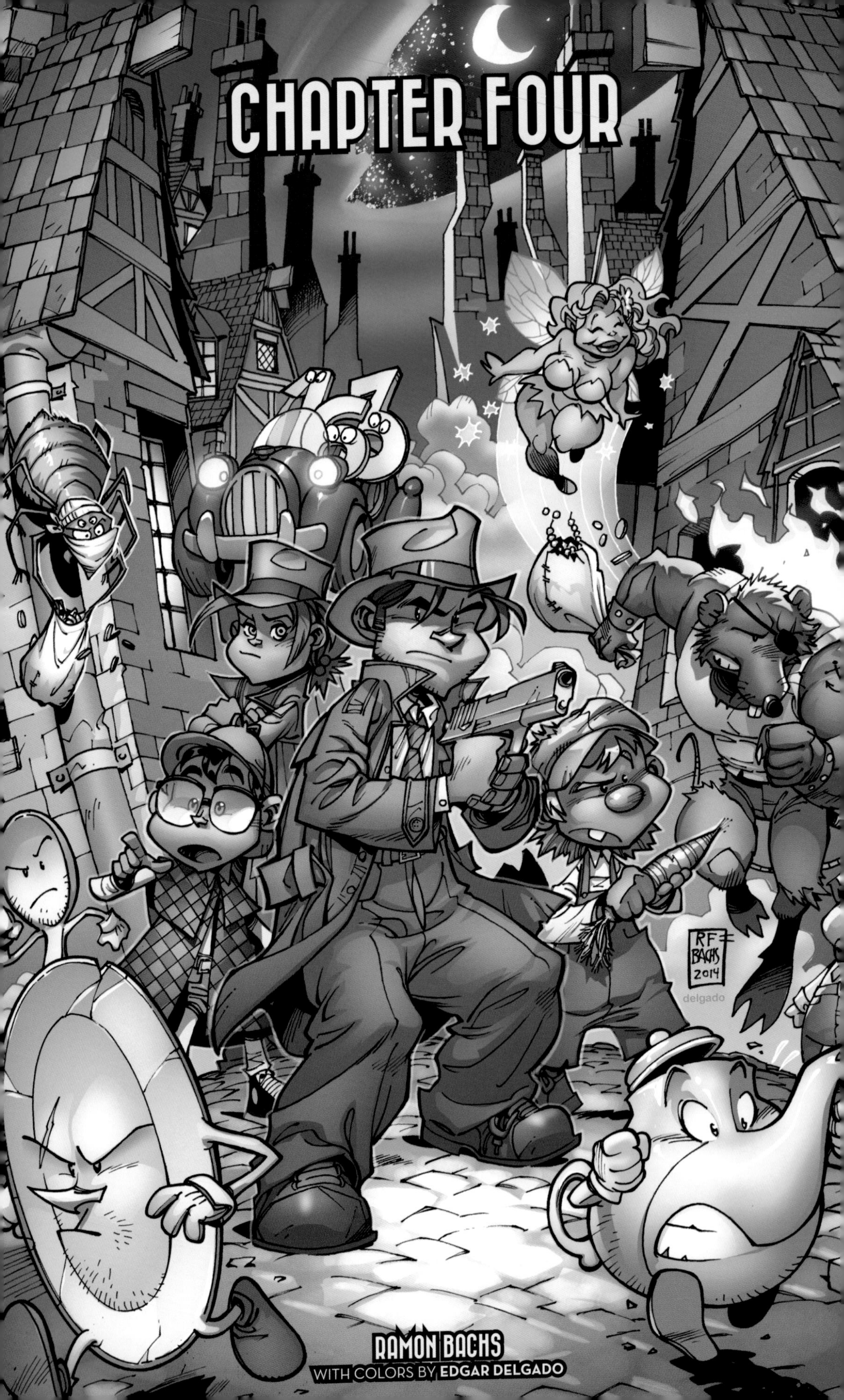
RF BACHS 2014
delgado

RAMON BACHS
WITH COLORS BY EDGAR DELGADO

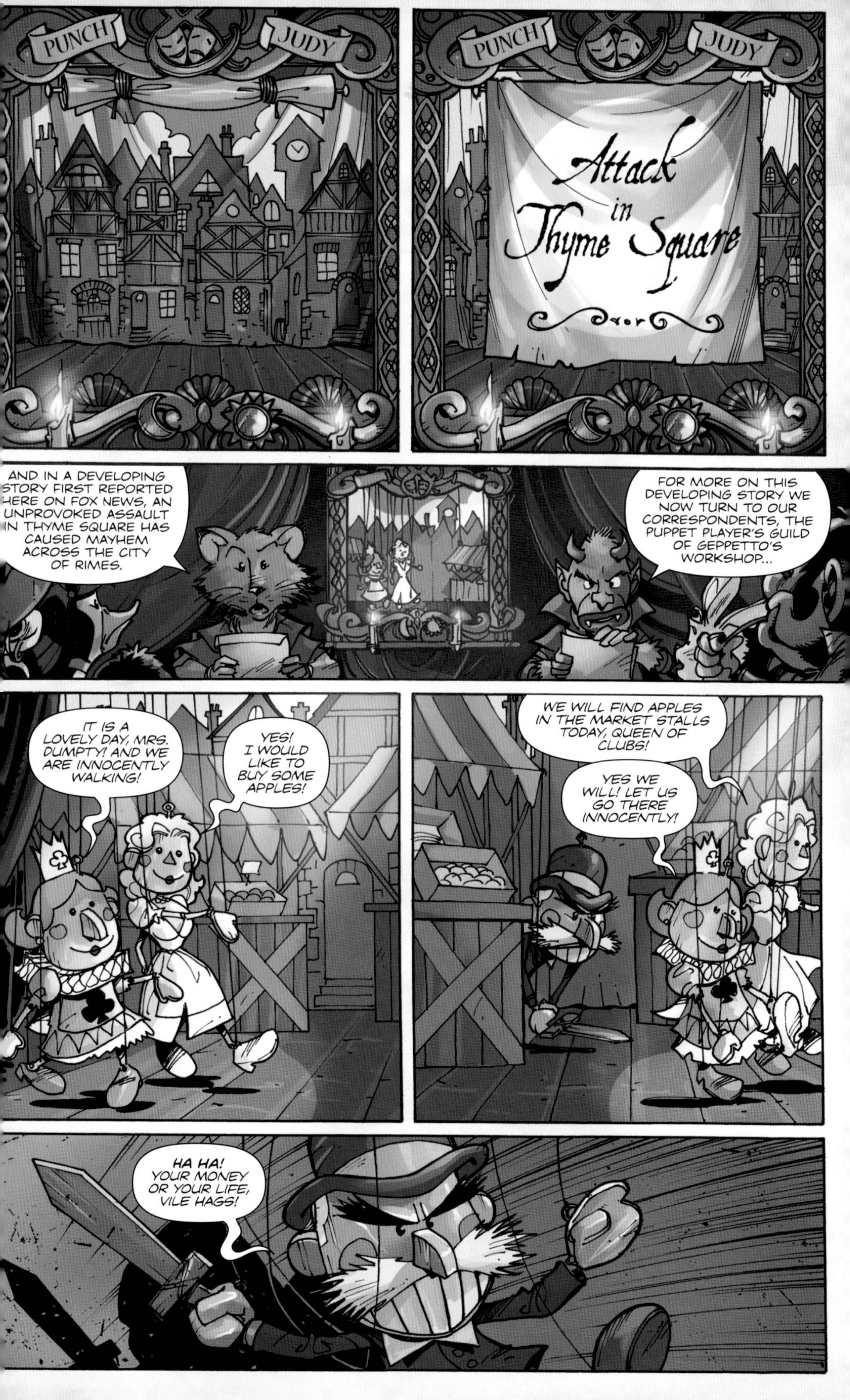
PUNCH
JUDY
PUNCH
JUDY
Attack in Thyme Square
AND IN A DEVELOPING STORY FIRST REPORTED HERE ON FOX NEWS, AN UNPROVOKED ASSAULT IN THYME SQUARE HAS CAUSED MAYHEM ACROSS THE CITY OF RIMES.
FOR MORE ON THIS DEVELOPING STORY WE NOW TURN TO OUR CORRESPONDENTS, THE PUPPET PLAYER'S GUILD OF GEPPETTO'S WORKSHOP...
IT IS A LOVELY DAY, MRS. DUMPTY! AND WE ARE INNOCENTLY WALKING!
YES! I WOULD LIKE TO BUY SOME APPLES!
WE WILL FIND APPLES IN THE MARKET STALLS TODAY, QUEEN OF CLUBS!
YES WE WILL! LET US GO THERE INNOCENTLY!
HA HA! YOUR MONEY OR YOUR LIFE, VILE HAGS!

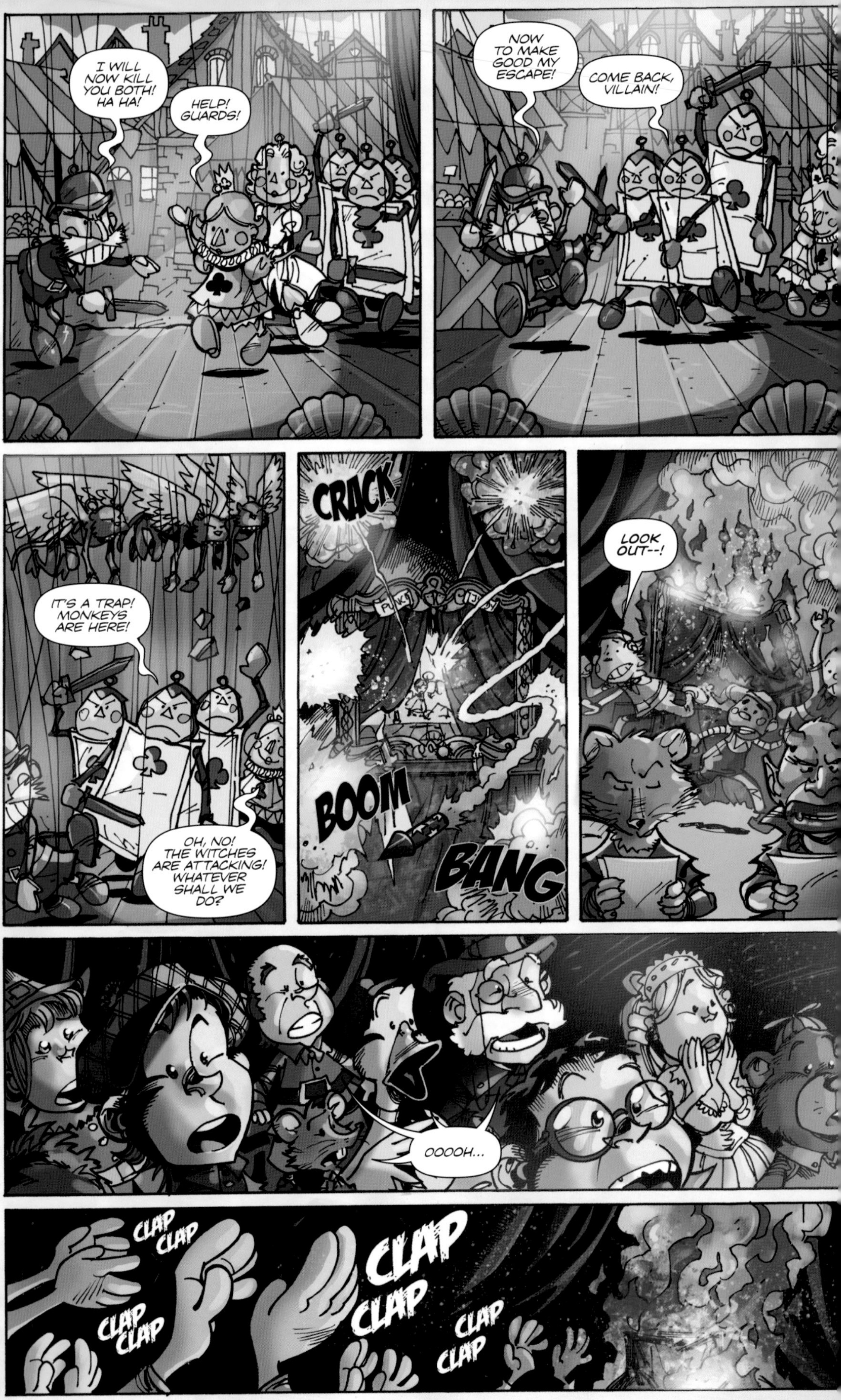

I WILL NOW KILL YOU BOTH! HA HA!
HELP! GUARDS!
NOW TO MAKE GOOD MY ESCAPE!
COME BACK, VILLAIN!
IT'S A TRAP! MONKEYS ARE HERE!
OH, NO! THE WITCHES ARE ATTACKING! WHATEVER SHALL WE DO?
CRACK
BOOM
BANG
LOOK OUT--!
OOOOH...
CLAP CLAP
CLAP CLAP
CLAP CLAP
CLAP CLAP

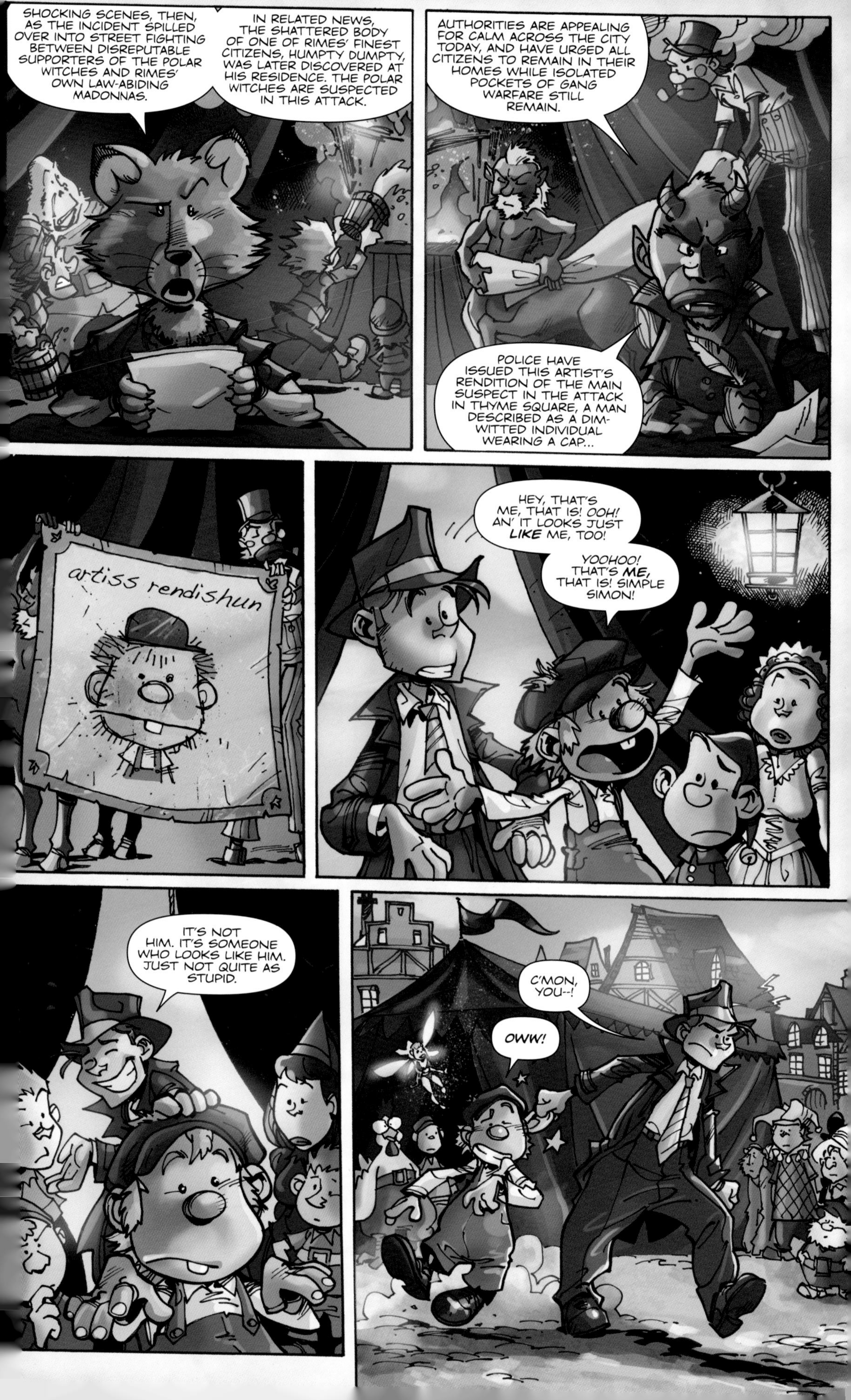
SHOCKING SCENES, THEN, AS THE INCIDENT SPILLED OVER INTO STREET FIGHTING BETWEEN DISREPUTABLE SUPPORTERS OF THE POLAR WITCHES AND RIMES' OWN LAW-ABIDING MADONNAS.
IN RELATED NEWS, THE SHATTERED BODY OF ONE OF RIMES' FINEST CITIZENS, HUMPTY DUMPTY, WAS LATER DISCOVERED AT HIS RESIDENCE. THE POLAR WITCHES ARE SUSPECTED IN THIS ATTACK.
AUTHORITIES ARE APPEALING FOR CALM ACROSS THE CITY TODAY, AND HAVE URGED ALL CITIZENS TO REMAIN IN THEIR HOMES WHILE ISOLATED POCKETS OF GANG WARFARE STILL REMAIN.
POLICE HAVE ISSUED THIS ARTIST'S RENDITION OF THE MAIN SUSPECT IN THE ATTACK IN THYME SQUARE, A MAN DESCRIBED AS A DIM-WITTED INDIVIDUAL WEARING A CAP...
artiss rendishun
HEY, THAT'S ME, THAT IS! OOH! AN' IT LOOKS JUST LIKE ME, TOO!
YOOHOO! THAT'S ME, THAT IS! SIMPLE SIMON!
IT'S NOT HIM. IT'S SOMEONE WHO LOOKS LIKE HIM. JUST NOT QUITE AS STUPID.
C'MON, YOU--!
OWW!

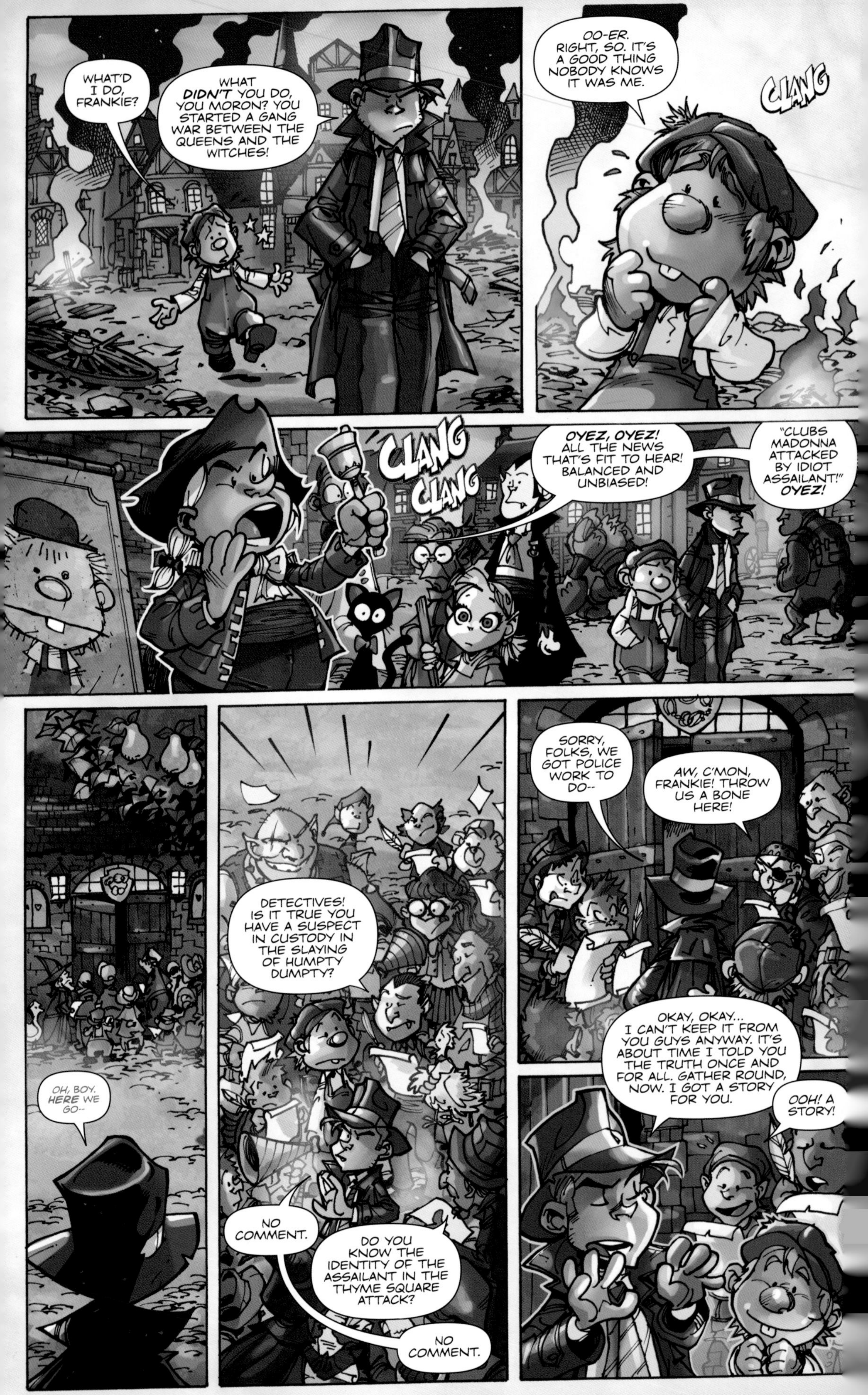

WHAT'D I DO, FRANKIE?
WHAT **DIDN'T** YOU DO, YOU MORON? YOU STARTED A GANG WAR BETWEEN THE QUEENS AND THE WITCHES!
OO-ER. RIGHT, SO. IT'S A GOOD THING NOBODY KNOWS IT WAS ME.
CLANG
CLANG
CLANG
OYEZ, OYEZ! ALL THE NEWS THAT'S FIT TO HEAR! BALANCED AND UNBIASED!
"CLUBS MADONNA ATTACKED BY IDIOT ASSAILANT!" ***OYEZ!***
OH, BOY. ***HERE*** WE GO--
DETECTIVES! IS IT TRUE YOU HAVE A SUSPECT IN CUSTODY IN THE SLAYING OF HUMPTY DUMPTY?
NO COMMENT.
DO YOU KNOW THE IDENTITY OF THE ASSAILANT IN THE THYME SQUARE ATTACK?
NO COMMENT.
SORRY, FOLKS, WE GOT POLICE WORK TO DO--
AW, C'MON, FRANKIE! THROW US A BONE HERE!
OKAY, OKAY... I CAN'T KEEP IT FROM YOU GUYS ANYWAY. IT'S ABOUT TIME I TOLD YOU THE TRUTH ONCE AND FOR ALL. GATHER ROUND, NOW. I GOT A STORY FOR YOU.
OOH! A STORY!

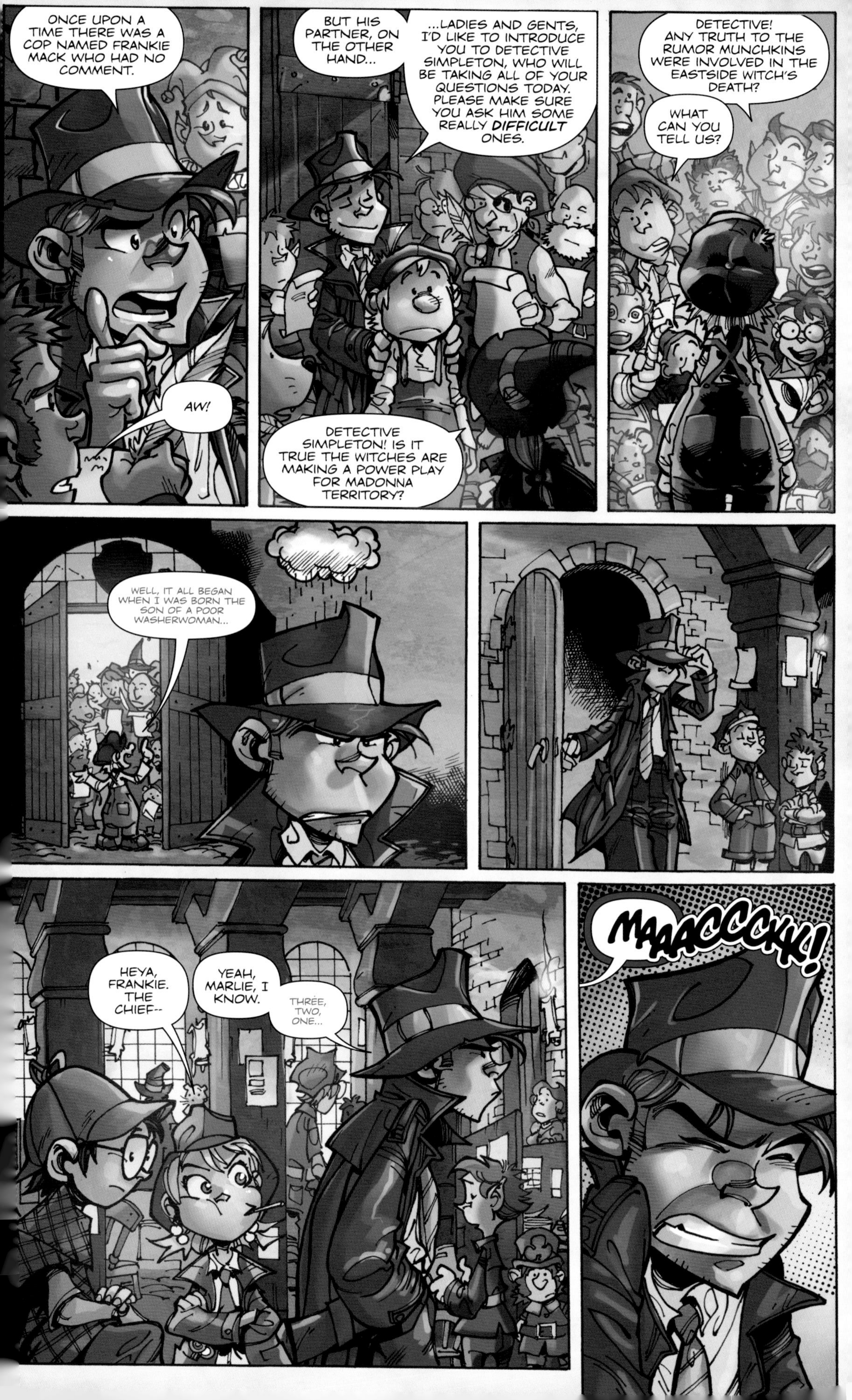
ONCE UPON A TIME THERE WAS A COP NAMED FRANKIE MACK WHO HAD NO COMMENT.
AW!
BUT HIS PARTNER, ON THE OTHER HAND...
...LADIES AND GENTS, I'D LIKE TO INTRODUCE YOU TO DETECTIVE SIMPLETON, WHO WILL BE TAKING ALL OF YOUR QUESTIONS TODAY. PLEASE MAKE SURE YOU ASK HIM SOME REALLY DIFFICULT ONES.
DETECTIVE SIMPLETON! IS IT TRUE THE WITCHES ARE MAKING A POWER PLAY FOR MADONNA TERRITORY?
DETECTIVE! ANY TRUTH TO THE RUMOR MUNCHKINS WERE INVOLVED IN THE EASTSIDE WITCH'S DEATH?
WHAT CAN YOU TELL US?
WELL, IT ALL BEGAN WHEN I WAS BORN THE SON OF A POOR WASHERWOMAN...
HEYA, FRANKIE. THE CHIEF--
YEAH, MARLIE, I KNOW.
THREE, TWO, ONE...
MAAACCCKK!

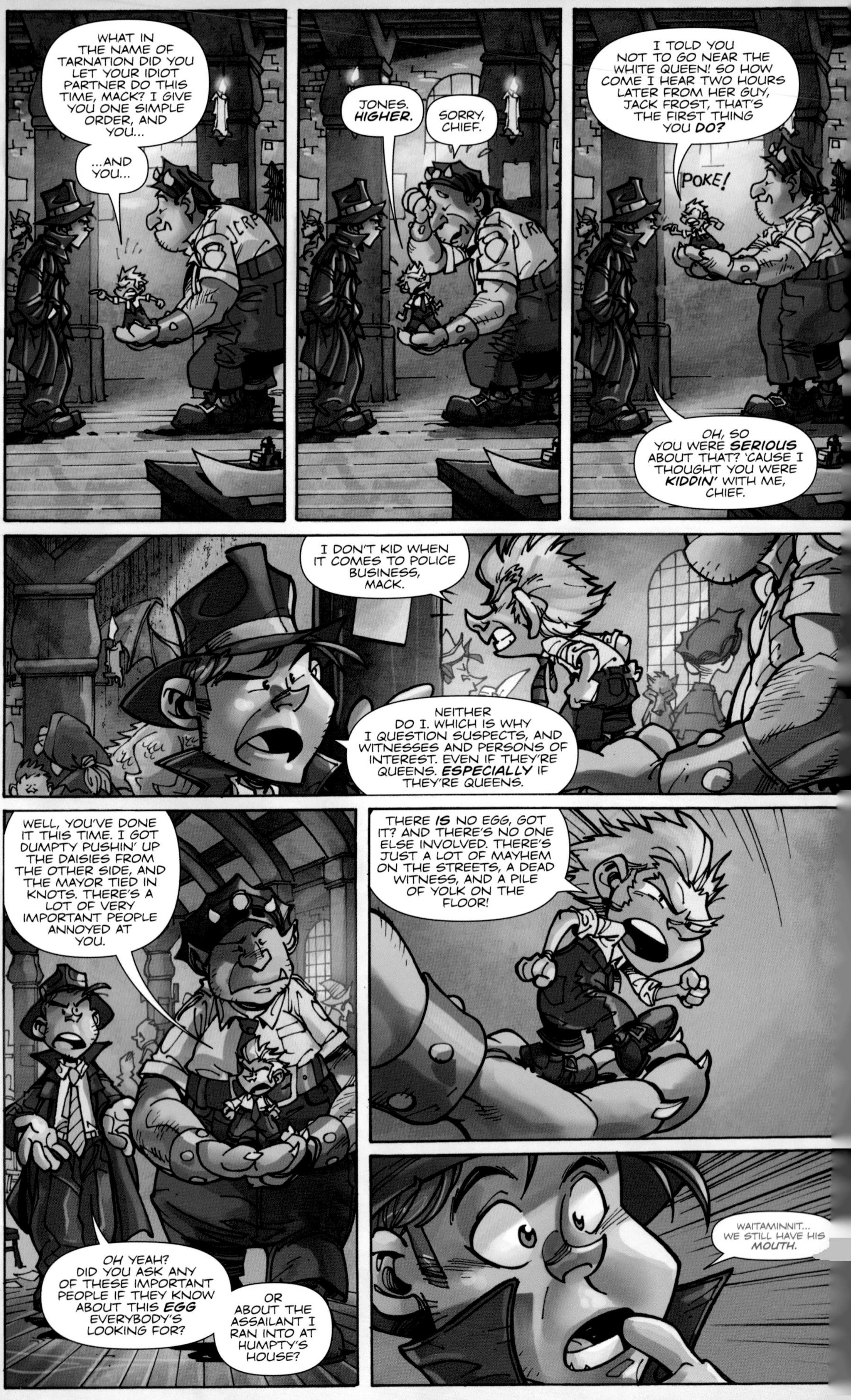
WHAT IN THE NAME OF TARNATION DID YOU LET YOUR IDIOT PARTNER DO THIS TIME, MACK? I GIVE YOU ONE SIMPLE ORDER, AND YOU...
...AND YOU...
JONES. HIGHER.
SORRY, CHIEF.
I TOLD YOU NOT TO GO NEAR THE WHITE QUEEN! SO HOW COME I HEAR TWO HOURS LATER FROM HER GUY, JACK FROST, THAT'S THE FIRST THING YOU DO?
POKE!
OH, SO YOU WERE SERIOUS ABOUT THAT? 'CAUSE I THOUGHT YOU WERE KIDDIN' WITH ME, CHIEF.
I DON'T KID WHEN IT COMES TO POLICE BUSINESS, MACK.
NEITHER DO I. WHICH IS WHY I QUESTION SUSPECTS, AND WITNESSES AND PERSONS OF INTEREST. EVEN IF THEY'RE QUEENS. ESPECIALLY IF THEY'RE QUEENS.
WELL, YOU'VE DONE IT THIS TIME. I GOT DUMPTY PUSHIN' UP THE DAISIES FROM THE OTHER SIDE, AND THE MAYOR TIED IN KNOTS. THERE'S A LOT OF VERY IMPORTANT PEOPLE ANNOYED AT YOU.
OH YEAH? DID YOU ASK ANY OF THESE IMPORTANT PEOPLE IF THEY KNOW ABOUT THIS EGG EVERYBODY'S LOOKING FOR?
OR ABOUT THE ASSAILANT I RAN INTO AT HUMPTY'S HOUSE?
THERE IS NO EGG, GOT IT? AND THERE'S NO ONE ELSE INVOLVED. THERE'S JUST A LOT OF MAYHEM ON THE STREETS, A DEAD WITNESS, AND A PILE OF YOLK ON THE FLOOR!
WAITAMINNIT... WE STILL HAVE HIS MOUTH.

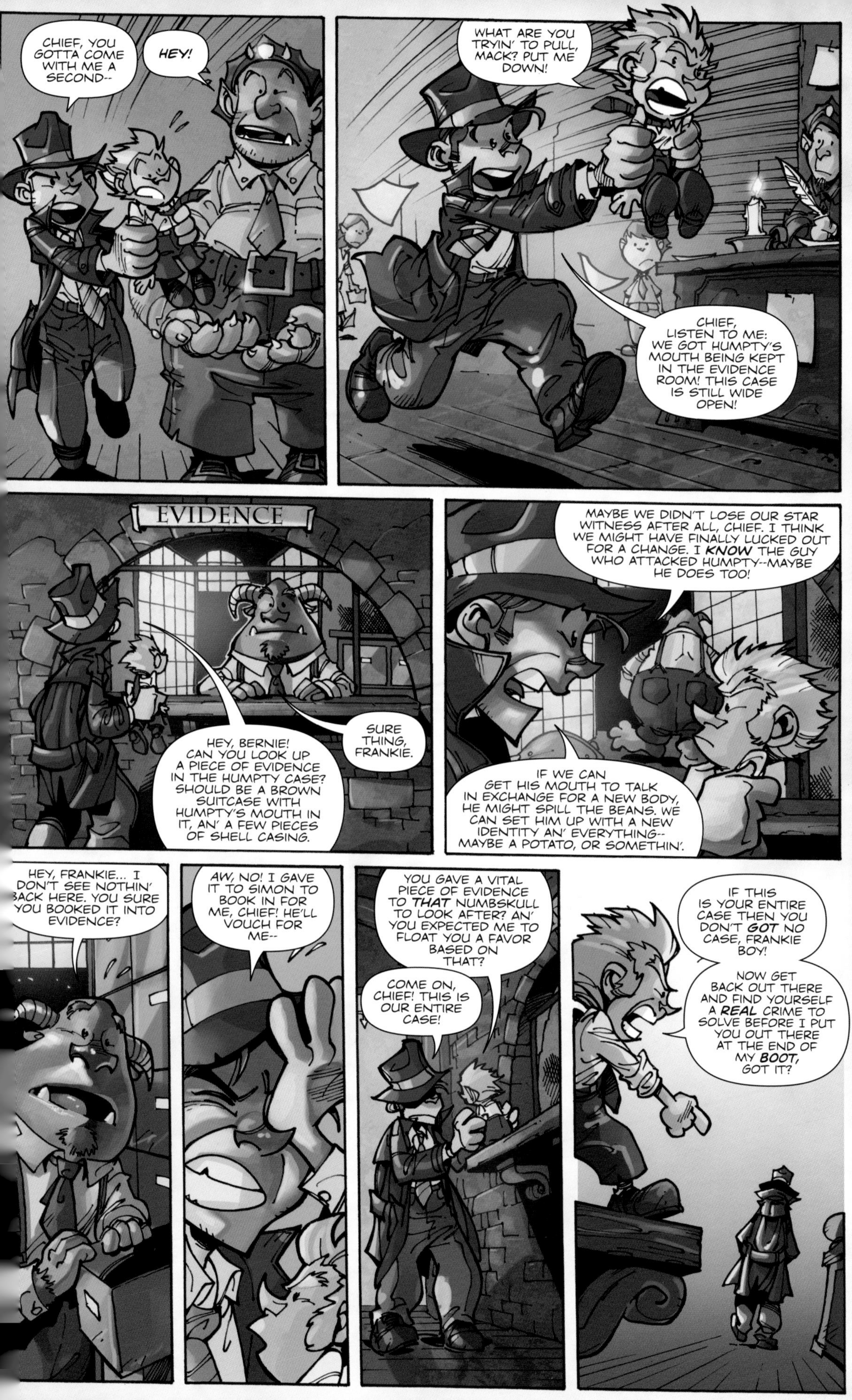

CHIEF, YOU GOTTA COME WITH ME A SECOND--
HEY!
WHAT ARE YOU TRYIN' TO PULL, MACK? PUT ME DOWN!
CHIEF, LISTEN TO ME: WE GOT HUMPTY'S MOUTH BEING KEPT IN THE EVIDENCE ROOM! THIS CASE IS STILL WIDE OPEN!
EVIDENCE
HEY, BERNIE! CAN YOU LOOK UP A PIECE OF EVIDENCE IN THE HUMPTY CASE? SHOULD BE A BROWN SUITCASE WITH HUMPTY'S MOUTH IN IT, AN' A FEW PIECES OF SHELL CASING.
SURE THING, FRANKIE.
MAYBE WE DIDN'T LOSE OUR STAR WITNESS AFTER ALL, CHIEF. I THINK WE MIGHT HAVE FINALLY LUCKED OUT FOR A CHANGE. I KNOW THE GUY WHO ATTACKED HUMPTY--MAYBE HE DOES TOO!
IF WE CAN GET HIS MOUTH TO TALK IN EXCHANGE FOR A NEW BODY, HE MIGHT SPILL THE BEANS. WE CAN SET HIM UP WITH A NEW IDENTITY AN' EVERYTHING-- MAYBE A POTATO, OR SOMETHIN'.
HEY, FRANKIE... I DON'T SEE NOTHIN' BACK HERE. YOU SURE YOU BOOKED IT INTO EVIDENCE?
AW, NO! I GAVE IT TO SIMON TO BOOK IN FOR ME, CHIEF! HE'LL VOUCH FOR ME--
YOU GAVE A VITAL PIECE OF EVIDENCE TO THAT NUMBSKULL TO LOOK AFTER? AN' YOU EXPECTED ME TO FLOAT YOU A FAVOR BASED ON THAT?
COME ON, CHIEF! THIS IS OUR ENTIRE CASE!
IF THIS IS YOUR ENTIRE CASE THEN YOU DON'T GOT NO CASE, FRANKIE BOY!
NOW GET BACK OUT THERE AND FIND YOURSELF A REAL CRIME TO SOLVE BEFORE I PUT YOU OUT THERE AT THE END OF MY BOOT, GOT IT?

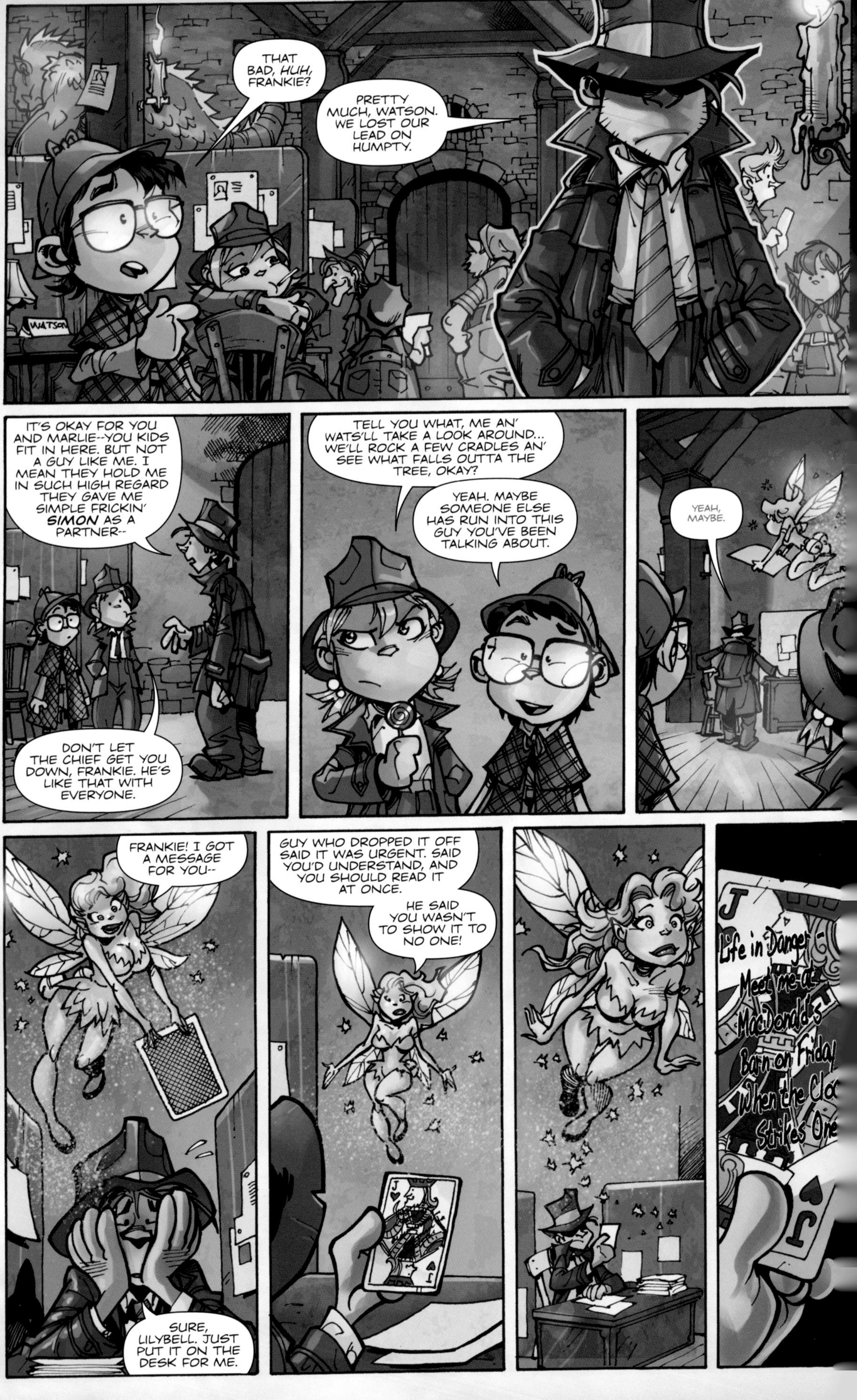
WATSON
THAT BAD, HUH, FRANKIE?
PRETTY MUCH, WATSON. WE LOST OUR LEAD ON HUMPTY.
IT'S OKAY FOR YOU AND MARLIE--YOU KIDS FIT IN HERE. BUT NOT A GUY LIKE ME. I MEAN THEY HOLD ME IN SUCH HIGH REGARD THEY GAVE ME SIMPLE FRICKIN' SIMON AS A PARTNER--
DON'T LET THE CHIEF GET YOU DOWN, FRANKIE. HE'S LIKE THAT WITH EVERYONE.
TELL YOU WHAT, ME AN' WATS'LL TAKE A LOOK AROUND... WE'LL ROCK A FEW CRADLES AN' SEE WHAT FALLS OUTTA THE TREE, OKAY?
YEAH. MAYBE SOMEONE ELSE HAS RUN INTO THIS GUY YOU'VE BEEN TALKING ABOUT.
YEAH, MAYBE.
FRANKIE! I GOT A MESSAGE FOR YOU--
SURE, LILYBELL. JUST PUT IT ON THE DESK FOR ME.
GUY WHO DROPPED IT OFF SAID IT WAS URGENT. SAID YOU'D UNDERSTAND, AND YOU SHOULD READ IT AT ONCE.
HE SAID YOU WASN'T TO SHOW IT TO NO ONE!
Life in Danger
Meet me at MacDonald's Barn on Friday When the Cloc Strikes One

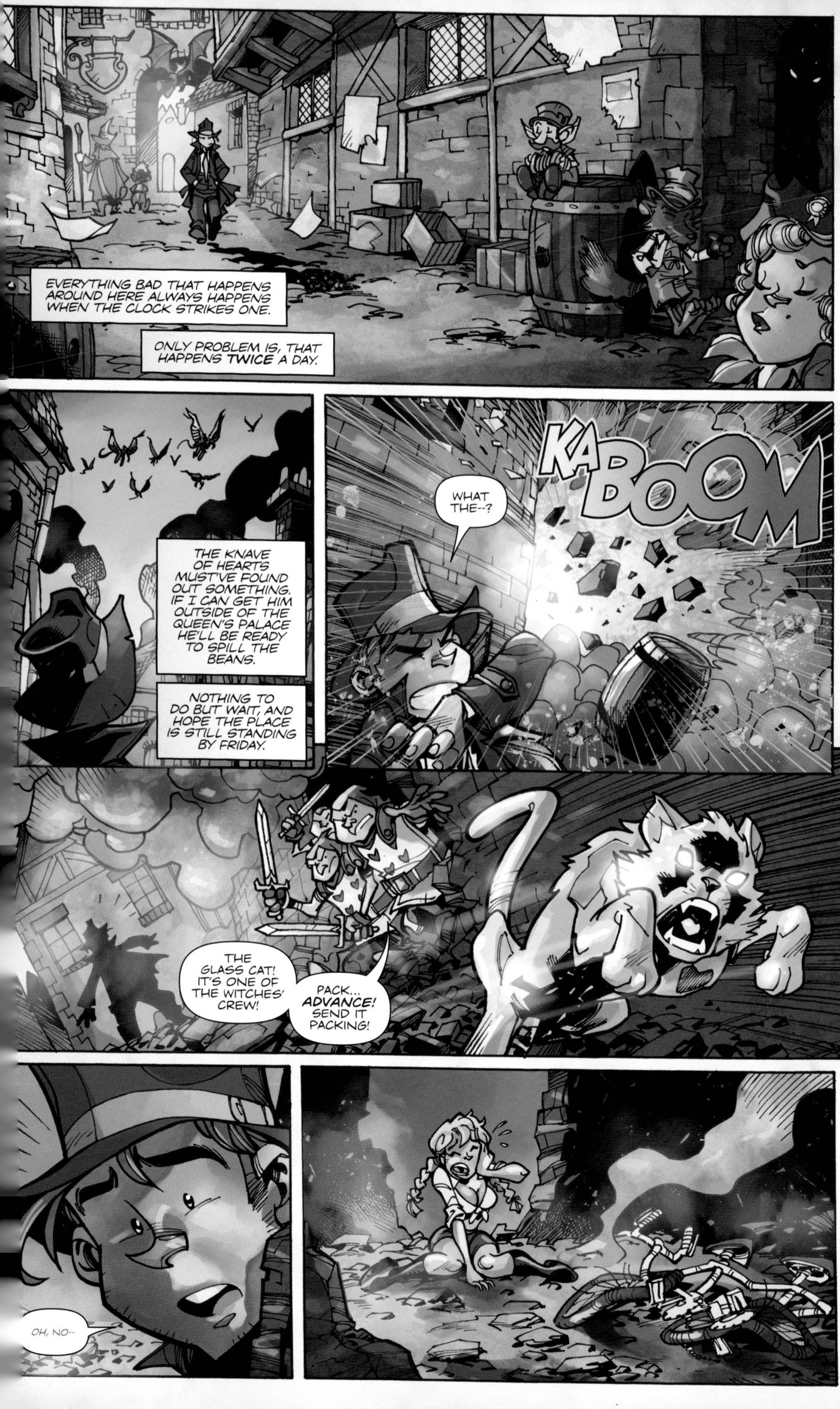
EVERYTHING BAD THAT HAPPENS AROUND HERE ALWAYS HAPPENS WHEN THE CLOCK STRIKES ONE.
ONLY PROBLEM IS, THAT HAPPENS **TWICE** A DAY.
THE KNAVE OF HEARTS MUST'VE FOUND OUT SOMETHING. IF I CAN GET HIM OUTSIDE OF THE QUEEN'S PALACE HE'LL BE READY TO SPILL THE BEANS.
NOTHING TO DO BUT WAIT, AND HOPE THE PLACE IS STILL STANDING BY FRIDAY.
KA BOOM
WHAT THE--?
THE GLASS CAT! IT'S ONE OF THE WITCHES' CREW!
PACK... **ADVANCE!** SEND IT PACKING!
OH, NO--

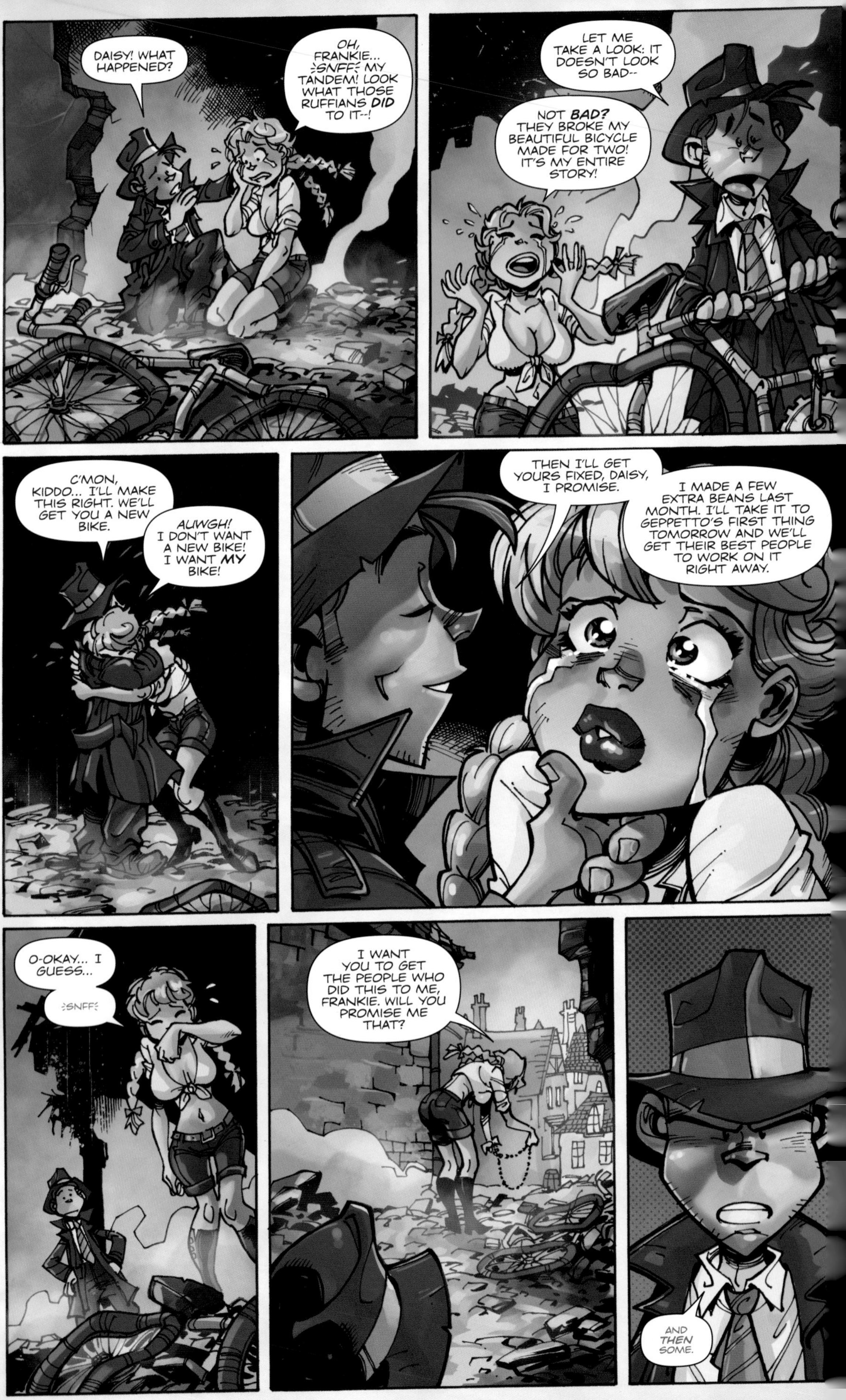

DAISY! WHAT HAPPENED?
OH, FRANKIE... ⸗SNFF⸗ MY TANDEM! LOOK WHAT THOSE RUFFIANS DID TO IT--!
LET ME TAKE A LOOK: IT DOESN'T LOOK SO BAD--
NOT BAD? THEY BROKE MY BEAUTIFUL BICYCLE MADE FOR TWO! IT'S MY ENTIRE STORY!
C'MON, KIDDO... I'LL MAKE THIS RIGHT. WE'LL GET YOU A NEW BIKE.
AUWGH! I DON'T WANT A NEW BIKE! I WANT MY BIKE!
THEN I'LL GET YOURS FIXED, DAISY, I PROMISE.
I MADE A FEW EXTRA BEANS LAST MONTH. I'LL TAKE IT TO GEPPETTO'S FIRST THING TOMORROW AND WE'LL GET THEIR BEST PEOPLE TO WORK ON IT RIGHT AWAY.
O-OKAY... I GUESS...
⸗SNFF⸗
I WANT YOU TO GET THE PEOPLE WHO DID THIS TO ME, FRANKIE. WILL YOU PROMISE ME THAT?
AND THEN SOME.

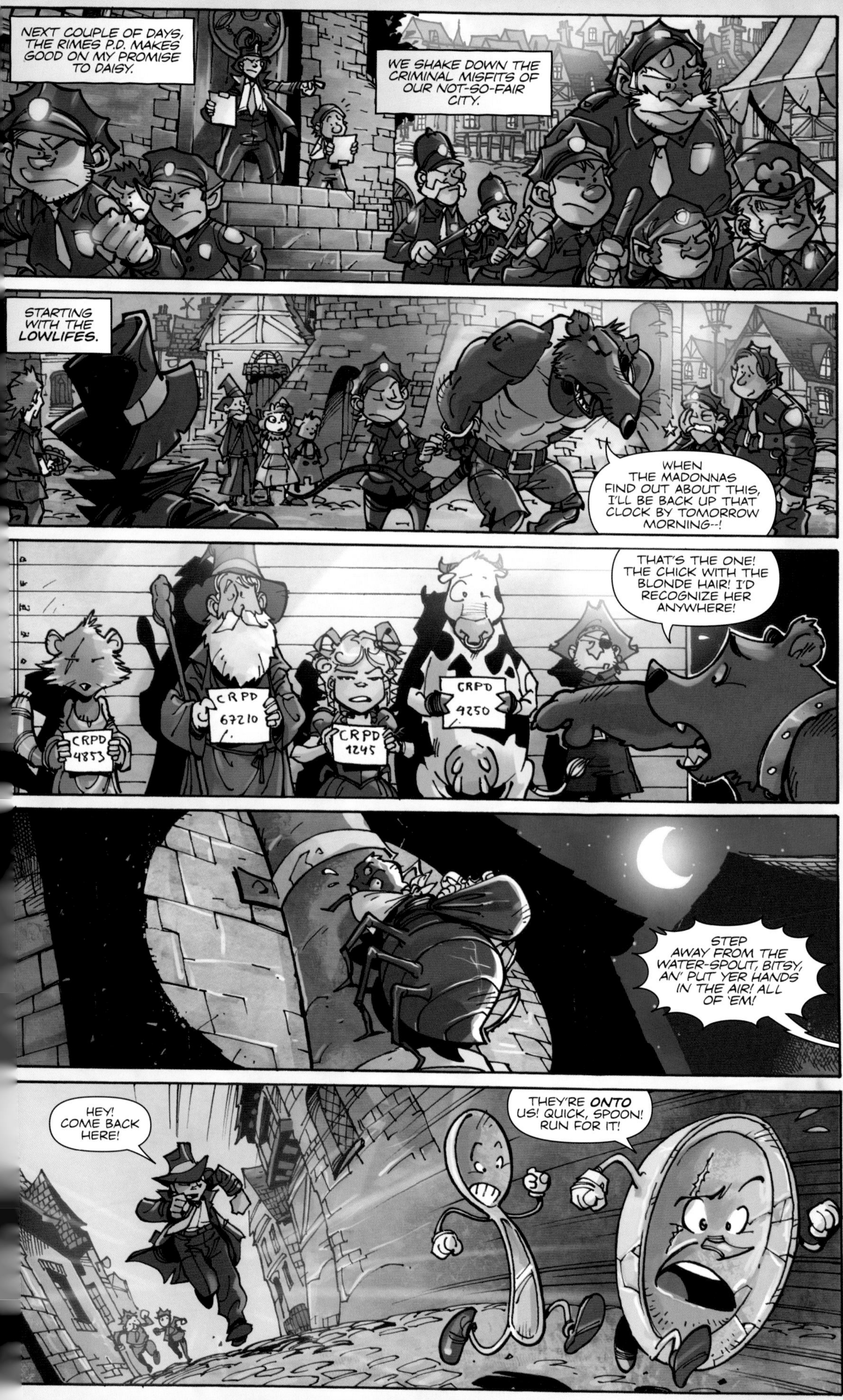
NEXT COUPLE OF DAYS, THE RIMES P.D. MAKES GOOD ON MY PROMISE TO DAISY.
WE SHAKE DOWN THE CRIMINAL MISFITS OF OUR NOT-SO-FAIR CITY.
STARTING WITH THE **LOWLIFES.**
WHEN THE MADONNAS FIND OUT ABOUT THIS, I'LL BE BACK UP THAT CLOCK BY TOMORROW MORNING--!
THAT'S THE ONE! THE CHICK WITH THE BLONDE HAIR! I'D RECOGNIZE HER ANYWHERE!
CRPD 4853
CRPD 67210
CRPD 1245
CRPD 9250
STEP AWAY FROM THE WATER-SPOUT, BITSY, AN' PUT YER HANDS IN THE AIR! ALL OF 'EM!
HEY! COME BACK HERE!
THEY'RE **ONTO** US! QUICK, SPOON! RUN FOR IT!

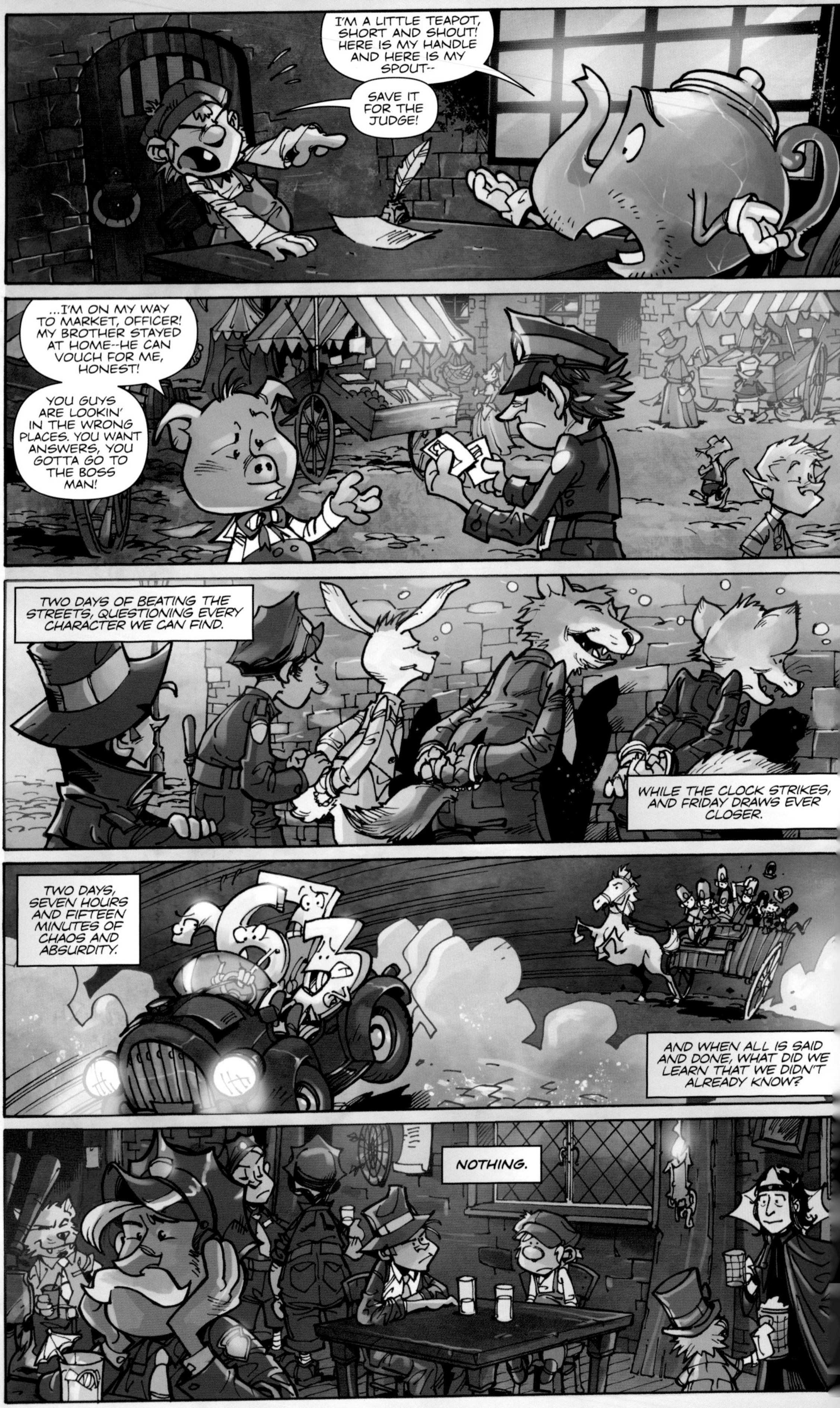
I'M A LITTLE TEAPOT, SHORT AND SHOUT! HERE IS MY HANDLE AND HERE IS MY SPOUT--
SAVE IT FOR THE JUDGE!
...I'M ON MY WAY TO MARKET, OFFICER! MY BROTHER STAYED AT HOME--HE CAN VOUCH FOR ME, HONEST!
YOU GUYS ARE LOOKIN' IN THE WRONG PLACES. YOU WANT ANSWERS, YOU GOTTA GO TO THE BOSS MAN!
TWO DAYS OF BEATING THE STREETS, QUESTIONING EVERY CHARACTER WE CAN FIND.
WHILE THE CLOCK STRIKES, AND FRIDAY DRAWS EVER CLOSER.
TWO DAYS, SEVEN HOURS AND FIFTEEN MINUTES OF CHAOS AND ABSURDITY.
AND WHEN ALL IS SAID AND DONE, WHAT DID WE LEARN THAT WE DIDN'T ALREADY KNOW?
NOTHING.

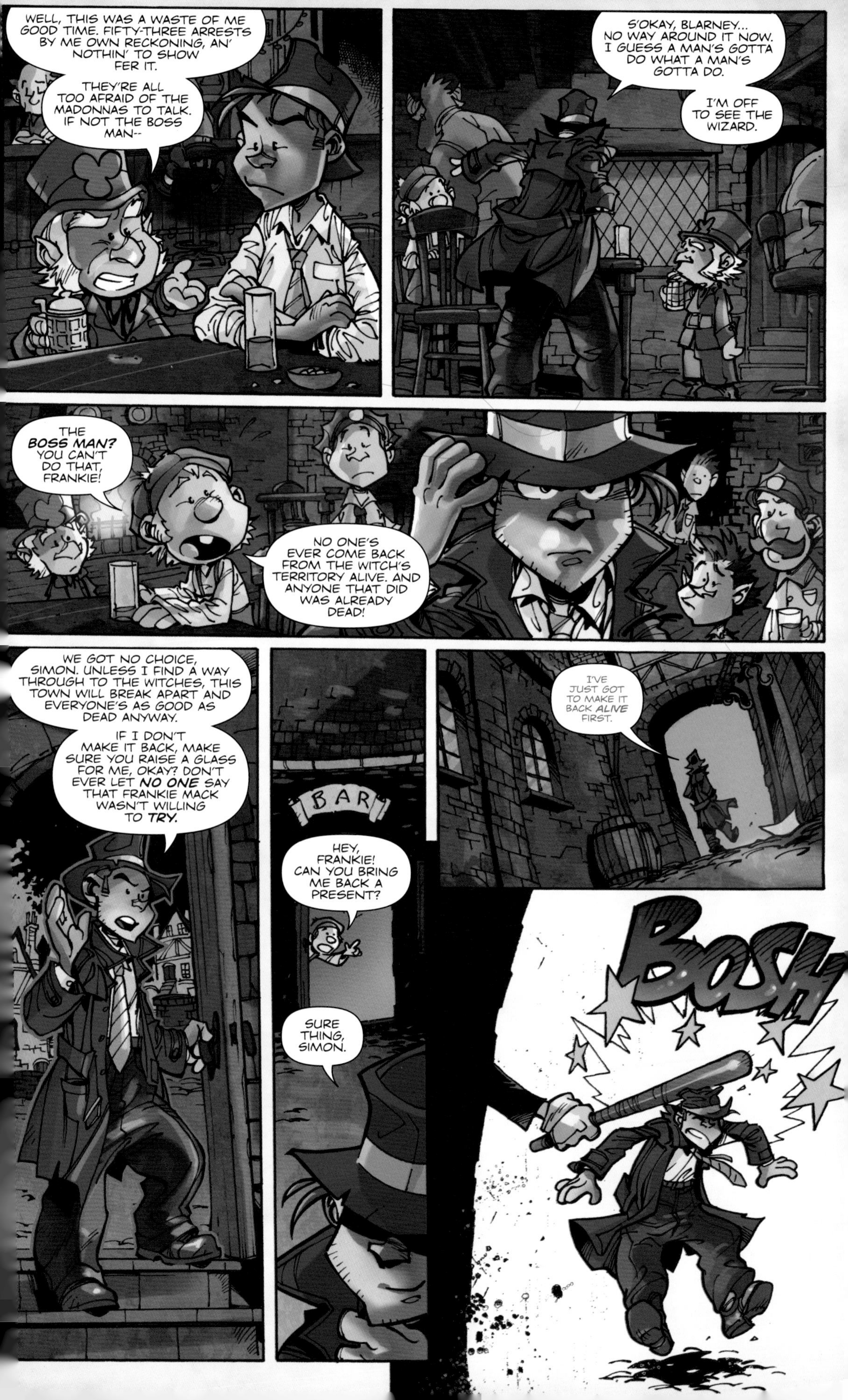
WELL, THIS WAS A WASTE OF ME GOOD TIME. FIFTY-THREE ARRESTS BY ME OWN RECKONING, AN' NOTHIN' TO SHOW FER IT.
THEY'RE ALL TOO AFRAID OF THE MADONNAS TO TALK. IF NOT THE BOSS MAN--
S'OKAY, BLARNEY... NO WAY AROUND IT NOW. I GUESS A MAN'S GOTTA DO WHAT A MAN'S GOTTA DO.
I'M OFF TO SEE THE WIZARD.
THE *BOSS MAN?* YOU CAN'T DO THAT, FRANKIE!
NO ONE'S EVER COME BACK FROM THE WITCH'S TERRITORY ALIVE. AND ANYONE THAT DID WAS ALREADY DEAD!
WE GOT NO CHOICE, SIMON. UNLESS I FIND A WAY THROUGH TO THE WITCHES, THIS TOWN WILL BREAK APART AND EVERYONE'S AS GOOD AS DEAD ANYWAY.
IF I DON'T MAKE IT BACK, MAKE SURE YOU RAISE A GLASS FOR ME, OKAY? DON'T EVER LET **NO ONE** SAY THAT FRANKIE MACK WASN'T WILLING TO ***TRY.***
BAR
HEY, FRANKIE! CAN YOU BRING ME BACK A PRESENT?
SURE THING, SIMON.
I'VE JUST GOT TO MAKE IT BACK *ALIVE* FIRST.
BOSH

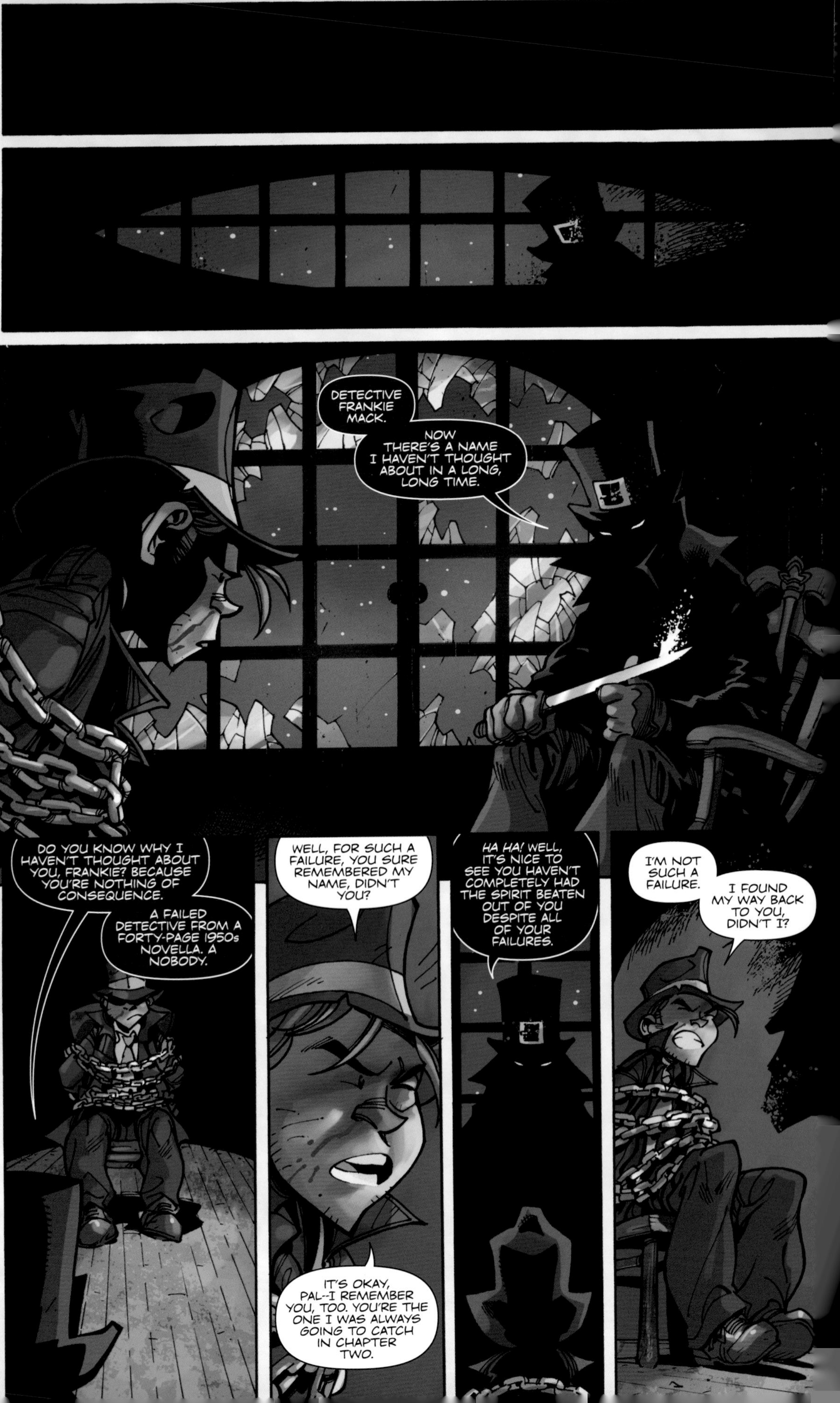
DETECTIVE FRANKIE MACK.
NOW THERE'S A NAME I HAVEN'T THOUGHT ABOUT IN A LONG, LONG TIME.
DO YOU KNOW WHY I HAVEN'T THOUGHT ABOUT YOU, FRANKIE? BECAUSE YOU'RE NOTHING OF CONSEQUENCE.
A FAILED DETECTIVE FROM A FORTY-PAGE 1950s NOVELLA. A NOBODY.
WELL, FOR SUCH A FAILURE, YOU SURE REMEMBERED MY NAME, DIDN'T YOU?
IT'S OKAY, PAL--I REMEMBER YOU, TOO. YOU'RE THE ONE I WAS ALWAYS GOING TO CATCH IN CHAPTER TWO.
HA HA! WELL, IT'S NICE TO SEE YOU HAVEN'T COMPLETELY HAD THE SPIRIT BEATEN OUT OF YOU DESPITE ALL OF YOUR FAILURES.
I'M NOT SUCH A FAILURE.
I FOUND MY WAY BACK TO YOU, DIDN'T I?

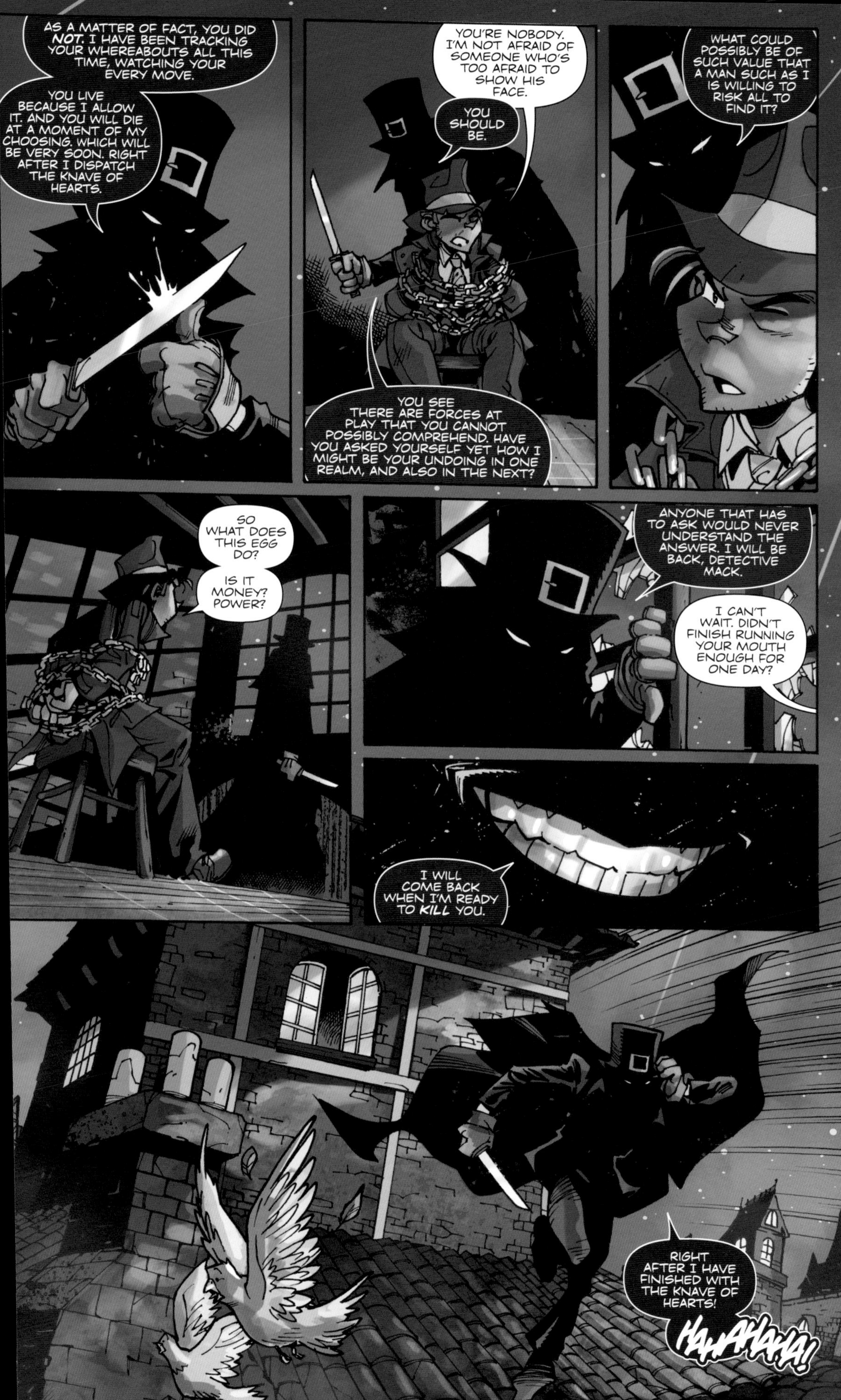

AS A MATTER OF FACT, YOU DID **NOT.** I HAVE BEEN TRACKING YOUR WHEREABOUTS ALL THIS TIME, WATCHING YOUR EVERY MOVE.
YOU LIVE BECAUSE I ALLOW IT. AND YOU WILL DIE AT A MOMENT OF MY CHOOSING. WHICH WILL BE VERY SOON. RIGHT AFTER I DISPATCH THE KNAVE OF HEARTS.
YOU'RE NOBODY. I'M NOT AFRAID OF SOMEONE WHO'S TOO AFRAID TO SHOW HIS FACE.
YOU SHOULD BE.
YOU SEE THERE ARE FORCES AT PLAY THAT YOU CANNOT POSSIBLY COMPREHEND. HAVE YOU ASKED YOURSELF YET HOW I MIGHT BE YOUR UNDOING IN ONE REALM, AND ALSO IN THE NEXT?
WHAT COULD POSSIBLY BE OF SUCH VALUE THAT A MAN SUCH AS I IS WILLING TO RISK ALL TO FIND IT?
SO WHAT DOES THIS EGG DO?
IS IT MONEY? POWER?
ANYONE THAT HAS TO ASK WOULD NEVER UNDERSTAND THE ANSWER. I WILL BE BACK, DETECTIVE MACK.
I CAN'T WAIT. DIDN'T FINISH RUNNING YOUR MOUTH ENOUGH FOR ONE DAY?
I WILL COME BACK WHEN I'M READY TO ***KILL*** YOU.
RIGHT AFTER I HAVE FINISHED WITH THE KNAVE OF HEARTS!
HAHAHAHA!

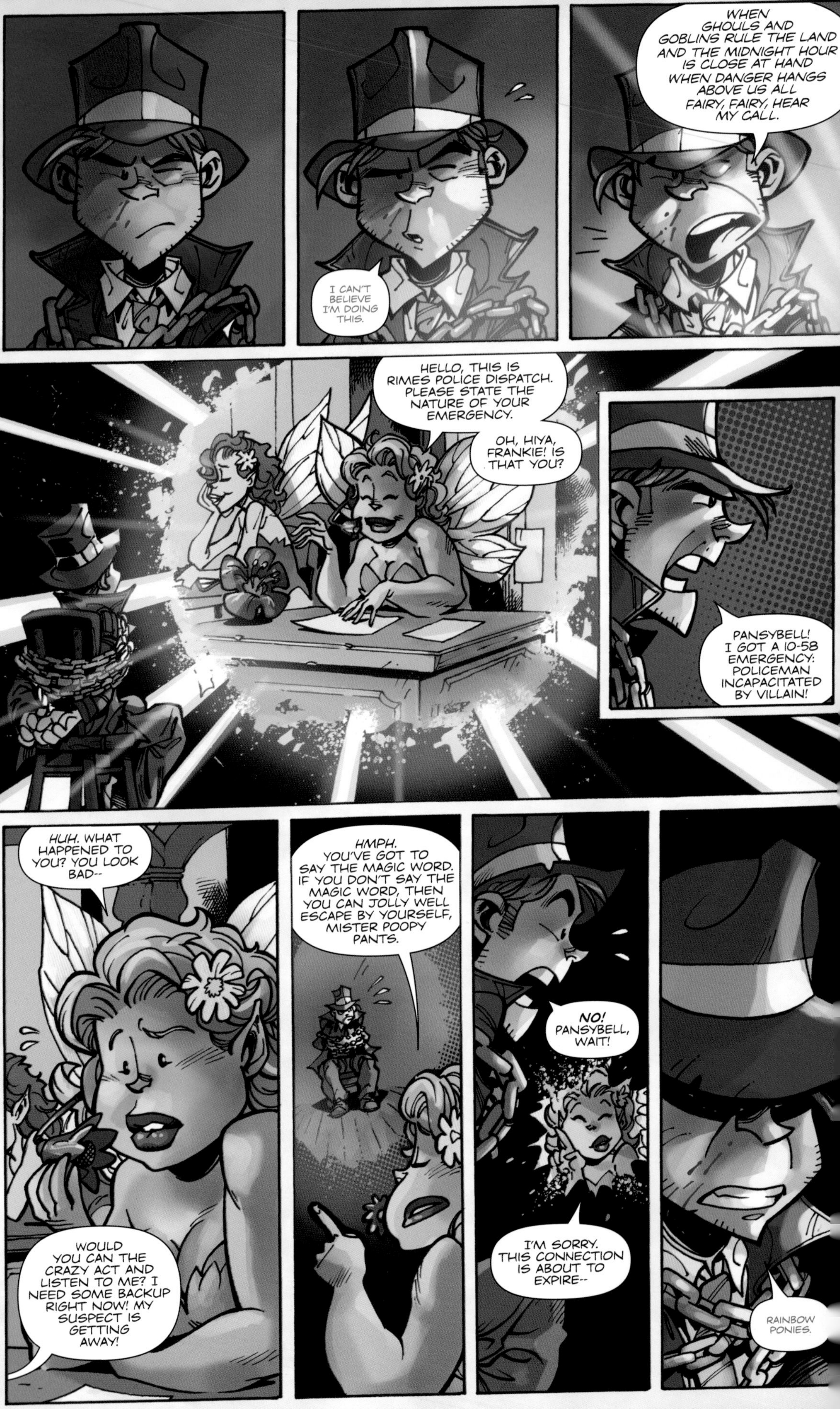
I CAN'T BELIEVE I'M DOING THIS.
WHEN GHOULS AND GOBLINS RULE THE LAND AND THE MIDNIGHT HOUR IS CLOSE AT HAND WHEN DANGER HANGS ABOVE US ALL FAIRY, FAIRY, HEAR MY CALL.
HELLO, THIS IS RIMES POLICE DISPATCH. PLEASE STATE THE NATURE OF YOUR EMERGENCY.
OH, HIYA, FRANKIE! IS THAT YOU?
PANSYBELL! I GOT A 10-58 EMERGENCY: POLICEMAN INCAPACITATED BY VILLAIN!
HUH. WHAT HAPPENED TO YOU? YOU LOOK BAD--
WOULD YOU CAN THE CRAZY ACT AND LISTEN TO ME? I NEED SOME BACKUP RIGHT NOW! MY SUSPECT IS GETTING AWAY!
HMPH. YOU'VE GOT TO SAY THE MAGIC WORD. IF YOU DON'T SAY THE MAGIC WORD, THEN YOU CAN JOLLY WELL ESCAPE BY YOURSELF, MISTER POOPY PANTS.
NO! PANSYBELL, WAIT!
I'M SORRY. THIS CONNECTION IS ABOUT TO EXPIRE--
RAINBOW PONIES.

RAINBOW PONIES! I *LOVE* RAINBOW PONIES!

WHAT'S THE PROBLEM? *OOH.* SOMEONE TIED YOU UP. THAT'S A 10-58!

YOU WANT ME TO HELP YOU ESCAPE, AM I RIGHT? I CAN DO MAGIC, AN' EVERYTHING!

OH, I'M SO HAPPY YOU CALLED ME, FRANKIE! *RAINBOW* PONIES!

PANSYBELL, LISTEN TO ME: MY GUY'S GETTING AWAY! I NEED TO GET OUT OF HERE AS QUICKLY AS POSSIBLE.

THE KNAVE OF HEARTS IS IN MORTAL DANGER. YOU GOTTA HELP ME.

SNAP!

THANKS, PANSY! GET A FIX ON THIS PLACE FOR ME, OKAY? TELL MARLIE AND WATSON TO BRING IN FORENSICS!

I WANT TO KNOW WHO RENTED OUT THIS PLACE, AND FOR HOW LONG!

HEY, FRANKIE! *RAINBOW* PONIES!

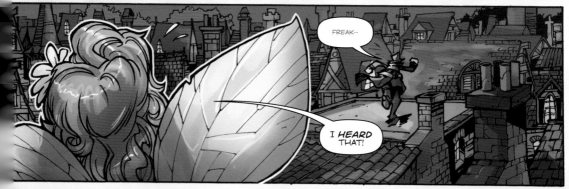

FREAK--

I *HEARD* THAT!

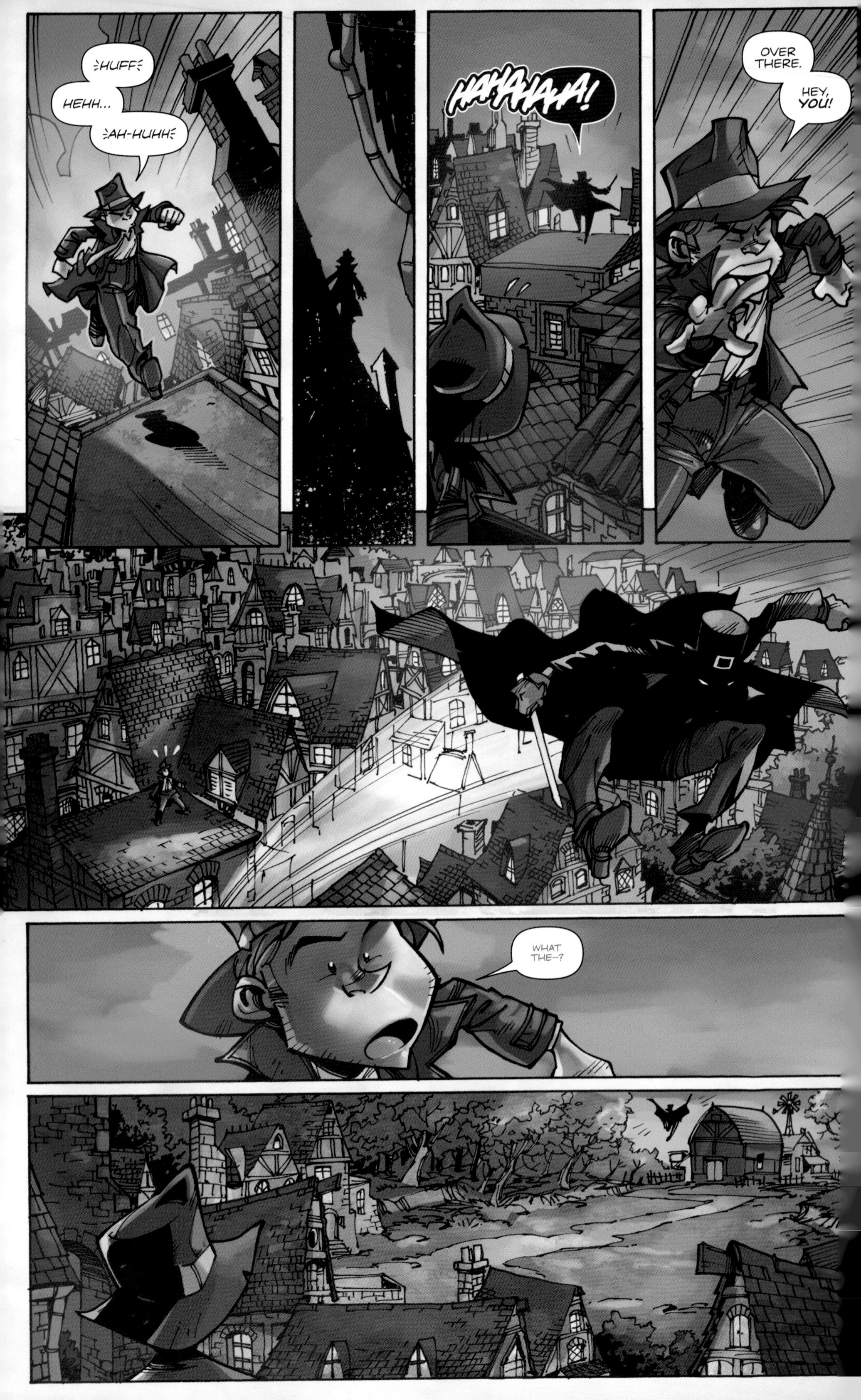
HUFF
HEHH...
AH-HUHH
HAHAHAHA!
OVER THERE.
HEY, YOU!
WHAT THE--?

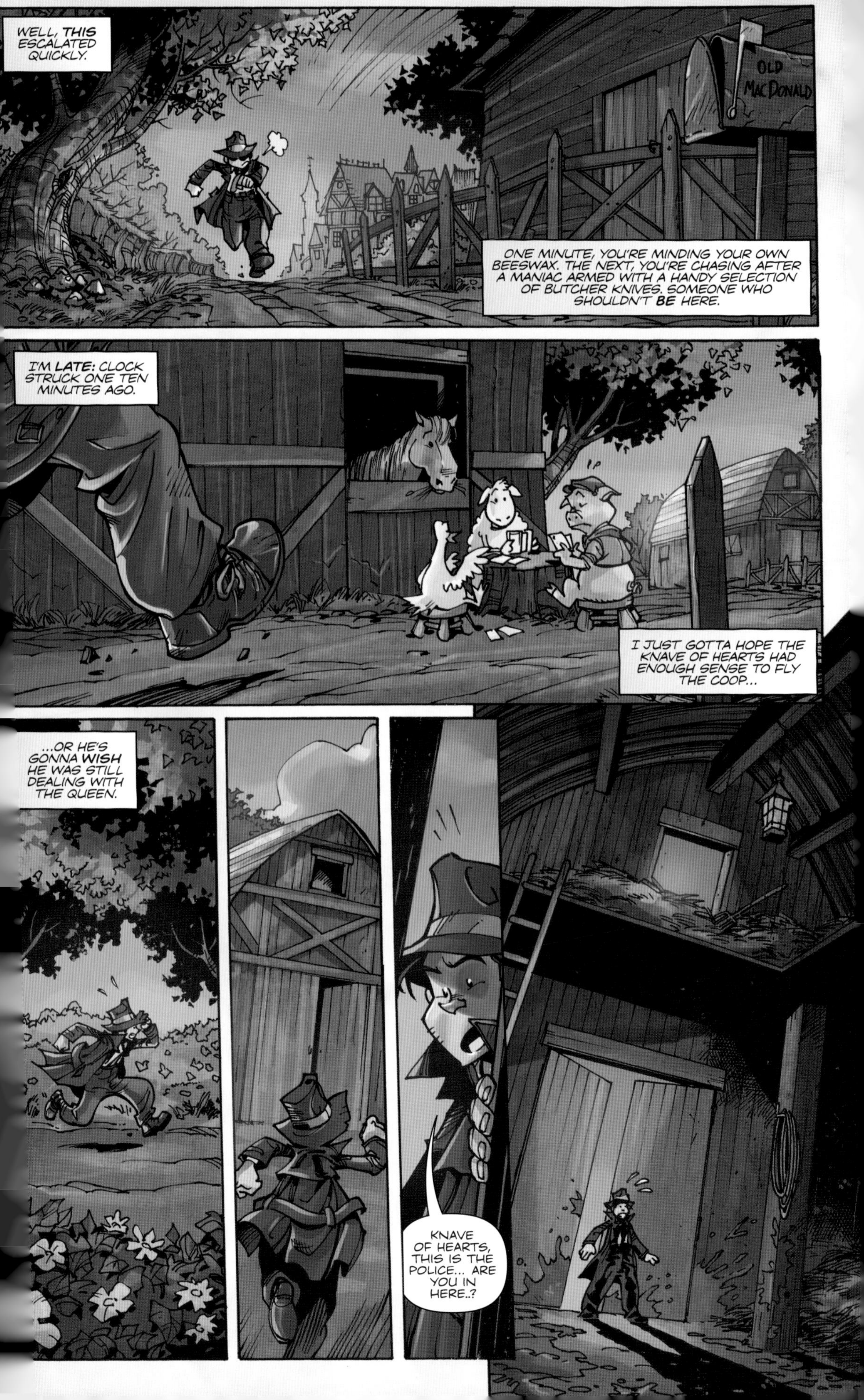
WELL, THIS ESCALATED QUICKLY.
OLD MacDONALD
ONE MINUTE, YOU'RE MINDING YOUR OWN BEESWAX. THE NEXT, YOU'RE CHASING AFTER A MANIAC ARMED WITH A HANDY SELECTION OF BUTCHER KNIVES. SOMEONE WHO SHOULDN'T BE HERE.
I'M LATE: CLOCK STRUCK ONE TEN MINUTES AGO.
I JUST GOTTA HOPE THE KNAVE OF HEARTS HAD ENOUGH SENSE TO FLY THE COOP...
...OR HE'S GONNA WISH HE WAS STILL DEALING WITH THE QUEEN.
KNAVE OF HEARTS, THIS IS THE POLICE... ARE YOU IN HERE..?

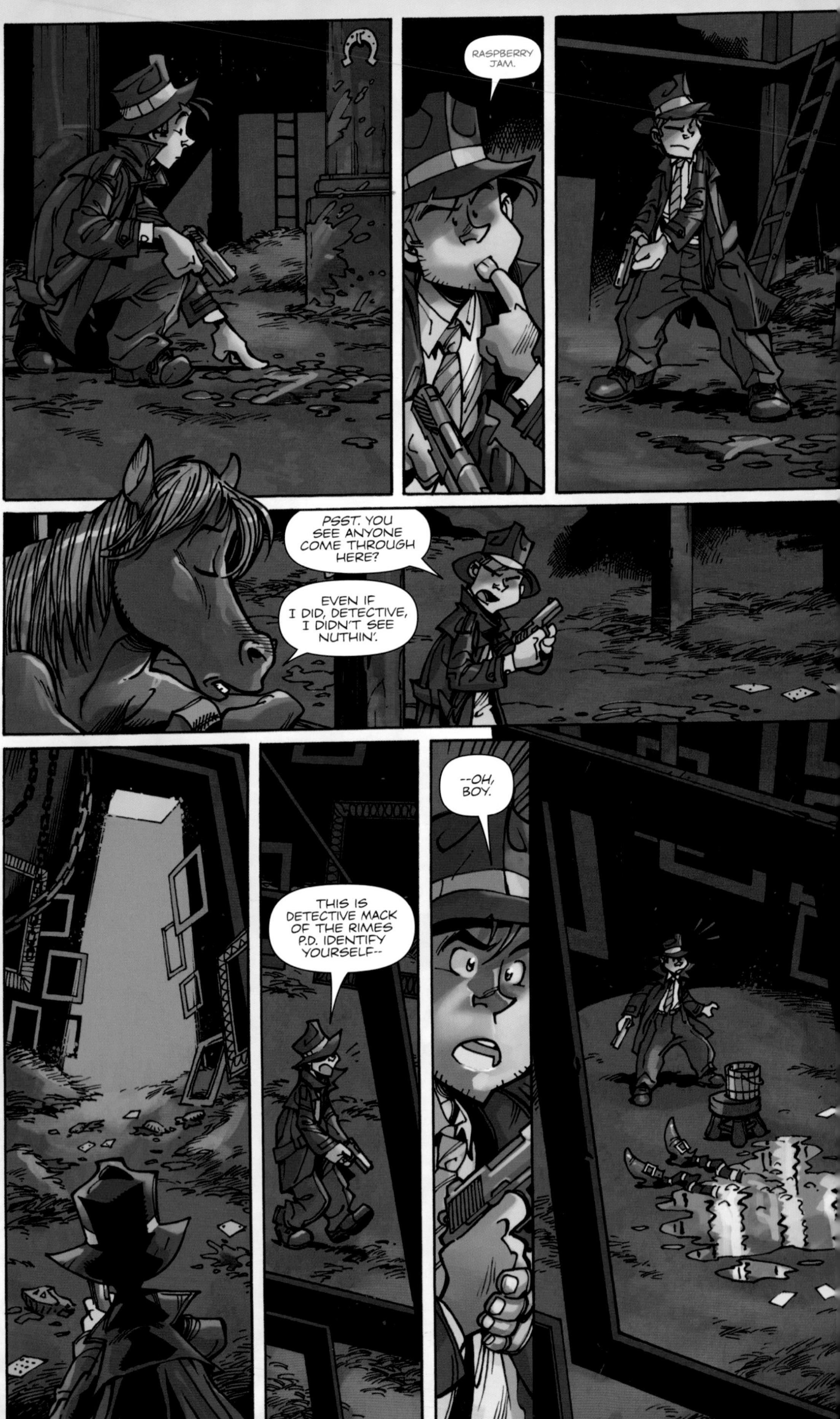
RASPBERRY JAM.
PSST. YOU SEE ANYONE COME THROUGH HERE?
EVEN IF I DID, DETECTIVE, I DIDN'T SEE NUTHIN'.
THIS IS DETECTIVE MACK OF THE RIMES P.D. IDENTIFY YOURSELF--
--OH, BOY.

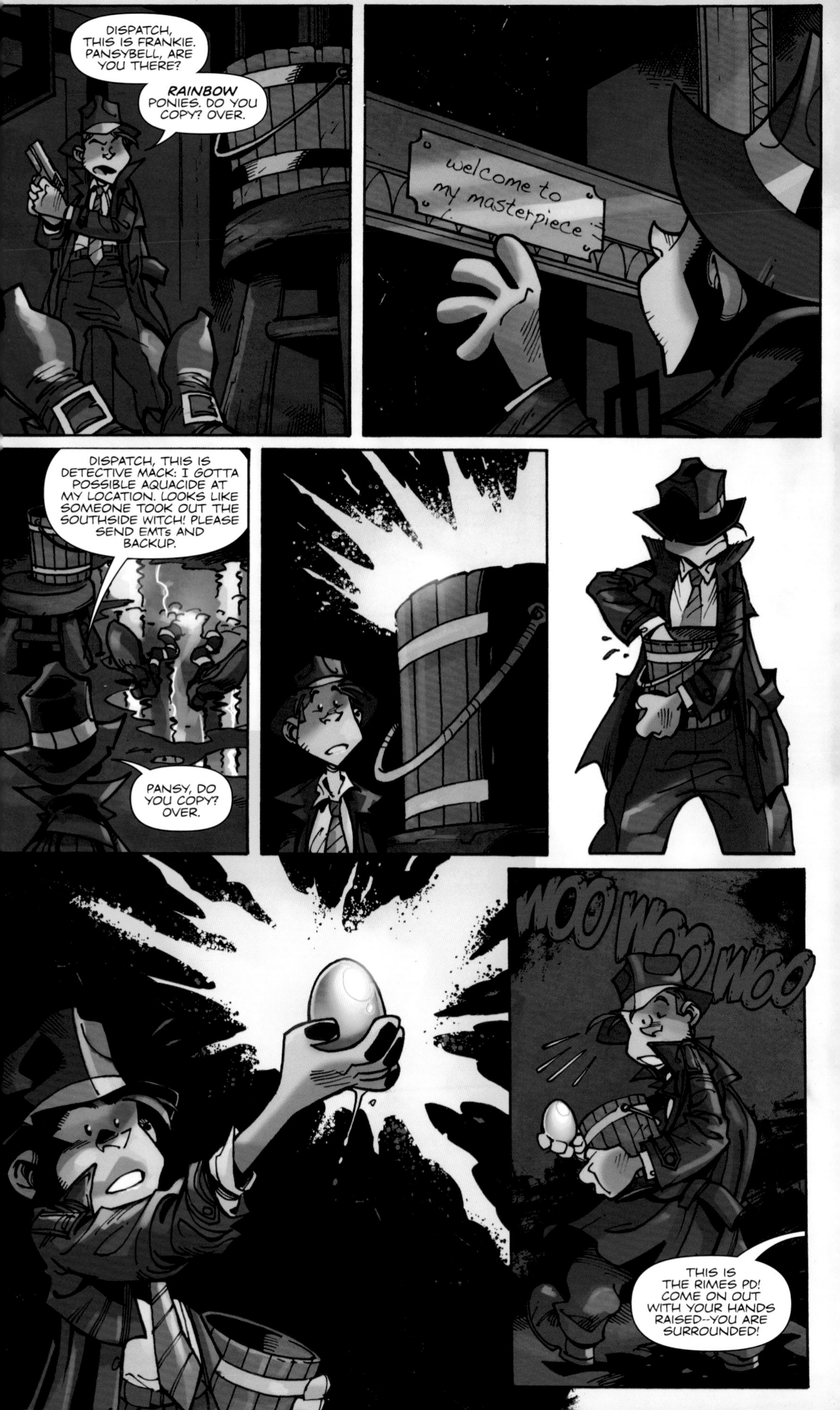

DISPATCH, THIS IS FRANKIE. PANSYBELL, ARE YOU THERE?
RAINBOW PONIES. DO YOU COPY? OVER.
welcome to my masterpiece
DISPATCH, THIS IS DETECTIVE MACK: I GOTTA POSSIBLE AQUACIDE AT MY LOCATION. LOOKS LIKE SOMEONE TOOK OUT THE SOUTHSIDE WITCH! PLEASE SEND EMTs AND BACKUP.
PANSY, DO YOU COPY? OVER.
WOO WOO WOO WOO
THIS IS THE RIMES PD! COME ON OUT WITH YOUR HANDS RAISED--YOU ARE SURROUNDED!

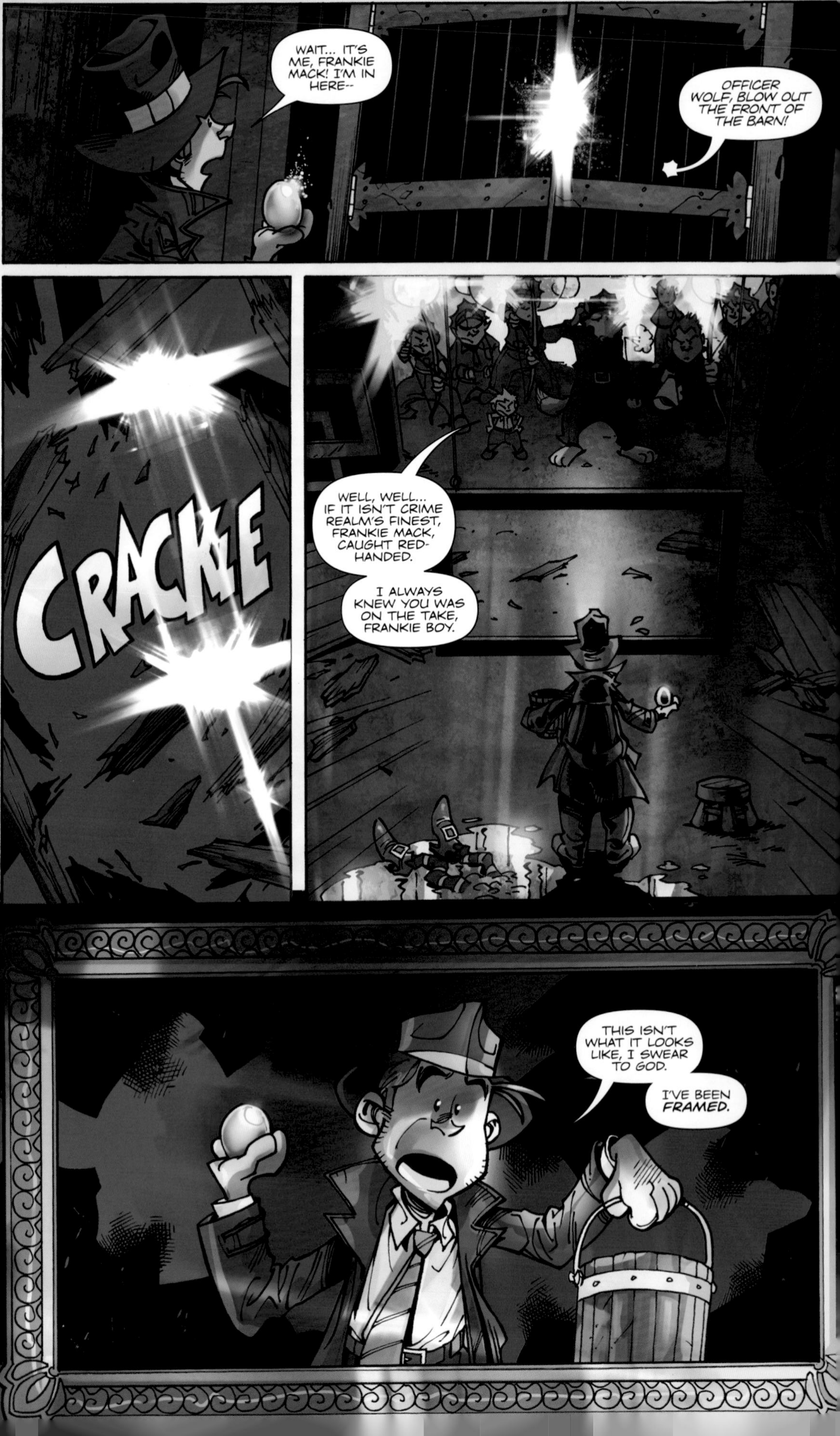
WAIT... IT'S ME, FRANKIE MACK! I'M IN HERE--
OFFICER WOLF, BLOW OUT THE FRONT OF THE BARN!
CRACKLE
WELL, WELL... IF IT ISN'T CRIME REALM'S FINEST, FRANKIE MACK, CAUGHT RED-HANDED.
I ALWAYS KNEW YOU WAS ON THE TAKE, FRANKIE BOY.
THIS ISN'T WHAT IT LOOKS LIKE, I SWEAR TO GOD.
I'VE BEEN **FRAMED.**

FICTION SQUAD
10¢
JENKINS
BACHS
BOOM!
MICHAEL DIALYNAS
ISSUE FOUR KICKSTARTER COVER

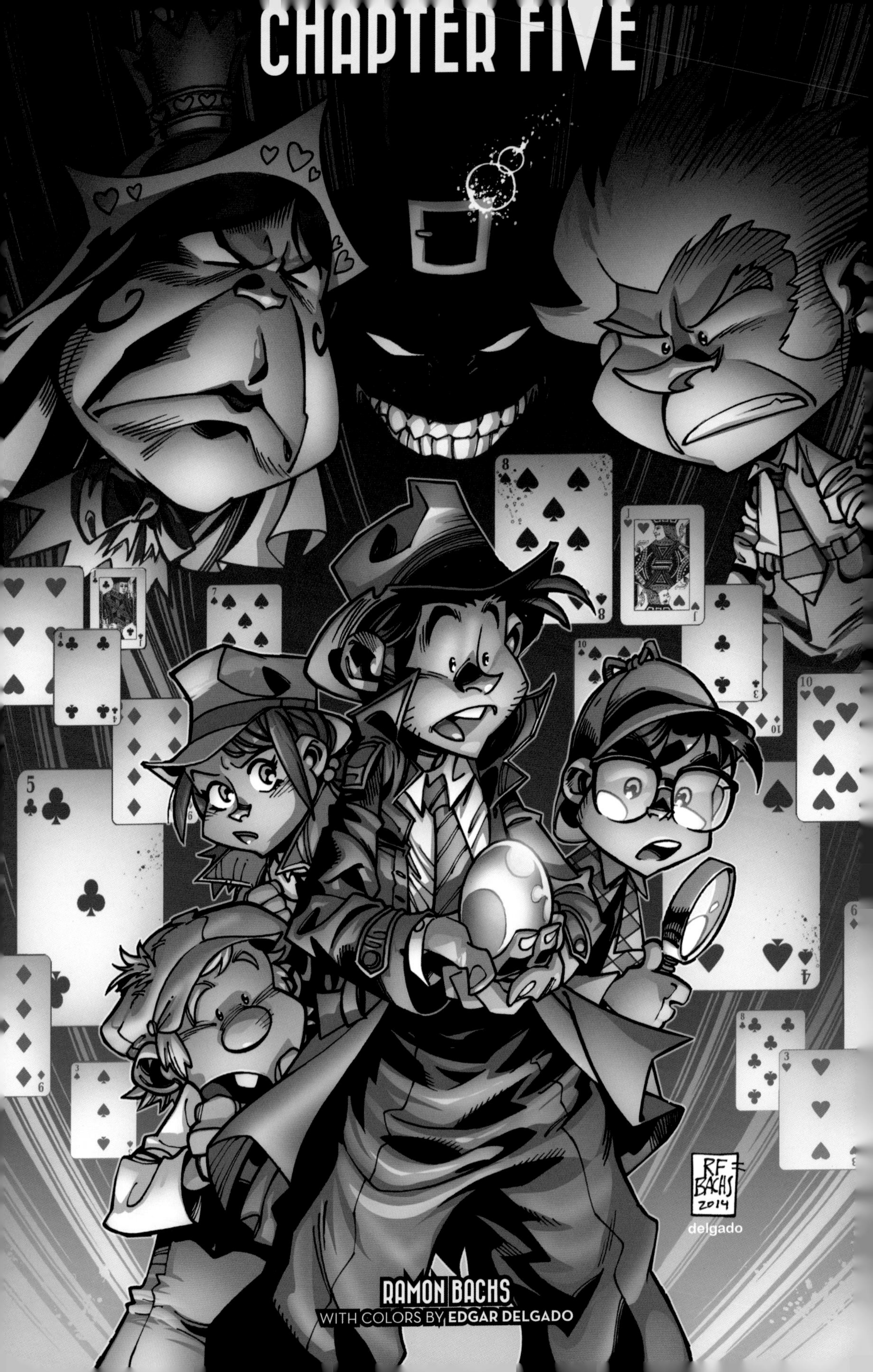
CHAPTER FIVE
RF BACHS 2014
delgado
RAMON BACHS
WITH COLORS BY EDGAR DELGADO

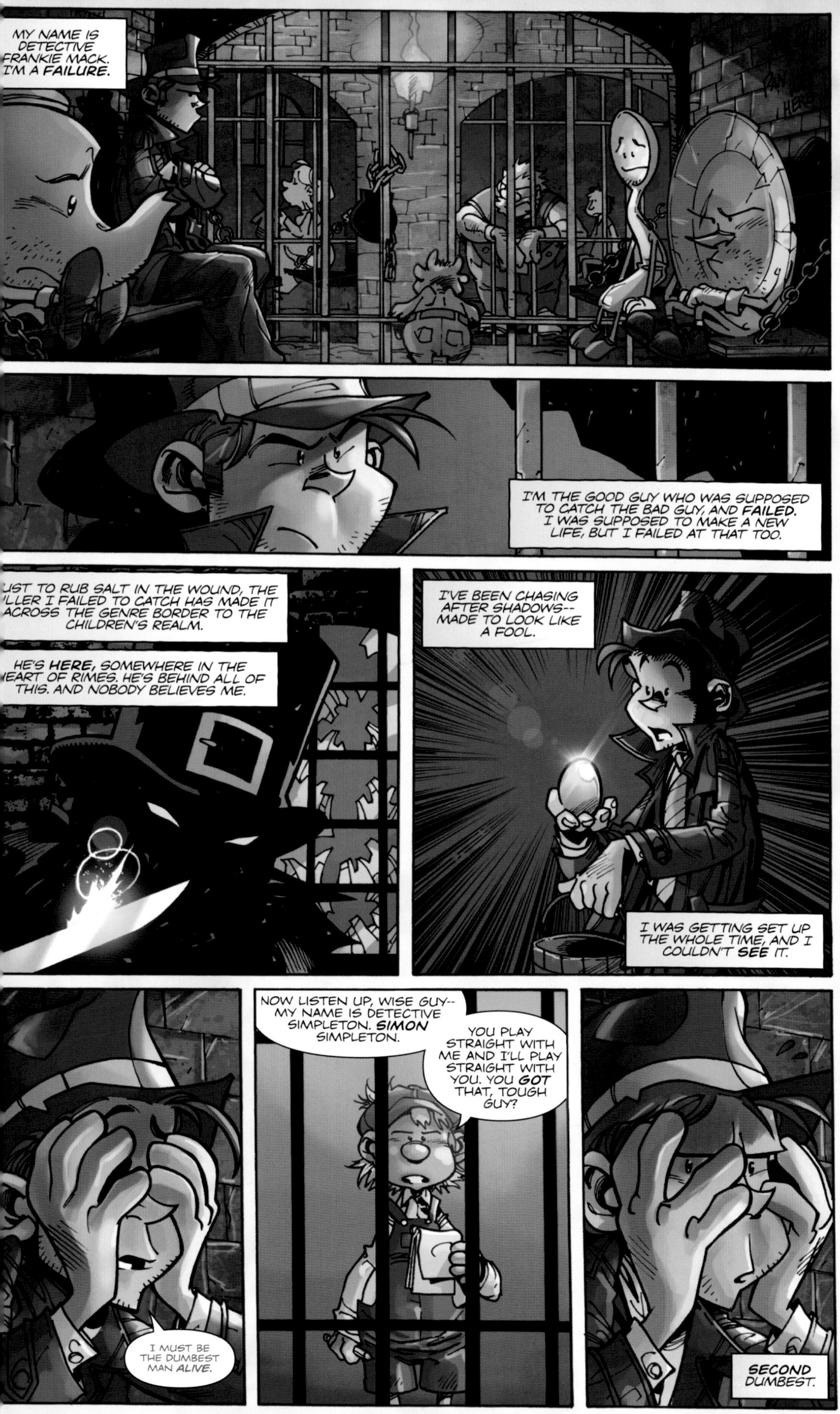
MY NAME IS DETECTIVE FRANKIE MACK. I'M A **FAILURE.**
I'M THE GOOD GUY WHO WAS SUPPOSED TO CATCH THE BAD GUY, AND **FAILED.** I WAS SUPPOSED TO MAKE A NEW LIFE, BUT I FAILED AT THAT TOO.
UST TO RUB SALT IN THE WOUND, THE ILLER I FAILED TO CATCH HAS MADE IT ACROSS THE GENRE BORDER TO THE CHILDREN'S REALM.
HE'S **HERE,** SOMEWHERE IN THE EART OF RIMES. HE'S BEHIND ALL OF THIS. AND NOBODY BELIEVES ME.
I'VE BEEN CHASING AFTER SHADOWS-- MADE TO LOOK LIKE A FOOL.
I WAS GETTING SET UP THE WHOLE TIME, AND I COULDN'T **SEE** IT.
I MUST BE THE DUMBEST MAN *ALIVE.*
NOW LISTEN UP, WISE GUY-- MY NAME IS DETECTIVE SIMPLETON. ***SIMON*** SIMPLETON.
YOU PLAY STRAIGHT WITH ME AND I'LL PLAY STRAIGHT WITH YOU. YOU ***GOT*** THAT, TOUGH GUY?
SECOND DUMBEST.

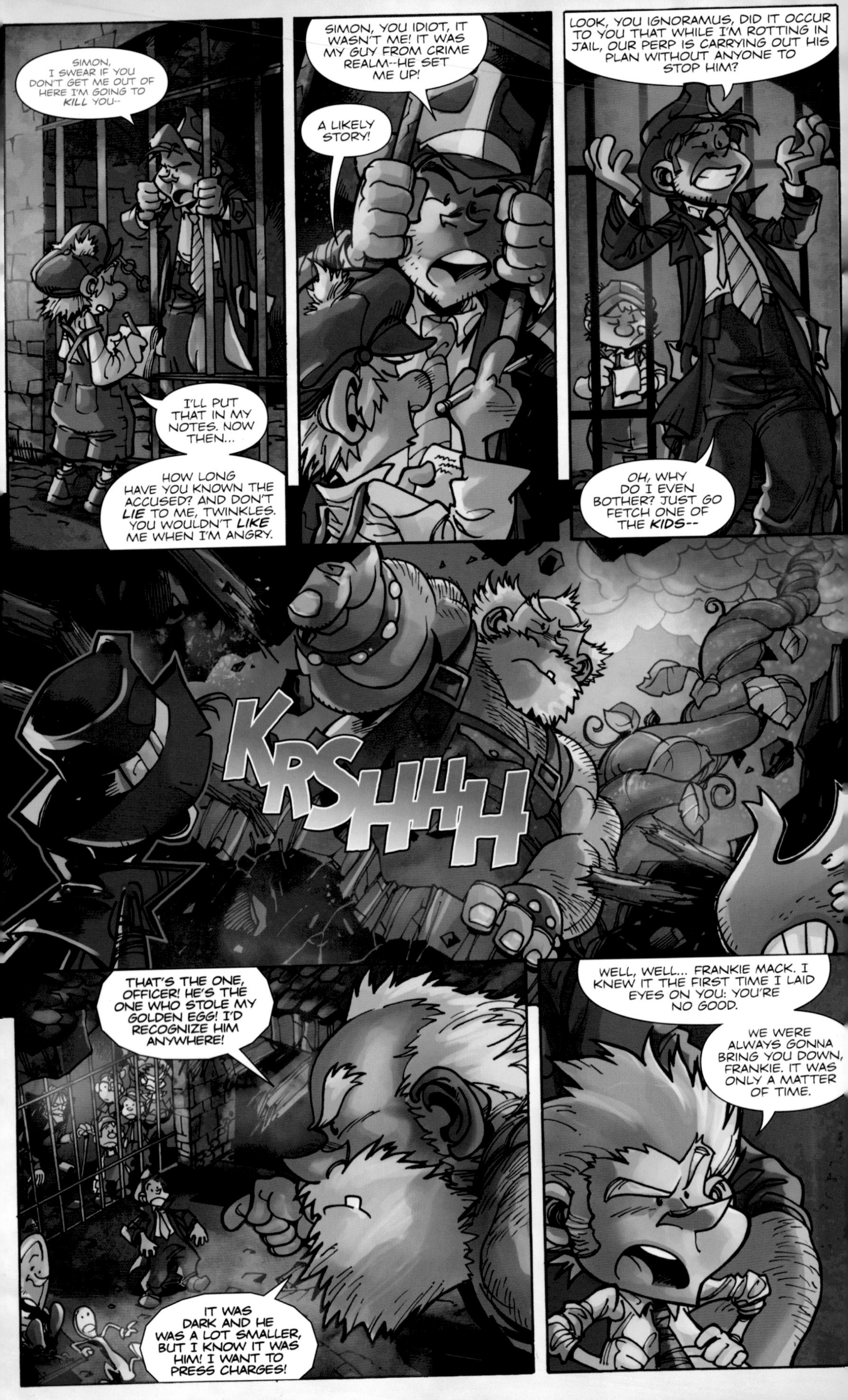
SIMON, I SWEAR IF YOU DON'T GET ME OUT OF HERE I'M GOING TO KILL YOU--
I'LL PUT THAT IN MY NOTES. NOW THEN...
HOW LONG HAVE YOU KNOWN THE ACCUSED? AND DON'T LIE TO ME, TWINKLES. YOU WOULDN'T LIKE ME WHEN I'M ANGRY.
SIMON, YOU IDIOT, IT WASN'T ME! IT WAS MY GUY FROM CRIME REALM--HE SET ME UP!
A LIKELY STORY!
LOOK, YOU IGNORAMUS, DID IT OCCUR TO YOU THAT WHILE I'M ROTTING IN JAIL, OUR PERP IS CARRYING OUT HIS PLAN WITHOUT ANYONE TO STOP HIM?
OH, WHY DO I EVEN BOTHER? JUST GO FETCH ONE OF THE KIDS--
KRSHHHH
THAT'S THE ONE, OFFICER! HE'S THE ONE WHO STOLE MY GOLDEN EGG! I'D RECOGNIZE HIM ANYWHERE!
IT WAS DARK AND HE WAS A LOT SMALLER, BUT I KNOW IT WAS HIM! I WANT TO PRESS CHARGES!
WELL, WELL... FRANKIE MACK. I KNEW IT THE FIRST TIME I LAID EYES ON YOU: YOU'RE NO GOOD.
WE WERE ALWAYS GONNA BRING YOU DOWN, FRANKIE. IT WAS ONLY A MATTER OF TIME.

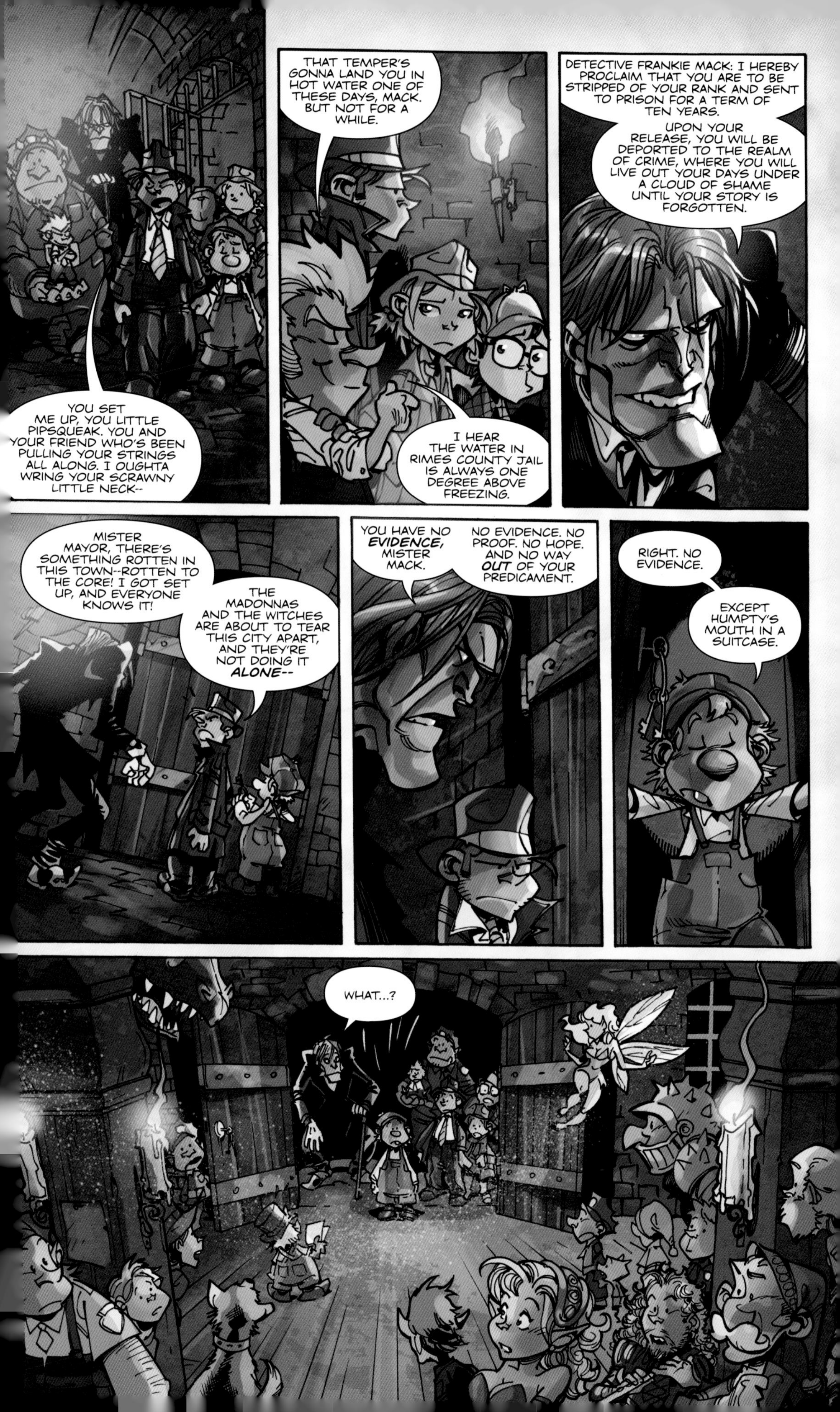
THAT TEMPER'S GONNA LAND YOU IN HOT WATER ONE OF THESE DAYS, MACK. BUT NOT FOR A WHILE.
YOU SET ME UP, YOU LITTLE PIPSQUEAK. YOU AND YOUR FRIEND WHO'S BEEN PULLING YOUR STRINGS ALL ALONG. I OUGHTA WRING YOUR SCRAWNY LITTLE NECK--
I HEAR THE WATER IN RIMES COUNTY JAIL IS ALWAYS ONE DEGREE ABOVE FREEZING.
DETECTIVE FRANKIE MACK: I HEREBY PROCLAIM THAT YOU ARE TO BE STRIPPED OF YOUR RANK AND SENT TO PRISON FOR A TERM OF TEN YEARS.
UPON YOUR RELEASE, YOU WILL BE DEPORTED TO THE REALM OF CRIME, WHERE YOU WILL LIVE OUT YOUR DAYS UNDER A CLOUD OF SHAME UNTIL YOUR STORY IS FORGOTTEN.
MISTER MAYOR, THERE'S SOMETHING ROTTEN IN THIS TOWN--ROTTEN TO THE CORE! I GOT SET UP, AND EVERYONE KNOWS IT!
THE MADONNAS AND THE WITCHES ARE ABOUT TO TEAR THIS CITY APART, AND THEY'RE NOT DOING IT ALONE--
YOU HAVE NO EVIDENCE, MISTER MACK.
NO EVIDENCE. NO PROOF. NO HOPE. AND NO WAY OUT OF YOUR PREDICAMENT.
RIGHT. NO EVIDENCE.
EXCEPT HUMPTY'S MOUTH IN A SUITCASE.
WHAT...?

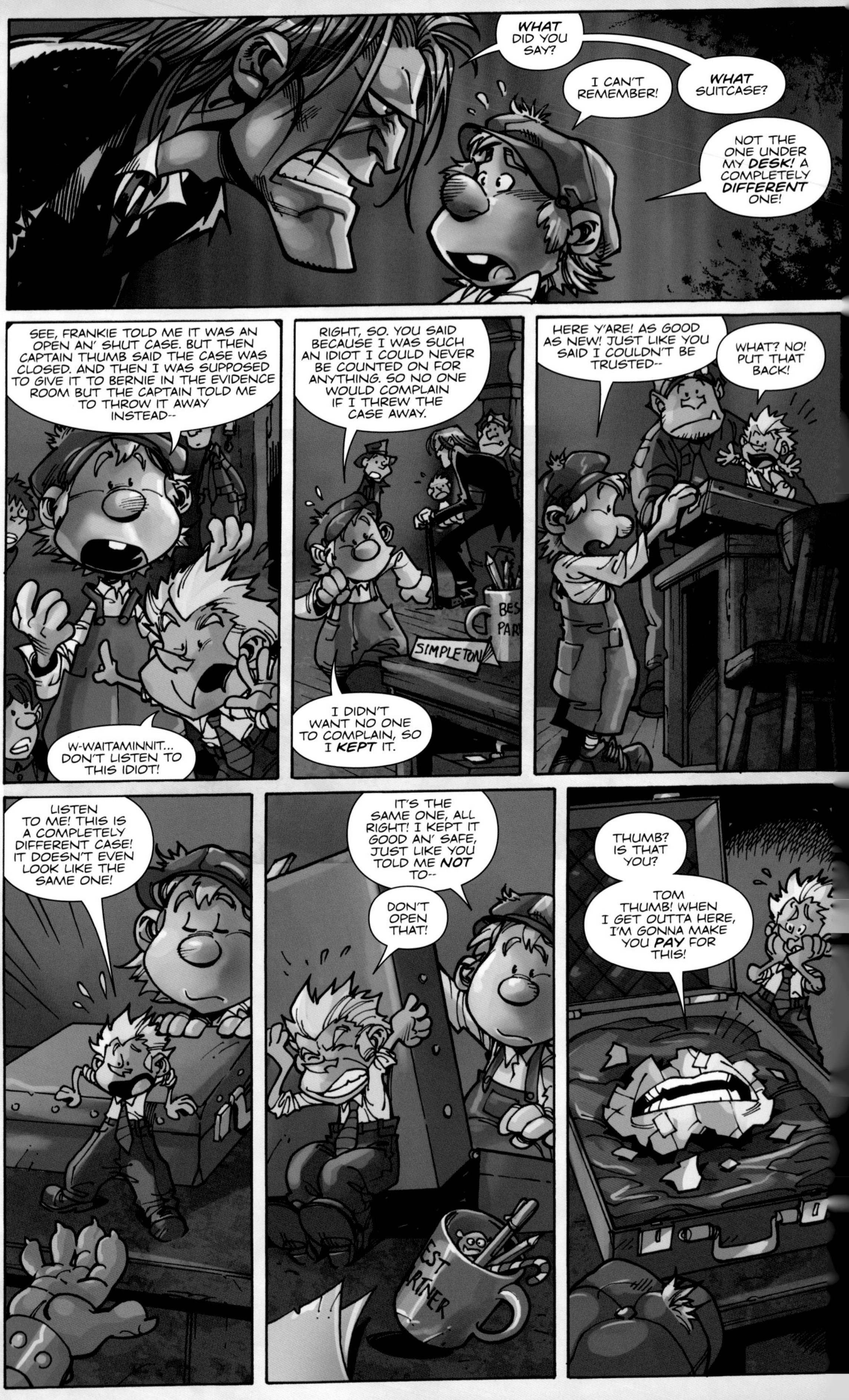
WHAT DID YOU SAY?
I CAN'T REMEMBER!
WHAT SUITCASE?
NOT THE ONE UNDER MY DESK! A COMPLETELY DIFFERENT ONE!
SEE, FRANKIE TOLD ME IT WAS AN OPEN AN' SHUT CASE. BUT THEN CAPTAIN THUMB SAID THE CASE WAS CLOSED. AND THEN I WAS SUPPOSED TO GIVE IT TO BERNIE IN THE EVIDENCE ROOM BUT THE CAPTAIN TOLD ME TO THROW IT AWAY INSTEAD--
W-WAITAMINNIT... DON'T LISTEN TO THIS IDIOT!
RIGHT, SO. YOU SAID BECAUSE I WAS SUCH AN IDIOT I COULD NEVER BE COUNTED ON FOR ANYTHING. SO NO ONE WOULD COMPLAIN IF I THREW THE CASE AWAY.
SIMPLETON
I DIDN'T WANT NO ONE TO COMPLAIN, SO I KEPT IT.
HERE Y'ARE! AS GOOD AS NEW! JUST LIKE YOU SAID I COULDN'T BE TRUSTED--
WHAT? NO! PUT THAT BACK!
LISTEN TO ME! THIS IS A COMPLETELY DIFFERENT CASE! IT DOESN'T EVEN LOOK LIKE THE SAME ONE!
IT'S THE SAME ONE, ALL RIGHT! I KEPT IT GOOD AN' SAFE, JUST LIKE YOU TOLD ME NOT TO--
DON'T OPEN THAT!
THUMB? IS THAT YOU?
TOM THUMB! WHEN I GET OUTTA HERE, I'M GONNA MAKE YOU PAY FOR THIS!

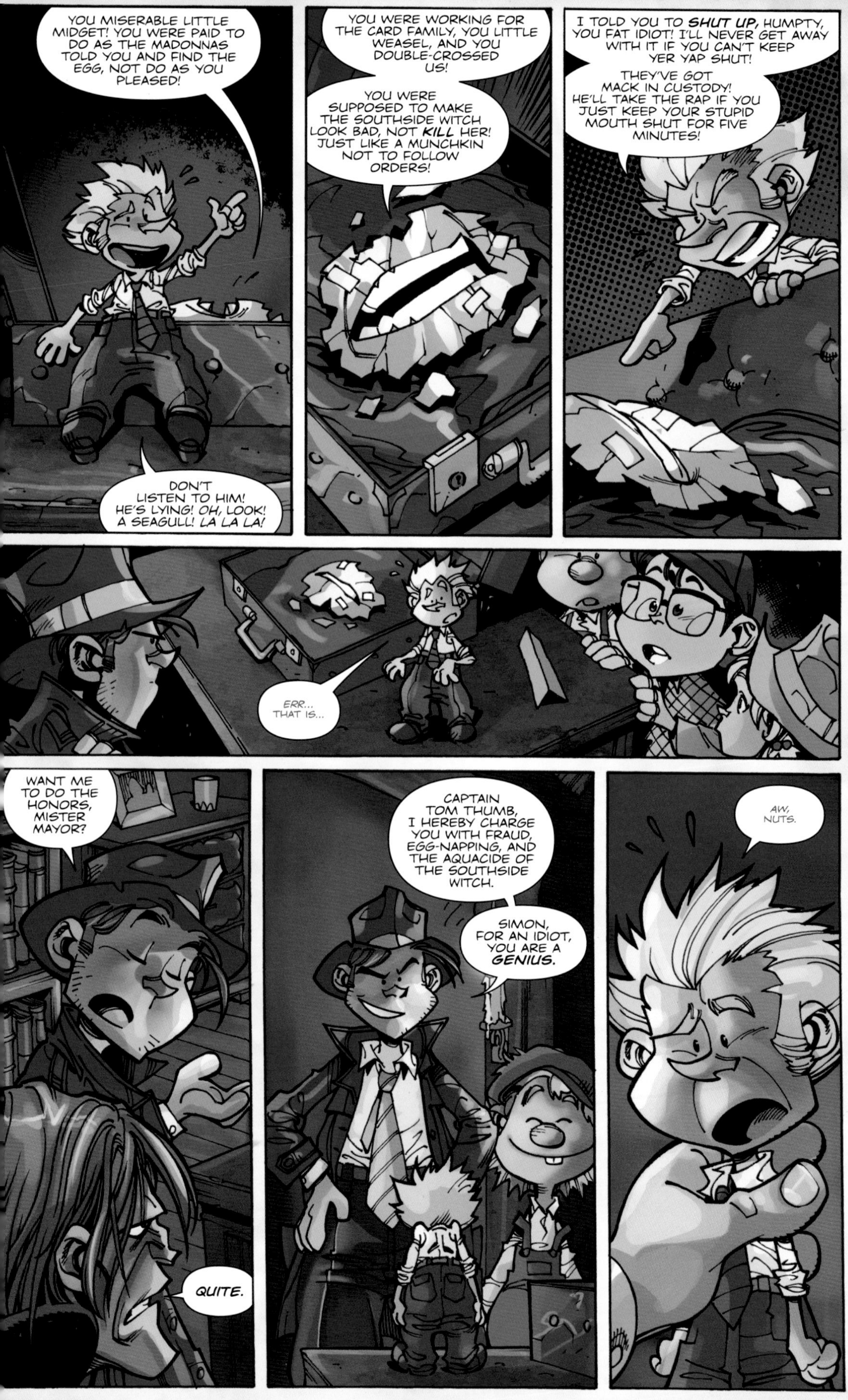
YOU MISERABLE LITTLE MIDGET! YOU WERE PAID TO DO AS THE MADONNAS TOLD YOU AND FIND THE EGG, NOT DO AS YOU PLEASED!
DON'T LISTEN TO HIM! HE'S LYING! OH, LOOK! A SEAGULL! LA LA LA!
YOU WERE WORKING FOR THE CARD FAMILY, YOU LITTLE WEASEL, AND YOU DOUBLE-CROSSED US!
YOU WERE SUPPOSED TO MAKE THE SOUTHSIDE WITCH LOOK BAD, NOT KILL HER! JUST LIKE A MUNCHKIN NOT TO FOLLOW ORDERS!
I TOLD YOU TO SHUT UP, HUMPTY, YOU FAT IDIOT! I'LL NEVER GET AWAY WITH IT IF YOU CAN'T KEEP YER YAP SHUT!
THEY'VE GOT MACK IN CUSTODY! HE'LL TAKE THE RAP IF YOU JUST KEEP YOUR STUPID MOUTH SHUT FOR FIVE MINUTES!
ERR... THAT IS...
WANT ME TO DO THE HONORS, MISTER MAYOR?
QUITE.
CAPTAIN TOM THUMB, I HEREBY CHARGE YOU WITH FRAUD, EGG-NAPPING, AND THE AQUACIDE OF THE SOUTHSIDE WITCH.
SIMON, FOR AN IDIOT, YOU ARE A GENIUS.
AW, NUTS.

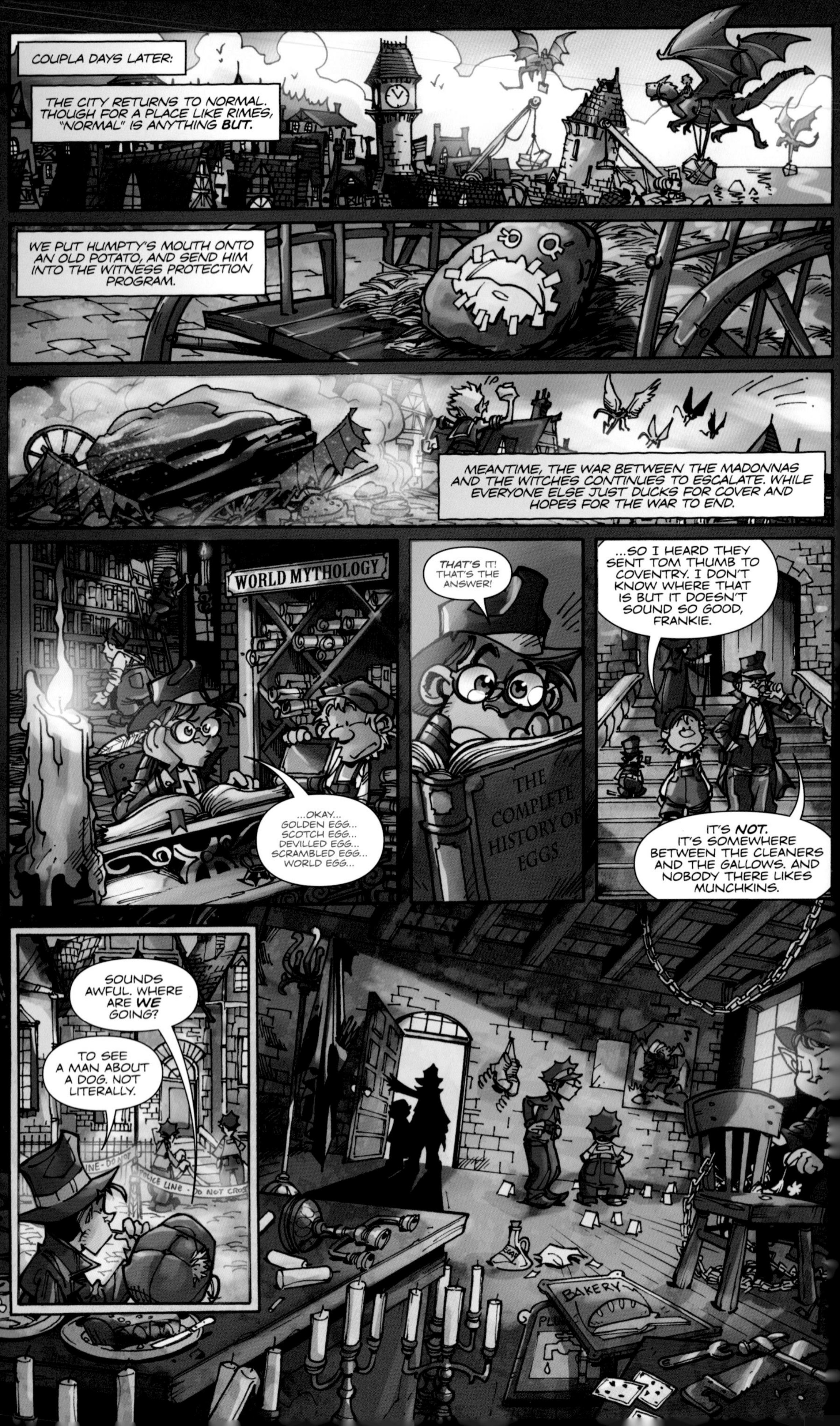
COUPLA DAYS LATER:
THE CITY RETURNS TO NORMAL. THOUGH FOR A PLACE LIKE RIMES, "NORMAL" IS ANYTHING BUT.
WE PUT HUMPTY'S MOUTH ONTO AN OLD POTATO, AND SEND HIM INTO THE WITNESS PROTECTION PROGRAM.
MEANTIME, THE WAR BETWEEN THE MADONNAS AND THE WITCHES CONTINUES TO ESCALATE. WHILE EVERYONE ELSE JUST DUCKS FOR COVER AND HOPES FOR THE WAR TO END.
WORLD MYTHOLOGY
...OKAY... GOLDEN EGG... SCOTCH EGG... DEVILLED EGG... SCRAMBLED EGG... WORLD EGG...
THAT'S IT! THAT'S THE ANSWER!
THE COMPLETE HISTORY OF EGGS
...SO I HEARD THEY SENT TOM THUMB TO COVENTRY. I DON'T KNOW WHERE THAT IS BUT IT DOESN'T SOUND SO GOOD, FRANKIE.
IT'S NOT. IT'S SOMEWHERE BETWEEN THE CLEANERS AND THE GALLOWS. AND NOBODY THERE LIKES MUNCHKINS.
SOUNDS AWFUL. WHERE ARE WE GOING?
TO SEE A MAN ABOUT A DOG. NOT LITERALLY.
POLICE LINE - DO NOT CROSS
BAKERY

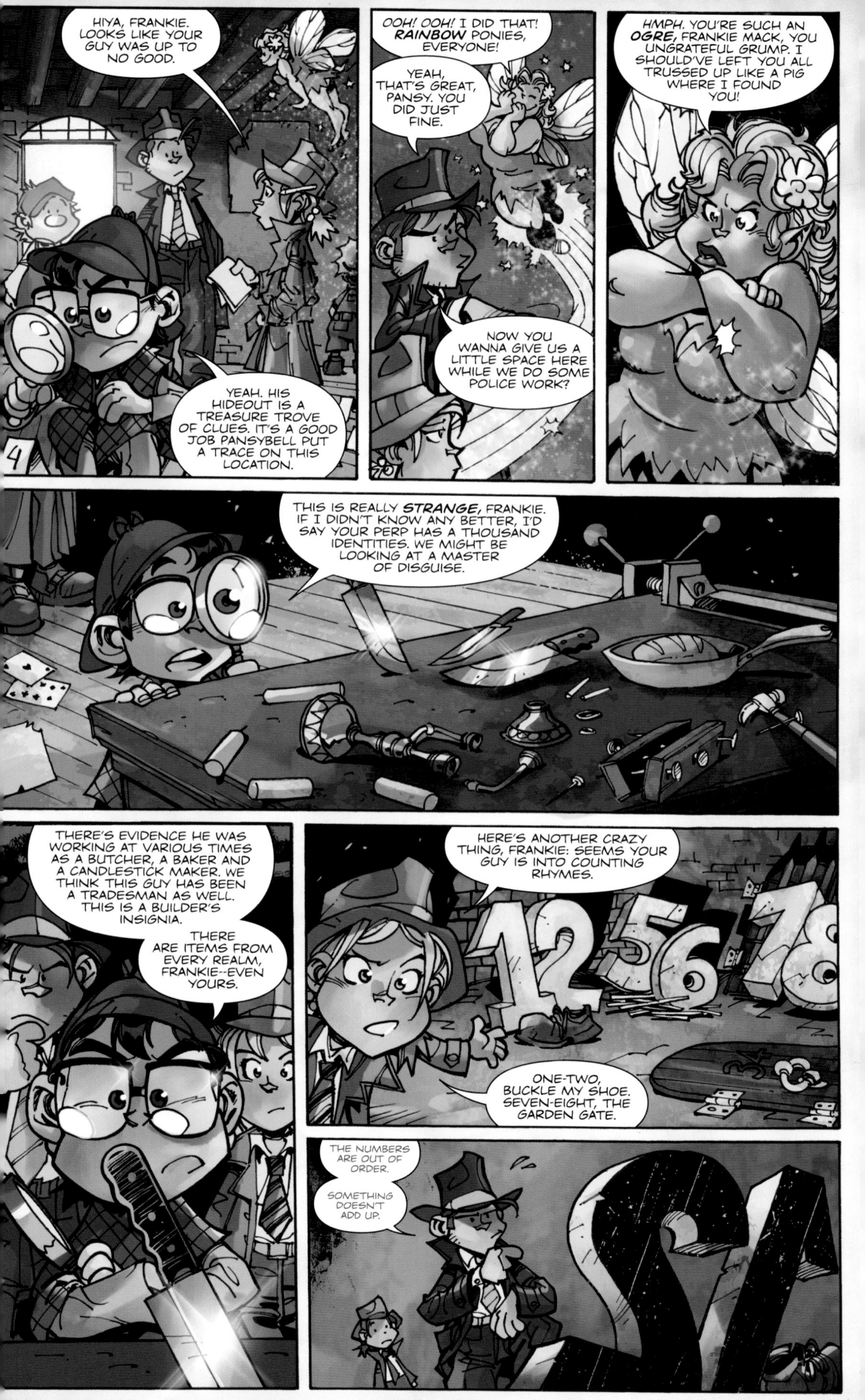
HIYA, FRANKIE. LOOKS LIKE YOUR GUY WAS UP TO NO GOOD.
YEAH. HIS HIDEOUT IS A TREASURE TROVE OF CLUES. IT'S A GOOD JOB PANSYBELL PUT A TRACE ON THIS LOCATION.
4
OOH! OOH! I DID THAT! RAINBOW PONIES, EVERYONE!
YEAH, THAT'S GREAT, PANSY. YOU DID JUST FINE.
NOW YOU WANNA GIVE US A LITTLE SPACE HERE WHILE WE DO SOME POLICE WORK?
HMPH. YOU'RE SUCH AN OGRE, FRANKIE MACK, YOU UNGRATEFUL GRUMP. I SHOULD'VE LEFT YOU ALL TRUSSED UP LIKE A PIG WHERE I FOUND YOU!
THIS IS REALLY STRANGE, FRANKIE. IF I DIDN'T KNOW ANY BETTER, I'D SAY YOUR PERP HAS A THOUSAND IDENTITIES. WE MIGHT BE LOOKING AT A MASTER OF DISGUISE.
THERE'S EVIDENCE HE WAS WORKING AT VARIOUS TIMES AS A BUTCHER, A BAKER AND A CANDLESTICK MAKER. WE THINK THIS GUY HAS BEEN A TRADESMAN AS WELL. THIS IS A BUILDER'S INSIGNIA.
THERE ARE ITEMS FROM EVERY REALM, FRANKIE--EVEN YOURS.
HERE'S ANOTHER CRAZY THING, FRANKIE: SEEMS YOUR GUY IS INTO COUNTING RHYMES.
ONE-TWO, BUCKLE MY SHOE. SEVEN-EIGHT, THE GARDEN GATE.
THE NUMBERS ARE OUT OF ORDER.
SOMETHING DOESN'T ADD UP.

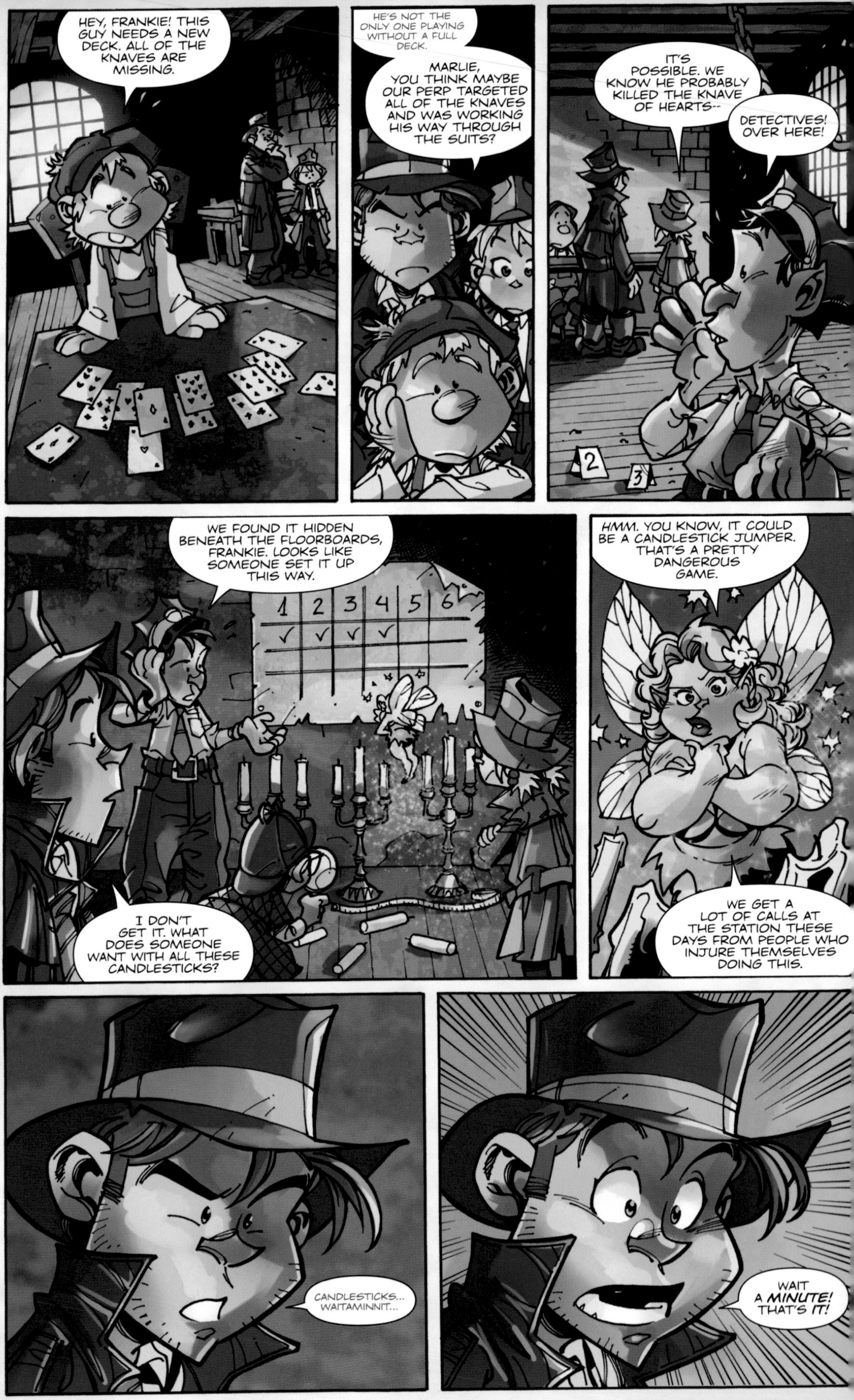
HEY, FRANKIE! THIS GUY NEEDS A NEW DECK. ALL OF THE KNAVES ARE MISSING.
HE'S NOT THE ONLY ONE PLAYING WITHOUT A FULL DECK.
MARLIE, YOU THINK MAYBE OUR PERP TARGETED ALL OF THE KNAVES AND WAS WORKING HIS WAY THROUGH THE SUITS?
IT'S POSSIBLE. WE KNOW HE PROBABLY KILLED THE KNAVE OF HEARTS--
DETECTIVES! OVER HERE!
2
3
WE FOUND IT HIDDEN BENEATH THE FLOORBOARDS, FRANKIE. LOOKS LIKE SOMEONE SET IT UP THIS WAY.
1 2 3 4 5 6
I DON'T GET IT. WHAT DOES SOMEONE WANT WITH ALL THESE CANDLESTICKS?
HMM. YOU KNOW, IT COULD BE A CANDLESTICK JUMPER. THAT'S A PRETTY DANGEROUS GAME.
WE GET A LOT OF CALLS AT THE STATION THESE DAYS FROM PEOPLE WHO INJURE THEMSELVES DOING THIS.
CANDLESTICKS... WAITAMINNIT...
WAIT A *MINUTE!* THAT'S *IT!*

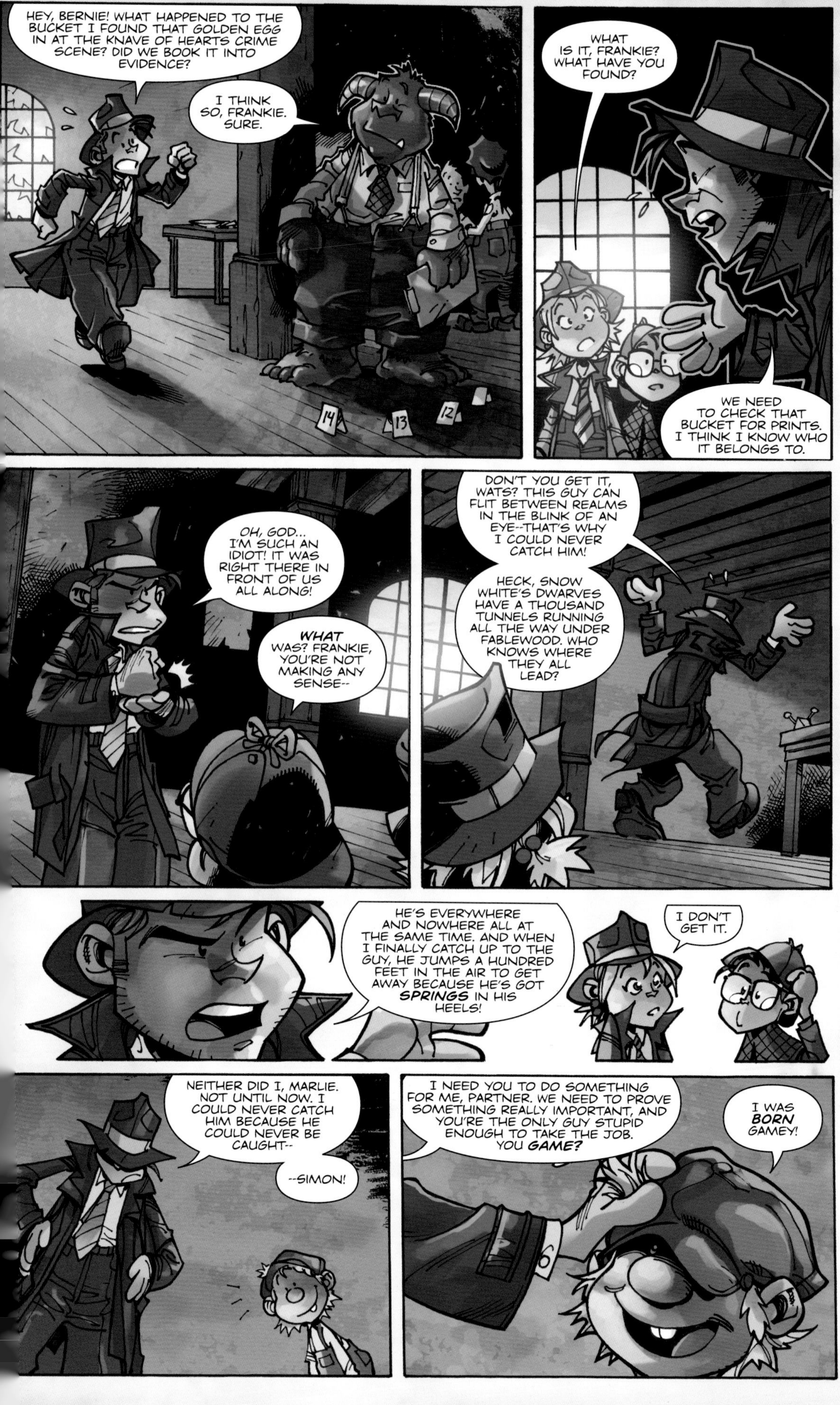

HEY, BERNIE! WHAT HAPPENED TO THE BUCKET I FOUND THAT GOLDEN EGG IN AT THE KNAVE OF HEARTS CRIME SCENE? DID WE BOOK IT INTO EVIDENCE?
I THINK SO, FRANKIE. SURE.
14
13
12
WHAT IS IT, FRANKIE? WHAT HAVE YOU FOUND?
WE NEED TO CHECK THAT BUCKET FOR PRINTS. I THINK I KNOW WHO IT BELONGS TO.
OH, GOD... I'M SUCH AN IDIOT! IT WAS RIGHT THERE IN FRONT OF US ALL ALONG!
WHAT WAS? FRANKIE, YOU'RE NOT MAKING ANY SENSE--
DON'T YOU GET IT, WATS? THIS GUY CAN FLIT BETWEEN REALMS IN THE BLINK OF AN EYE--THAT'S WHY I COULD NEVER CATCH HIM!
HECK, SNOW WHITE'S DWARVES HAVE A THOUSAND TUNNELS RUNNING ALL THE WAY UNDER FABLEWOOD. WHO KNOWS WHERE THEY ALL LEAD?
HE'S EVERYWHERE AND NOWHERE ALL AT THE SAME TIME. AND WHEN I FINALLY CATCH UP TO THE GUY, HE JUMPS A HUNDRED FEET IN THE AIR TO GET AWAY BECAUSE HE'S GOT *SPRINGS* IN HIS HEELS!
I DON'T GET IT.
NEITHER DID I, MARLIE. NOT UNTIL NOW. I COULD NEVER CATCH HIM BECAUSE HE COULD NEVER BE CAUGHT--
--SIMON!
I NEED YOU TO DO SOMETHING FOR ME, PARTNER. WE NEED TO PROVE SOMETHING REALLY IMPORTANT, AND YOU'RE THE ONLY GUY STUPID ENOUGH TO TAKE THE JOB. YOU *GAME?*
I WAS *BORN* GAMEY!

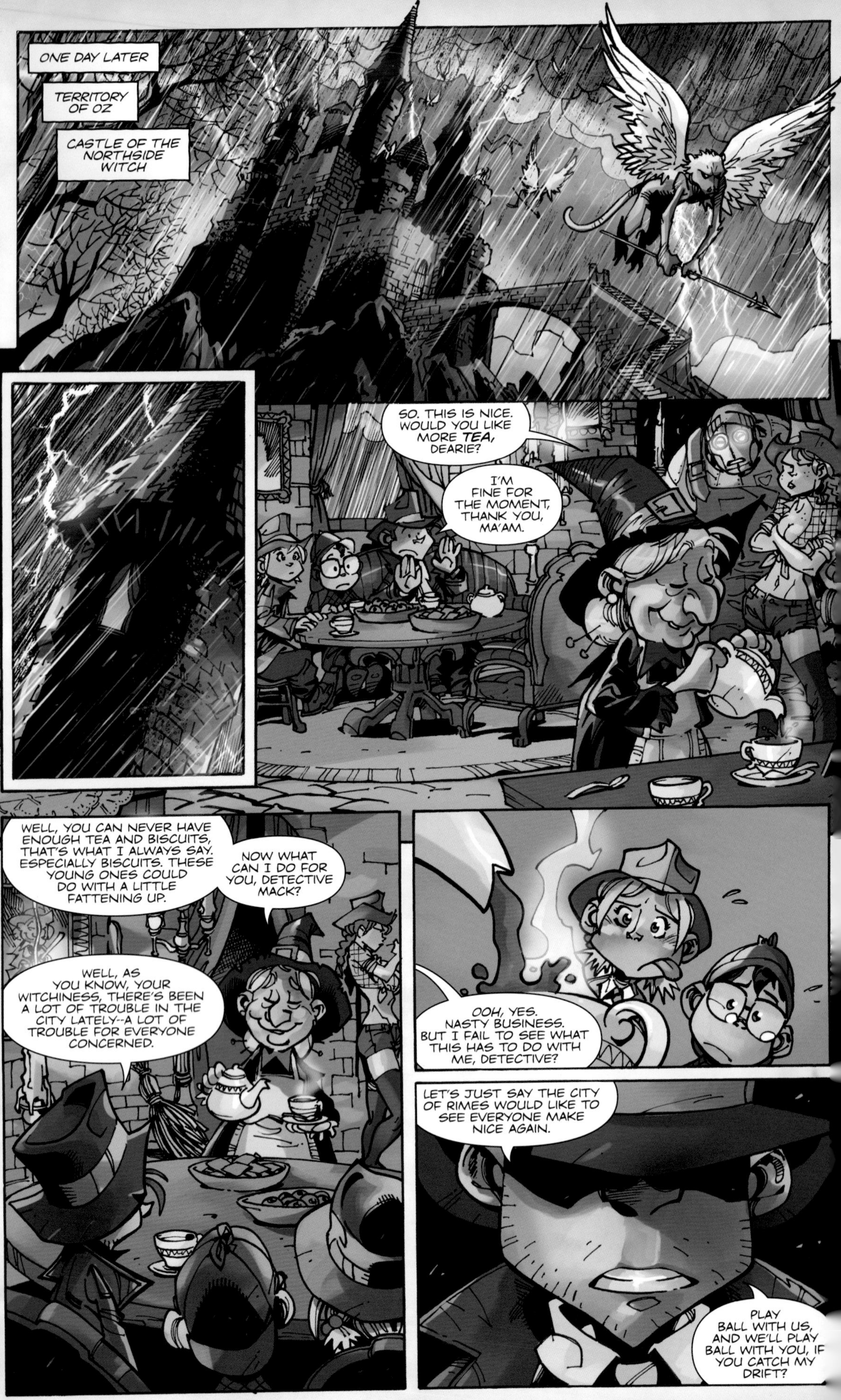

ONE DAY LATER
TERRITORY OF OZ
CASTLE OF THE NORTHSIDE WITCH
SO. THIS IS NICE. WOULD YOU LIKE MORE TEA, DEARIE?
I'M FINE FOR THE MOMENT, THANK YOU, MA'AM.
WELL, YOU CAN NEVER HAVE ENOUGH TEA AND BISCUITS, THAT'S WHAT I ALWAYS SAY. ESPECIALLY BISCUITS. THESE YOUNG ONES COULD DO WITH A LITTLE FATTENING UP.
NOW WHAT CAN I DO FOR YOU, DETECTIVE MACK?
WELL, AS YOU KNOW, YOUR WITCHINESS, THERE'S BEEN A LOT OF TROUBLE IN THE CITY LATELY--A LOT OF TROUBLE FOR EVERYONE CONCERNED.
OOH, YES. NASTY BUSINESS. BUT I FAIL TO SEE WHAT THIS HAS TO DO WITH ME, DETECTIVE?
LET'S JUST SAY THE CITY OF RIMES WOULD LIKE TO SEE EVERYONE MAKE NICE AGAIN.
PLAY BALL WITH US, AND WE'LL PLAY BALL WITH YOU, IF YOU CATCH MY DRIFT?

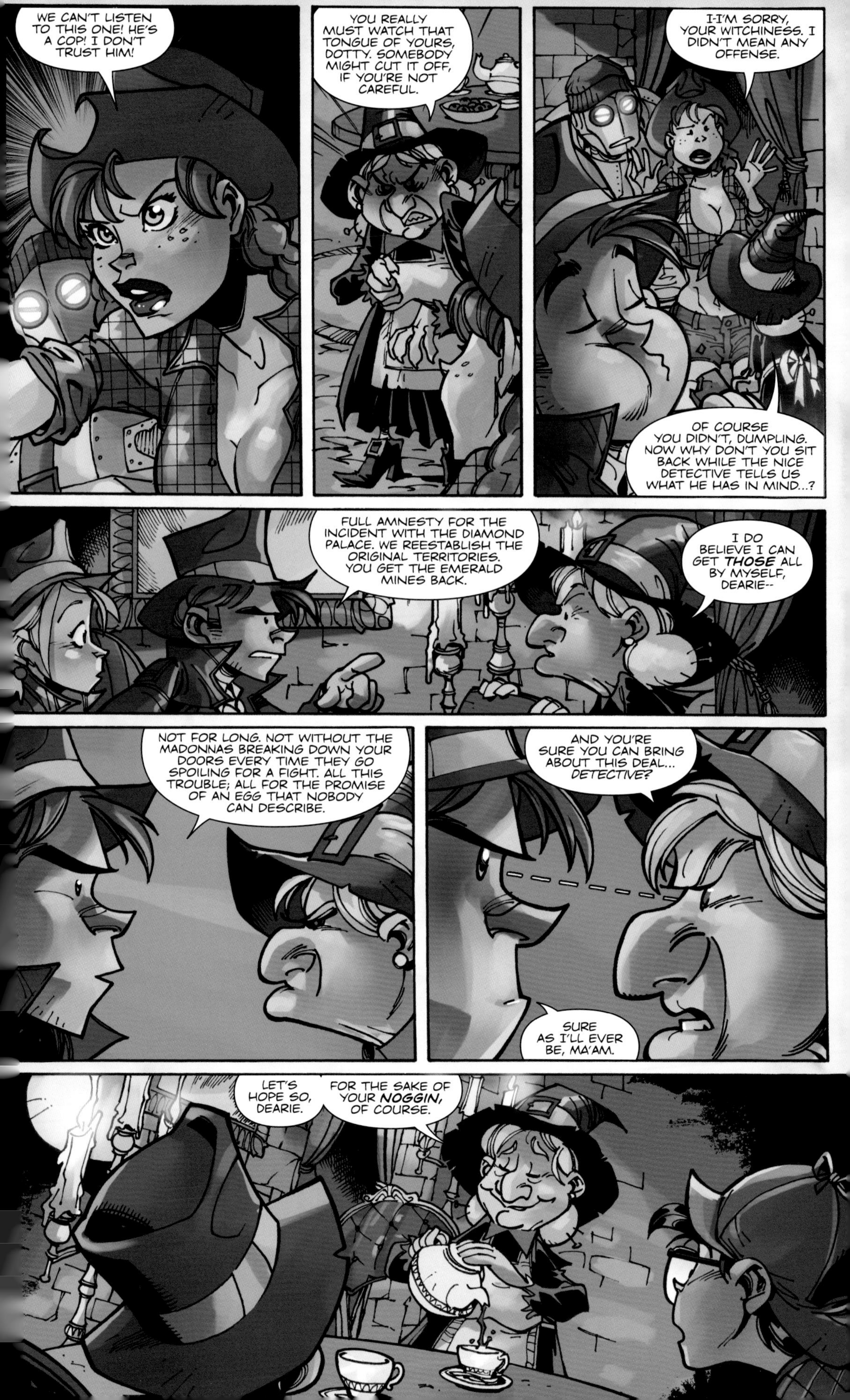
WE CAN'T LISTEN TO THIS ONE! HE'S A COP! I DON'T TRUST HIM!
YOU REALLY MUST WATCH THAT TONGUE OF YOURS, DOTTY. SOMEBODY MIGHT CUT IT OFF, IF YOU'RE NOT CAREFUL.
I-I'M SORRY, YOUR WITCHINESS. I DIDN'T MEAN ANY OFFENSE.
OF COURSE YOU DIDN'T, DUMPLING. NOW WHY DON'T YOU SIT BACK WHILE THE NICE DETECTIVE TELLS US WHAT HE HAS IN MIND...?
FULL AMNESTY FOR THE INCIDENT WITH THE DIAMOND PALACE. WE REESTABLISH THE ORIGINAL TERRITORIES. YOU GET THE EMERALD MINES BACK.
I DO BELIEVE I CAN GET ***THOSE*** ALL BY MYSELF, DEARIE--
NOT FOR LONG. NOT WITHOUT THE MADONNAS BREAKING DOWN YOUR DOORS EVERY TIME THEY GO SPOILING FOR A FIGHT. ALL THIS TROUBLE; ALL FOR THE PROMISE OF AN EGG THAT NOBODY CAN DESCRIBE.
AND YOU'RE SURE YOU CAN BRING ABOUT THIS DEAL... *DETECTIVE?*
SURE AS I'LL EVER BE, MA'AM.
LET'S HOPE SO, DEARIE.
FOR THE SAKE OF YOUR ***NOGGIN,*** OF COURSE.

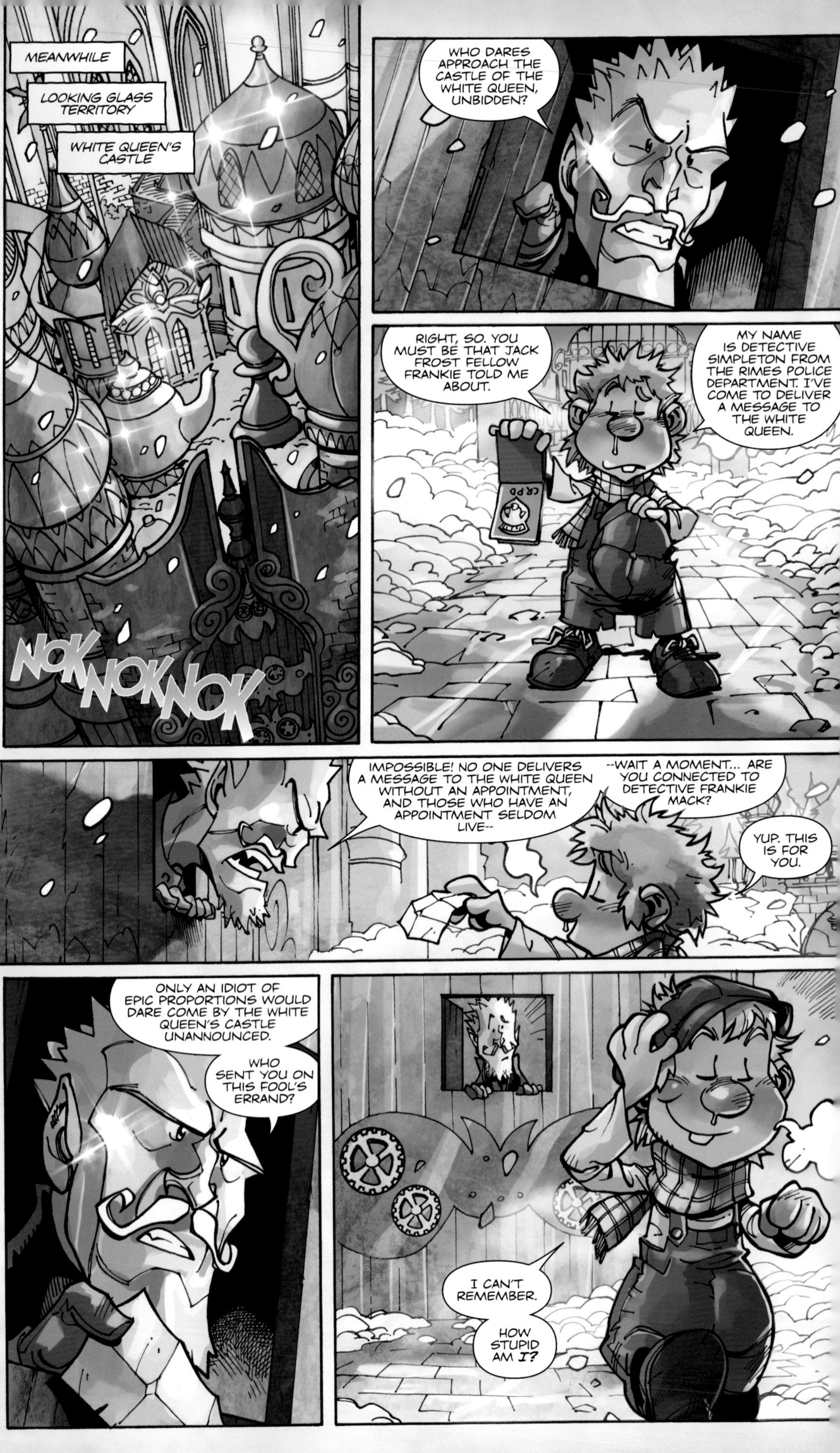
MEANWHILE
LOOKING GLASS TERRITORY
WHITE QUEEN'S CASTLE
NOKNOKNOK
WHO DARES APPROACH THE CASTLE OF THE WHITE QUEEN, UNBIDDEN?
RIGHT, SO. YOU MUST BE THAT JACK FROST FELLOW FRANKIE TOLD ME ABOUT.
MY NAME IS DETECTIVE SIMPLETON FROM THE RIMES POLICE DEPARTMENT. I'VE COME TO DELIVER A MESSAGE TO THE WHITE QUEEN.
CRPD
IMPOSSIBLE! NO ONE DELIVERS A MESSAGE TO THE WHITE QUEEN WITHOUT AN APPOINTMENT, AND THOSE WHO HAVE AN APPOINTMENT SELDOM LIVE--
--WAIT A MOMENT... ARE YOU CONNECTED TO DETECTIVE FRANKIE MACK?
YUP. THIS IS FOR YOU.
ONLY AN IDIOT OF EPIC PROPORTIONS WOULD DARE COME BY THE WHITE QUEEN'S CASTLE UNANNOUNCED.
WHO SENT YOU ON THIS FOOL'S ERRAND?
I CAN'T REMEMBER.
HOW STUPID AM *I?*

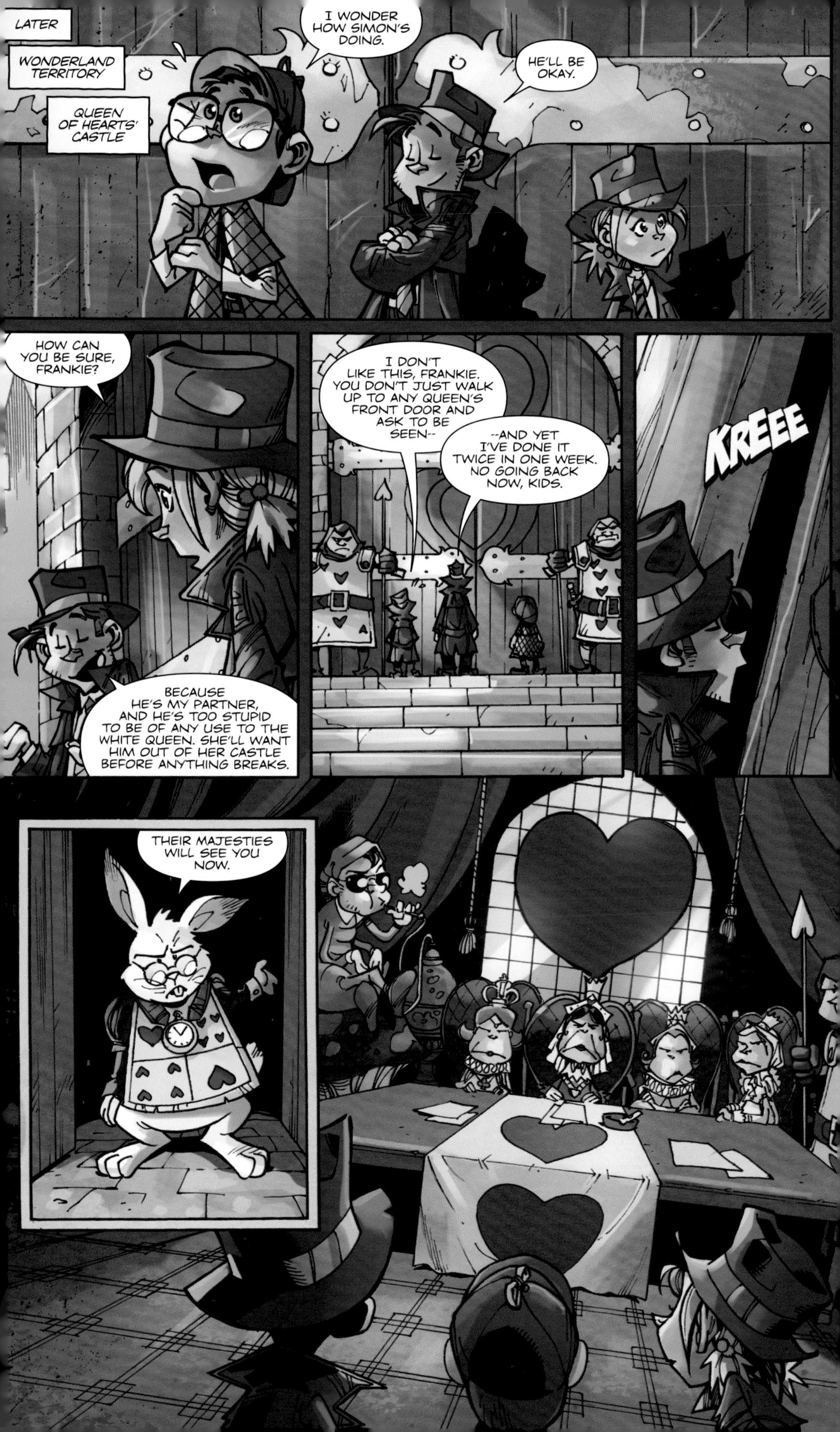
LATER
WONDERLAND TERRITORY
QUEEN OF HEARTS' CASTLE
I WONDER HOW SIMON'S DOING.
HE'LL BE OKAY.
HOW CAN YOU BE SURE, FRANKIE?
BECAUSE HE'S MY PARTNER, AND HE'S TOO STUPID TO BE OF ANY USE TO THE WHITE QUEEN. SHE'LL WANT HIM OUT OF HER CASTLE BEFORE ANYTHING BREAKS.
I DON'T LIKE THIS, FRANKIE. YOU DON'T JUST WALK UP TO ANY QUEEN'S FRONT DOOR AND ASK TO BE SEEN--
--AND YET I'VE DONE IT TWICE IN ONE WEEK. NO GOING BACK NOW, KIDS.
KREEE
THEIR MAJESTIES WILL SEE YOU NOW.

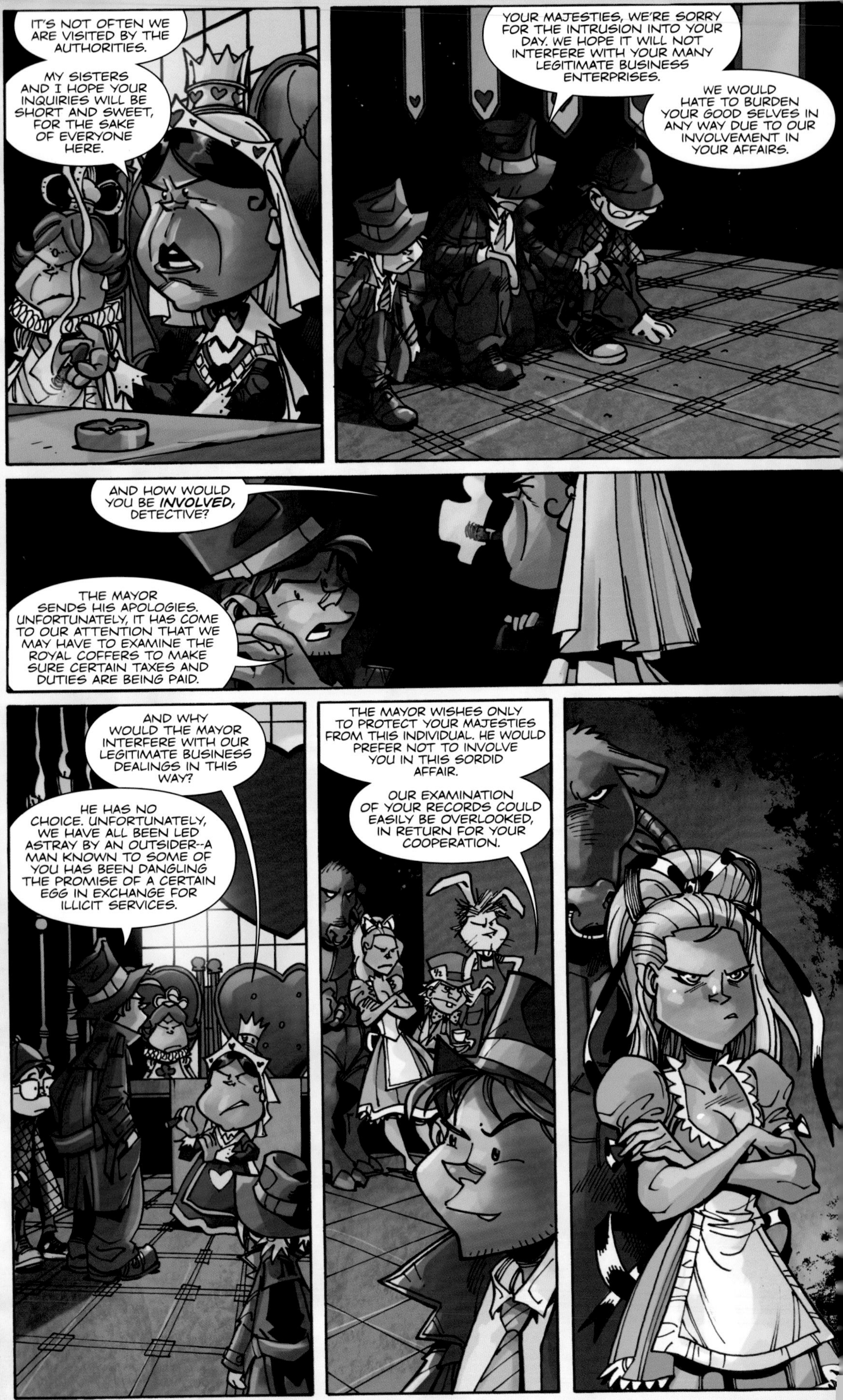
IT'S NOT OFTEN WE ARE VISITED BY THE AUTHORITIES.
MY SISTERS AND I HOPE YOUR INQUIRIES WILL BE SHORT AND SWEET, FOR THE SAKE OF EVERYONE HERE.
YOUR MAJESTIES, WE'RE SORRY FOR THE INTRUSION INTO YOUR DAY. WE HOPE IT WILL NOT INTERFERE WITH YOUR MANY LEGITIMATE BUSINESS ENTERPRISES.
WE WOULD HATE TO BURDEN YOUR GOOD SELVES IN ANY WAY DUE TO OUR INVOLVEMENT IN YOUR AFFAIRS.
AND HOW WOULD YOU BE ***INVOLVED,*** DETECTIVE?
THE MAYOR SENDS HIS APOLOGIES. UNFORTUNATELY, IT HAS COME TO OUR ATTENTION THAT WE MAY HAVE TO EXAMINE THE ROYAL COFFERS TO MAKE SURE CERTAIN TAXES AND DUTIES ARE BEING PAID.
AND WHY WOULD THE MAYOR INTERFERE WITH OUR LEGITIMATE BUSINESS DEALINGS IN THIS WAY?
HE HAS NO CHOICE. UNFORTUNATELY, WE HAVE ALL BEEN LED ASTRAY BY AN OUTSIDER--A MAN KNOWN TO SOME OF YOU HAS BEEN DANGLING THE PROMISE OF A CERTAIN EGG IN EXCHANGE FOR ILLICIT SERVICES.
THE MAYOR WISHES ONLY TO PROTECT YOUR MAJESTIES FROM THIS INDIVIDUAL. HE WOULD PREFER NOT TO INVOLVE YOU IN THIS SORDID AFFAIR.
OUR EXAMINATION OF YOUR RECORDS COULD EASILY BE OVERLOOKED, IN RETURN FOR YOUR COOPERATION.

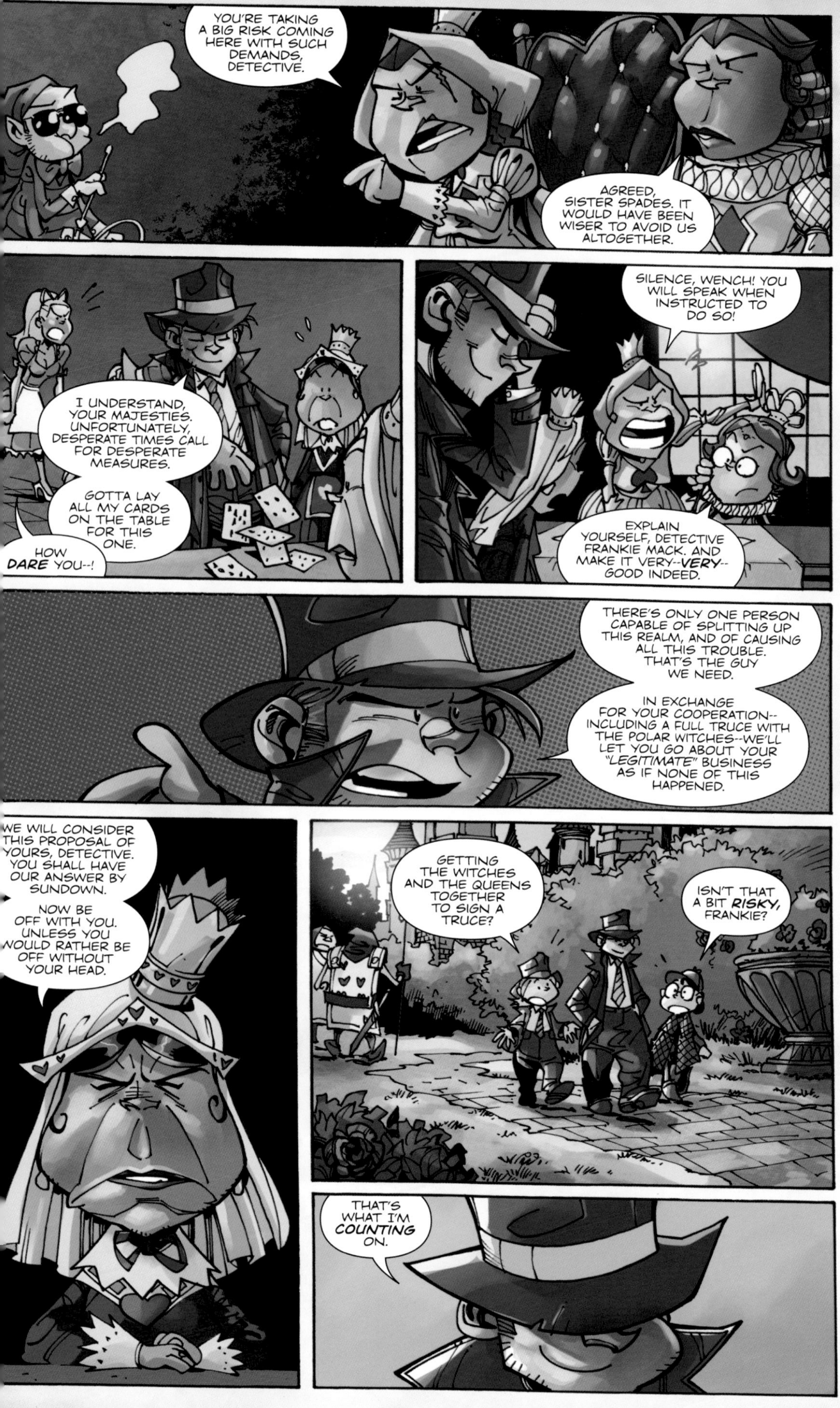
YOU'RE TAKING A BIG RISK COMING HERE WITH SUCH DEMANDS, DETECTIVE.
AGREED, SISTER SPADES. IT WOULD HAVE BEEN WISER TO AVOID US ALTOGETHER.
I UNDERSTAND, YOUR MAJESTIES. UNFORTUNATELY, DESPERATE TIMES CALL FOR DESPERATE MEASURES.
GOTTA LAY ALL MY CARDS ON THE TABLE FOR THIS ONE.
HOW DARE YOU--!
SILENCE, WENCH! YOU WILL SPEAK WHEN INSTRUCTED TO DO SO!
EXPLAIN YOURSELF, DETECTIVE FRANKIE MACK. AND MAKE IT VERY--VERY--GOOD INDEED.
THERE'S ONLY ONE PERSON CAPABLE OF SPLITTING UP THIS REALM, AND OF CAUSING ALL THIS TROUBLE. THAT'S THE GUY WE NEED.
IN EXCHANGE FOR YOUR COOPERATION--INCLUDING A FULL TRUCE WITH THE POLAR WITCHES--WE'LL LET YOU GO ABOUT YOUR "LEGITIMATE" BUSINESS AS IF NONE OF THIS HAPPENED.
WE WILL CONSIDER THIS PROPOSAL OF YOURS, DETECTIVE. YOU SHALL HAVE OUR ANSWER BY SUNDOWN.
NOW BE OFF WITH YOU. UNLESS YOU WOULD RATHER BE OFF WITHOUT YOUR HEAD.
GETTING THE WITCHES AND THE QUEENS TOGETHER TO SIGN A TRUCE?
ISN'T THAT A BIT RISKY, FRANKIE?
THAT'S WHAT I'M COUNTING ON.

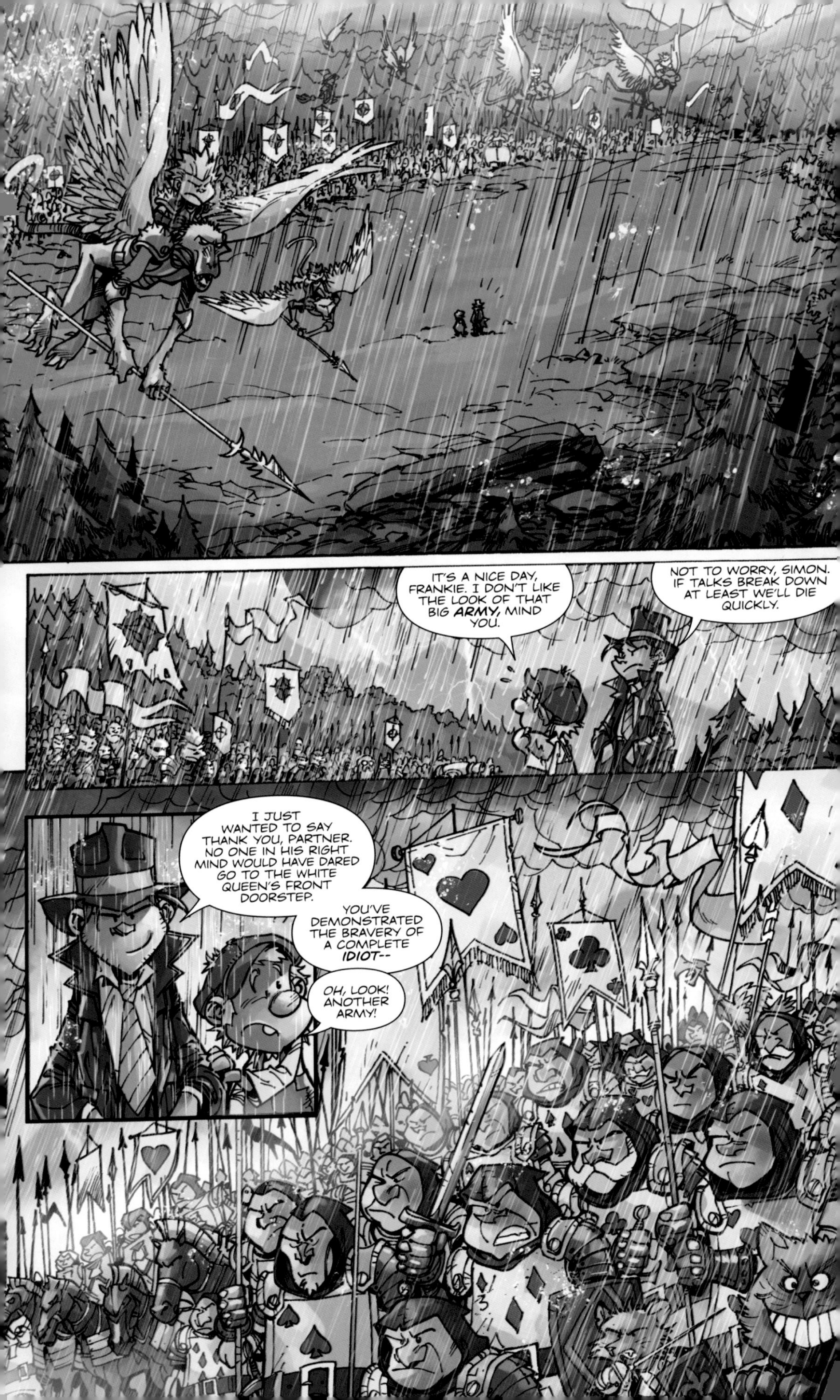
IT'S A NICE DAY, FRANKIE. I DON'T LIKE THE LOOK OF THAT BIG ARMY, MIND YOU.
NOT TO WORRY, SIMON. IF TALKS BREAK DOWN AT LEAST WE'LL DIE QUICKLY.
I JUST WANTED TO SAY THANK YOU, PARTNER. NO ONE IN HIS RIGHT MIND WOULD HAVE DARED GO TO THE WHITE QUEEN'S FRONT DOORSTEP.
YOU'VE DEMONSTRATED THE BRAVERY OF A COMPLETE IDIOT--
OH, LOOK! ANOTHER ARMY!

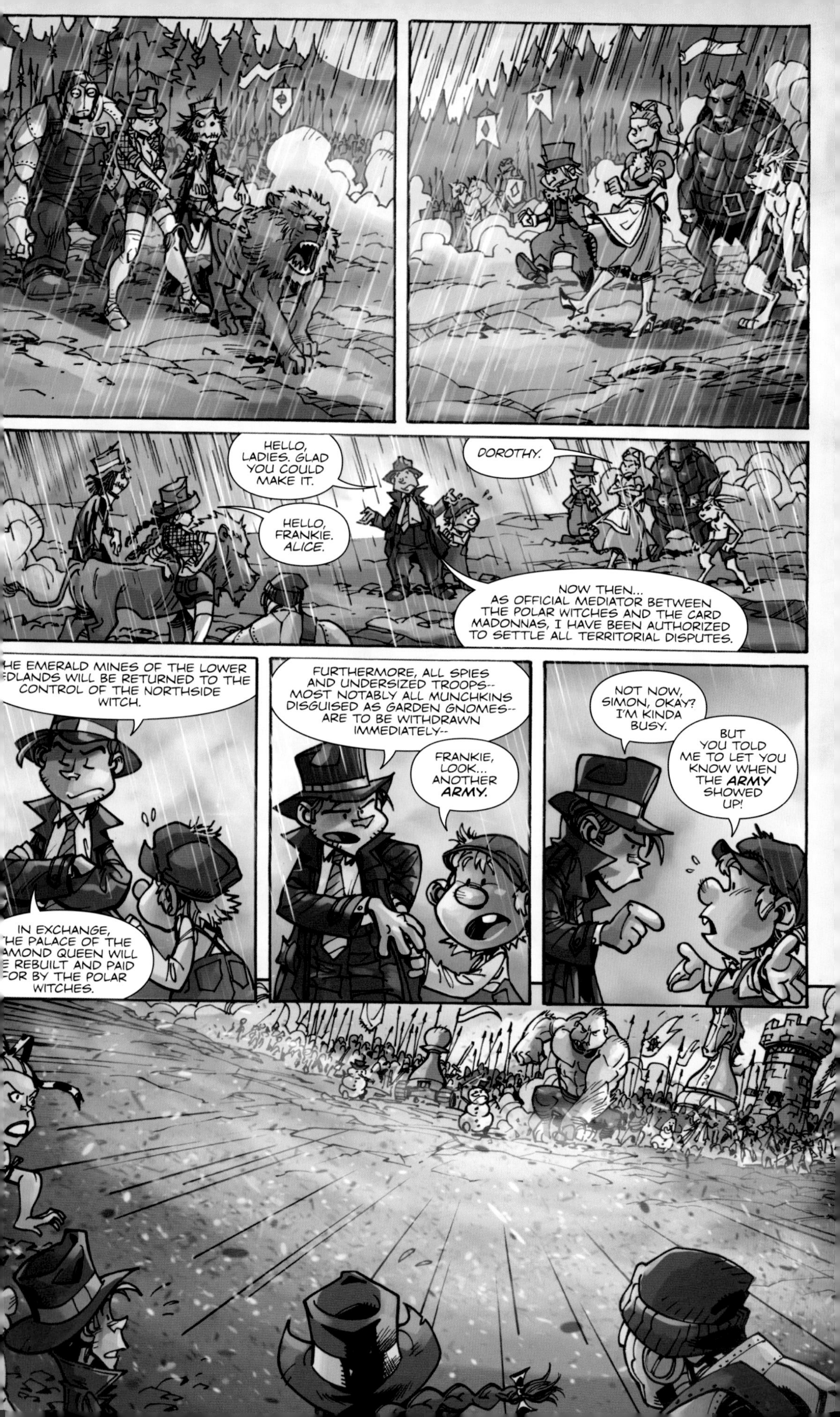
HELLO, LADIES. GLAD YOU COULD MAKE IT.
HELLO, FRANKIE. ALICE.
DOROTHY.
NOW THEN... AS OFFICIAL MEDIATOR BETWEEN THE POLAR WITCHES AND THE CARD MADONNAS, I HAVE BEEN AUTHORIZED TO SETTLE ALL TERRITORIAL DISPUTES.
HE EMERALD MINES OF THE LOWER EDLANDS WILL BE RETURNED TO THE CONTROL OF THE NORTHSIDE WITCH.
IN EXCHANGE, THE PALACE OF THE AMOND QUEEN WILL E REBUILT AND PAID FOR BY THE POLAR WITCHES.
FURTHERMORE, ALL SPIES AND UNDERSIZED TROOPS-- MOST NOTABLY ALL MUNCHKINS DISGUISED AS GARDEN GNOMES-- ARE TO BE WITHDRAWN IMMEDIATELY--
FRANKIE, LOOK... ANOTHER **ARMY.**
NOT NOW, SIMON, OKAY? I'M KINDA BUSY.
BUT YOU TOLD ME TO LET YOU KNOW WHEN THE **ARMY** SHOWED UP!

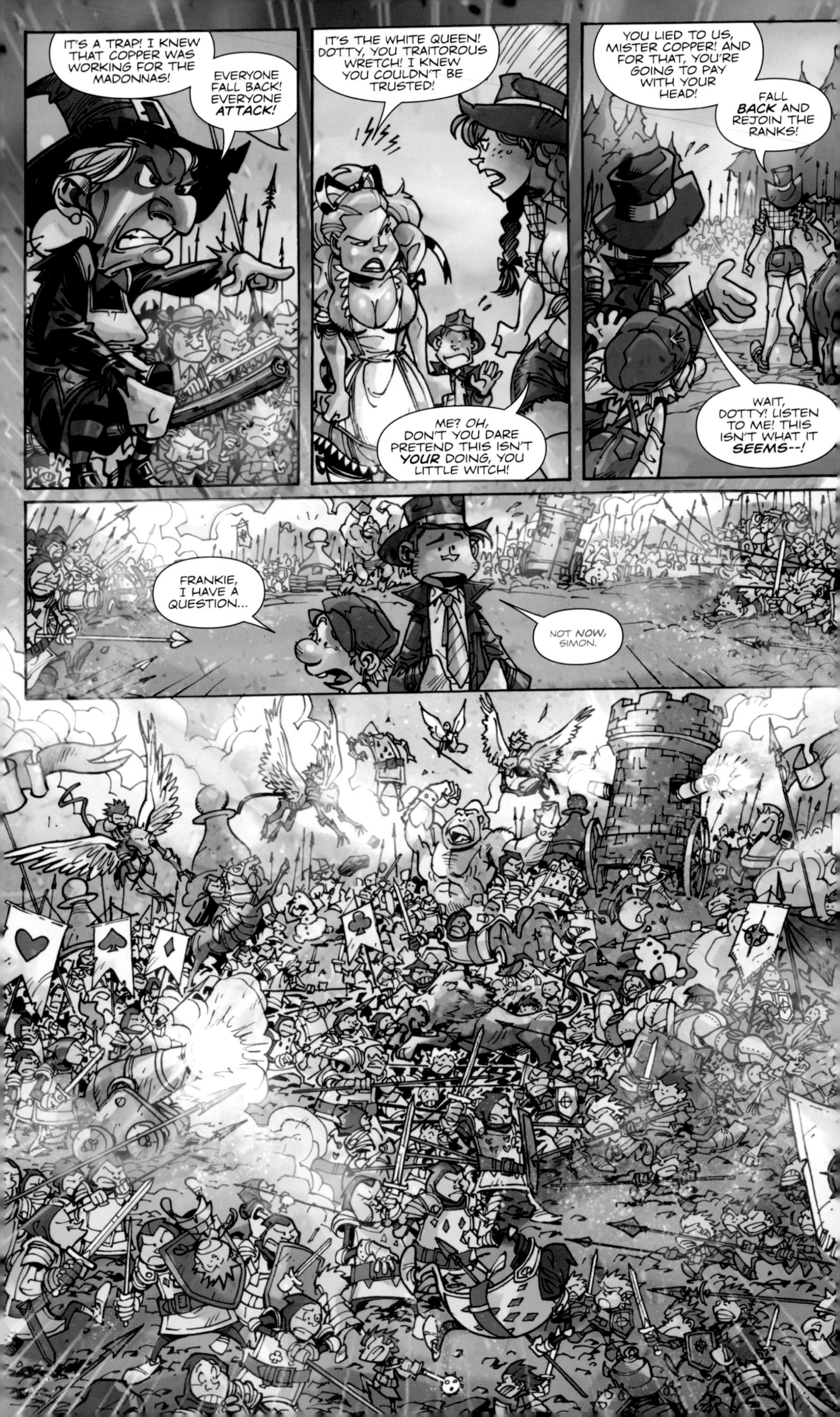

IT'S A TRAP! I KNEW THAT COPPER WAS WORKING FOR THE MADONNAS!
EVERYONE FALL BACK! EVERYONE ATTACK!
IT'S THE WHITE QUEEN! DOTTY, YOU TRAITOROUS WRETCH! I KNEW YOU COULDN'T BE TRUSTED!
ME? OH, DON'T YOU DARE PRETEND THIS ISN'T YOUR DOING, YOU LITTLE WITCH!
YOU LIED TO US, MISTER COPPER! AND FOR THAT, YOU'RE GOING TO PAY WITH YOUR HEAD!
FALL BACK AND REJOIN THE RANKS!
WAIT, DOTTY! LISTEN TO ME! THIS ISN'T WHAT IT SEEMS--!
FRANKIE, I HAVE A QUESTION...
NOT NOW, SIMON.

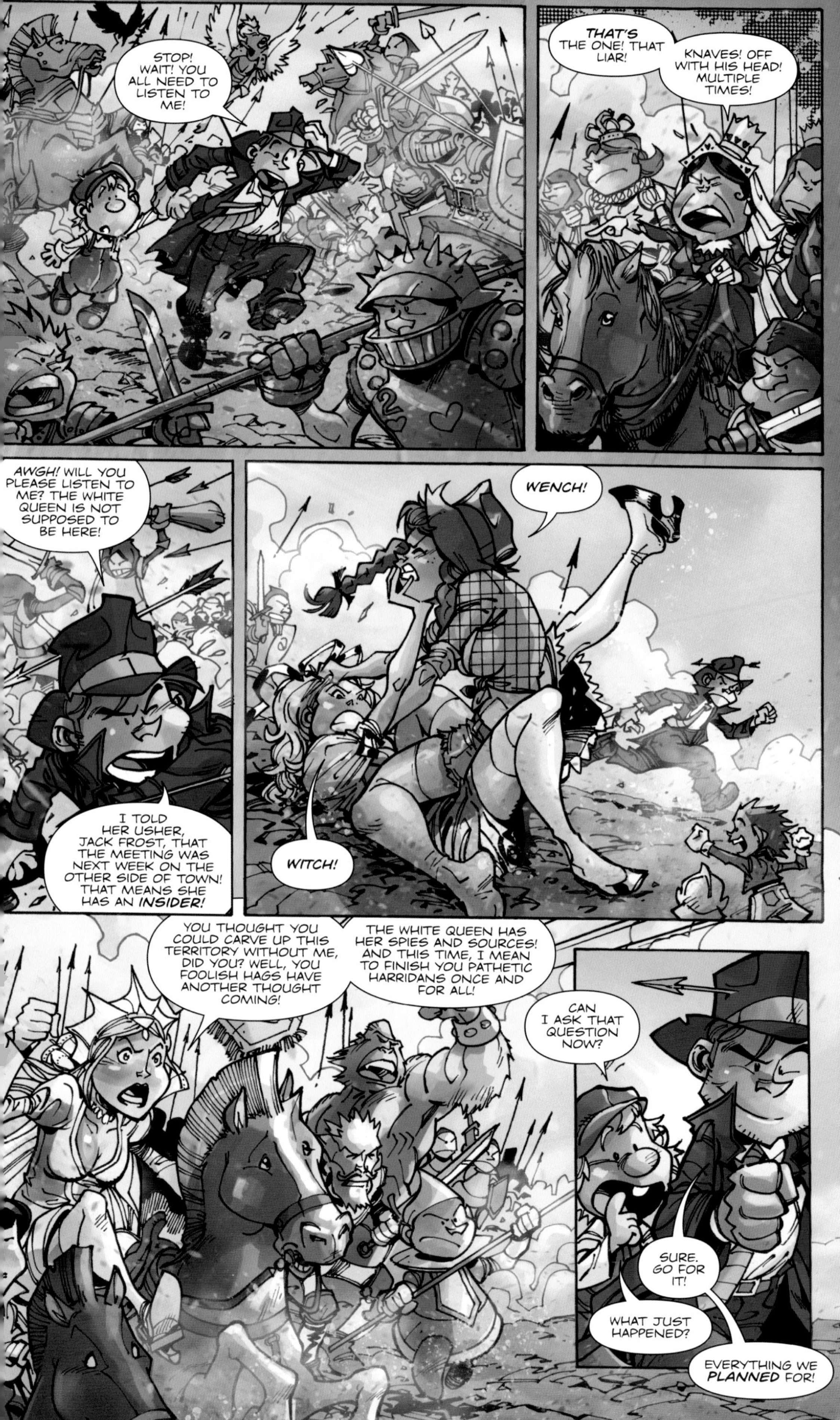
STOP! WAIT! YOU ALL NEED TO LISTEN TO ME!
THAT'S THE ONE! THAT LIAR!
KNAVES! OFF WITH HIS HEAD! MULTIPLE TIMES!
AWGH! WILL YOU PLEASE LISTEN TO ME? THE WHITE QUEEN IS NOT SUPPOSED TO BE HERE!
I TOLD HER USHER, JACK FROST, THAT THE MEETING WAS NEXT WEEK ON THE OTHER SIDE OF TOWN! THAT MEANS SHE HAS AN INSIDER!
WENCH!
WITCH!
YOU THOUGHT YOU COULD CARVE UP THIS TERRITORY WITHOUT ME, DID YOU? WELL, YOU FOOLISH HAGS HAVE ANOTHER THOUGHT COMING!
THE WHITE QUEEN HAS HER SPIES AND SOURCES! AND THIS TIME, I MEAN TO FINISH YOU PATHETIC HARRIDANS ONCE AND FOR ALL!
CAN I ASK THAT QUESTION NOW?
SURE. GO FOR IT!
WHAT JUST HAPPENED?
EVERYTHING WE PLANNED FOR!

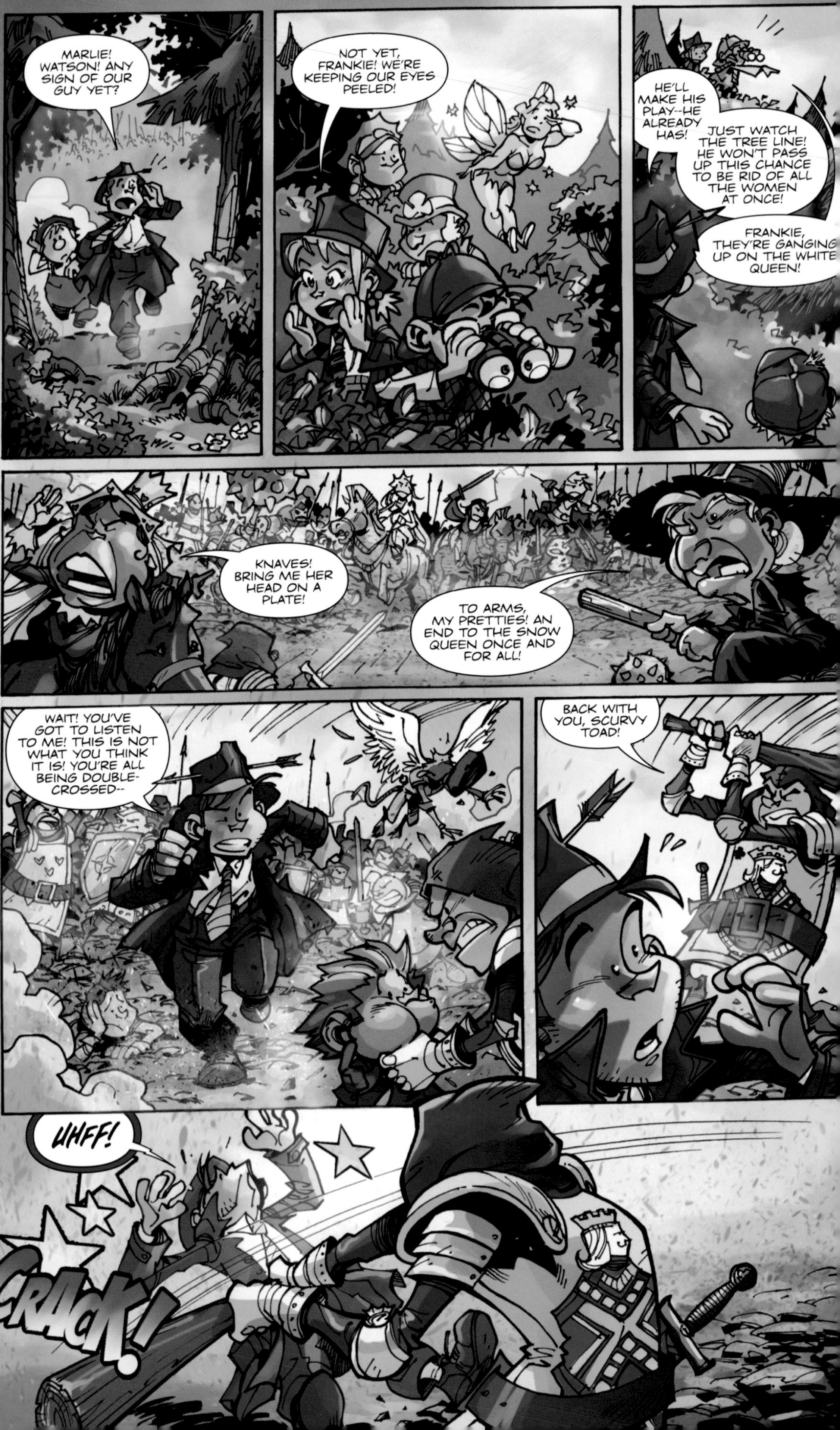
MARLIE! WATSON! ANY SIGN OF OUR GUY YET?
NOT YET, FRANKIE! WE'RE KEEPING OUR EYES PEELED!
HE'LL MAKE HIS PLAY--HE ALREADY HAS!
JUST WATCH THE TREE LINE! HE WON'T PASS UP THIS CHANCE TO BE RID OF ALL THE WOMEN AT ONCE!
FRANKIE, THEY'RE GANGING UP ON THE WHITE QUEEN!
KNAVES! BRING ME HER HEAD ON A PLATE!
TO ARMS, MY PRETTIES! AN END TO THE SNOW QUEEN ONCE AND FOR ALL!
WAIT! YOU'VE GOT TO LISTEN TO ME! THIS IS NOT WHAT YOU THINK IT IS! YOU'RE ALL BEING DOUBLE-CROSSED--
BACK WITH YOU, SCURVY TOAD!
UHFF!
CRACK!

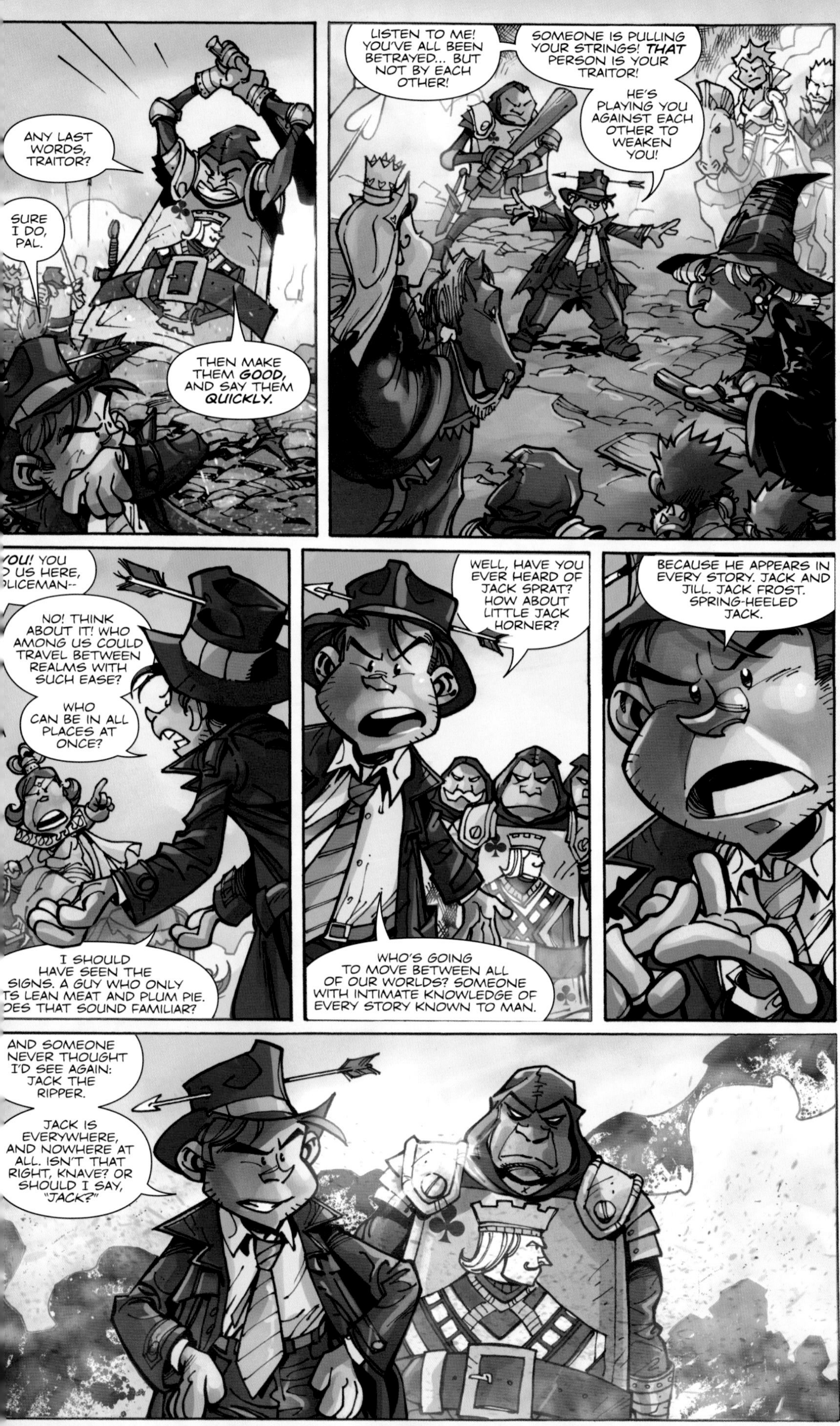

ANY LAST WORDS, TRAITOR?
SURE I DO, PAL.
THEN MAKE THEM **GOOD,** AND SAY THEM **QUICKLY.**
LISTEN TO ME! YOU'VE ALL BEEN BETRAYED... BUT NOT BY EACH OTHER!
SOMEONE IS PULLING YOUR STRINGS! ***THAT*** PERSON IS YOUR TRAITOR!
HE'S PLAYING YOU AGAINST EACH OTHER TO WEAKEN YOU!
OU! YOU
D US HERE,
LICEMAN--
NO! THINK ABOUT IT! WHO AMONG US COULD TRAVEL BETWEEN REALMS WITH SUCH EASE?
WHO CAN BE IN ALL PLACES AT ONCE?
I SHOULD HAVE SEEN THE SIGNS. A GUY WHO ONLY
TS LEAN MEAT AND PLUM PIE.
DES THAT SOUND FAMILIAR?
WELL, HAVE YOU EVER HEARD OF JACK SPRAT? HOW ABOUT LITTLE JACK HORNER?
WHO'S GOING TO MOVE BETWEEN ALL OF OUR WORLDS? SOMEONE WITH INTIMATE KNOWLEDGE OF EVERY STORY KNOWN TO MAN.
BECAUSE HE APPEARS IN EVERY STORY. JACK AND JILL. JACK FROST. SPRING-HEELED JACK.
AND SOMEONE I NEVER THOUGHT I'D SEE AGAIN: JACK THE RIPPER.
JACK IS EVERYWHERE, AND NOWHERE AT ALL. ISN'T THAT RIGHT, KNAVE? OR SHOULD I SAY, *"JACK?"*

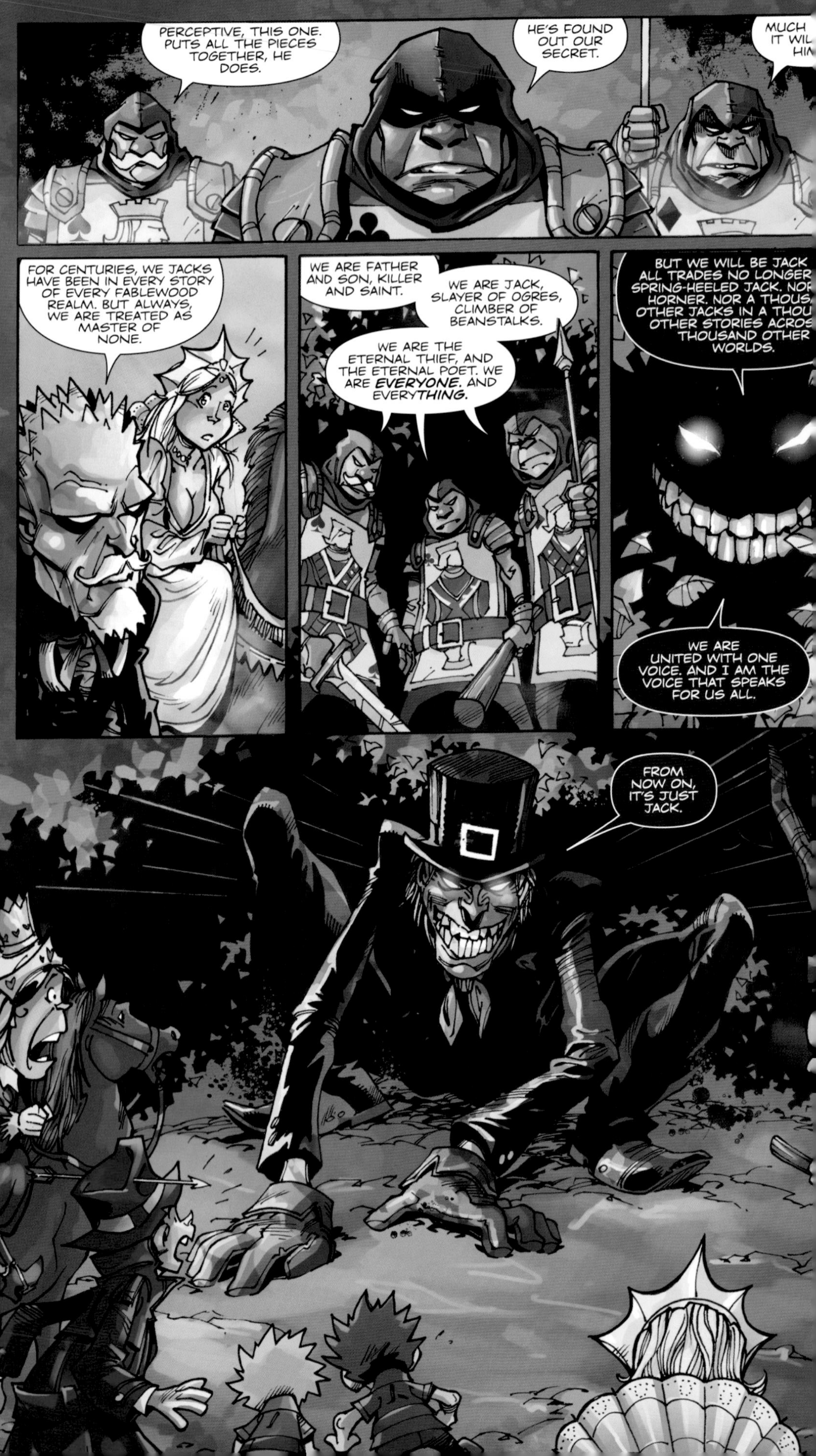
PERCEPTIVE, THIS ONE. PUTS ALL THE PIECES TOGETHER, HE DOES.
HE'S FOUND OUT OUR SECRET.
MUCH IT WIL HIM
FOR CENTURIES, WE JACKS HAVE BEEN IN EVERY STORY OF EVERY FABLEWOOD REALM. BUT ALWAYS, WE ARE TREATED AS MASTER OF NONE.
WE ARE FATHER AND SON, KILLER AND SAINT.
WE ARE JACK, SLAYER OF OGRES, CLIMBER OF BEANSTALKS.
WE ARE THE ETERNAL THIEF, AND THE ETERNAL POET. WE ARE ***EVERYONE***. AND EVERY***THING***.
BUT WE WILL BE JACK ALL TRADES NO LONGER SPRING-HEELED JACK. NOR HORNER. NOR A THOUS OTHER JACKS IN A THOU OTHER STORIES ACROS THOUSAND OTHER WORLDS.
WE ARE UNITED WITH ONE VOICE. AND I AM THE VOICE THAT SPEAKS FOR US ALL.
FROM NOW ON, IT'S JUST JACK.

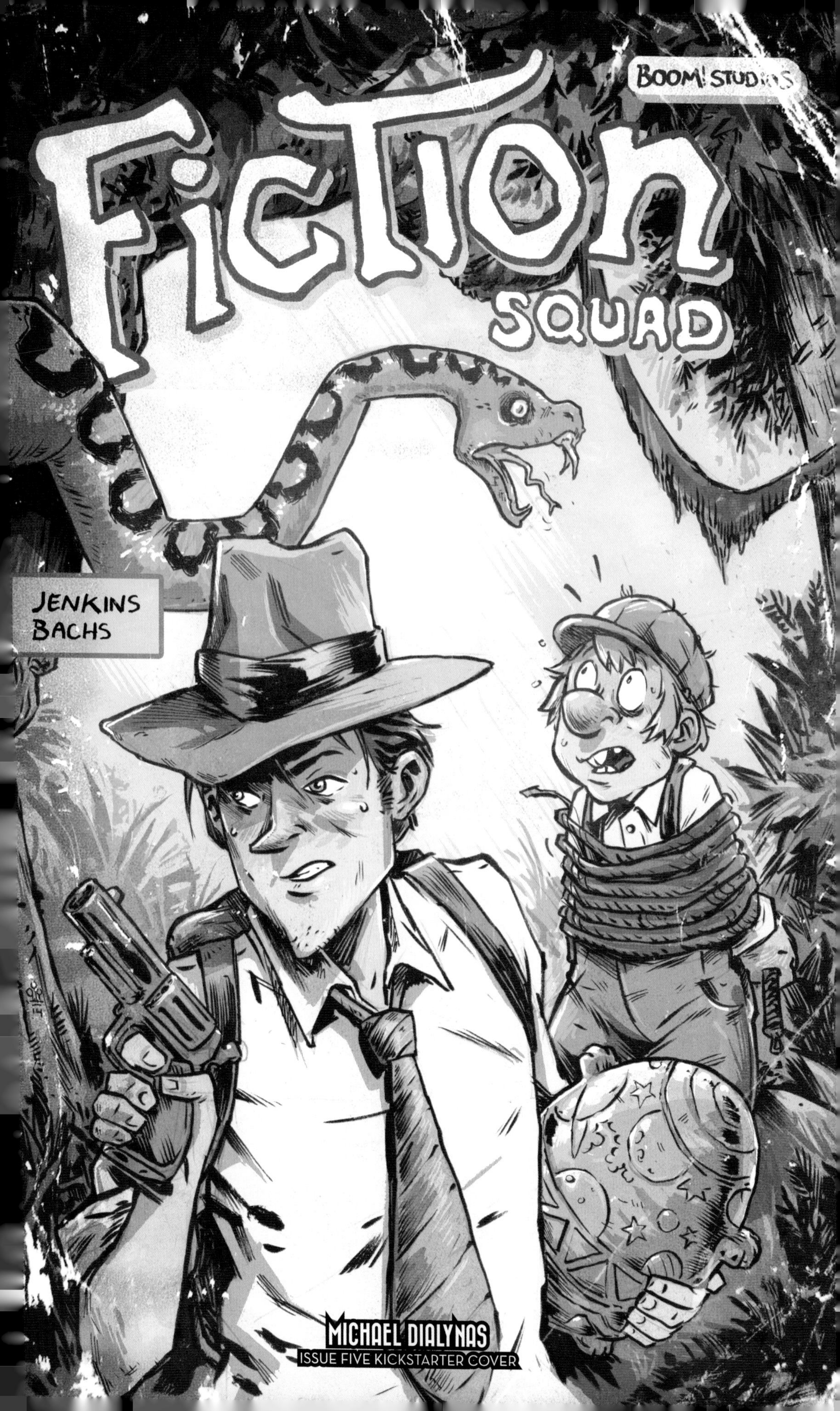
BOOM! STUDIOS
FICTION SQUAD
JENKINS
BACHS
MICHAEL DIALYNAS
ISSUE FIVE KICKSTARTER COVER

CHAPTER SIX

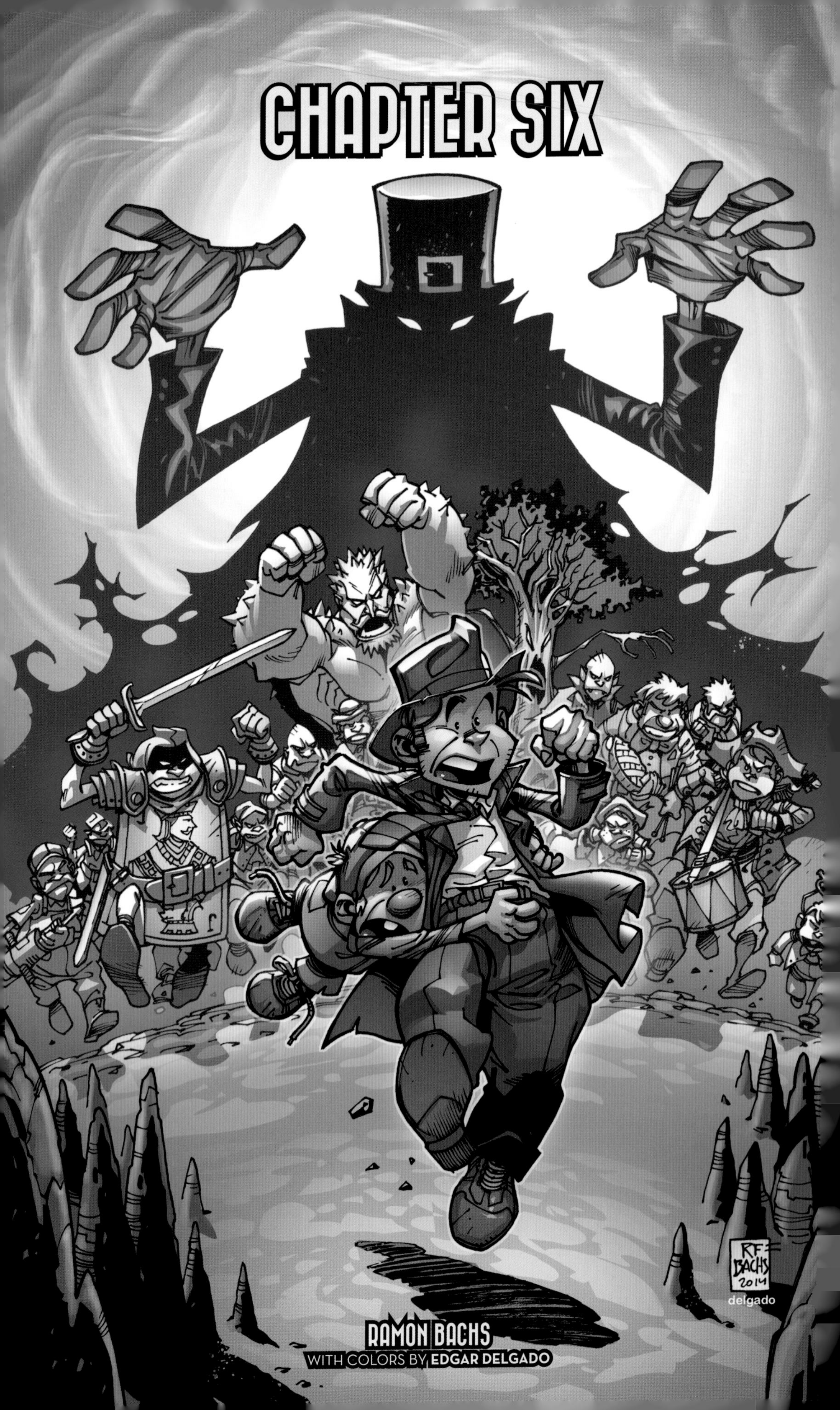
RF BACHS 2014
delgado

RAMON BACHS
WITH COLORS BY EDGAR DELGADO

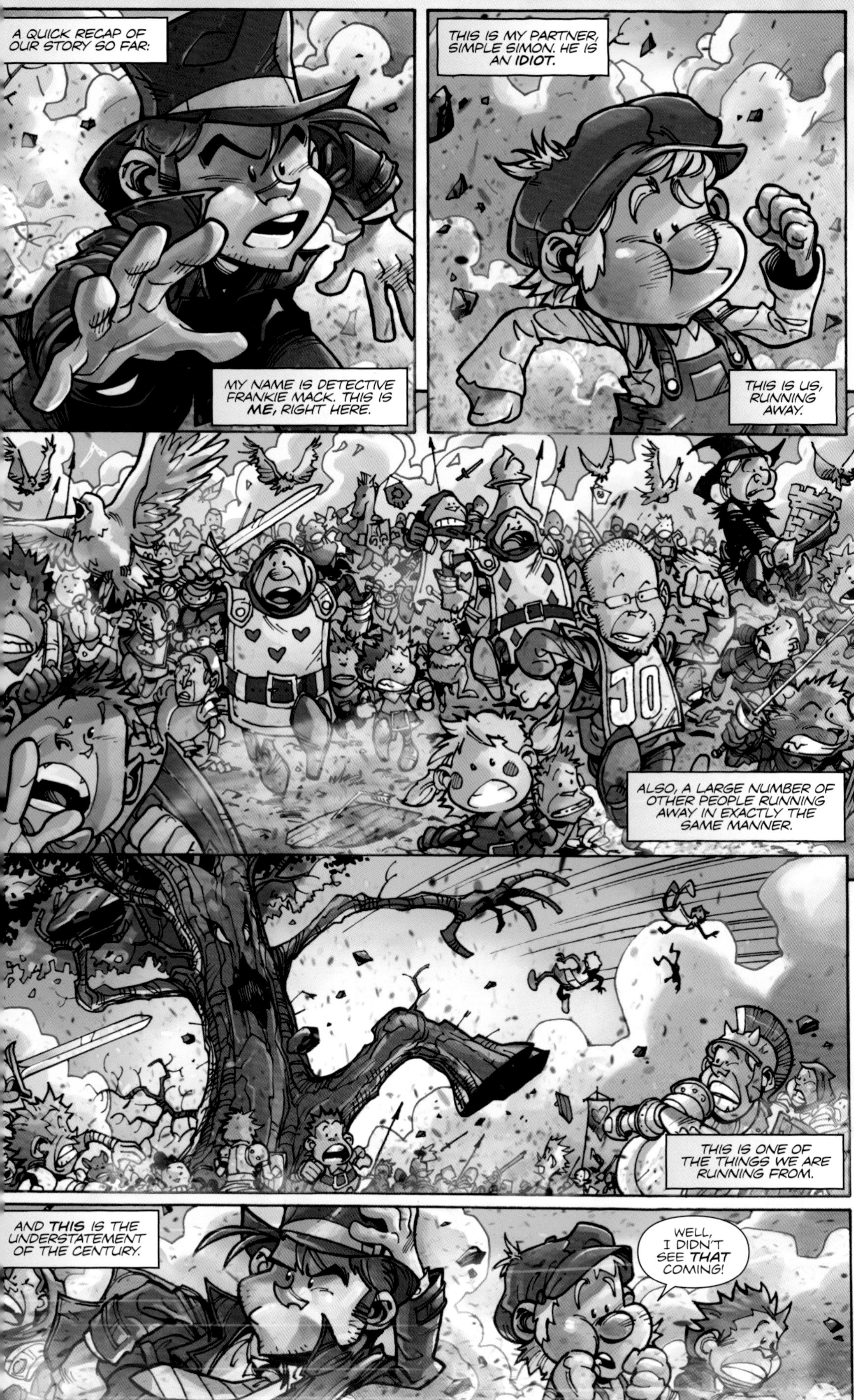

A QUICK RECAP OF OUR STORY SO FAR:
MY NAME IS DETECTIVE FRANKIE MACK. THIS IS ME, RIGHT HERE.
THIS IS MY PARTNER, SIMPLE SIMON. HE IS AN IDIOT.
THIS IS US, RUNNING AWAY.
ALSO, A LARGE NUMBER OF OTHER PEOPLE RUNNING AWAY IN EXACTLY THE SAME MANNER.
THIS IS ONE OF THE THINGS WE ARE RUNNING FROM.
AND THIS IS THE UNDERSTATEMENT OF THE CENTURY.
WELL, I DIDN'T SEE THAT COMING!

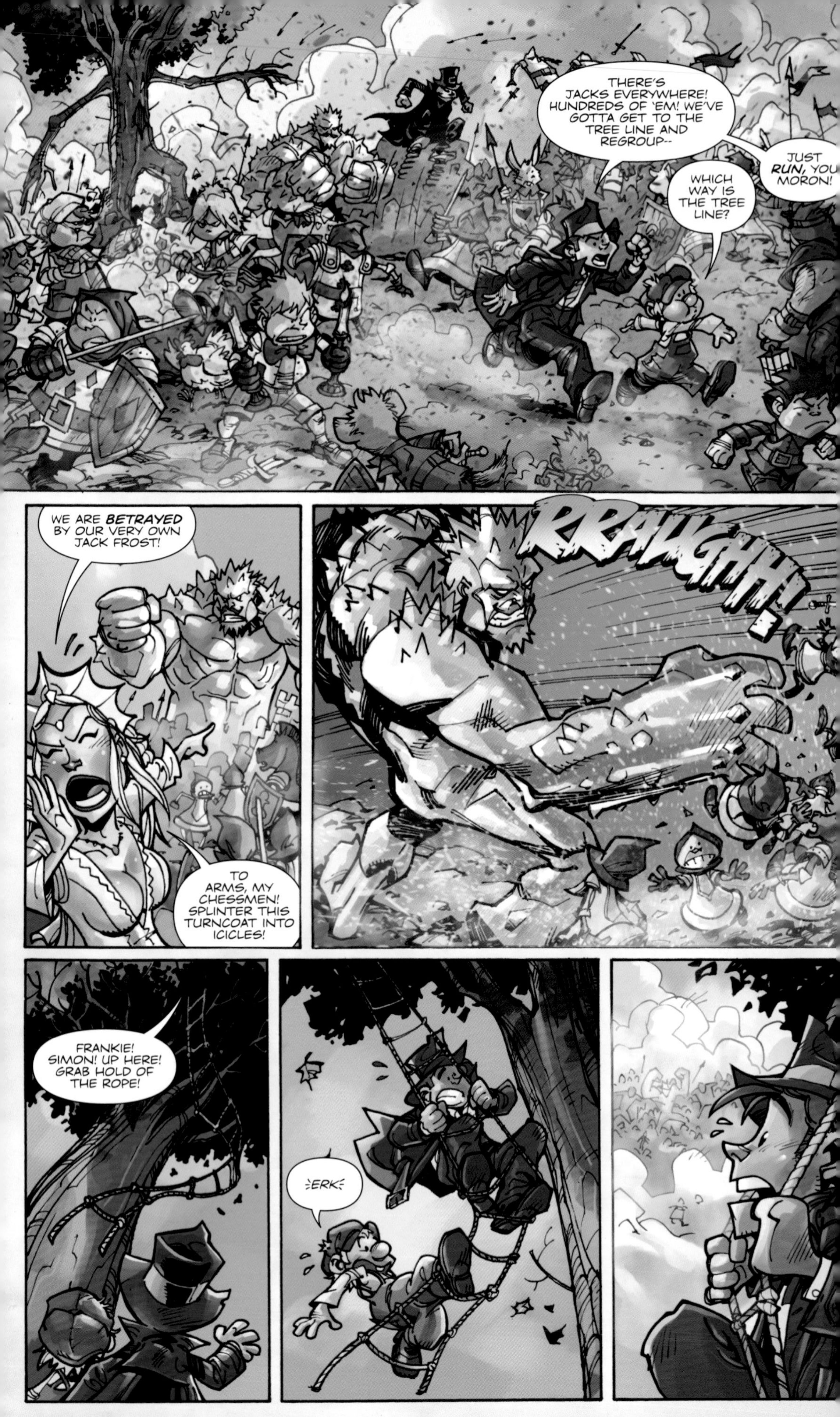
THERE'S JACKS EVERYWHERE! HUNDREDS OF 'EM! WE'VE GOTTA GET TO THE TREE LINE AND REGROUP--
WHICH WAY IS THE TREE LINE?
JUST RUN, YOU MORON!
WE ARE BETRAYED BY OUR VERY OWN JACK FROST!
TO ARMS, MY CHESSMEN! SPLINTER THIS TURNCOAT INTO ICICLES!
RRAUGH!!
FRANKIE! SIMON! UP HERE! GRAB HOLD OF THE ROPE!
ERK

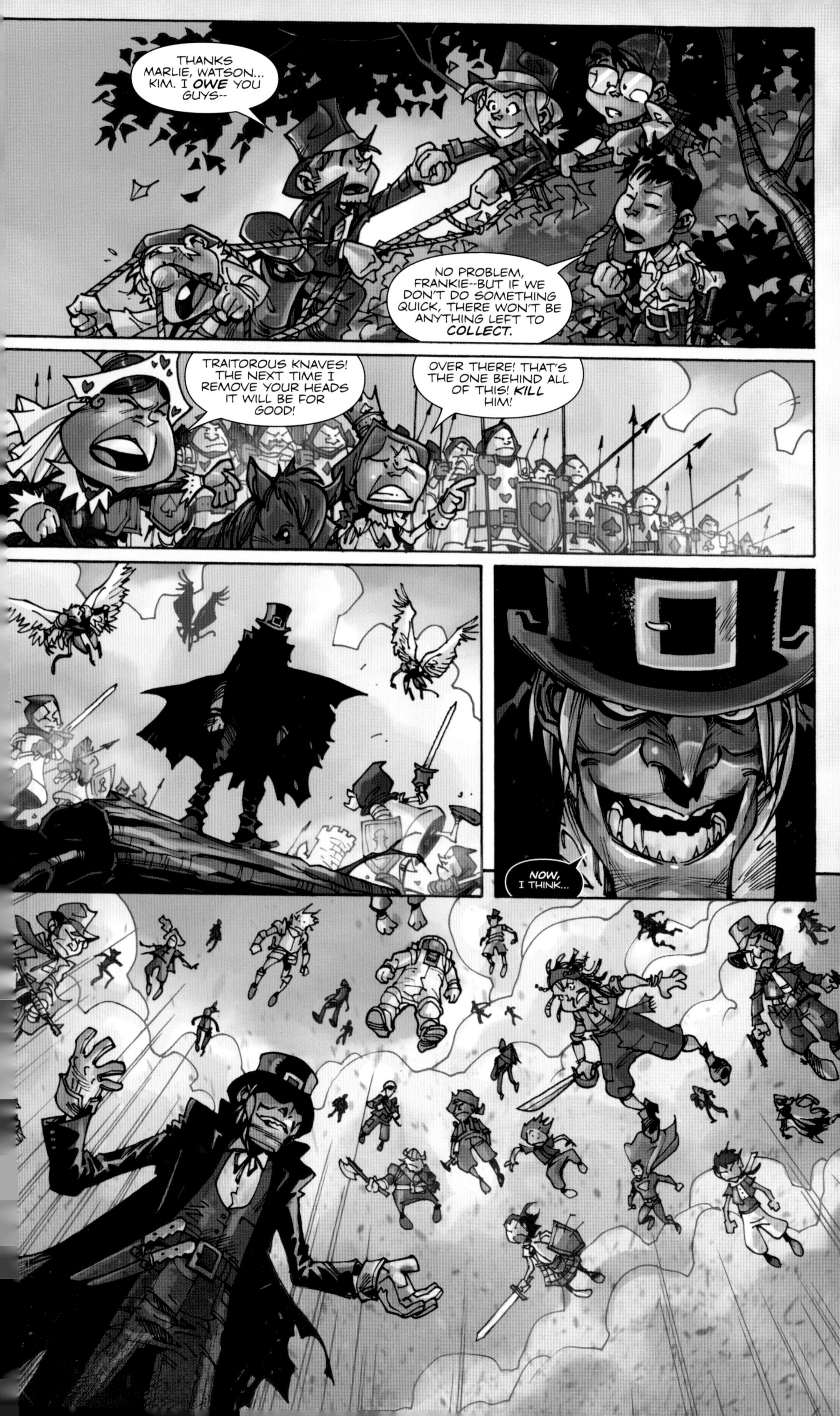
THANKS MARLIE, WATSON... KIM. I OWE YOU GUYS--
NO PROBLEM, FRANKIE--BUT IF WE DON'T DO SOMETHING QUICK, THERE WON'T BE ANYTHING LEFT TO COLLECT.
TRAITOROUS KNAVES! THE NEXT TIME I REMOVE YOUR HEADS IT WILL BE FOR GOOD!
OVER THERE! THAT'S THE ONE BEHIND ALL OF THIS! KILL HIM!
NOW, I THINK...

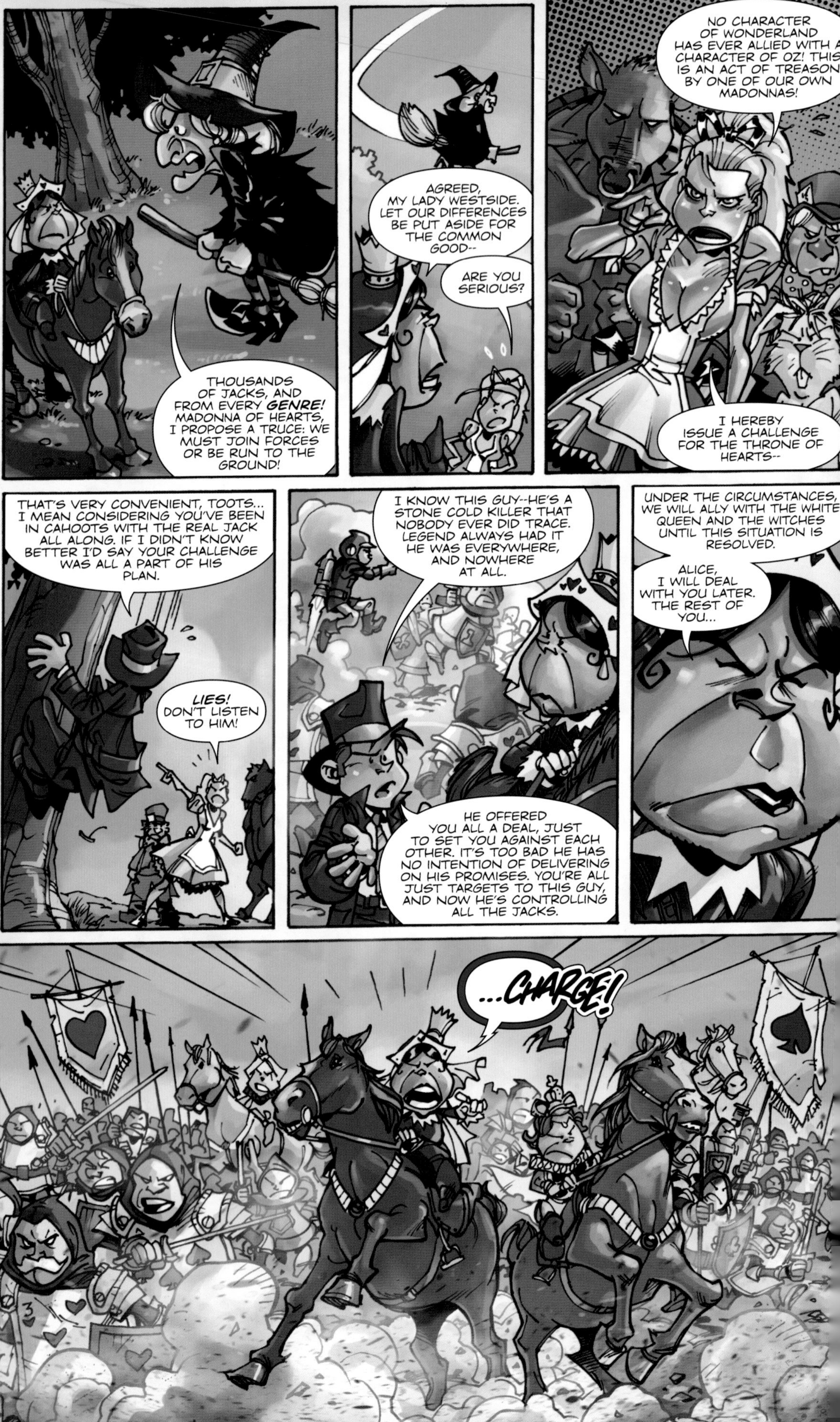
THOUSANDS OF JACKS, AND FROM EVERY GENRE! MADONNA OF HEARTS, I PROPOSE A TRUCE: WE MUST JOIN FORCES OR BE RUN TO THE GROUND!
AGREED, MY LADY WESTSIDE. LET OUR DIFFERENCES BE PUT ASIDE FOR THE COMMON GOOD--
ARE YOU SERIOUS?
NO CHARACTER OF WONDERLAND HAS EVER ALLIED WITH A CHARACTER OF OZ! THIS IS AN ACT OF TREASON BY ONE OF OUR OWN MADONNAS!
I HEREBY ISSUE A CHALLENGE FOR THE THRONE OF HEARTS--
THAT'S VERY CONVENIENT, TOOTS... I MEAN CONSIDERING YOU'VE BEEN IN CAHOOTS WITH THE REAL JACK ALL ALONG. IF I DIDN'T KNOW BETTER I'D SAY YOUR CHALLENGE WAS ALL A PART OF HIS PLAN.
LIES! DON'T LISTEN TO HIM!
I KNOW THIS GUY--HE'S A STONE COLD KILLER THAT NOBODY EVER DID TRACE. LEGEND ALWAYS HAD IT HE WAS EVERYWHERE, AND NOWHERE AT ALL.
HE OFFERED YOU ALL A DEAL, JUST TO SET YOU AGAINST EACH OTHER. IT'S TOO BAD HE HAS NO INTENTION OF DELIVERING ON HIS PROMISES. YOU'RE ALL JUST TARGETS TO THIS GUY, AND NOW HE'S CONTROLLING ALL THE JACKS.
UNDER THE CIRCUMSTANCES, WE WILL ALLY WITH THE WHITE QUEEN AND THE WITCHES UNTIL THIS SITUATION IS RESOLVED.
ALICE, I WILL DEAL WITH YOU LATER. THE REST OF YOU...
...CHARGE!

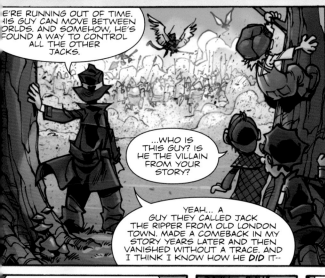

E'RE RUNNING OUT OF TIME. HIS GUY CAN MOVE BETWEEN ORLDS. AND SOMEHOW, HE'S FOUND A WAY TO CONTROL ALL THE OTHER JACKS.

...WHO IS THIS GUY? IS HE THE VILLAIN FROM YOUR STORY?

YEAH... A GUY THEY CALLED JACK THE RIPPER FROM OLD LONDON TOWN. MADE A COMEBACK IN MY STORY YEARS LATER AND THEN VANISHED WITHOUT A TRACE. AND I THINK I KNOW HOW HE *DID* IT--

--OVER *THERE!*

PARTNER, I NEED YOU TO STAY BACK HERE FOR ME, OKAY? I'M GOING TO TRY AN' BRING THIS GUY IN ONCE AN' FOR ALL.

WHAT DO YOU WANT *ME* TO DO?

I NEED A DISTRACTION. JUST BE YOURSELF--

HEY, EVERYBODY! LET'S SING A WAR SHANTY! ALL TOGETHER NOW!

"BRAVE SHIP'S CAP-TAIN... ON THE SEVEN SEAS..." ♪♪♪

ATTABOY.

WHAT ON EARTH IS THAT FOOL *DOING* OVER THERE--?

≀UHHF!≀

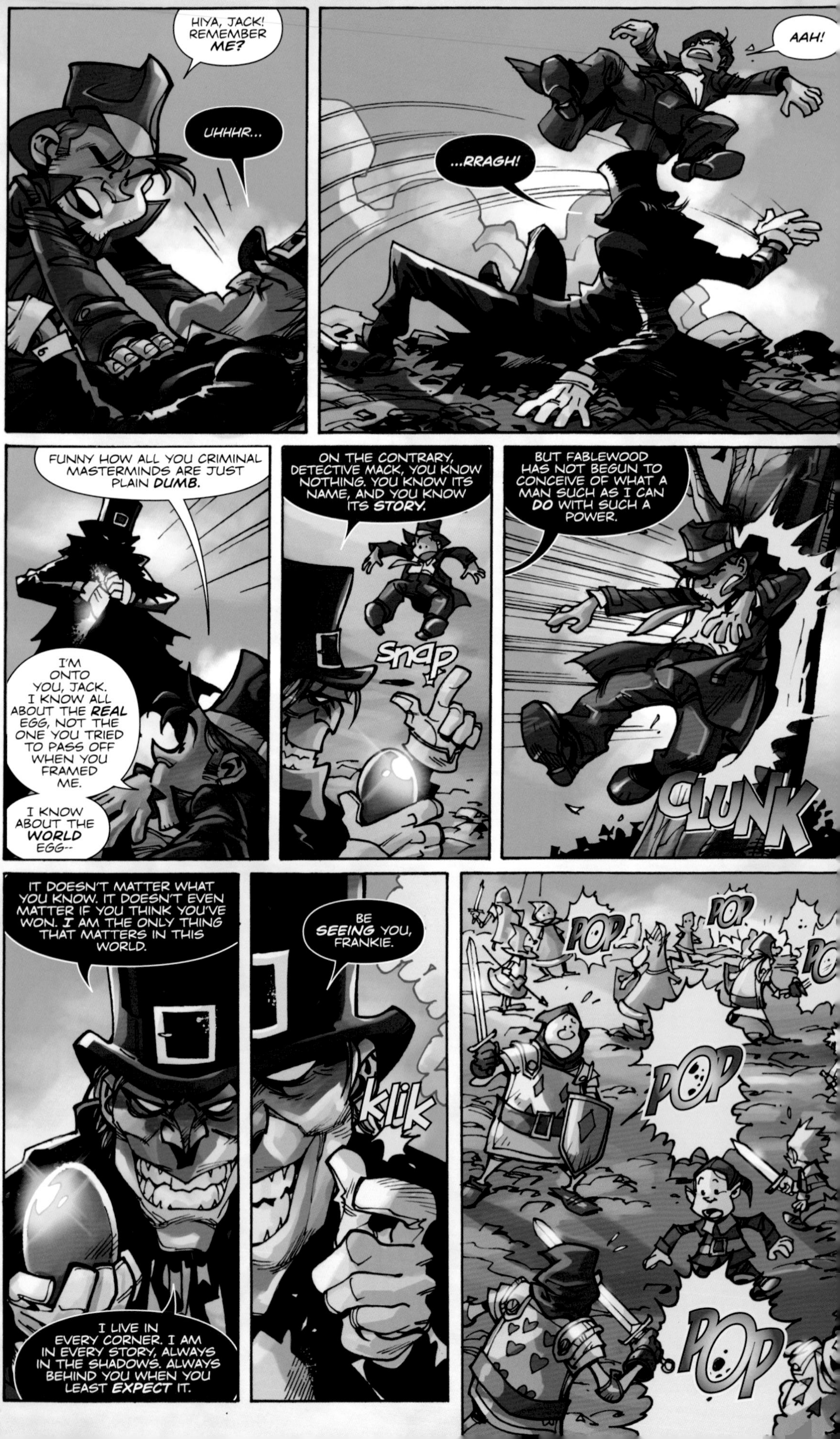
HIYA, JACK! REMEMBER ME?
UHHHR...
...RRAGH!
AAH!
FUNNY HOW ALL YOU CRIMINAL MASTERMINDS ARE JUST PLAIN DUMB.
I'M ONTO YOU, JACK. I KNOW ALL ABOUT THE REAL EGG, NOT THE ONE YOU TRIED TO PASS OFF WHEN YOU FRAMED ME.
I KNOW ABOUT THE WORLD EGG--
ON THE CONTRARY, DETECTIVE MACK, YOU KNOW NOTHING. YOU KNOW ITS NAME, AND YOU KNOW ITS STORY.
snap
BUT FABLEWOOD HAS NOT BEGUN TO CONCEIVE OF WHAT A MAN SUCH AS I CAN DO WITH SUCH A POWER.
CLUNK
IT DOESN'T MATTER WHAT YOU KNOW. IT DOESN'T EVEN MATTER IF YOU THINK YOU'VE WON. I AM THE ONLY THING THAT MATTERS IN THIS WORLD.
I LIVE IN EVERY CORNER. I AM IN EVERY STORY, ALWAYS IN THE SHADOWS. ALWAYS BEHIND YOU WHEN YOU LEAST EXPECT IT.
BE SEEING YOU, FRANKIE.
klik
POP
POP
POP
POP

WHAT HAPPENED? WHERE DID THEY GO?

I DON'T KNOW. THEY JUST DISAPPEARED.

"...AND SAIL THE SEVEN SEAS... A-PIRATING WE WILL GO...!" ♪

THEY DIDN'T JUST DISAPPEAR--

--SIMON, YOU CAN SHUT UP NOW--

OH. RIGHT, SO.

--JACK'S USING THE WORLD EGG TO RESHAPE EVENTS IN ANY WAY HE WANTS.

IT IS A GOOD THING THAT YOU HAVE DONE, DETECTIVE. A GOOD THING--

WITH RESPECT, YOUR MAJESTY, I DIDN'T DO ANYTHING. THIS GUY CAN REWRITE THE ENTIRE STORYBOOK. HE LEFT BECAUSE HE WANTED TO.

WE'LL HAVE TO ACT FAST. I'VE GOT TO FIND OUT WHERE HE TOOK ALL THE OTHER JACKS--

mmmmUUmmmmmmmmmBBBBBle

LOOK OUT ABOVE!

KRASH

KRAAAK

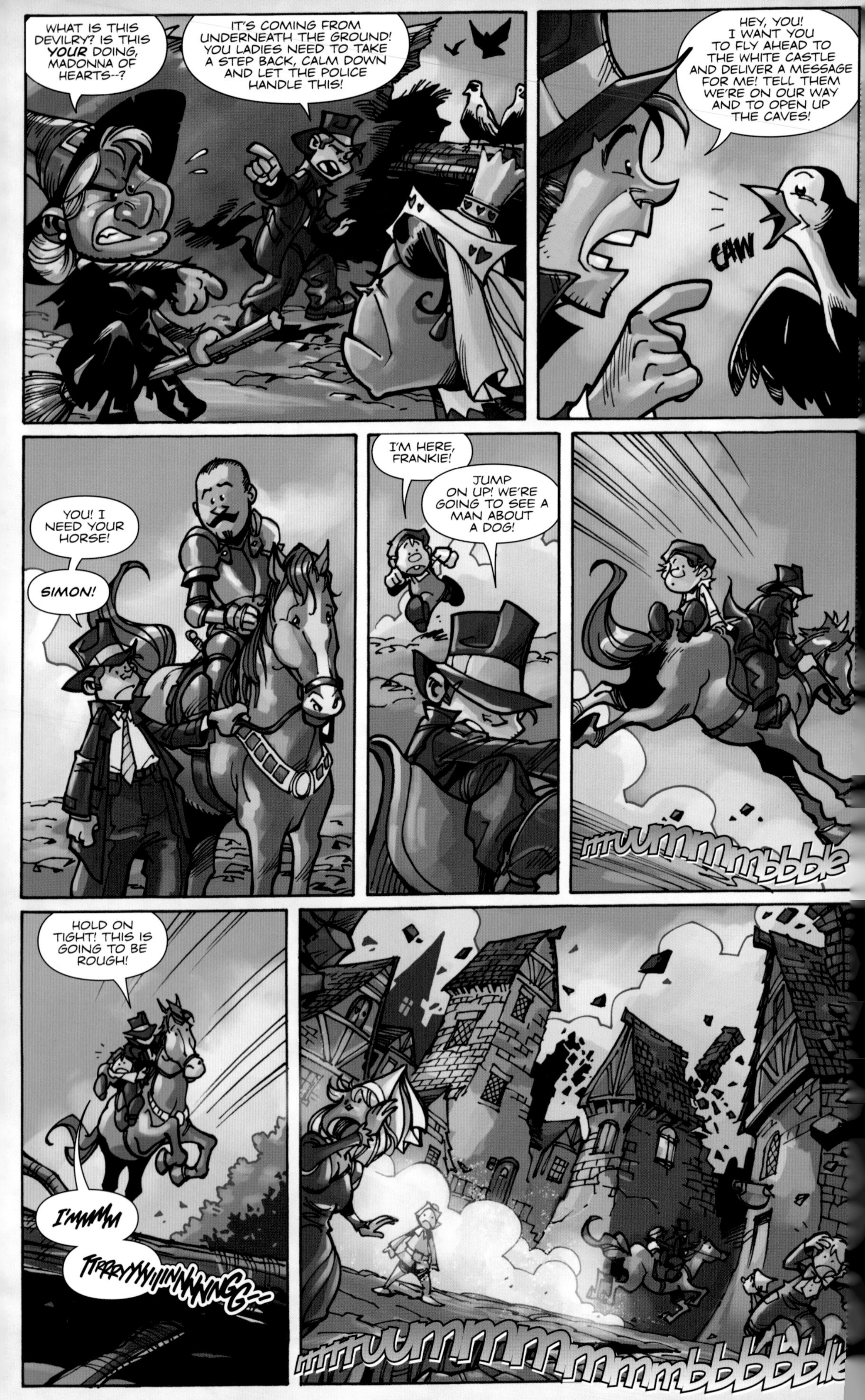
WHAT IS THIS DEVILRY? IS THIS YOUR DOING, MADONNA OF HEARTS--?
IT'S COMING FROM UNDERNEATH THE GROUND! YOU LADIES NEED TO TAKE A STEP BACK, CALM DOWN AND LET THE POLICE HANDLE THIS!
HEY, YOU! I WANT YOU TO FLY AHEAD TO THE WHITE CASTLE AND DELIVER A MESSAGE FOR ME! TELL THEM WE'RE ON OUR WAY AND TO OPEN UP THE CAVES!
CAW
YOU! I NEED YOUR HORSE!
SIMON!
I'M HERE, FRANKIE!
JUMP ON UP! WE'RE GOING TO SEE A MAN ABOUT A DOG!
rrrruummmmbbble
HOLD ON TIGHT! THIS IS GOING TO BE ROUGH!
I'MMMM
TRRRYYYIIINNNNNGG--
rrrrruummmmmmmmbbbbbble

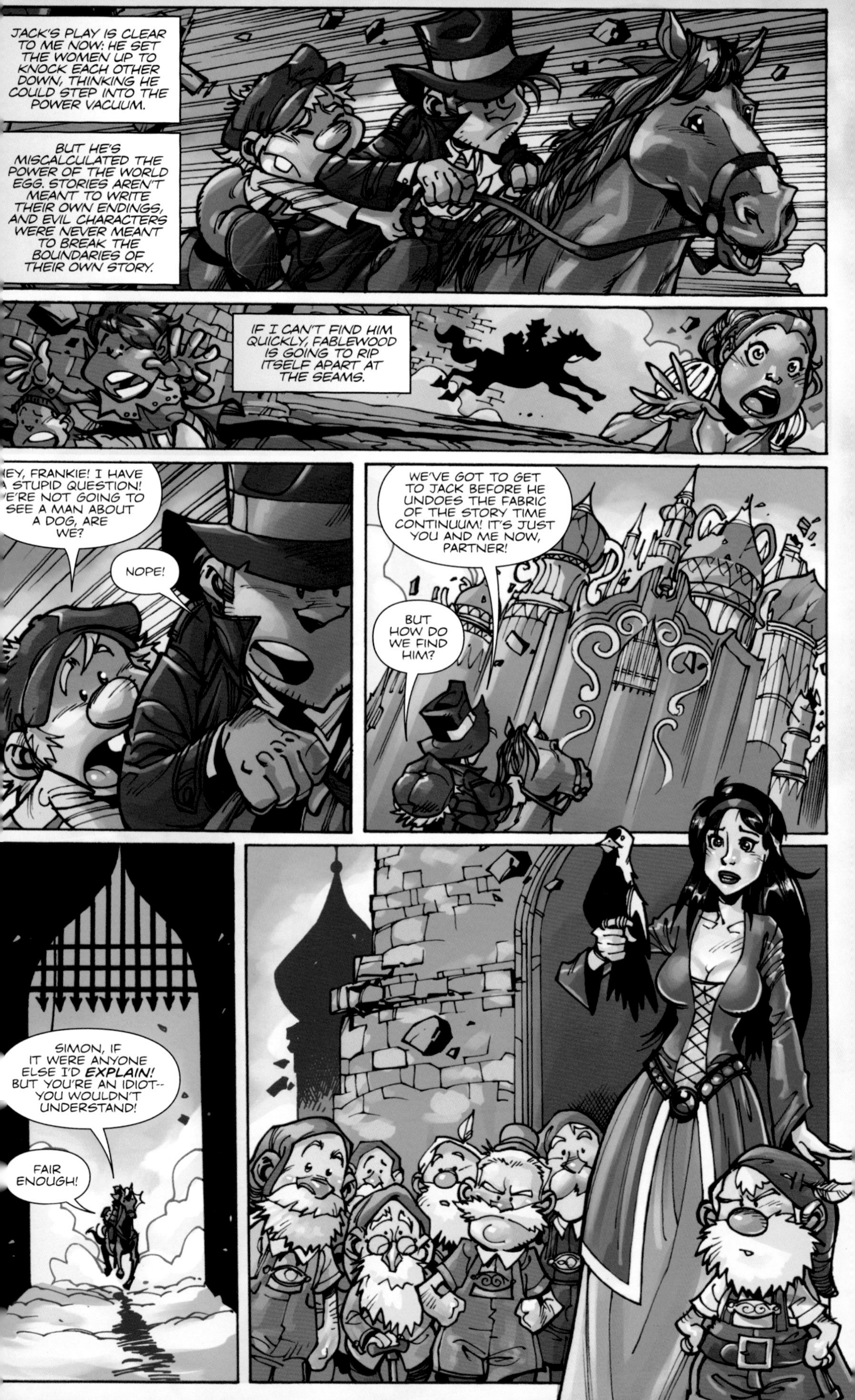

JACK'S PLAY IS CLEAR TO ME NOW: HE SET THE WOMEN UP TO KNOCK EACH OTHER DOWN, THINKING HE COULD STEP INTO THE POWER VACUUM.
BUT HE'S MISCALCULATED THE POWER OF THE WORLD EGG. STORIES AREN'T MEANT TO WRITE THEIR OWN ENDINGS, AND EVIL CHARACTERS WERE NEVER MEANT TO BREAK THE BOUNDARIES OF THEIR OWN STORY.
IF I CAN'T FIND HIM QUICKLY, FABLEWOOD IS GOING TO RIP ITSELF APART AT THE SEAMS.
EY, FRANKIE! I HAVE A STUPID QUESTION! E'RE NOT GOING TO SEE A MAN ABOUT A DOG, ARE WE?
NOPE!
WE'VE GOT TO GET TO JACK BEFORE HE UNDOES THE FABRIC OF THE STORY TIME CONTINUUM! IT'S JUST YOU AND ME NOW, PARTNER!
BUT HOW DO WE FIND HIM?
SIMON, IF IT WERE ANYONE ELSE I'D *EXPLAIN!* BUT YOU'RE AN IDIOT-- YOU WOULDN'T UNDERSTAND!
FAIR ENOUGH!

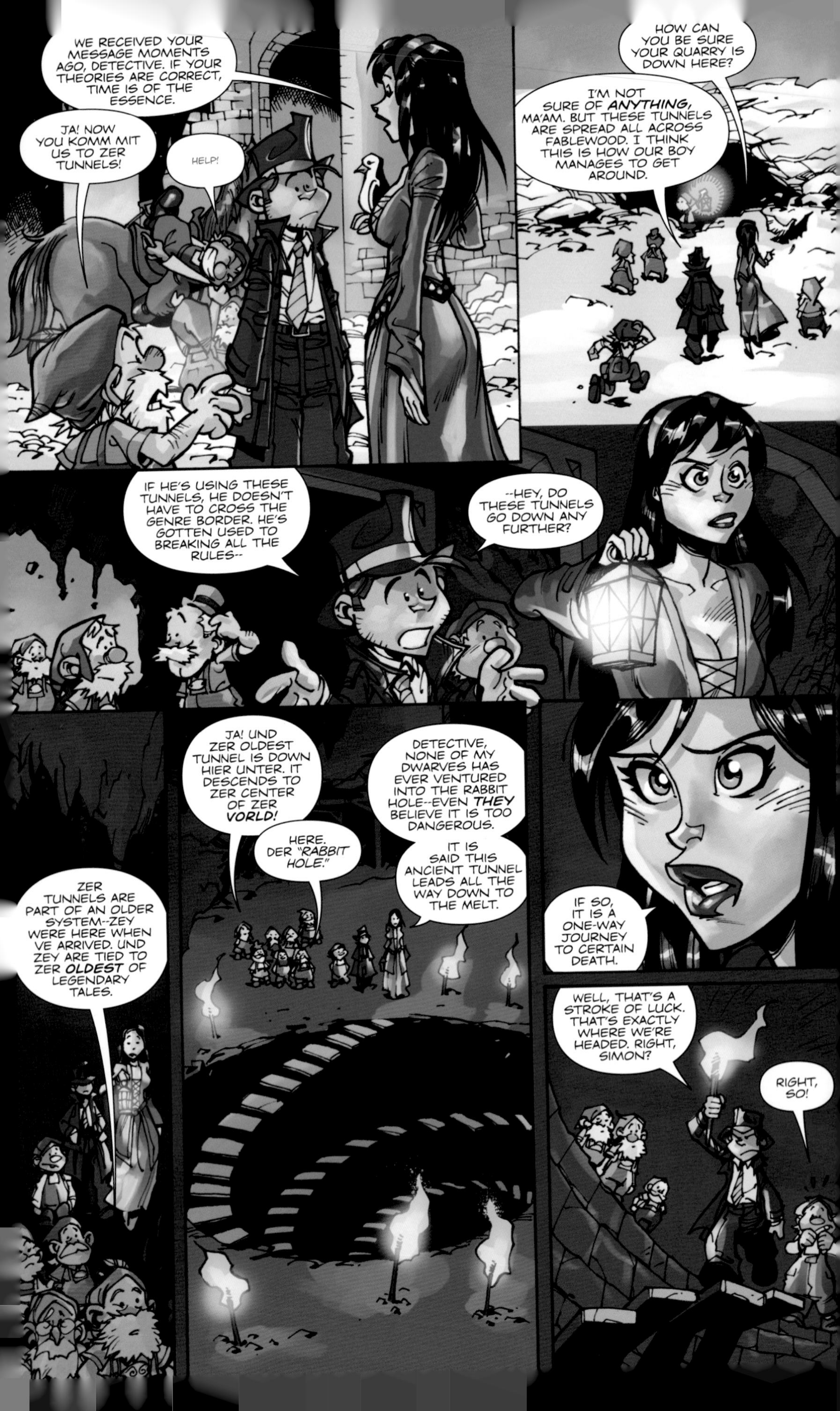

WE RECEIVED YOUR MESSAGE MOMENTS AGO, DETECTIVE. IF YOUR THEORIES ARE CORRECT, TIME IS OF THE ESSENCE.
JA! NOW YOU KOMM MIT US TO ZER TUNNELS!
HELP!
HOW CAN YOU BE SURE YOUR QUARRY IS DOWN HERE?
I'M NOT SURE OF ANYTHING, MA'AM. BUT THESE TUNNELS ARE SPREAD ALL ACROSS FABLEWOOD. I THINK THIS IS HOW OUR BOY MANAGES TO GET AROUND.
IF HE'S USING THESE TUNNELS, HE DOESN'T HAVE TO CROSS THE GENRE BORDER. HE'S GOTTEN USED TO BREAKING ALL THE RULES--
--HEY, DO THESE TUNNELS GO DOWN ANY FURTHER?
ZER TUNNELS ARE PART OF AN OLDER SYSTEM--ZEY WERE HERE WHEN VE ARRIVED. UND ZEY ARE TIED TO ZER OLDEST OF LEGENDARY TALES.
JA! UND ZER OLDEST TUNNEL IS DOWN HIER UNTER. IT DESCENDS TO ZER CENTER OF ZER VORLD!
HERE. DER "RABBIT HOLE."
DETECTIVE, NONE OF MY DWARVES HAS EVER VENTURED INTO THE RABBIT HOLE--EVEN THEY BELIEVE IT IS TOO DANGEROUS.
IT IS SAID THIS ANCIENT TUNNEL LEADS ALL THE WAY DOWN TO THE MELT.
IF SO, IT IS A ONE-WAY JOURNEY TO CERTAIN DEATH.
WELL, THAT'S A STROKE OF LUCK. THAT'S EXACTLY WHERE WE'RE HEADED. RIGHT, SIMON?
RIGHT, SO!

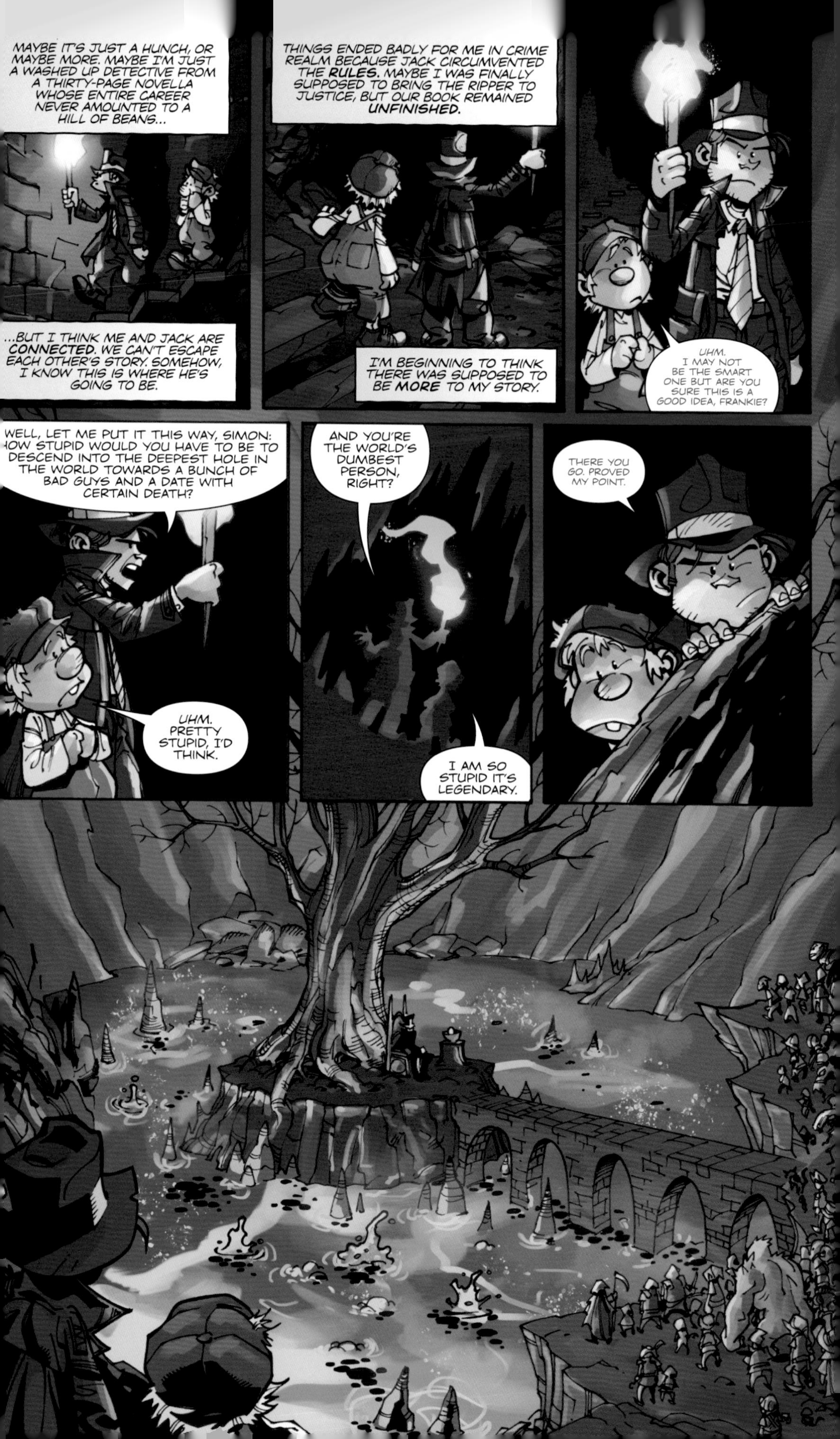

MAYBE IT'S JUST A HUNCH, OR MAYBE MORE. MAYBE I'M JUST A WASHED UP DETECTIVE FROM A THIRTY-PAGE NOVELLA WHOSE ENTIRE CAREER NEVER AMOUNTED TO A HILL OF BEANS...
...BUT I THINK ME AND JACK ARE CONNECTED. WE CAN'T ESCAPE EACH OTHER'S STORY. SOMEHOW, I KNOW THIS IS WHERE HE'S GOING TO BE.
THINGS ENDED BADLY FOR ME IN CRIME REALM BECAUSE JACK CIRCUMVENTED THE RULES. MAYBE I WAS FINALLY SUPPOSED TO BRING THE RIPPER TO JUSTICE, BUT OUR BOOK REMAINED UNFINISHED.
I'M BEGINNING TO THINK THERE WAS SUPPOSED TO BE MORE TO MY STORY.
UHM. I MAY NOT BE THE SMART ONE BUT ARE YOU SURE THIS IS A GOOD IDEA, FRANKIE?
WELL, LET ME PUT IT THIS WAY, SIMON: HOW STUPID WOULD YOU HAVE TO BE TO DESCEND INTO THE DEEPEST HOLE IN THE WORLD TOWARDS A BUNCH OF BAD GUYS AND A DATE WITH CERTAIN DEATH?
UHM. PRETTY STUPID, I'D THINK.
AND YOU'RE THE WORLD'S DUMBEST PERSON, RIGHT?
I AM SO STUPID IT'S LEGENDARY.
THERE YOU GO. PROVED MY POINT.

THERE MUST BE MILLIONS OF THEM. OUR GUY'S OVER ACROSS THE FAR SIDE OF THAT BRIDGE, SEE?

THAT'S A BIG TREE.

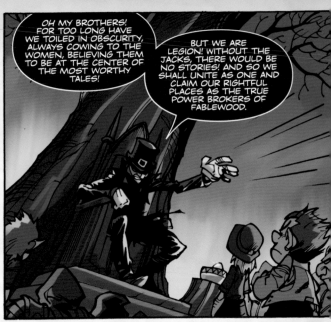

OH MY BROTHERS! FOR TOO LONG HAVE WE TOILED IN OBSCURITY, ALWAYS COWING TO THE WOMEN, BELIEVING THEM TO BE AT THE CENTER OF THE MOST WORTHY TALES!

BUT WE ARE LEGION! WITHOUT THE JACKS, THERE WOULD BE NO STORIES! AND SO WE SHALL UNITE AS ONE AND CLAIM OUR RIGHTFUL PLACES AS THE TRUE POWER BROKERS OF FABLEWOOD.

I MIGHT BE DUMBER THAN A PLANK, BUT HE'S MORE THAN TWICE AS HALF-MENTAL AS THE BOTH OF US.

THAT'S THE FIRST SENSIBLE THING YOU'VE SAID ALL DAY--

--BINGO!

THIS, OH MY BROTHERS, IS THE WORLD EGG, FALLEN FROM THE TREE OF LIFE. IT IS AN ORIGINAL LEGEND THAT WILL GRANT US THE POWER TO ALTER OUR TALES.

IN EVERY STORY, THERE WILL NOW BE A JACK. AND IN EVERY STORY, JACK SHALL NOW PREVAIL.

WYAAAAHHHH!

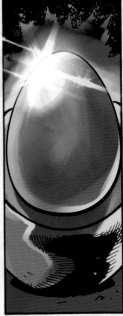

CRAZIER THAN A BANDERSNATCH.

WE'VE GOT TO BRING THIS GUY IN.

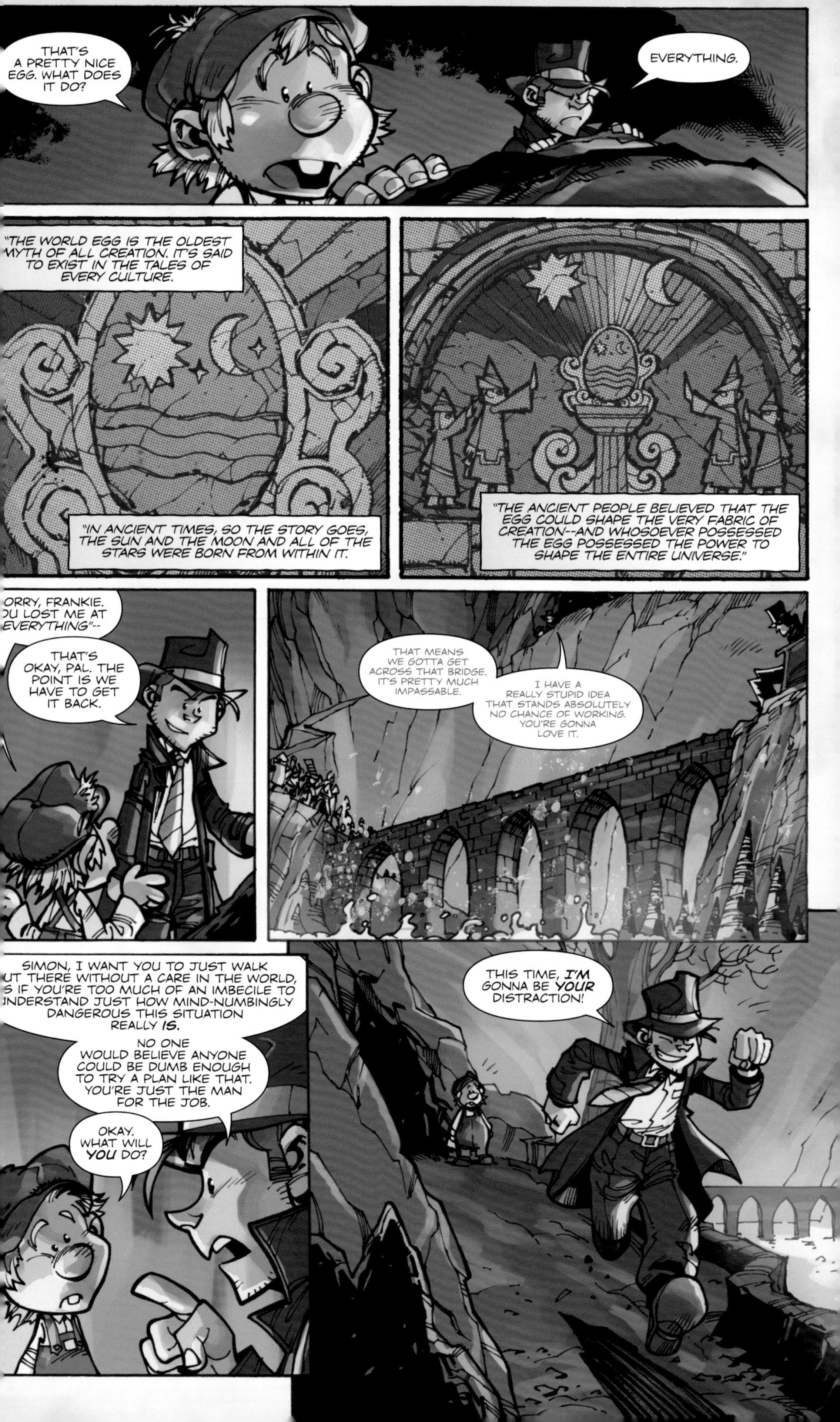
THAT'S A PRETTY NICE EGG. WHAT DOES IT DO?
EVERYTHING.
"THE WORLD EGG IS THE OLDEST MYTH OF ALL CREATION. IT'S SAID TO EXIST IN THE TALES OF EVERY CULTURE.
"IN ANCIENT TIMES, SO THE STORY GOES, THE SUN AND THE MOON AND ALL OF THE STARS WERE BORN FROM WITHIN IT.
"THE ANCIENT PEOPLE BELIEVED THAT THE EGG COULD SHAPE THE VERY FABRIC OF CREATION--AND WHOSOEVER POSSESSED THE EGG POSSESSED THE POWER TO SHAPE THE ENTIRE UNIVERSE."
ORRY, FRANKIE. OU LOST ME AT "EVERYTHING"--
THAT'S OKAY, PAL. THE POINT IS WE HAVE TO GET IT BACK.
THAT MEANS WE GOTTA GET ACROSS THAT BRIDGE. IT'S PRETTY MUCH IMPASSABLE.
I HAVE A REALLY STUPID IDEA THAT STANDS ABSOLUTELY NO CHANCE OF WORKING. YOU'RE GONNA LOVE IT.
SIMON, I WANT YOU TO JUST WALK UT THERE WITHOUT A CARE IN THE WORLD, S IF YOU'RE TOO MUCH OF AN IMBECILE TO UNDERSTAND JUST HOW MIND-NUMBINGLY DANGEROUS THIS SITUATION REALLY IS.
NO ONE WOULD BELIEVE ANYONE COULD BE DUMB ENOUGH TO TRY A PLAN LIKE THAT. YOU'RE JUST THE MAN FOR THE JOB.
OKAY. WHAT WILL YOU DO?
THIS TIME, I'M GONNA BE YOUR DISTRACTION!

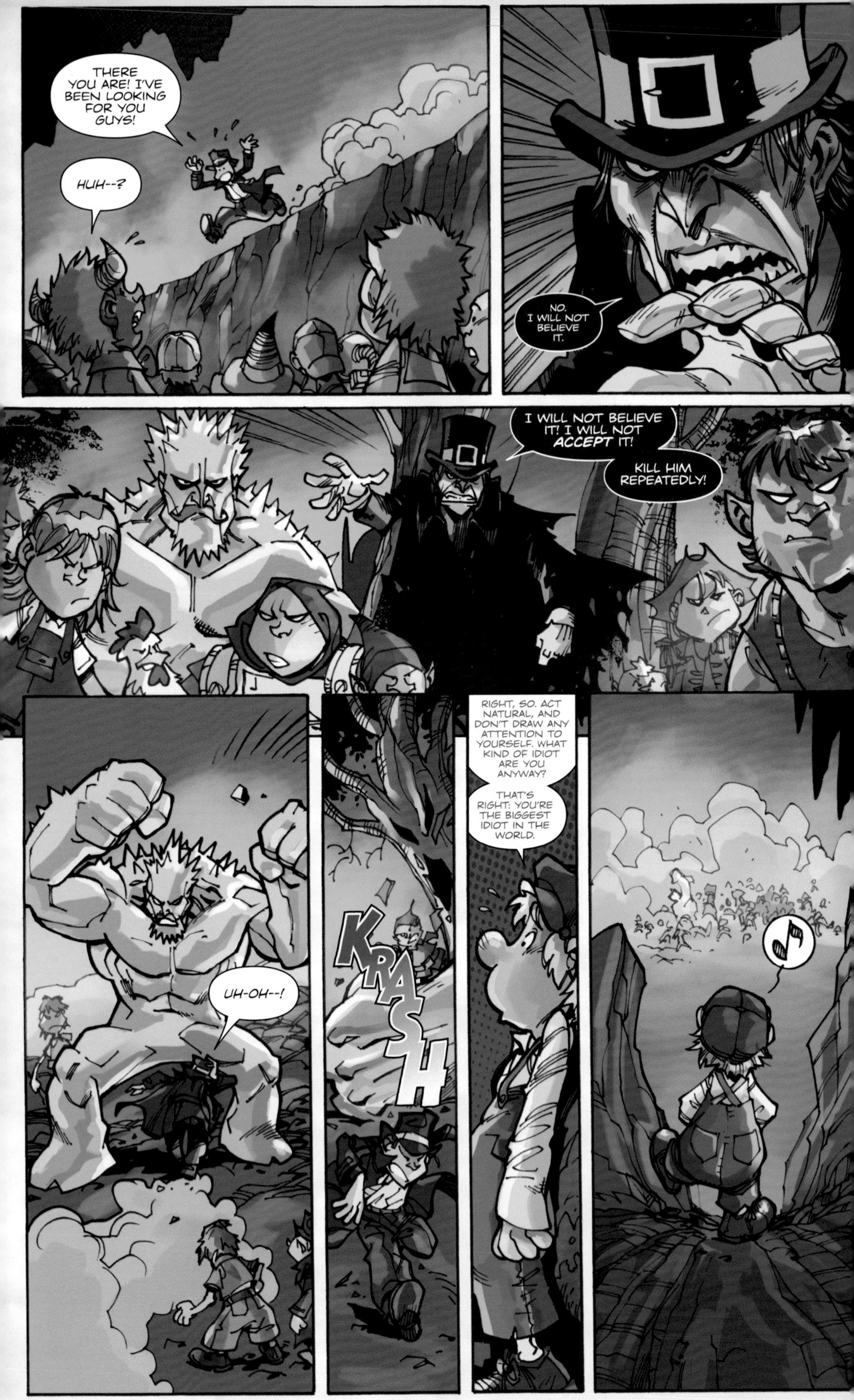
THERE YOU ARE! I'VE BEEN LOOKING FOR YOU GUYS!
HUH--?
NO. I WILL NOT BELIEVE IT.
I WILL NOT BELIEVE IT! I WILL NOT *ACCEPT* IT!
KILL HIM REPEATEDLY!
UH-OH--!
KRASH
RIGHT, SO. ACT NATURAL, AND DON'T DRAW ANY ATTENTION TO YOURSELF. WHAT KIND OF IDIOT ARE YOU ANYWAY?
THAT'S RIGHT: YOU'RE THE BIGGEST IDIOT IN THE WORLD.

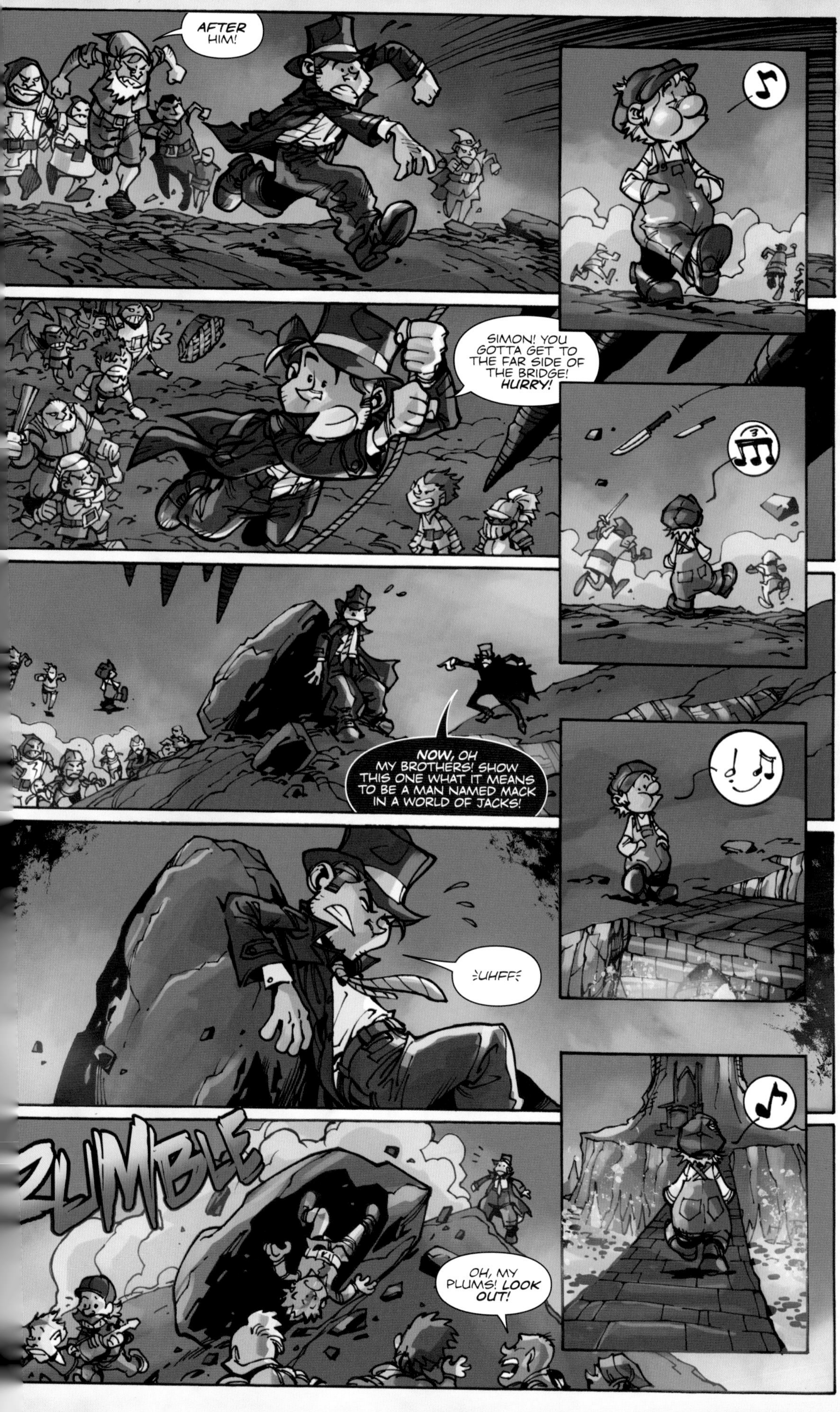
AFTER HIM!
SIMON! YOU GOTTA GET TO THE FAR SIDE OF THE BRIDGE! HURRY!
NOW, OH MY BROTHERS! SHOW THIS ONE WHAT IT MEANS TO BE A MAN NAMED MACK IN A WORLD OF JACKS!
UHFF
ZLUMBLE
OH, MY PLUMS! LOOK OUT!

BRING YOUR SPADE--WE GOTTA GET OVER THERE! COME ON!
HELLO, LADS! NICE DAY FOR A KILLING, EH?
WHO WAS THAT IDIOT?
I DUNNO. MUST BE A NEW GUY.
AA-AHH!
JUST A FEW MOMENTS MORE, DETECTIVE. THIS IS WHERE YOUR STORY ABRUPTLY ENDS.
HEY, FRANKIE!
IS IT THIS ONE?

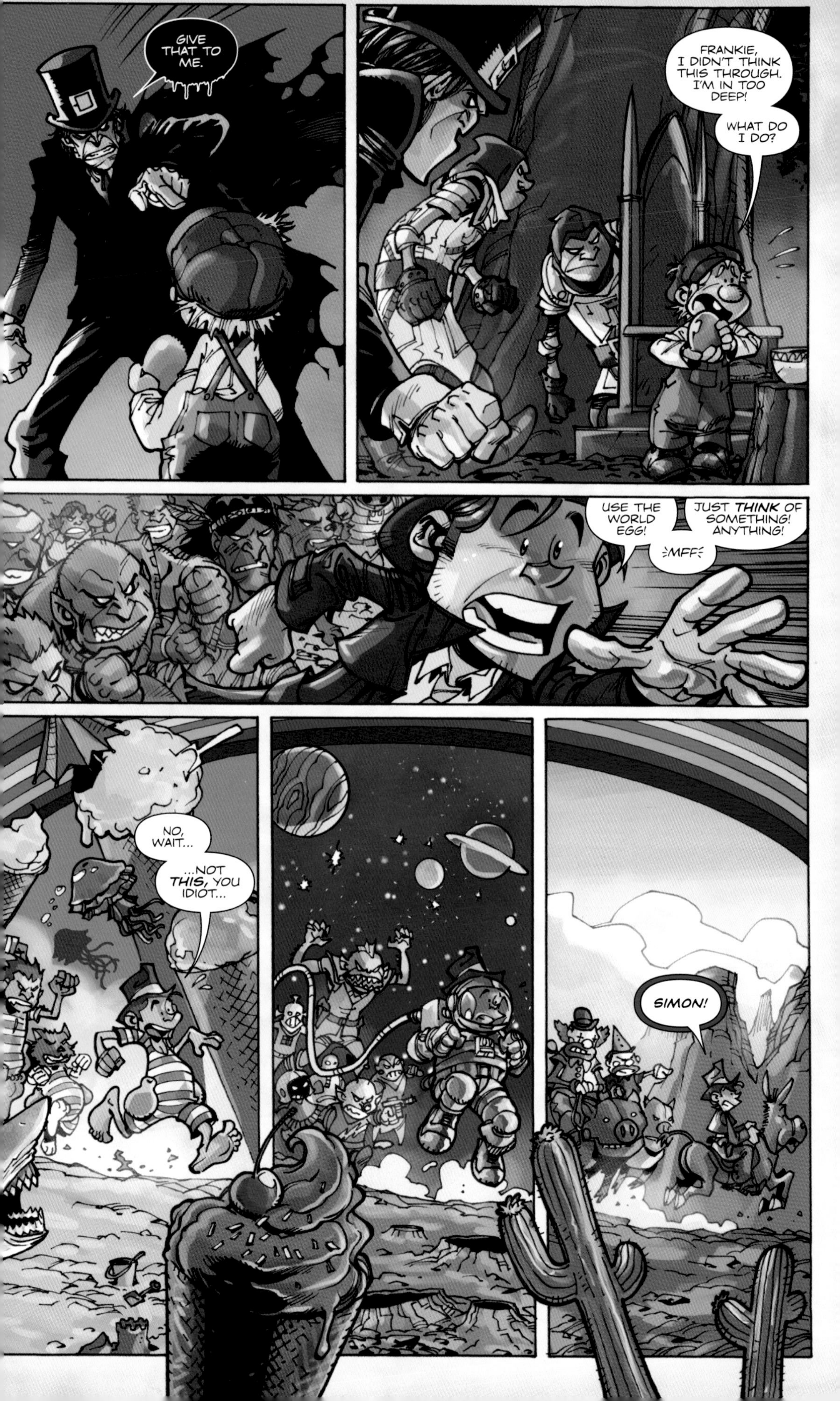
GIVE THAT TO ME.
FRANKIE, I DIDN'T THINK THIS THROUGH. I'M IN TOO DEEP!
WHAT DO I DO?
USE THE WORLD EGG!
JUST THINK OF SOMETHING! ANYTHING!
MFF
NO, WAIT...
...NOT THIS, YOU IDIOT...
SIMON!

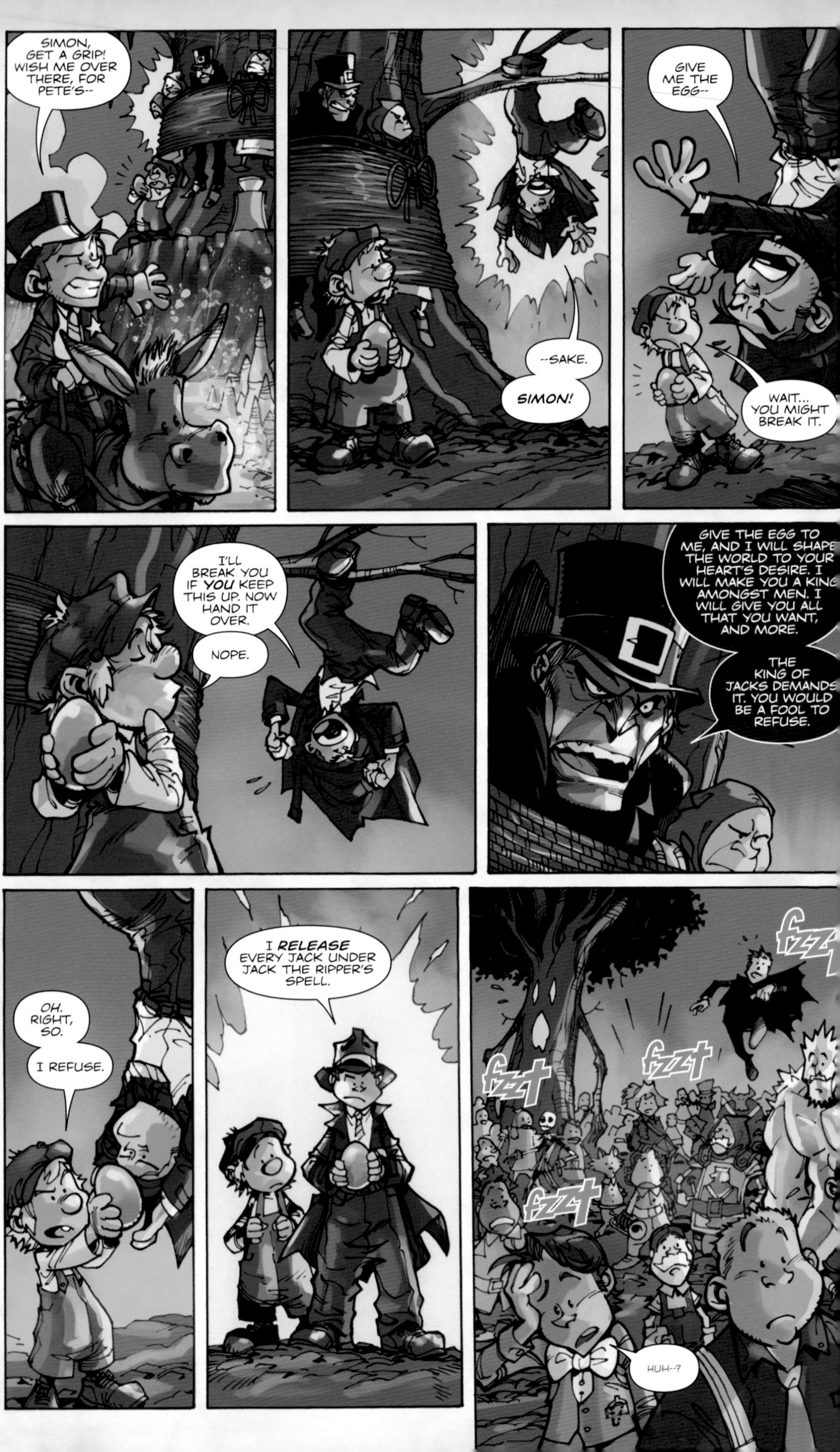
SIMON, GET A GRIP! WISH ME OVER THERE, FOR PETE'S--
--SAKE.
SIMON!
GIVE ME THE EGG--
WAIT... YOU MIGHT BREAK IT.
I'LL BREAK YOU IF YOU KEEP THIS UP. NOW HAND IT OVER.
NOPE.
GIVE THE EGG TO ME, AND I WILL SHAPE THE WORLD TO YOUR HEART'S DESIRE. I WILL MAKE YOU A KING AMONGST MEN. I WILL GIVE YOU ALL THAT YOU WANT, AND MORE.
THE KING OF JACKS DEMANDS IT. YOU WOULD BE A FOOL TO REFUSE.
OH. RIGHT, SO.
I REFUSE.
I RELEASE EVERY JACK UNDER JACK THE RIPPER'S SPELL.
fzzt
fzzt
fzzt
fzzt
HUH--?

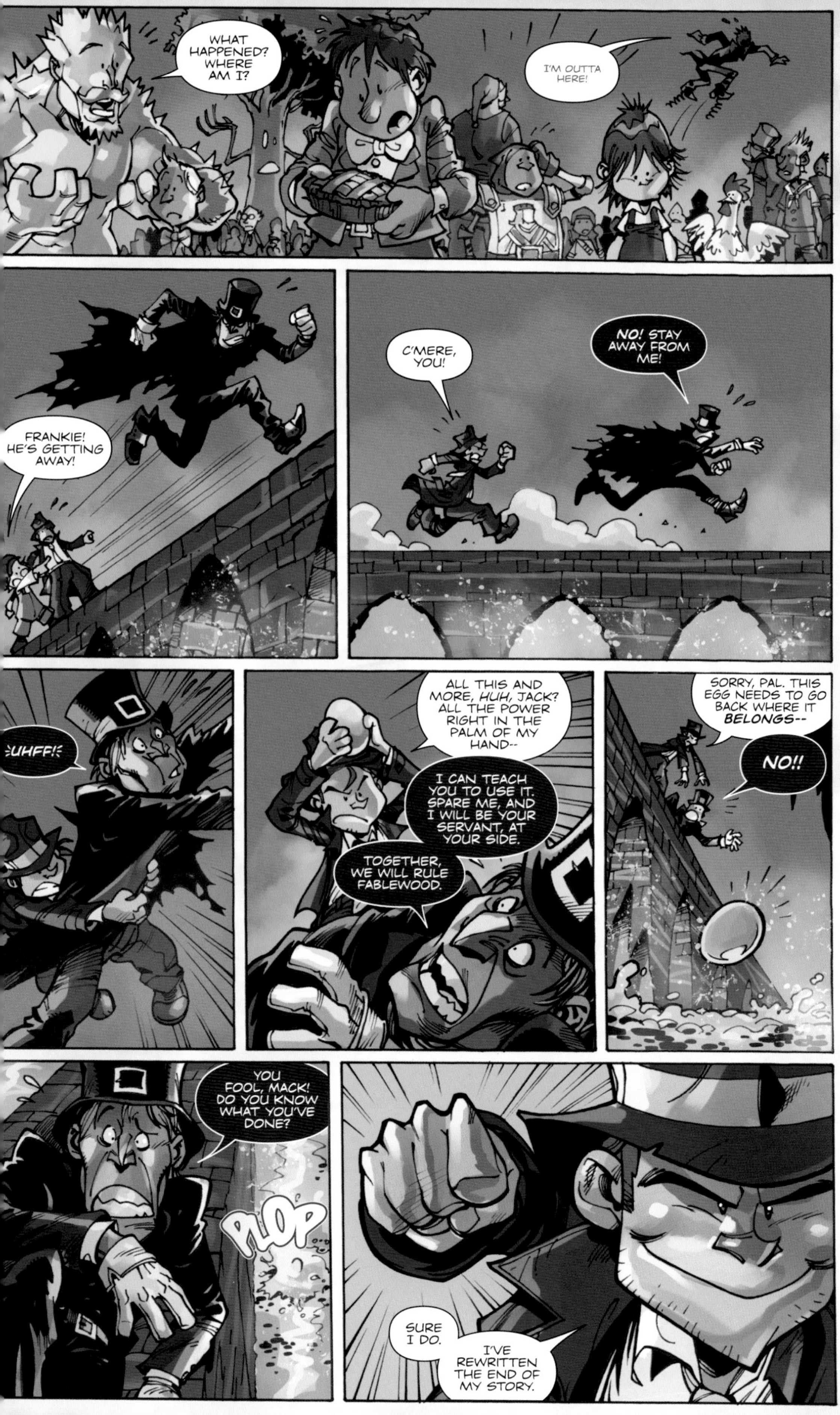
WHAT HAPPENED? WHERE AM I?
I'M OUTTA HERE!
FRANKIE! HE'S GETTING AWAY!
C'MERE, YOU!
NO! STAY AWAY FROM ME!
UHFF!
ALL THIS AND MORE, HUH, JACK? ALL THE POWER RIGHT IN THE PALM OF MY HAND--
I CAN TEACH YOU TO USE IT. SPARE ME, AND I WILL BE YOUR SERVANT, AT YOUR SIDE.
TOGETHER, WE WILL RULE FABLEWOOD.
SORRY, PAL. THIS EGG NEEDS TO GO BACK WHERE IT BELONGS--
NO!!
YOU FOOL, MACK! DO YOU KNOW WHAT YOU'VE DONE?
PLOP
SURE I DO.
I'VE REWRITTEN THE END OF MY STORY.

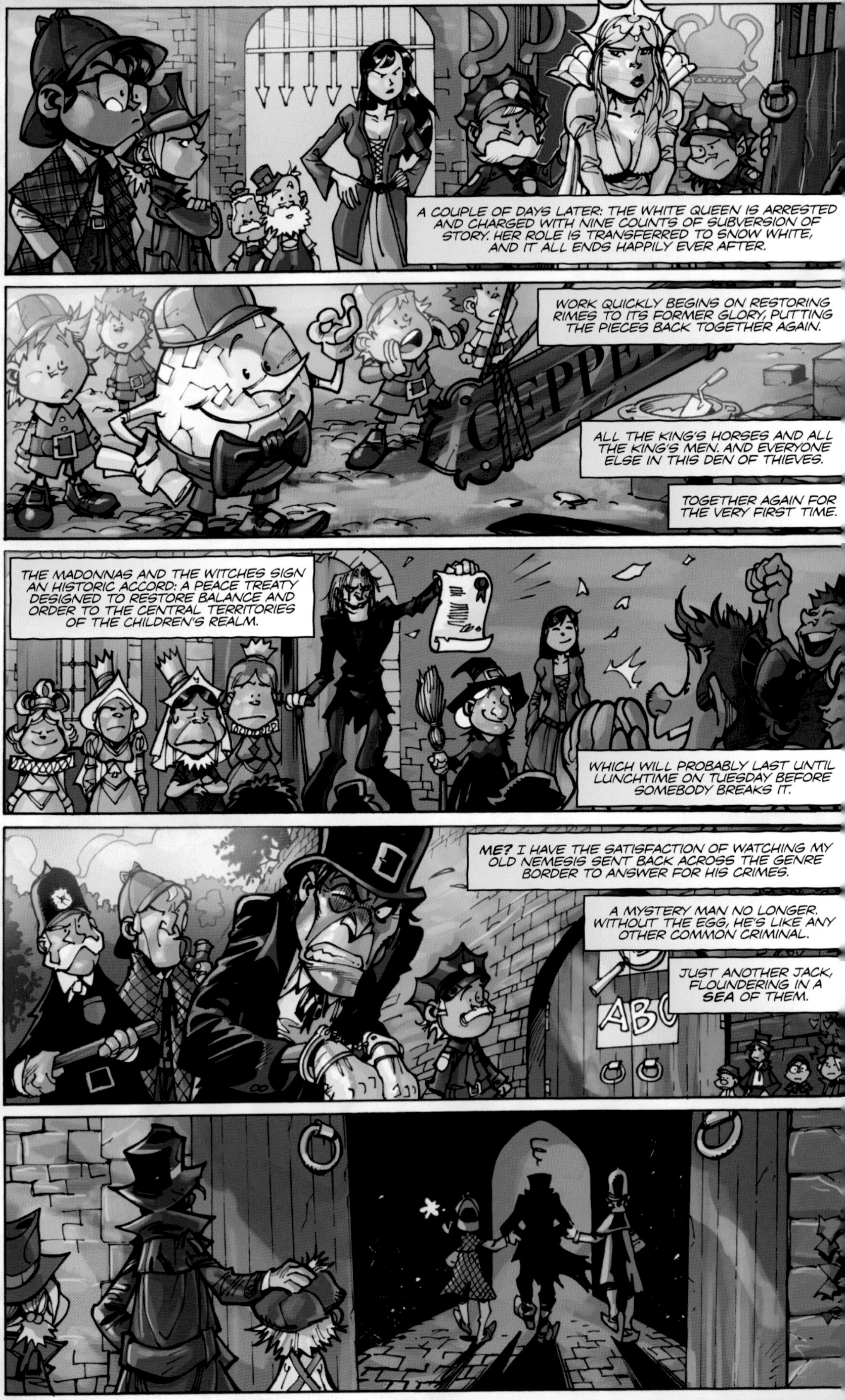
A COUPLE OF DAYS LATER: THE WHITE QUEEN IS ARRESTED AND CHARGED WITH NINE COUNTS OF SUBVERSION OF STORY. HER ROLE IS TRANSFERRED TO SNOW WHITE, AND IT ALL ENDS HAPPILY EVER AFTER.
WORK QUICKLY BEGINS ON RESTORING RIMES TO ITS FORMER GLORY, PUTTING THE PIECES BACK TOGETHER AGAIN.
GEPPE
ALL THE KING'S HORSES AND ALL THE KING'S MEN. AND EVERYONE ELSE IN THIS DEN OF THIEVES.
TOGETHER AGAIN FOR THE VERY FIRST TIME.
THE MADONNAS AND THE WITCHES SIGN AN HISTORIC ACCORD: A PEACE TREATY DESIGNED TO RESTORE BALANCE AND ORDER TO THE CENTRAL TERRITORIES OF THE CHILDREN'S REALM.
WHICH WILL PROBABLY LAST UNTIL LUNCHTIME ON TUESDAY BEFORE SOMEBODY BREAKS IT.
ME? I HAVE THE SATISFACTION OF WATCHING MY OLD NEMESIS SENT BACK ACROSS THE GENRE BORDER TO ANSWER FOR HIS CRIMES.
A MYSTERY MAN NO LONGER. WITHOUT THE EGG, HE'S LIKE ANY OTHER COMMON CRIMINAL.
JUST ANOTHER JACK, FLOUNDERING IN A SEA OF THEM.
ABC

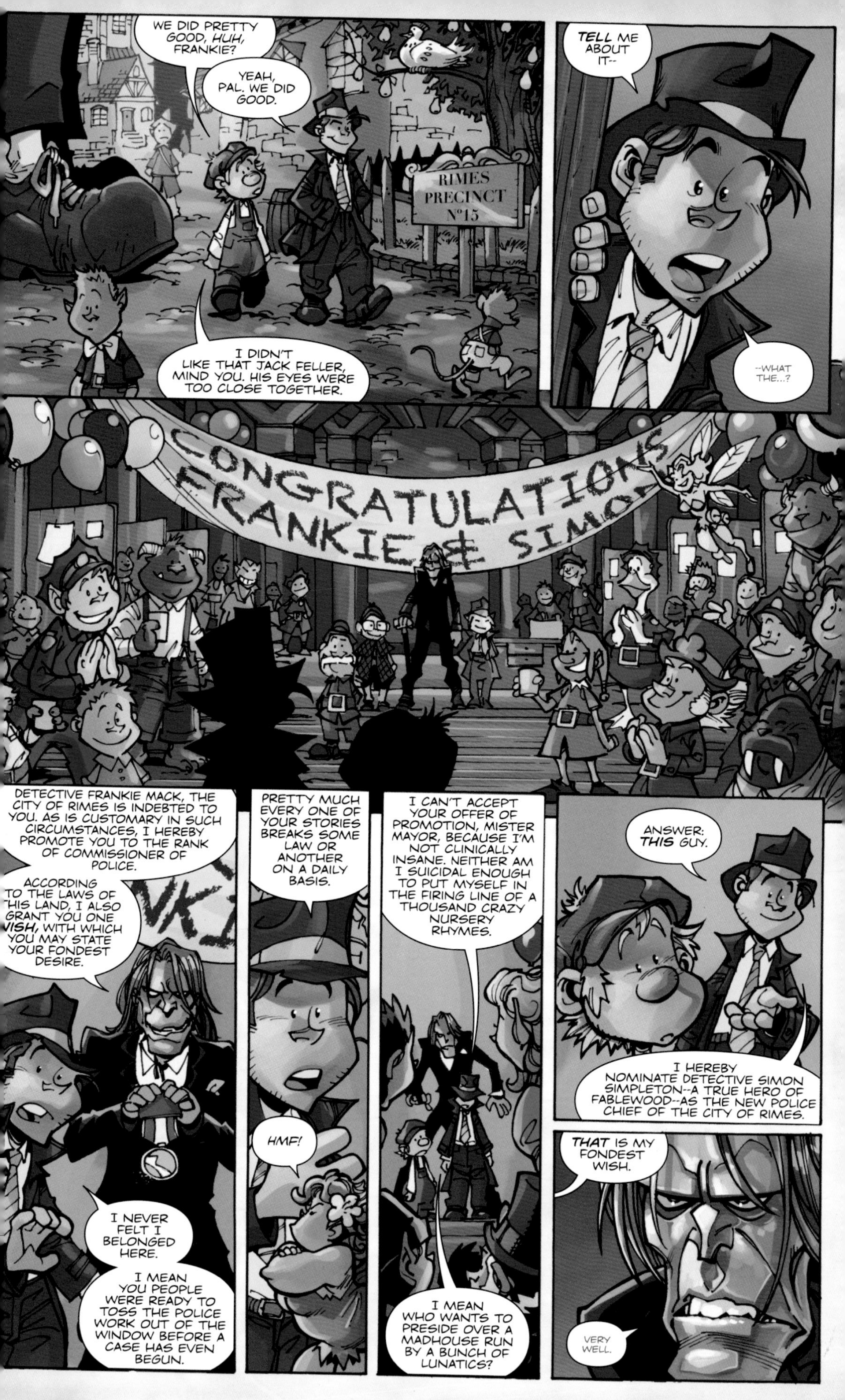

WE DID PRETTY GOOD, HUH, FRANKIE?
YEAH, PAL. WE DID GOOD.
RIMES PRECINCT Nº15
I DIDN'T LIKE THAT JACK FELLER, MIND YOU. HIS EYES WERE TOO CLOSE TOGETHER.
TELL ME ABOUT IT--
--WHAT THE...?
CONGRATULATIONS FRANKIE & SIMO
DETECTIVE FRANKIE MACK, THE CITY OF RIMES IS INDEBTED TO YOU. AS IS CUSTOMARY IN SUCH CIRCUMSTANCES, I HEREBY PROMOTE YOU TO THE RANK OF COMMISSIONER OF POLICE.
ACCORDING TO THE LAWS OF THIS LAND, I ALSO GRANT YOU ONE WISH, WITH WHICH YOU MAY STATE YOUR FONDEST DESIRE.
I NEVER FELT I BELONGED HERE.
I MEAN YOU PEOPLE WERE READY TO TOSS THE POLICE WORK OUT OF THE WINDOW BEFORE A CASE HAS EVEN BEGUN.
PRETTY MUCH EVERY ONE OF YOUR STORIES BREAKS SOME LAW OR ANOTHER ON A DAILY BASIS.
HMF!
I CAN'T ACCEPT YOUR OFFER OF PROMOTION, MISTER MAYOR, BECAUSE I'M NOT CLINICALLY INSANE. NEITHER AM I SUICIDAL ENOUGH TO PUT MYSELF IN THE FIRING LINE OF A THOUSAND CRAZY NURSERY RHYMES.
I MEAN WHO WANTS TO PRESIDE OVER A MADHOUSE RUN BY A BUNCH OF LUNATICS?
ANSWER: THIS GUY.
I HEREBY NOMINATE DETECTIVE SIMON SIMPLETON--A TRUE HERO OF FABLEWOOD--AS THE NEW POLICE CHIEF OF THE CITY OF RIMES.
THAT IS MY FONDEST WISH.
VERY WELL.

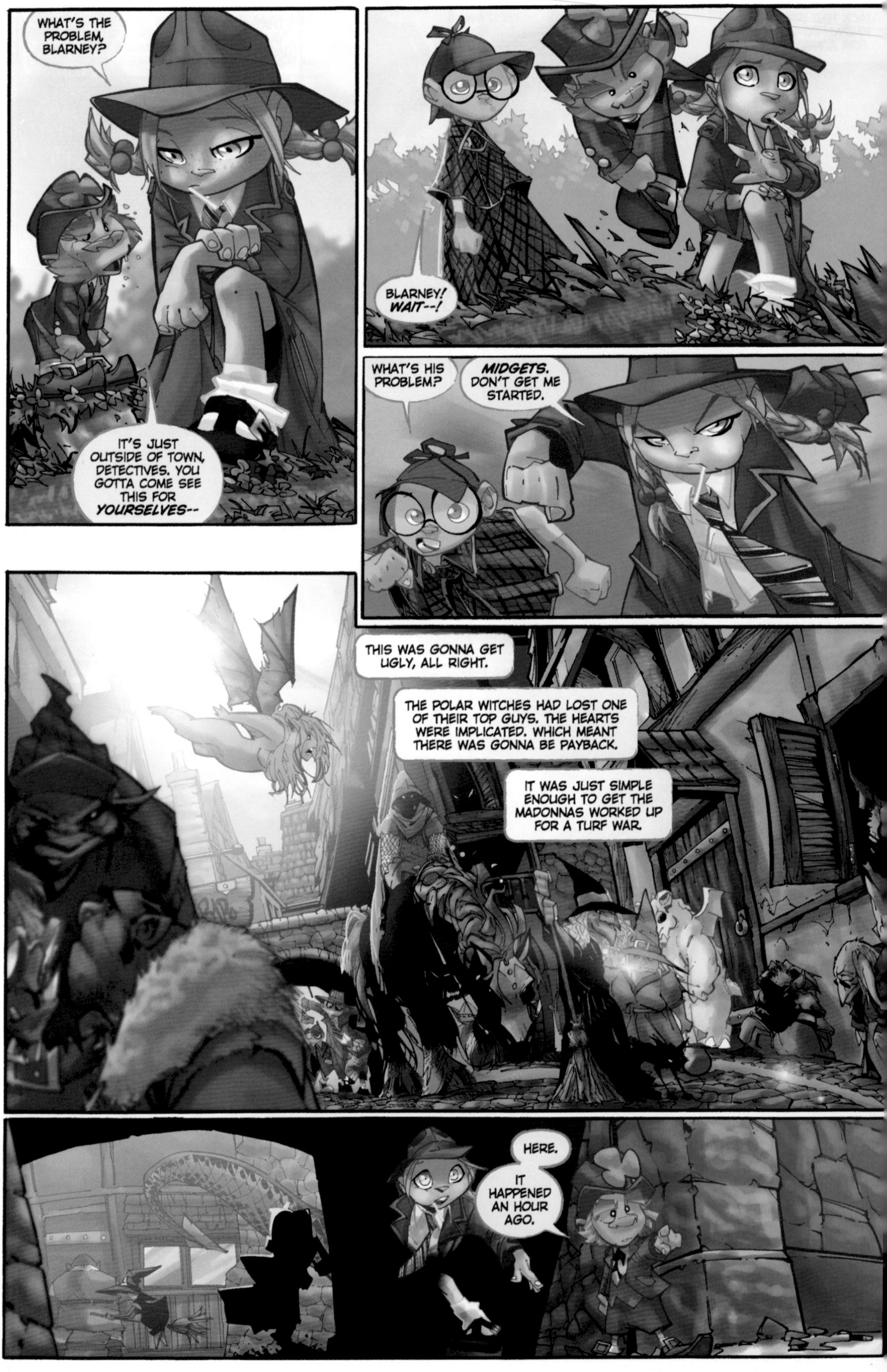

WHAT'S THE PROBLEM, BLARNEY?
IT'S JUST OUTSIDE OF TOWN, DETECTIVES. YOU GOTTA COME SEE THIS FOR *YOURSELVES--*
BLARNEY! *WAIT--!*
WHAT'S HIS PROBLEM?
MIDGETS. DON'T GET ME STARTED.
THIS WAS GONNA GET UGLY, ALL RIGHT.
THE POLAR WITCHES HAD LOST ONE OF THEIR TOP GUYS. THE HEARTS WERE IMPLICATED. WHICH MEANT THERE WAS GONNA BE PAYBACK.
IT WAS JUST SIMPLE ENOUGH TO GET THE MADONNAS WORKED UP FOR A TURF WAR.
HERE.
IT HAPPENED AN HOUR AGO.

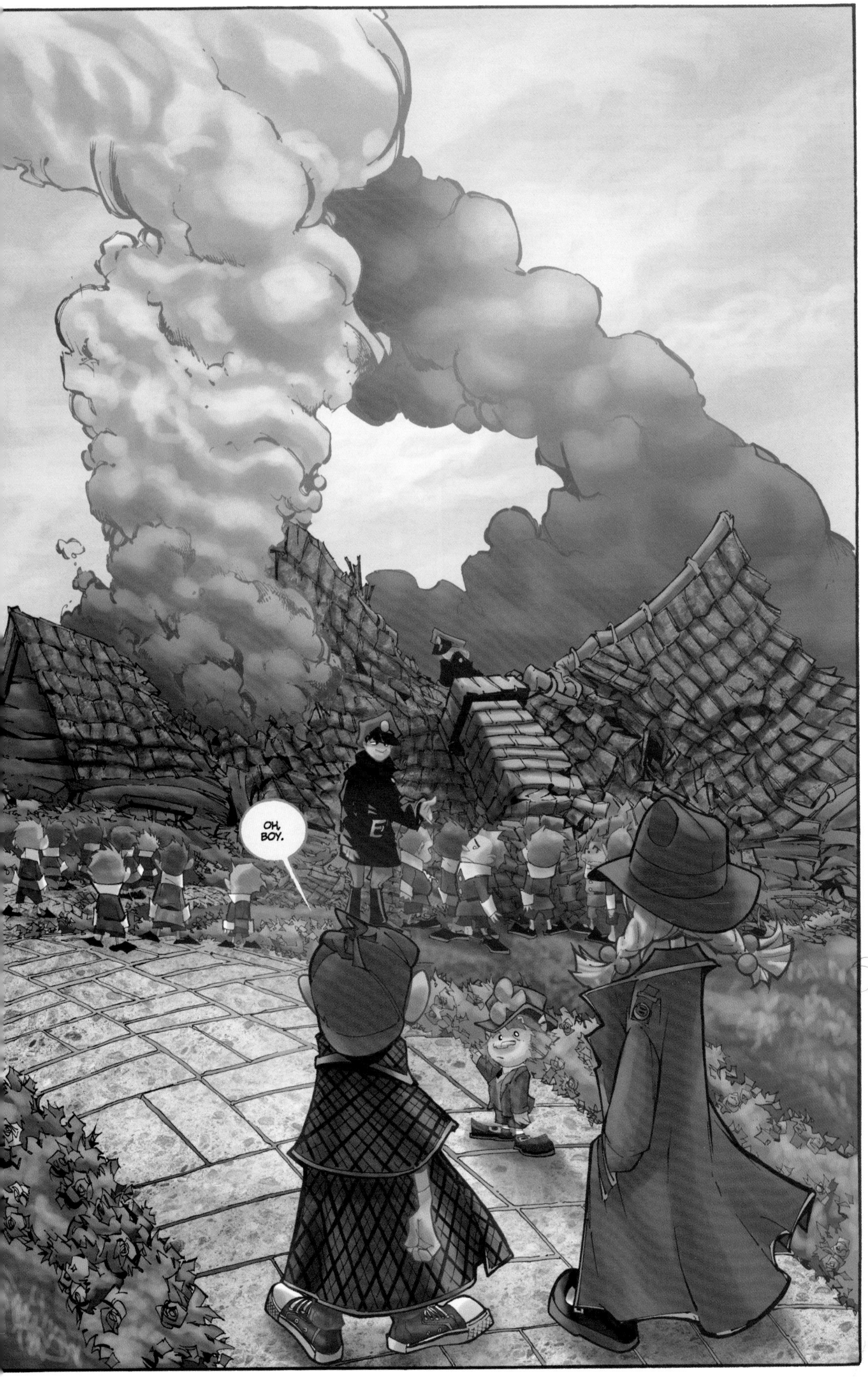
OH, BOY.

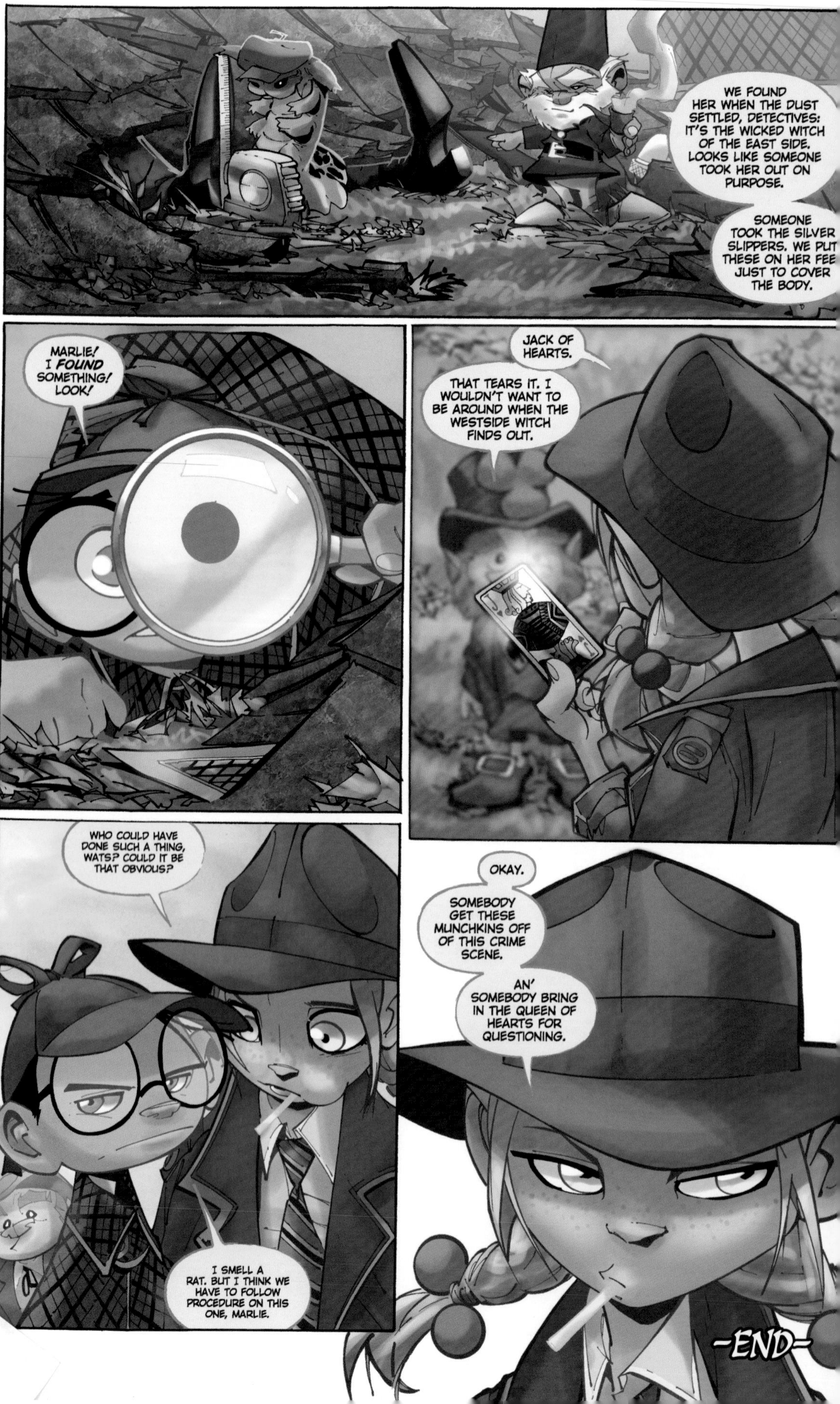
WE FOUND HER WHEN THE DUST SETTLED, DETECTIVES: IT'S THE WICKED WITCH OF THE EAST SIDE. LOOKS LIKE SOMEONE TOOK HER OUT ON PURPOSE.
SOMEONE TOOK THE SILVER SLIPPERS. WE PUT THESE ON HER FEE JUST TO COVER THE BODY.
MARLIE! I FOUND SOMETHING! LOOK!
JACK OF HEARTS.
THAT TEARS IT. I WOULDN'T WANT TO BE AROUND WHEN THE WESTSIDE WITCH FINDS OUT.
WHO COULD HAVE DONE SUCH A THING, WATS? COULD IT BE THAT OBVIOUS?
I SMELL A RAT. BUT I THINK WE HAVE TO FOLLOW PROCEDURE ON THIS ONE, MARLIE.
OKAY.
SOMEBODY GET THESE MUNCHKINS OFF OF THIS CRIME SCENE.
AN' SOMEBODY BRING IN THE QUEEN OF HEARTS FOR QUESTIONING.
-END-

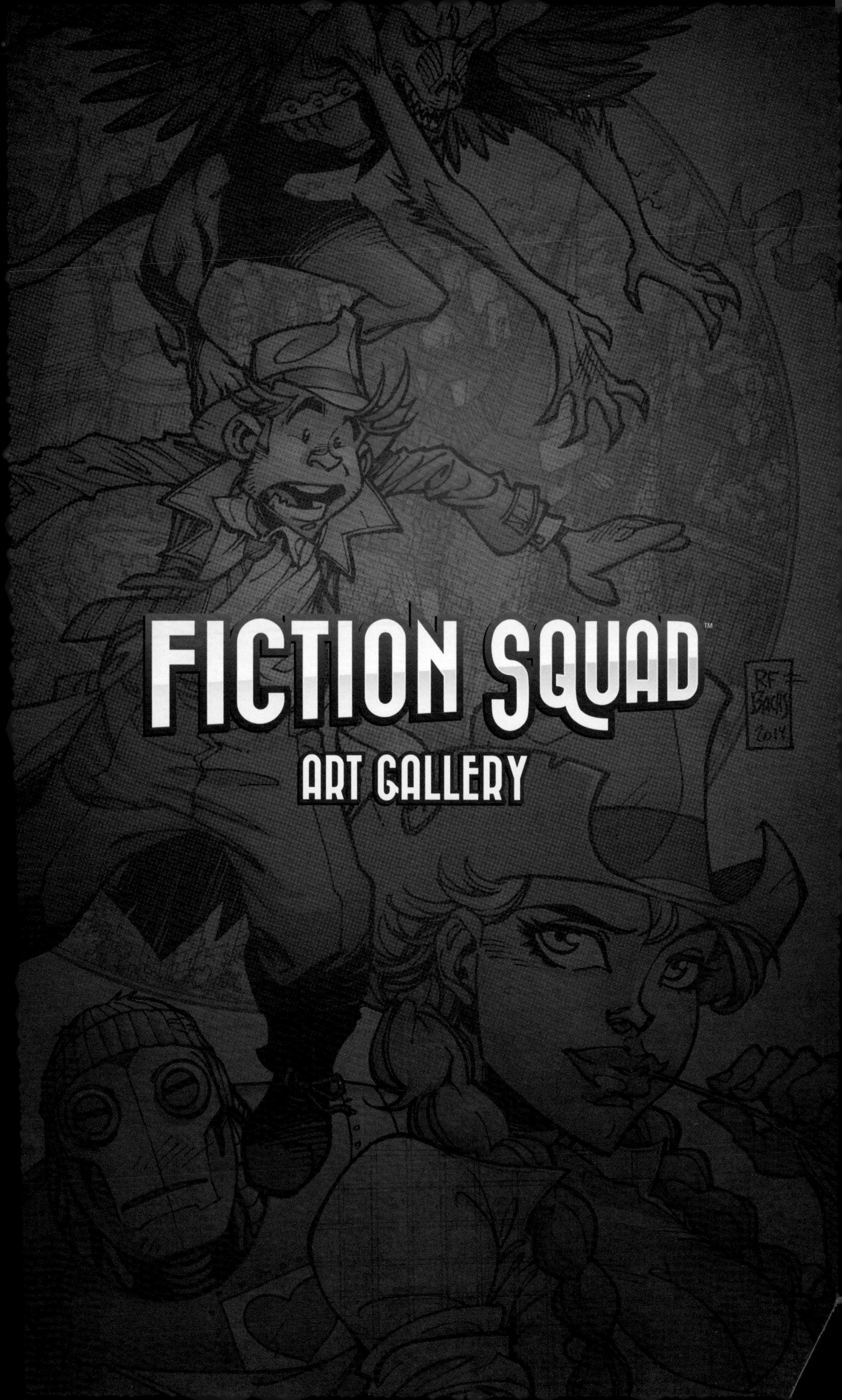
FICTION SQUAD™
ART GALLERY
RF BACHS 2014

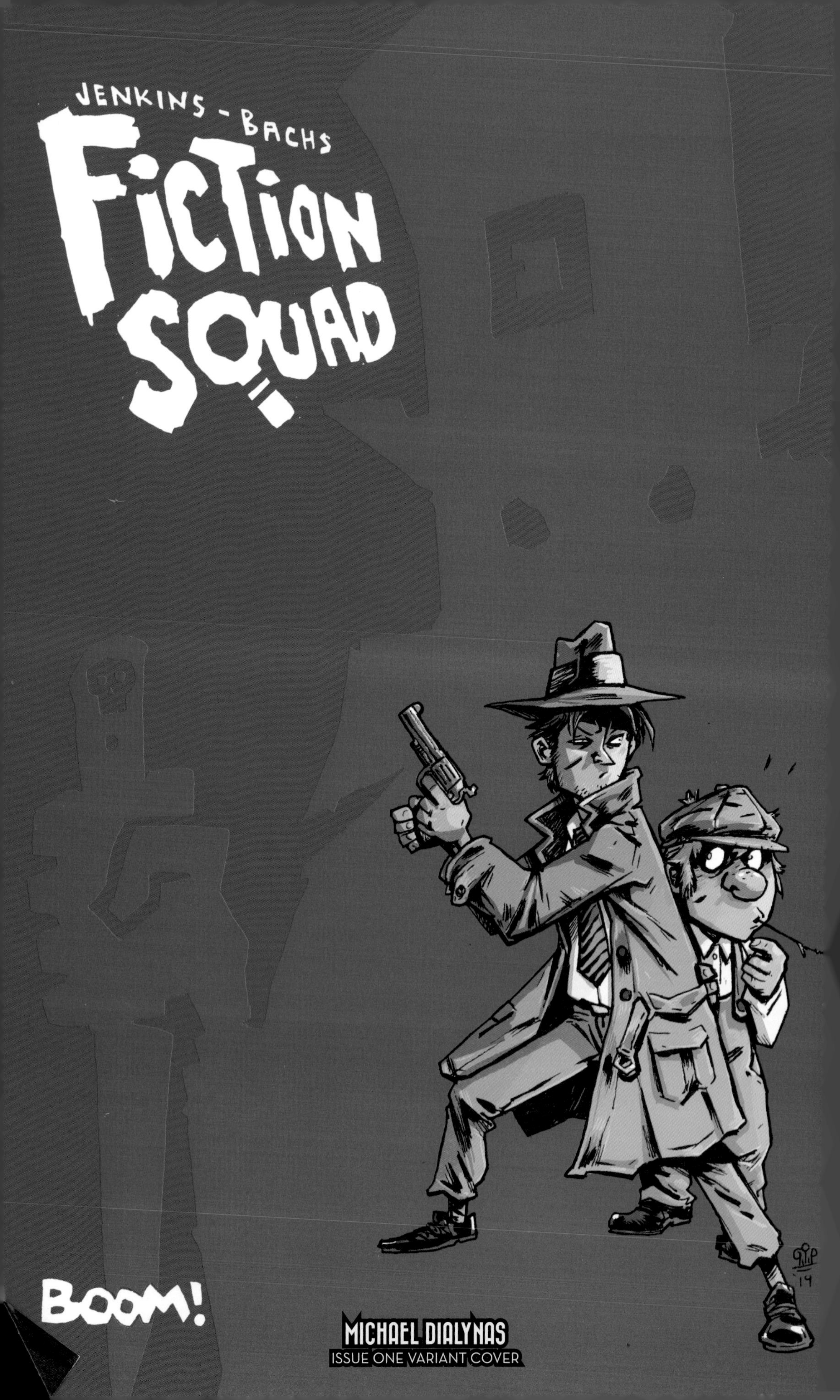
JENKINS - BACHS
FICTION SQUAD
BOOM!
MICHAEL DIALYNAS
ISSUE ONE VARIANT COVER

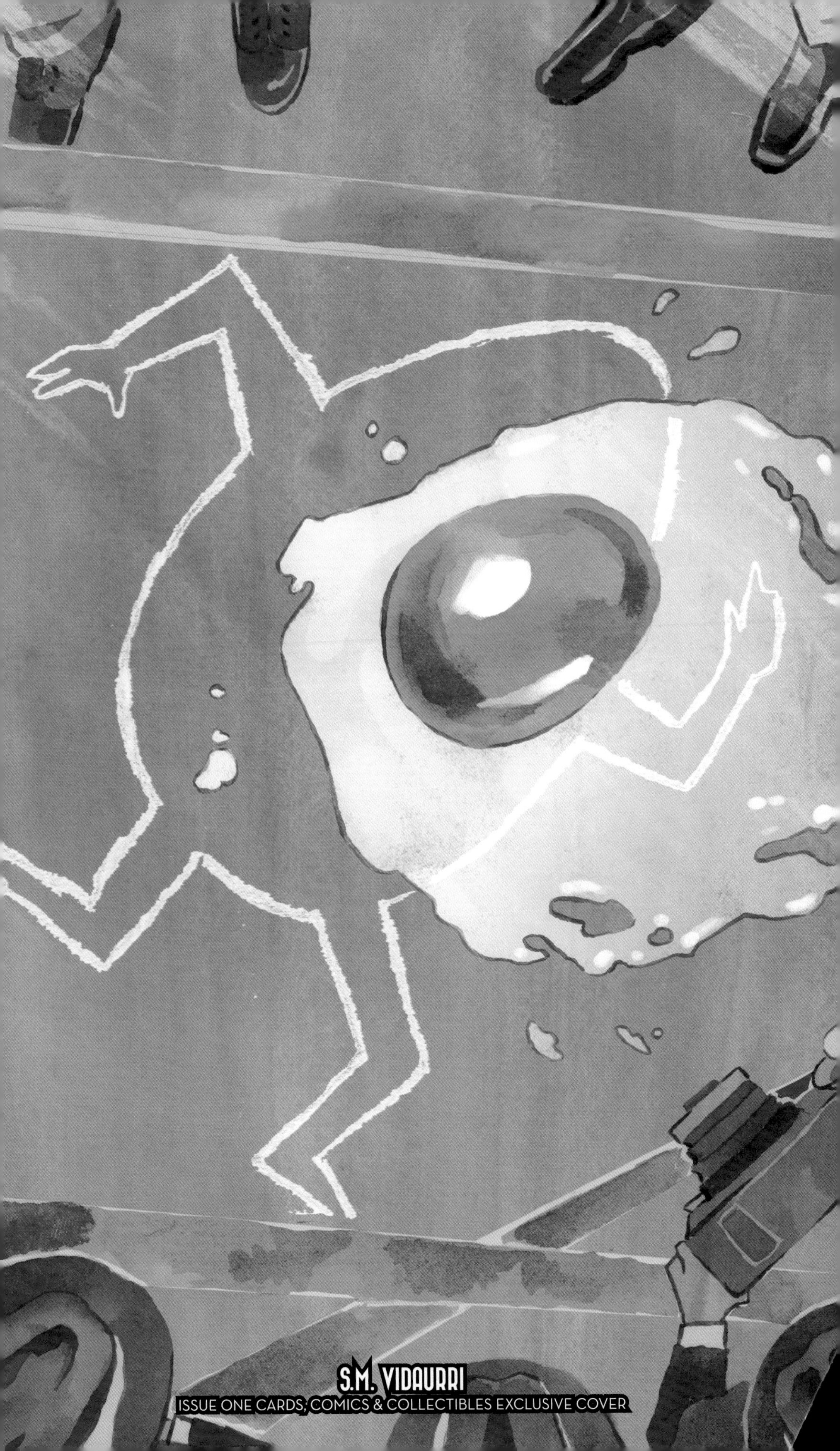

S.M. VIDAURRI

ISSUE ONE CARDS, COMICS & COLLECTIBLES EXCLUSIVE COVER

RAMON BACHS
CHARACTER DESIGN GALLERY

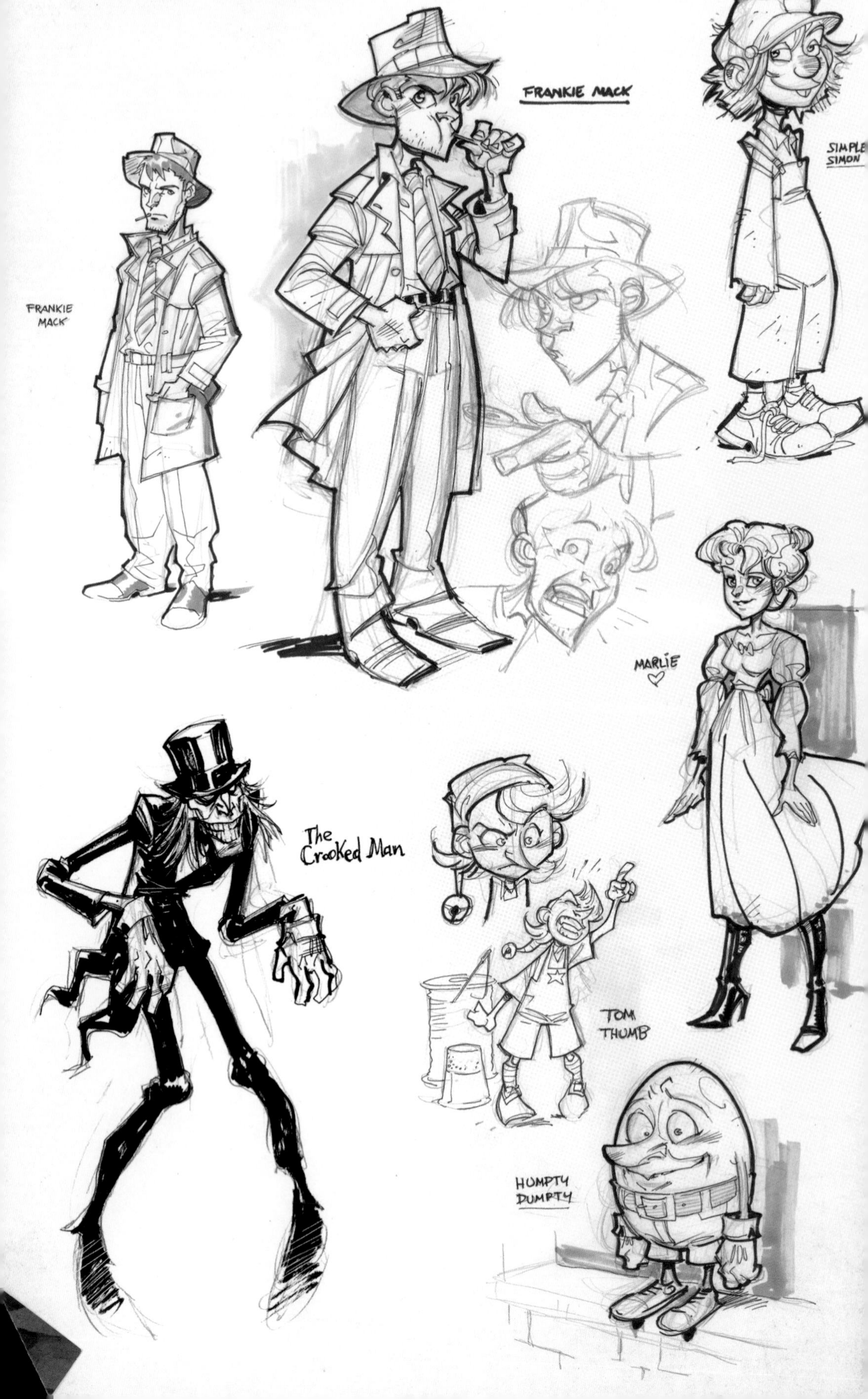
FRANKIE MACK
FRANKIE MACK
SIMPLE SIMON
MARLIE
The Crooked Man
TOM THUMB
HUMPTY DUMPTY

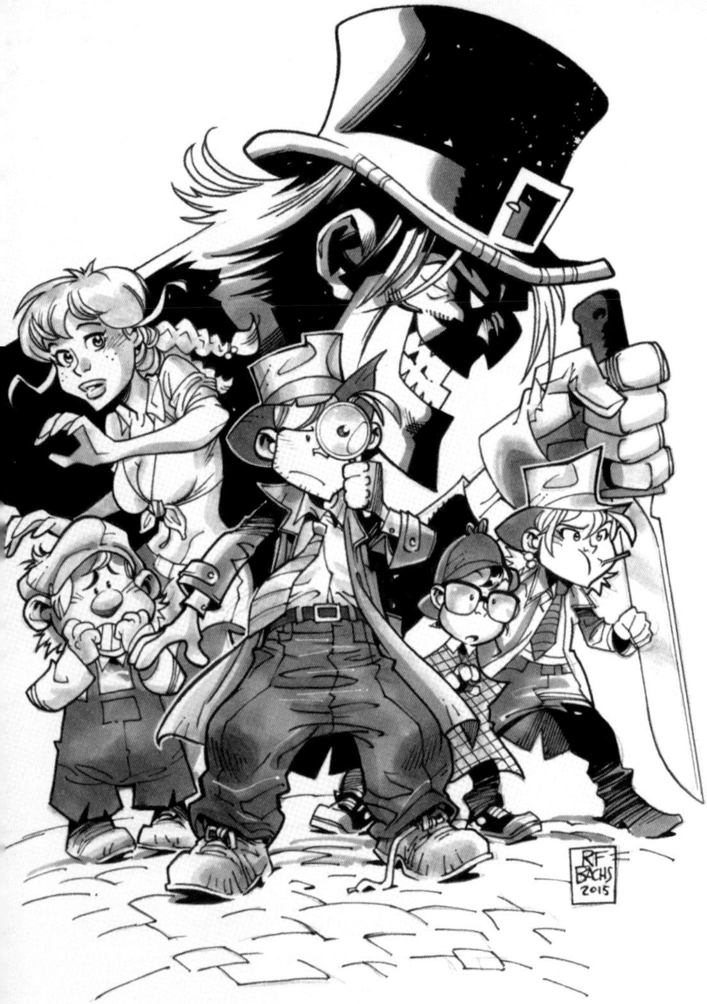
RF
BACHS
2015

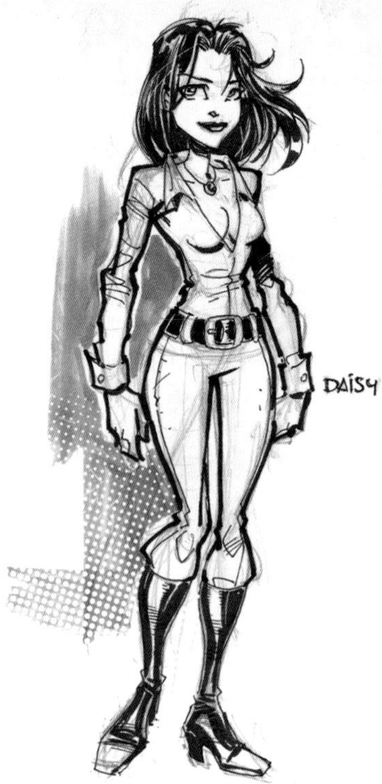
DAISY

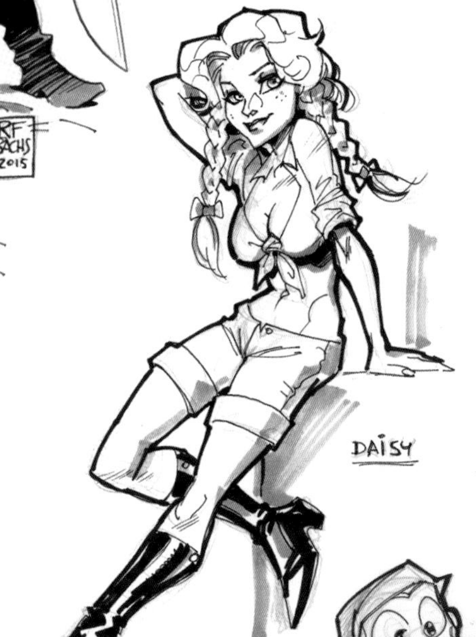
DAISY

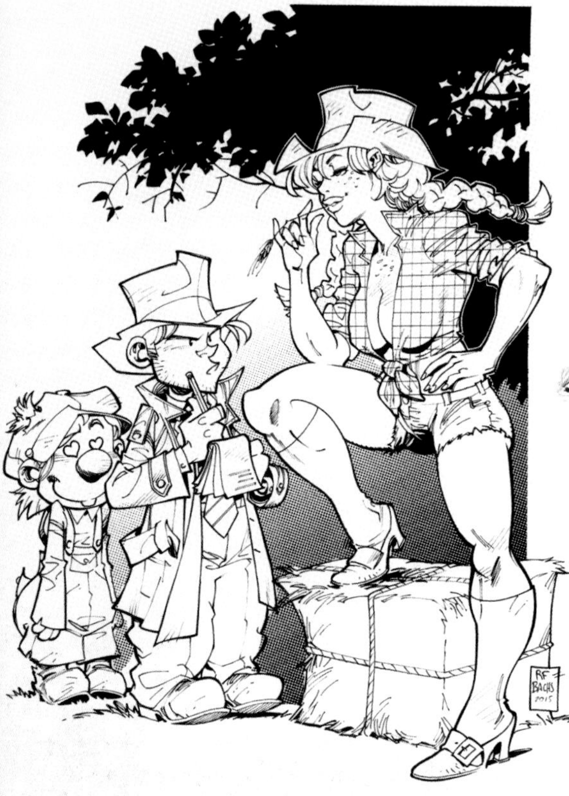
RF
BACHS
2015

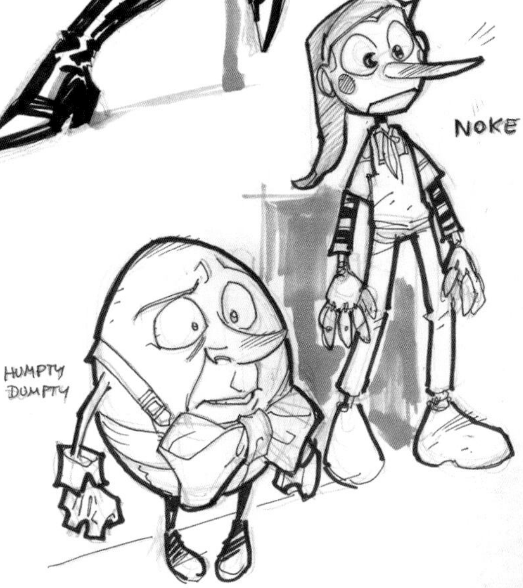
NOKE
HUMPTY
DUMPTY

HUMBERTO RAMOS
CHARACTER DESIGN GALLERY

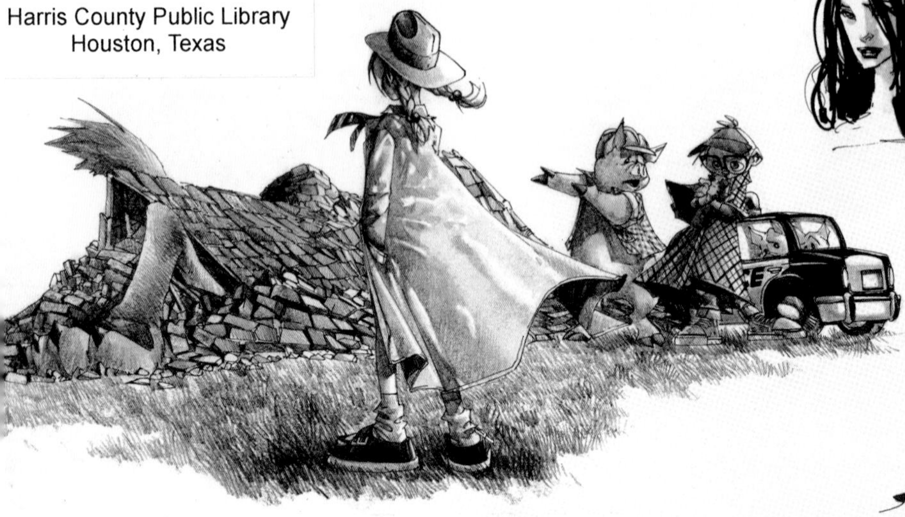

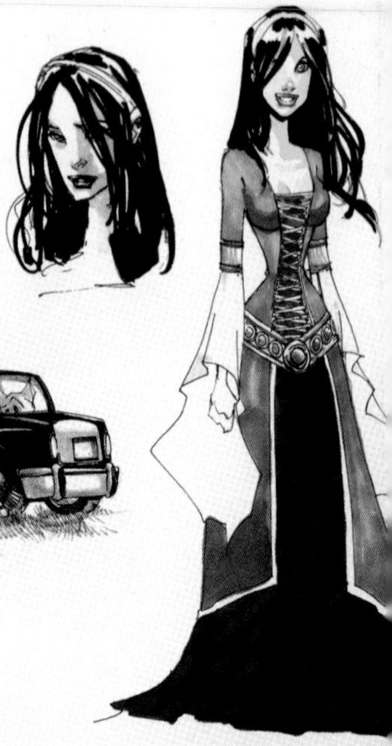

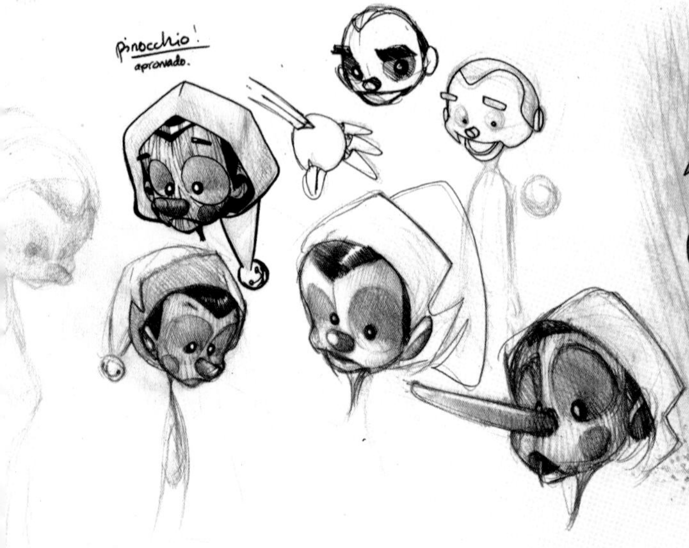
pinocchio!
aprovado.

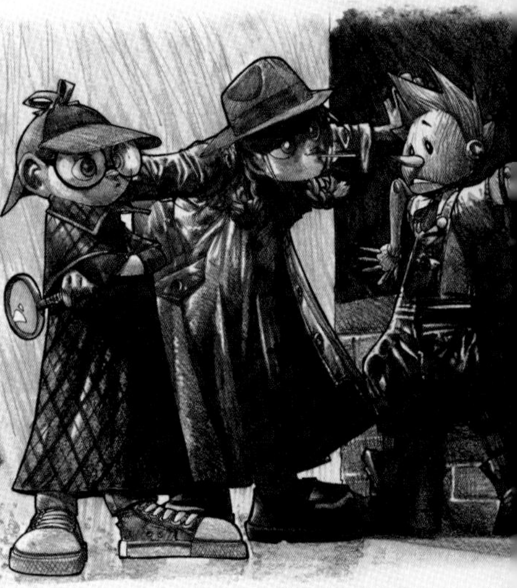

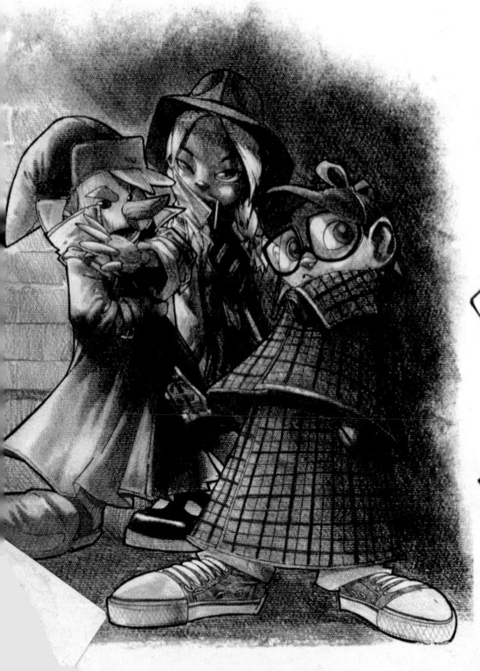

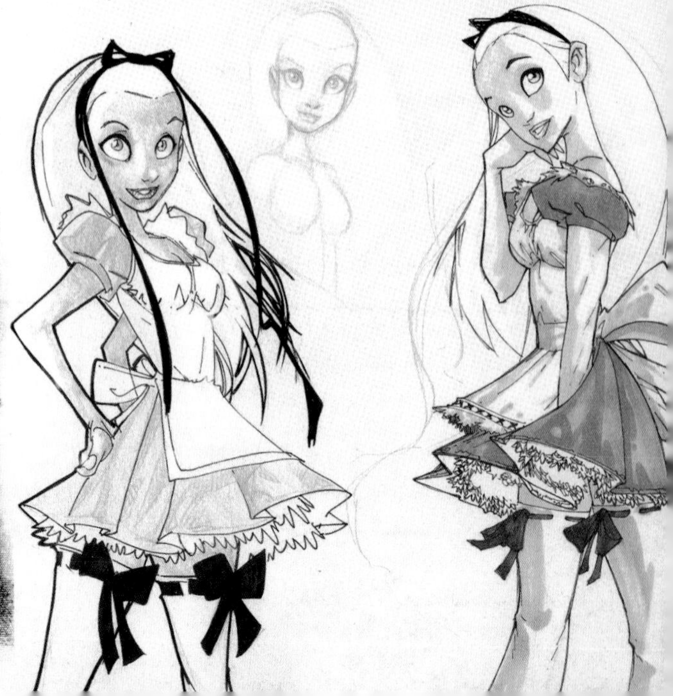